Biological and Artificial Intelligence Environments

Organizing-Scientific Commitee

Referees

Sponsoring Institutions

International Institute for Advanced Scientific Studies (IIASS) "E.R. Caianiello"
Dip. di Fisica "E.R. Caianiello", University of Salerno
Dip. di Matematica ed Informatica, University of Salerno
University of Milano
Dip. di Scienze dell'Informazione, University of Milano
Società Italiana Reti Neuroniche (SIREN)
IEEE Neural Network Society, Italian Chapter
INNS, SIG Italy
Istituto Italiano per gli Studi Filosofici, Napoli

Biological and Artificial Intelligence Environments

15th Italian Workshop on Neural Nets, WIRN VIETRI 2004

Edited by

Bruno Apolloni
Università di Milano, Italy

Maria Marinaro
Università di Salerno, Fisciano (SA), Italy

and

Roberto Tagliaferri
Università di Salerno, Fisciano (SA) Italy

Springer

A C.I.P. Catalogue record for this book is available from the Library of Congress.

ISBN 13 978-90-481-6863-7 (PB)
ISBN 13 978-1-4020-3432-9 (e-book)

Published by Springer,
P.O. Box 17, 3300 AA Dordrecht, The Netherlands.

www.springeronline.com

Printed on acid-free paper

Printed in the Netherlands.

Table of Contents

Preface

This volume reports the proceedings of the 15th Italian Workshop on Neural Nets WIRN04. The workshop, held in Perugia from September 14th to 17th 2004 has been jointly organized by the International Institute for Advanced Scientific Studies "Eduardo R. Caianiello" (IIASS) and the Società Italiana Reti Neuroniche (SIREN).

This year the Conference has constituted a joint event of three associations: Associazione Italiana per l'Intelligenza Artificiale (AIIA), Gruppo Italiano di Ricercatori in Pattern Recognition (GIRPR), Società Italiana Reti Neuroniche (SIREN) within the conference CISI-04 (Conferenza Italiana sui Sistemi Intelligenti - 2004) combining the three associations' annual meetings. The aim was to examine Intelligent Systems as a joint topic, pointing out synergies and differences between the various approaches.

The volume covers this matter from the Neural Networks and related fields perspective. It contains invited review papers and selected original contributions presented in either oral or poster sessions by both Italian and foreign researchers. The contributions have been assembled, for reading convenience, into five sections. The first two collect papers from pre-WIRN workshops focused on Computational Intelligence Methods for Bioinformatics and Biostatistics, and Computational Intelligence on Hardware, respectively. The remaining sections concern Architectures and Algorithms, Models, and Applications.

The Editors would like to thank the invited speakers and all the contributors whose highly qualified papers helped the success of the Workshop. Finally, special thanks go to the referees for their accurate work.

December 2004

Bruno Apolloni
Maria Marinaro
Roberto Tagliaferri

Acknowledgments

Special thanks go to Angelo Ciaramella and Antonino Staiano for their contribution in editing and collecting the papers, and to Simone Bassis for the web management. Furthermore thanks go to Tina Nappi and Ornella De Pasquale for their secretarial work and to Michele Donnarumma for his technical work.

PROGENGRID: A GRID FRAMEWORK FOR BIOINFORMATICS

Giovanni Aloisio, Massimo Cafaro, Sandro Fiore, and Maria Mirto
CACT, University of Lecce, Italy & SPACI Consortium, Italy
{ giovanni.aloisio, massimo.cafaro, sandro.fiore, maria.mirto } @unile.it

Abstract Important issues in bioinformatics are the difficulties for non computer experts to use bioinformatics tools, the transparent access to large biological data sets, and the exploitation of large computing power. Moreover, often such tools and databases are developed by independent groups, so the task of enabling their composition and cooperation is even more difficult. Integrating Computational Grid and Web Services technologies can be a key solution to simplify interaction between bioinformatics tools and biological databases. This paper presents ProGenGrid (Proteomics & Genomics Grid), a distributed and ubiquitous grid environment, accessible through the web, for supporting *"in silico"* experiments in bioinformatics.

Keywords: Bioinformatics, Drug Design, Workflow, Grid Computing, Computational Grid, Web Services.

1. Introduction

The growing access to large biological data sets, plus rapidly developing theory behind pathways, such as systems biology, genomics, proteomics, and so on, will give rise to large-scale *"in silico"* models. The combination of such different competences and knowledge will have an enormous impact. To realize this effect life scientists need tools to produce data, keep track of it, run it in models, and more. A series of new techniques and tools will help such users (e.g. biologists) feel this forward momentum in bioinformatics. Information technology can play a significant role by transforming those data into knowledge that will drive new advancements in the industry. One solution for handling and analyzing so much disparate data comes from Computational Grid [Foster and Kesselman, 1998], which connects many computers within and between institutions through middleware software.

One of the main problems in bioinformatics is the increasing availability of different, often heterogeneous, biological data sets. Indeed, different data sets

B. Apolloni et al. (eds.), Biological and Artificial Intelligence Environments, 1–9

may contain different aspects of the same object. Data integration should give a homogeneous view of information contained in different databases, and should allow working with a single virtual biological data source. As a result, scientists need tools that keep track of data and relate one data set to another. High performance, data integration and collaboration requirements can be satisfied by Computational Grids. The Life Science Grid Research Group [LSG-RG, 2003] established under the Global Grid Forum, underlined as a Grid framework, enhanced through specific services, could satisfy bioinformatics requirements. Indeed, some emerging Bioinformatics Grids, such as Asia Pacific BioGRID and myGrid [myGrid Project, 2001], aim to allow: (i) deployment, distribution and management of needed biological software components; (ii) harmonized standard integration of various software layers and services; (iii) powerful, flexible policy definition, control and negotiation mechanism for a collaborative grid environment. So, bioinformatics platforms need to offer powerful and high level modelling techniques to ease the work of e-scientists, and should exploit Computational Grids transparently and efficiently. The proposed solution aims to satisfy those requirements and is based on the following key approaches: web/grid services, workflow, ontologies and data integration through the Grid.

The rest of the paper is organized as follows. Section 2 presents the ProGenGrid architecture, and describes its main components, such as data access, ontology, workflow modelling layers. Section 3 describes an initial prototype, Section 4 discusses a simple case study through which an high level service, namely drug design, is offered. Section 5 concludes the paper and discusses future work.

2. System Architecture

ProGenGrid (see Fig. 1) is a software platform exploiting a Service Oriented Architecture (SOA) that wraps programs and data as Web Services and offers tools for their composition to provide ease of use, re-use and better quality of results. Services are divided in two classes:

Application-level services, that allow (i) Composition of complex activities using Workflow technology for designing, scheduling and controlling bioinformatics services; (ii) Collaborative working for the sharing of experimental results.

Middleware-level services, that allow (iii) Biological database access: interaction with distributed biological data sources accessible through a uniform and standard front-end; (iv) Discovery and use of existing analysis tools available as Web Services for their sharing; (v) Access control list to carry out the authorization process for a specific data bank. Such services will be used by the developers to build enhanced services and will be available in a first prototype,

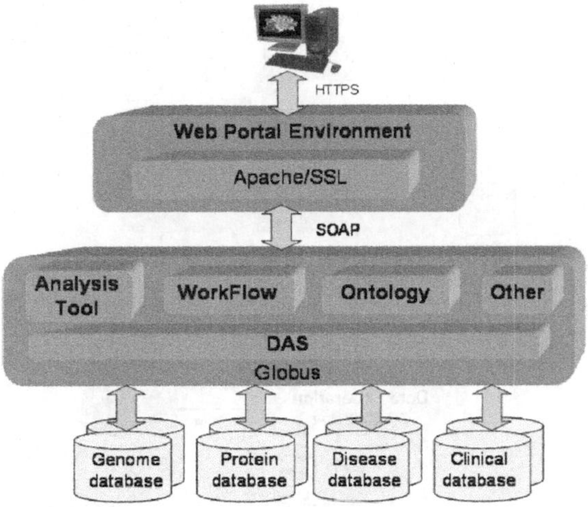

Figure 1. ProGenGrid Architecture

through a web portal. The main components of the system (see Fig. 1), that are built on top of Globus Toolkit [Foster and Kesselman, 1997] and are based on Web Services technology, are: Data Access Service, Ontology, Workflow, and Web Portal. To date, the overall system has been designed and the WorkFlow Management System has been developed.

2.1 Data Access Service

In order to access heterogeneous biological data sources (stored either in flat files or in relational databases), a Data Access Service (DAS) offering data integration and data federation services has been planned (see Fig. 2).
Data integration is responsible for mapping high level user's requests to low level SQL queries. This mapping leverages the Metadata Ontology Repository which contains semantic information about proteomics and genomics data sources. This level provides a first step in the data virtualization process, structuring or restructuring data coming from different sources, thus managing complex queries. At the lowest level the access to physical data sources is granted by specific wrappers created at run-time.
Data federation is responsible for allowing interconnections between application and data sources. Often works with brokers which bridge the gap between data source and requester. This process provides local references to data sources and basic support for data result aggregation.

To date, in our infrastructure the integration service is not completely developed whereas the federation broker is based on the GRelC [Aloisio et al., 2004b] Server (a basic component of the GRelC toolkit), which has to hide,

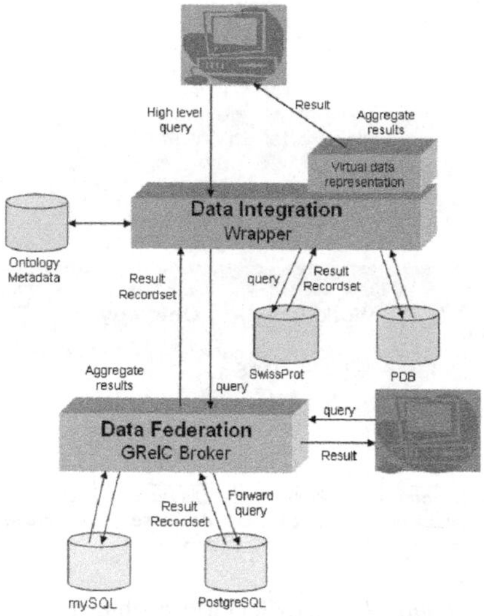

Figure 2. Data Access Service (DAS) Architecture

in a grid environment, the database heterogeneity and other low level details, providing secure access to data sources by means of the Globus Toolkit Grid Security Infrastructure [Tuecke, 2001]. It offers a robust, efficient and transparent access front end to relational (e.g. MySQL, Postgres, Oracle, are supported DBMS) and not-relational data sources (e.g. flat files). The queries are executed on a remote DBMS and the results returned by the wrapper and broker are then combined and returned to the application in a single XML recordset. Regarding the integration service, we plan to model the semantics of data sources and their relations through ontologies: the goal is to support the work of the wrapper module so that the translation from an abstract query into a set of data source specific commands can be driven by the ontology.

2.2 Ontology

In our system, the ontology is used at two levels: *Workflow Validation* during the composition of tasks without known applications details (such as data type, etc.) and conversion of input data, if needed. In particular we classified ProGenGrid components as: data banks, bioinformatics algorithms, graphics tools, drug design tools and input data types. This initial ontology, written in DAML+OIL [Daml, 2000], has been stored in a relational database; *Data Access*, in particular for guaranteeing: (i) Semantic integration of different data sources as explained in the previous Section. Currently we are using GeneOntology; (ii) Analysis of stored output data coming from different experiments.

2.3 WorkFlow

We use workflow technology to model and design complex *"in silico"* experiments composed by different web/grid services. WorkFlow Management Systems (WFMSs) support the enactment of processes by coordinating the temporal and logical order of the elementary process activities and supplying the data resources necessary for the execution of the functions. A WFMS: (i) allows a clear business process (biological experiment) definition and reproducibility because the process, the input parameters and the program versions used are clearly defined and these have not to be redefined at any time; (ii) and performs complex computations which are executed repeatedly by one or more scientists. It automatically executes large computations as needed for automated optimization or robustness evaluation.

3. ProGenGrid Implementation

We implemented a first prototype of the system (see Fig. 3) that supports the phases of application design, execution and monitoring, as described in the following.

1 **Component discovery.** It discovers available bioinformatics tools, data banks and graphics tools modeled through the ontology. Since we are considering such components as grid services, we plan to extend the GridLab MDS web services [Aloisio et al., 2003] to manage registration and retrieval of such grid services.

2 **Workflow editing.** Discovered components are made available to a semantic editor that allows the design (i.e. the activities are modeled using UML) of an experiment (abstract workflow). During workflow creation the abstract workflow is validated through rules derived by metadata and ontology.

3 **Execution Plan.** The abstract workflow is translated into an "execution plan" (concrete workflow) containing the activities order and the logical name of the resources (needed for their discovery in a Grid environment). The execution plan (EP) is coded through a set of XML instructions extending the GGF workflow specification [Bivens, 2001].

4 **Application execution.** The ProGenGrid scheduler schedules the concrete workflow in a computational grid. It discovers the needed services querying the GridLab Monitoring and Discovery Service (MDS), built on top of the Globus MDS [MDS, 1998]. Such services are registered

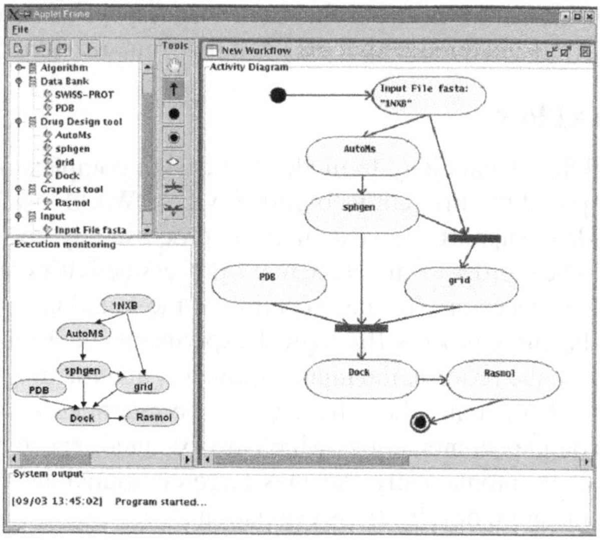

Figure 3. Snapshot of ProGenGrid prototype

through the MDS GridLab Web Services and are classified using an ontology. The scheduler invokes the Web Services related to each activity, and updates the EP reflecting the workflow status.

5 **Application monitoring.** Whenever workflow activities are started/finished, the system visualizes the advancement of the workflow execution using a graphical utility.

Fig. 3 shows a snapshot of ProGenGrid: the left upper frame shows the available resources installed on the testbed Grid; the left bottom frame shows graphically the status of application execution; the right frame shows the designed workflow using the UML notation [Eshuis and Wieringa, 2002] [OMG, 2003]; and finally the bottom central frame shows the application execution log. The current version is available as a Java Applet and we plan to integrate it in our web portal.

4. Drug Design

An important service offered by our system is drug design. This process involves various steps beginning from the synthesis in laboratory of a compound, candidate drug, to the introduction of the therapeutic agent or drug into market. Using a traditional approach this process can take many years (12 - 15) due to clinical testing for establishing the toxicology and possible side effects.

The R&D sections of many pharmaceutical companies aim at reducing the research timeline in the discovery stage. In particular, molecular modelling has emerged as a popular methodology for drug design combining different disciplines such as computational chemistry and computer graphics. It can be redesigned as a distributed system involving many resources for the screening of a large number (of the order of a million) of ligand records or molecules of compounds in a chemical database to identify those that are potential drugs, taking advantage of HPC technologies such as clusters and Grids for large-scale data exploration. This process is called molecular docking and predicts how small molecules, drug candidates, bind to an enzyme or a protein receptor of known three-dimensional (3D) structure. The receptor/ligand binding is a compute and data intensive task due to the large data sets of compounds to be screened.

Our goal is to use Grid technologies to provide large-scale parallel screening and docking, reducing the total computation time and costs of the process. So, scientists simulate receptor-ligand docking and get a score as a criterion for screening. As an example, we model the drug design application with our workflow editor (Fig. 3) involving the needed software in this process. In particular, we consider the DOCK [Ewing and Kuntz, 1996] software, a popular tool for receptor-ligand docking. It takes as input files of ligand and receptor and outputs a score and 3D structure of docked ligand. In particular the workflow starts with crystal coordinates of target receptor, i.e $< IDProtein >$ or its FASTA format (in this example, the protein target is 1NXB), then the AutoMs [AutoMS, 1996] tool is used to generate molecular surface for receptor and Sphgen [Sphgen, 1996] generates spheres to fill in the active site (the centers of the spheres become potential locations for ligand atoms). The DOCK software matches the sphere centers to the ligand atoms (extracted by structural databases such as PDB [Berman et al., 2000]), and uses scoring grid (generated by the grid program) to determine possible orientations for the ligand. Finally the Rasmol [Sayle and Milner-White, 1995] tool visualizes the docked ligand protein. The main issues raised by this kind of application are due to the computation and to the heterogeneity of the interfaces to the involved tools. Indeed the screening can involve million of ligands and hence requires high performance computing resources, the size of repositories containing these ligands often is in the range of gigabytes and the involved tools must be compiled and installed. To solve partially the computational time issue, we would like to transform the DOCK program (but also other existing molecular docking applications, such as GAMESS - General Atomic and Molecular Electronic Structure System - [Schmidt et al., 1993] and AUTODOCK - Automated Docking of Flexible Ligand to Micromolecules - [Goodsell et al., 1996]) into a parameter sweep application, for execution on distributed systems. It is worth noting here that we do not intend to update the existing sequential docking application but to partition the input data files to submit each dock job using our libraries, GRB and GRB-GSIFTP [Aloisio et al., 2001]. Moreover, we are developing a unique front-end to enable access to ligand molecules in the 3D-structure databases from remote resources (that are stored on a few grid nodes given the large storage required), including related indexing mechanisms to facilitate reading the compounds [Aloisio et al., 2004a], while a resource broker is used for scheduling and on-demand processing of docking jobs on grid resources. Finally, to solve the interface heterogeneity issue, the docking tools will be available as Web Services, so the bioinformaticians will not need to know details about installation or configuration of these tools.

5. Conclusions and Future Work

ProGenGrid is a software platform allowing the composition of existing bioinformatics resources, wrapped as Web Services, to create complex workflows. It offers tools for services composition, workflow execution and monitoring. Moreover, it uses a data integration and federation approach to simplify access to heterogeneous biological databases. The overall architecture and a first prototype have been described. Currently the architecture is partly implemented and future work will provide the full implementation that will be validated measuring the performances with respect to other approaches of high throughput applications in the field of drug design [Buyya et al., 2003]. Moreover, future work will regard the implementation of an efficient workflow scheduler that dynamically querying the GridLab MDS will be able to choose among different available Web Services to obtain an effective schedule.

References

Aloisio, G., Blasi, E., Cafaro, M., and Epicoco, I. (2001). The GRB library: Grid Computing with Globus in C. In *Proceedings of HPCN Europe 2001*, volume 2110 of *Lecture Notes in Computer Science*, pages 133–140. Springer-Verlag.

Aloisio, G., Cafaro, M., Epicoco, I., Lezzi, D., Mirto, M., and Mocavero, S. (2003). The Design and Implementation of the GridLab Information Service. In *Proceedings of the Second International Workshop on Grid and Cooperative Computing (GCC 2003)*, volume 3032 of *Lecture Notes in Computer Science*, pages 131–138. Springer-Verlag.

Aloisio, G., Cafaro, M., Fiore, S., and Mirto, M. (2004a). Bioinformatics Data Access Service in the ProGenGrid System. In *OTM Workshops*, volume 3292 of *Lecture Notes in Computer Science*, pages 211–221. Springer-Verlag.

Aloisio, G., Cafaro, M., Fiore, S., and Mirto, M. (2004b). The GRelC Project: Towards GRID-DBMS. In *Parallel and Distributed Computing and Networks (PDCN) IASTED*.

AutoMS (1996). AutoMS. http://dock.compbio.ucsf.edu/dock4/html/Manual.23.html#33.

Berman, H.M., Westbrook, J., amd G. Gilliland, Z. Feng, Bhat, T.N., Weissig, H., Shindyalov, I.N., and Bourne, P.E. (2000). The Protein Data Bank. *Nucleic Acids Research*, 28(1):235–242.

Bivens, H.P. (2001). Grid Workflow. *Grid Computing Environments Working Group Document.* http://dps.uibk.ac.at/uploads/101/draft-bivens-grid-workflow.pdf.

Buyya, R., Branson, K., Giddy, J., and Abramson, D. (2003). The Virtual laboratory: a toolset to enable distributed molecular modelling for drug design on the World-Wide Grid. *Concurrency and Computation: Practice and Experience*, 15(1):1–25.

Daml (2000). Daml+oil language. http://www.daml.org/2001/03/reference.html.

Eshuis, R. and Wieringa, R. (2002). Verification support for workflow design with UML activity graphs. In *Proceedings of the 24th International Conference on Software Engineering (ICSE)*, pages 166–176. ACM Press.

Ewing, T. J. A. and Kuntz, I.D. (1996). Critical Evaluation of Search Algorithms for Automated Molecular Docking and Database Screening. *J. of Computational Chem.*, 18(9):1175–1189.

Foster, I. and Kesselman, C. (1997). Globus: A Metacomputing Infrastructure Toolkit. *Intl J. Supercomputer Applications*, 11(2):115–128.

Foster, I. and Kesselman, C. (1998). *The Grid: Blueprint for a New Computing Infrastructure.* Morgan Kaufmann.

Goodsell, D.S., Morris, G.M., and Olson, A.J. (1996). Automated docking of Flexible Ligands: Applications of AutoDock. *J. Mol. Recognition*, 9(1):1–5. http://www.scripps.edu/pub/olson-web/doc/autodock/.

LSG-RG (2003). Life Sciences Grid - Research Group. http://www.ggf.org/7_APM/LSG.htm.

MDS (1998). Monitoring Discovery Service. http://www.globus.org/mds/.

myGrid Project (2001). myGrid Project. http://mygrid.man.ac.uk/.

OMG (2003). Uml- unified modeling language: Extensions for workflow process definition. http://www.omg.org/uml/.

Sayle, Roger A. and Milner-White, E. J. (1995). RasMol: Biomolecular graphics for all. *Trends in Biochemical Science (TIBS)*, 20(9):374.

Schmidt, M.W., Baldridge, K.K., Boatz, J.A., Elbert, S.T., Gordon, M.S., Jensen, J.H., Koseki, S., Matsunaga, N., Nguyen, K.A., Su, S., Windus, T.L., Dupuis, M., and Montgomery, J.A. (1993). General Atomic and Molecular Electronic Structure System. *J. of Computational Chem.*, 14(11):1347–1363. http://www.msg.ameslab.gov/GAMESS/GAMESS.html.

Sphgen (1996). Sphgen. http://dock.compbio.ucsf.edu/dock4/html/Manual.20.html#17338.

Tuecke, S. (2001). Grid Security Infrastructure (GSI) Roadmap. Technical report. www.gridforum.org/security/ggf1_2001-03/drafts/draft-ggf-gsi-roadmap-02.pdf.

A PRELIMINARY INVESTIGATION ON CONNECTING GENOTYPE TO ORAL CANCER DEVELOPMENT THROUGH XCS

Flavio Baronti,[1] Valentina Maggini,[2] Alessio Micheli,[1] Alessandro Passaro,[1] Anna Maria Rossi,[2] and Antonina Starita[1]

[1]*Dipartimento di Informatica, Università di Pisa*
*Via Buonarroti, 2 — 56100 Pisa (Italy)**
{baronti,passaro}@di.unipi.it

[2]*Dipartimento di Scienze dell'Uomo & dell'Ambiente - DSUA*
Università di Pisa

Abstract Head and neck squamous cell carcinoma (HNSCC) has already been proved to be linked with smoking and alcohol drinking habits. However the individual risk could be modified by genetic polymorphisms of enzymes involved in the metabolism of tobacco carcinogens and in the DNA repair mechanisms. To study this relationship, a data set comprising clinical (age, smoke, alcohol) and genetic data (the genetic polymorphism of 11 genes) was built; an XCS system was then developed in order to analyze it. XCS appears well suited to this problem since it can seamlessly accept missing values, and be adapted to deal with different data types (real, integer, and class). Moreover, it produces human-readable rules - which is fundamental in order to make the system useful to physicians. First results showed interesting rules, suggesting that this approach is viable and deserves deeper research.

Keywords: Learning classifier systems, XCS, genetic data, oral cancer.

1. Introduction

People are different. Physicians re-discover this basic rule every day: very often the statistics classify as equal two persons (same sex, age, lifestyle), but their predisposition (and reaction) to certain diseases varies greatly. This problem seems to have had a push towards better understanding in the last years: the DNA analysis techniques make it possible to explain these differences, by

*This work has been carried out in the framework of the BIOPATTERN European Network of Excellence.

B. Apolloni et al. (eds.), Biological and Artificial Intelligence Environments, 11–19

adding genetic information to clinical data. DNA appears to regulate most of the inner workings of the human body; it can be however very difficult to establish a clear gene-action relationship, as the biochemical effects are hard to trace through the human body. Moreover, genes often interact with each other, and some singularly "detrimental" or ineffective alleles can become beneficial when found together. These issues suggest the use of machine learning algorithms which can extract complex patterns from the observed data, and present them to the physicians in a human-readable form, amenable to further investigation.

In this work we consider the development of head and neck squamous cell carcinoma (HNSCC). This kind of cancer is mainly associated with smoking and alcohol drinking, but genetic polymorphism of enzymes involved in the metabolism of tobacco carcinogens and in the DNA repair mechanisms can influence the risk factor. The patients were thus described with a combination of clinical data (sex, age, smoking and drinking habits) and genetic data (the polymorphism of eleven genes believed to be relevant to this disease) — along with a single value which stated if they had cancer or not when the database was compiled.

We developed an XCS classifier system tailored to work with the different types of values found in this data set (boolean, integer, real and gene-class). This kind of classifier system was chosen for its capability to build very general accurate rules [Kovacs, 1997], whose interpretation is immediate. We then extended it with a ruleset reduction algorithm, in order to obtain a small set of mixed clinical and genetic rules that could suggest to physicians which genes promote or prevent oral cancer, and the direction to follow for more focused genetic research.

2. The problem

The data set we analyzed was designed to explore the influence of genotype on the chance to develop head and neck squamous cell carcinoma (HNSCC). It is already well-known that this kind of cancer is strictly connected with smoking and alcohol-drinking habits, along with age and sex. The individual risk however could be modified by genetic factors; thus the data was enriched with genotype information, regarding eleven genes involved with carcinogen-metabolizing (`CCND1`, `NQO1`, `EPHX1`, `CYP2A6`, `CYP2D6`, `CYP2E1`, `NAT1`, `NAT2`, `GSTP1`) and DNA repair systems (`OGG1`, `XPD`).

Nine of these genes have two allelic variants; let's call them a_1 and a_2. Since the DNA contains two copies of each gene, there exist three possible combinations: a_1a_1, a_2a_2 (the homozygotes) and a_1a_2 (the heterozygote — order does not matter). The homozygotes where represented with values 0 and 2, while the heterozygote with 1. Due to dominance, the heterozygote is in fact equivalent to one of the homozygotes; however, for many of the considered genes this dominance is not known. So class 1 can be either equivalent to class 0, or to class 2. The remaining two genes have 4 allelic variants, which result in 9 combinations; they were sorted by their activity level, and put on an integer scale from 0 to 8.

The full data consists of 355 records, with 124 positive elements and 231 negative. They were collected with different purposes and in different periods; this has led to many missing data among the genotypic information of patients. Actually only 122 elements have complete genotypic description; the remaining 233 have missing values ranging from 1 to 9, with the average being 3.58. As an overall figure, of the $11 \times 355 = 3905$ genotype values, just 3070 are present: 21% of the genotype information is missing.

3. XCS

Classical machine learning offers a few algorithms which comply with our requirements (such as decision tree induction [Quinlan, 1986], inductive logic programming [Muggleton, 1991], or bayesian networks [Heckerman et al., 1995]); we choose to employ a relatively new algorithm: XCS.

In [Wilson, 1995] and then in [Wilson, 1998], Wilson proposes XCS as an evolution of Holland's Learning Classifier Systems (LCS) [Holland, 1976], a machine learning technique which combines reinforcement learning, evolutionary computing and other heuristics to produce adaptive systems. Similarly to its ancestors, an XCS maintains and evolves a population of classifiers (rules) through a genetic algorithm. These rules are used to match environmental inputs and choose subsequent actions. Environment's reward to the actions is then used to modify the classifiers in a reinforcement learning process.

XCS introduces a measure of classifiers' fitness based on their accuracy, i.e. the reliability of their prediction of the expected payoff, and applies the GA only on the action set, the subset of classifiers which lead to the choice of the action. This gives the system a strong tendency to develop accurate and general rules to cover problem space and allow the system's "knowledge" to be clearly seen. In the following we provide a brief description of XCS. For full details see [Butz and Wilson, 2001].

System description

The core component of XCS is a set of classifiers, that is condition-action-prediction rules, where the **condition** specifies a pattern over the input states provided by the environment, the **action** is the action proposed (e.g. a classification), and the **prediction** is the payoff expected by the system in response to the action. Additionally each classifiers has associated an estimate of the **error** made in payoff predictions, and a **fitness** value.

XCS implements a reinforcement learning process: at every step the system is presented an individual from the data set and it examines its set of classifiers to select those matching the input situation. These classifiers form the *match set*. Then for each possible action the system uses the fitness–weighted average prediction of the corresponding classifiers to estimate environmental reward. At this point, the XCS can choose the best action looking for the highest predicted reward. However, during learning, the action is usually selected alternating the previous criterion with random choice, useful to better explore the problem space. The actual reward returned by the environment is then used to update the classifiers in the *action set*, i.e. the subset of the *match set* corresponding to the selected action. A genetic algorithm is also executed on this set to discover new interesting classifiers.

To reduce the number of rules developed, XCS implements various techniques, such as the use of macroclassifiers, the subsumption and the deletion mechanisms. In fact the system uses a population of macroclassifiers, i.e. normal classifiers with a **numerosity** parameter, representing the number of their instances (microclassifiers). This helps in keeping track of the most useful rules and improves computational performance at no cost.

Subsumption is used to help generalization: when the GA creates a new classifier with a condition logically subsumed by his parent (i.e. matching a subset of the inputs matched by the parent's) it is not added to the population, but the parent's numerosity is incremented. A similar check is also occasionally done among all the classifiers in the current action set.

Finally the deletion mechanism keeps the number of microclassifiers under a fixed bound. The classifier to be removed is chosen with a roulette wheel selection biased towards low–fitness individuals and assuring approximately equal number of classifiers in each action set.

As already stated this process leads to the evolution of more and more general rules. For each classifier we can define a measure of generality following [Wilson, 2001b], ranging from 0 (most specific) to 1 (most general). A possible termination criterion is to stop evolution when the average generality value of the population gets stable.

4. Adaptation to the problem

In facing the problem of HNSCC development prediction from clinical and genetic data, we looked for a method which could provide a meaningful insight of its classification process, instead of focusing only on accuracy. In this regard, XCS showed many advantages over other well-established classification systems (for experimental comparison between XCS and other machine learning algorhitms, see for instance [Bagnall and Cawley, 2003]). As seen in Wilson's works on Wisconsin Breast Cancer data [Wilson, 2001b] and Holmes' ones on epidemiologic surveillance data [Holmes, 2000] (using EpiCS, a similar classifier system), the use of explicit rules to match the input data allows an easy visualization of the criteria the system employs in each classification and a comparison with physicians' previous knowledge.

As we have seen above, the data set is characterized by the massive presence of missing data, especially in the genotype part. In these cases, essentially every classification technique is expected to experience a degradation of performance. However XCS allows at least their seamless management: an individual with missing data is matched only by those classifiers which have a wildcard on that value. The rationale underlying this choice is to avoid taking decisions based on data we do not have. This is different from Holmes' approach in [Holmes and Bilker, 2002], where missing values are matched by every classifier — thus producing a kind of average value for that data.

Data type integration

Another key aspect which lead us to choose XCS was the easiness of integration of different kind of data. In fact, the type of the information contained in the data set varies from binary (i.e. sex), to continuous-valued (i.e. age, indicators of smoking and alcohol-drinking habits), and to a special class data for the genotype. Whilst the original formulation of XCS is targeted to binary input, the shift to other data types, such as real or integer ones, has already been proved to be very easy (see respectively [Wilson, 2001b; Wilson, 2000]).

For the integer and real data types, our implementation is based on those proposed in the cited literature. But for the genotypic values we needed a slightly different treatment. Nine of the genes considered have two allelic variants, thus we need three classes (considering also the heterozygote) for the input values, but the classifiers have in fact to merge the heterozygote with either one of the homozygotes. So the values we used are the following: as input we have 00 for a_1a_1, 11 for a_1a_2, and 22 for a_2a_2; in classifiers 11 is not allowed, but we admit 01 (matching 00 and 11), 12 (matching 11 and 22) and ## (matching all values).

Ruleset reduction

During learning XCS tends to evolve an accurate and complete mapping of condition-action-prediction rules matching the data. Consequently, in particular on a very sparse data set as in our study, the final number of rules is quite high. Similar problems, which break the knowledge visibility property, were experienced in other studies on "real" data sets [Wilson, 2001b; Wilson, 2001a]. These works suggest to let the system evolve many steps after reaching the maximum performance, and then to extract a small subset of rules which reach the same performance level. This is the function of the *Compact Ruleset*

Algorithm (CRA), first proposed by Wilson [Wilson, 2001a], which we implemented with minor modifications.

5. First results

We had two aims in testing the system: evaluating its ability to correctly classify unseen data after training and checking if it could find interesting rules. We applied a ten–fold cross–validation, running the XCS ten times on each fold, in order to obtain average results (independent of a particular random seed). Each experiment was allowed to run for $500,000$ steps, as a few tests showed that the generality value reached its maximum at this point. Moreover we employed a crossover rate of 0.80 and a mutation rate of 0.04, while the other parameters were chosen following [Butz and Wilson, 2001]. The experiments were run twice, with a population of 800 and 6400 microclassifiers. Final results are summarized in Table 1, while the evolution of the system is plotted in Figs. 1 and 2.

In the test with 6400 classifiers the accuracy on the training set reached almost optimal value, quite better than in the 800 test. However the accuracy on the test set was comparable and even slightly better in the 800 test. This suggests that the high accuracy of the 6400 test is due to overfitting and lower population sizes are preferable.

The graphs show a quite unexpected result regarding generality: in fact while this value increases, there is not a corresponding increase in generalization, since the accuracy on the test set remains stable or even gets slightly worse.

The CRA successfully extracted a small subset of the original rules which maintained the maximum performance on the training set, while not getting worse significantly on the test set. Actually it could be more interesting to apply a pruning algorithm to the original population, designed to reduce the model complexity in order to achieve better generalization. Differently from CRA, such an algorithm should be allowed to lose some accuracy on the training set, in order to perform better on the test set.

Nevertheless the small sets of rules extracted made it feasible to manually look for possibly interesting rules. As an example we provide in Table 2 two of such rules in human readable form. The first rule is common knowledge rediscovered by the system. Instead the second one has been judged interesting by physicians: in fact previous studies already reported an increased lung cancer risk associated to `GSTP1` in combination with `EPHX1` polymorphisms [To-Figueras et al., 2001], so it will be interesting to investigate on the role of these genes in relation to HNSCC risk.

Table 1. Summary of the ten 10-fold cross validation experiments. Specificity and sensitivity are both relative to the test set.

Max rules	6400		800	
CRA	Before	After	Before	After
Rules	1659±91.9	47±5.6	403±10.7	47±5.8
Acc. (train)	99.4±0.4%	99.4±0.4%	93.2±0.3%	93.2±0.3%
Acc. (test)	75.3±5.2%	74.2±1.8%	76.9±2.8%	74.4±2.4%
Specificity	89.9±2.2%	76.9±3.5%	86.8±2.8%	81.5±2.4%
Sensitivity	50.1±9.3%	64.5±4.4%	60.2±5.1%	62.9±6.0%

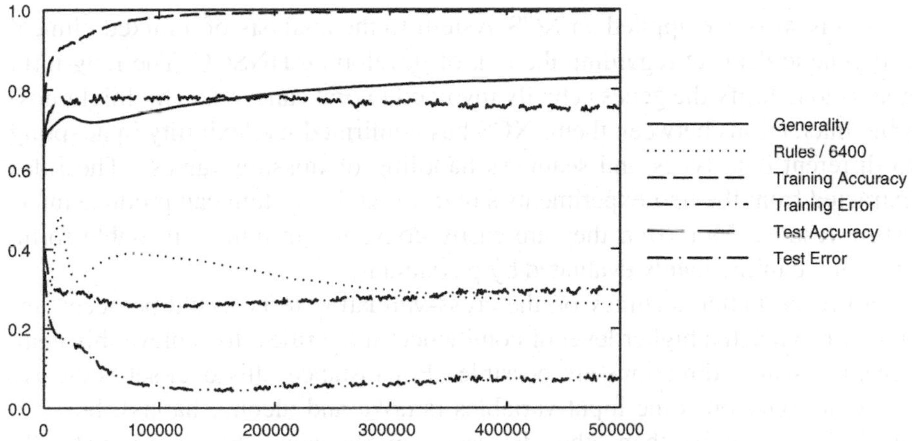

Figure 1. Plot of average evolution in the 6400 experiments.

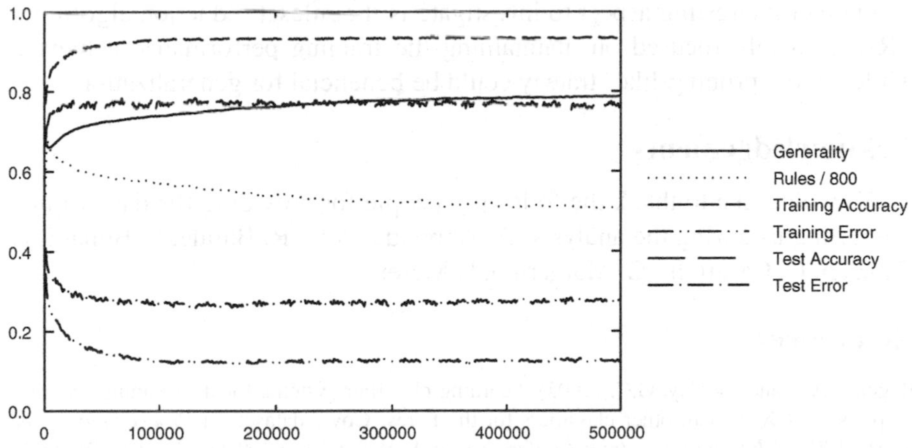

Figure 2. Plot of average evolution in the 800 experiments.

Table 2. Examples of rules extracted by the system, with their correct/matched ratio.

IF *age* ≤ 40 THEN *cancer=false*	(26/26)
IF *smoke*≥ 12 AND *EPHX1*$\in \{11, 22\}$ AND *GSTP1*$= 00$ THEN *cancer=true*	(38/40)

6. Conclusions and future developments

In this work we applied an XCS system to the analysis of a mixed clinical and genetic data set regarding the risk of developing HNSCC. The long-term goal is to identify the genes actually involved in oral cancer, and highlight possible interactions between them. XCS has confirmed its flexibility in adapting to different data types and seamless handling of missing values. The rules extracted from the first experiments suggest that the system can produce interesting results. Moreover, they are easily converted in human-readable form, and can be immediately evaluated by physicians.

However, better accuracy on the cross-validation tests would be necessary in order to reach a higher level of confidence in the rules; to achieve this goal, several research directions are possible. For instance, this data set is clearly noisy not only on some input variables (smoke and alcohol habits), but also on the target: more than other diseases, cancer cannot be deterministically predicted. Regarding the first issue, it would be useful to perform some tests on the effects of noise in XCS. Concerning the target variable, a possible direction is prediction of a risk factor instead of a raw class, as in [Holmes, 2000].

Another interesting aspect to investigate is the ruleset reduction algorithm: CRA is mainly focused on maintaining the training performance achieved, while a more pruning-like strategy could be beneficial for generalization.

Acknowledgements

We would like to thank the following people for providing the data set and supporting us during the analysis: A. Abbondandolo, R. Barale, S. Bonatti, F. Canzian, G. Casartelli, G. Margarino, P. Mereu.

References

Bagnall, A.J. and Cawley, G.C. (2003). Learning classifier systems for data mining: A comparison of XCS with other classifiers for the Forest Cover dataset. In *Proceedings of the IEEE/INNS International Joint Conference on Artificial Neural Networks (IJCNN-2003)*, volume 3, pages 1802–1807. IEEE Press.

Butz, Martin V. and Wilson, Stewart W. (2001). An algorithmic description of XCS. In Lanzi, P. L. and et al., editors, *IWLCS 2000*, volume 1996 of *LNAI*, pages 253–272. Springer-Verlag.

Heckerman, D., Geiger, D., and Chickering, D. M. (1995). Learning bayesian networks: The combination of knowledge and statistical data. *Machine Learning*, 20(3):197–243.

Holland, John H. (1976). Adaptation. In Rosen, R. and Snell, F. M., editors, *Progress in theoretical biology, 4*. New York: Plenum.

Holmes, John H. (2000). Learning classifier systems applied to knowledge discovery in clinical research databases. In Lanzi et al., editor, *Learning Classifier Systems. From Foundations to Applications*, volume 1813 of *LNAI*, pages 243–261. Springer-Verlag.

Holmes, John H. and Bilker, Warren B. (2002). The effect of missing data on learning classifier system learning rate and classification performance. In Lanzi et al., editor, *IWLCS 2002*, volume 2661 of *LNAI*, pages 46–60. Springer-Verlag.

Kovacs, Tim (1997). XCS classifier system reliably evolves accurate, complete, and minimal representations for boolean functions. Technical Report CSRP-97-19, University of Birmingham.

Muggleton, Stephen (1991). Inductive logic programming. *New Gen. Comp.*, 8(4):295–318.

Quinlan, J. Ross (1986). Induction of decision trees. *Machine Learning*, 1:81 – 106.

To-Figueras, J., Gene, M., Gomez-Catalan, J., Pique, E., Borrego, N., and Corbella, J. (2001). Lung cancer susceptibility in relation to combined polymorphisms of microsomal epoxide hydrolase and glutathione s-transferase p1. *Cancer Letters*, 173(2):155–162.

Wilson, Stewart W. (1995). Classifier fitness based on accuracy. *Evolutionary Computation*, 3(2).

Wilson, Stewart W. (1998). Generalization in the XCS classifier system. In Koza, John R. and et al., editors, *Genetic Programming 1998: Proceedings of the Third Annual Conference*, pages 665–674, University of Wisconsin, USA. Morgan Kaufmann.

Wilson, Stewart W. (2000). Get real! XCS with continuous-valued inputs. In Lanzi et al., editor, *Learning Classifier Systems. From Foundations to Applications*, volume 1813 of *LNAI*, pages 209–219. Springer-Verlag.

Wilson, Stewart W. (2001a). Compact rulesets from XCSI. In Lanzi, P. L. and et al., editors, *IWLCS 2001*, volume 2321, pages 197–210. Springer-Verlag.

Wilson, Stewart W. (2001b). Mining oblique data with XCS. In Lanzi, P. L. and et al., editors, *IWLCS 2000*, volume 1996 of *LNAI*, pages 158–174. Springer-Verlag.

MASS SPECTROMETRY DATA ANALYSIS FOR EARLY DETECTION OF INHERITED BREAST CANCER

Francesco Baudi[1], Mario Cannataro[1], Rita Casadonte[1], Francesco Costanzo[1], Giovanni Cuda[1], Maria Concetta Faniello[1], Marco Gaspari[1], Pietro Hiram Guzzi[1], Tommaso Mazza[1], Barbara Quaresima[1], Pierosandro Tagliaferri[1], Giuseppe Tradigo[1], Pierangelo Veltri[1] and Salvatore Venuta[1]

[1]*University Magna Græcia of Catanzaro, Catanzaro, Italy*

Abstract Mass Spectrometry (MS) can be used as a detector in High Performance Liquid Chromatography (HPLC) systems or as a tool for direct protein/peptides profiling from biological samples. Data Mining (DM) is the semi-automated extraction of patterns representing knowledge implicitly stored in large databases. The combined use of MS with DM is a novel approach in proteomic pattern analysis and is emerging as an effective method for the early diagnosis of diseases. We describe the workflow of a proteomic experiment for early detection of cancer which combines MS and DM, giving details of sample treatment and preparation, MS data generation, MS data preprocessing, data clustering and classification.

Keywords: Proteomics, Mass Spectrometry, Data Mining, Breast Cancer, Biomarkers

1. Introduction

Proteomics analysis is becoming a powerful, widely used technique in order to identify different molecular targets in different pathological conditions. In particular, cancer is one of the most diffuse and dangerous diseases and for this reason it is object of some scrupulous proteomic studies trying to exceed the limitations of the conventional diagnostic strategies. The aim is to identify some important markers for the prevention, the diagnosis and the treatment of several kind of cancer.

Breast cancer is one of the most common type of cancer in women, although it is known to affect men producing the same devastating effects. Recently, through studying blood samples of families in which there is a history of breast cancer, scientists have isolated and identified a gene linked to breast cancer. A person who has this modified gene, labelled BRCA1 (meaning Breast Cancer

B. Apolloni et al. (eds.), Biological and Artificial Intelligence Environments, 21–28

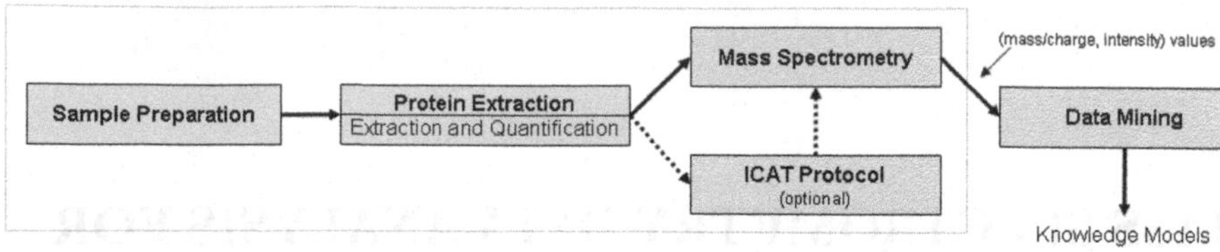

Figure 1. Workflow of the proteomics experiment

1), has an 85% lifetime risk of developing breast cancer, as well as a significantly higher risk of ovarian cancer. Being able to identify these genes through particular markers associated with the gene, we will know which individuals are more susceptible to cancer and therefore can follow the proper procedure. Scientists have successfully identified the gene, but presently there is no way to *repair* it. The recent isolation of the BRCA1 gene has prompted investigators to identify other genes that may contribute to breast cancer, ovarian cancer and the breast-ovarian cancer syndrome. By isolating such modified genes, we might develop a genetic test to identify altered gene allowing early detection of breast cancer.

The main goal of our research is to characterize different classes of patients affected by breast cancer through their proteom profiles by combining Mass Spectrometry and Data Mining. In particular our goal is to find the following classes starting from MS data: (i) Diseased Patients ($BRCA^+$), (ii) Diseased Patients ($BRCA^-$), (iii) Healthy Patients ($BRCA^+$) *(Carriers)*, (iv) Healthy Patients. In such a way, using an initial training set of known samples, a new unknown sample could be classified with respect to such classes. After describing the workflow of the experiment we present a bioinformatic platform for data mining analysis of mass spectrometry data. Initially, the training set for platform tuning will exclusively be composed by publicly available SELDI-TOF mass spectrometry data, from National Cancer Institute NCI (USA) [Petricoin et al., 2002], [Conrads et al., 2003].

2. Mass Spectrometry Analysis

Our proteomics experiment (see Fig. 1) comprises two main phases: (i) Mass Spectrometry analysis, that receives in input a set of biological samples (e.g. cells, tissues, serum), and produces as output a set of raw data (spectra); and (ii) Data Mining analysis, which comprises three main phases: data preprocessing, data clustering and data classification.

The Mass Spectrometry analysis [Aebersold and Mann, 2003] [Glish and Vachet, 2003] can be decomposed in four sub-phases (see Fig. 1): (i) Sample Preparation (e.g. Cell Culture, Tissue, Serum); (ii) Proteins Extractions; (iii) ICAT protocol: and (iv) Mass Spectrometry processing.

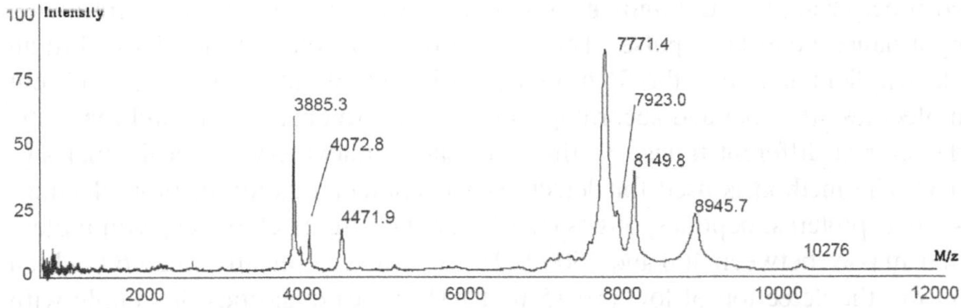

Figure 2. Peptide/Protein profile of a biological sample, Low Mw window:1000-12000 *m/z*

Sample Preparation. In the overall experiment we use three kind of samples: serum, tissue, cell culture. Cell culture is the technique used for maintaining in life, *in vitro*, some cells obtained by some animals or vegetable tissues, usually because of the enzymatic breakup. The cellular lines are called HCC1937 and are extracted both from healthy and diseased patients. In the first experiment, a HCC1937 line in which the BRCA1 is mutated is used, and another line in which the gene has been transfected (wild-type) and in which it works as oncosuppressor is employed. Both are kept in cultivation to obtain 2.500.000 cells.

Proteins Extraction. Proteins, because of cellular threadbare, are extracted by a buffer. The cellular threadbare is obtained because of Freez and Thaw process. This procedure implies the immersion in liquid nitrogen for one minute and the crystal formation that cracks the membranes. Centrifuging fourteen thousand times for 53 minutes proteins are ready to be extracted from the surnatant. The quantification is performed because the ICAT protocol previews at least 100 micrograms of proteins are tied with the reagent. ICAT is applied to every cellular line.

ICAT Protocol. The Isotope-Coded Affinity Tag-labeling procedure (ICAT) is used in protein separation. After the denaturation with SDS, triton and tris buffer, it needs: (i) the reduction of the disulphide bridges S-S with TCEP; (ii) the reaction of labeling with cleavable ICAT reagents (in according to the protocols supplied in the Cleavable ICAT Reagents Protein Labeling); (iii) the split of the protein in different peptides (approximately 10 peptides), at lysine and arginine, because of the trypsin. The sample containing the peptide is eluated in order to purify the marked peptides from those not marked. This operation is achieved with a cation-exchange cartridge.

Mass Spectrometry Processing. The sample, opportunely processed, is analyzed through Liquid Chromatography mass spectrometry (LC MS) or Matrix-Assisted Laser Desorption / Ionisation - Time Of Flight mass spectrometry (MALDI-TOF MS). MALDI-TOF is a relatively novel technique in which a co-precipitate of an UV-light absorbing matrix and a biomolecule is irradiated by a nanosecond laser pulse. The ionized biomolecules are accelerated in an electric field and enter the flight tube. During the flight in this tube, different molecules are separated according to their mass to charge ratio and reach the detector at different times. In this way each molecule yields a distinct signal. The method is used for detection and characterization of biomolecules, such as proteins, peptides, oligosaccharides and oligonucleotides, with molecular masses between 400 and 350000 Da. It is a very sensitive method, which allows the detection of low (10-15 to 10-18 mole) quantities of sample with an accuracy of 0.1 - 0.01%. Mass Spectrometry data is represented, at a first stage, as a (large) sequence of value pairs, where each pair contains a measured intensity, which depends on the quantity of the detected biomolecules, and a mass to charge ratio (*m/z*), which depends on the molecular mass of detected biomolecules. Due to the large number of (*m/z*) data contained in mass spectra obtained by real samples, analysis by manual inspection is not feasible. Mass spectra are usually represented in a graphical form as in Fig. 2.

3. Data Mining and Bioinformatics Analysis

The Data Mining analysis comprises the following sub-phases (see Fig. 3): (i) Data preprocessing, (ii) Clustering, (iii) Classification. In particular (supervised) classification is useful for disease classification and its main goal is to produce, starting from a training set of samples, a classifier able to assign new unknown samples to one of the classes. Conversely (unsupervised) clustering, a way to perform a descriptive modelling of data by partitioning samples into *k* groups, could be useful to find novel and potentially interesting clusters. For example, healthy patients with or without a cancer biomarker, depending on BRCA1 mutations. We currently implemented only the classification procedure, thus no clustering procudure is shown in Fig. 3.

Recently, a number of algorithms have been developed to find spectral differences between mass spectra of samples taken from two separate conditions. Such a discrimination is a goal for Mass Spectrometry Classification Algorithms (MSCAs). Although several MSCAs have been developed [Ball et al., 2002] [Lilien et al., 2003], these tools face only the data analysis aspect, without take into account the different phases of a MS experiment, from sample preparation to result interpretation. With this motivation we developed PROTEUS, a grid-based problem solving environment for proteomics data analysis [Cannataro et al., 2004]. It will be used to perform early disease diagnosis as well as monitoring disease progression, regression, and recurrence of inherited breast cancer [Cuda et al., 2003], by using different data mining and bioinformatics tools selected through domain ontologies (e.g. proteomic and breast cancer domains) and combined through workflow paradigm.

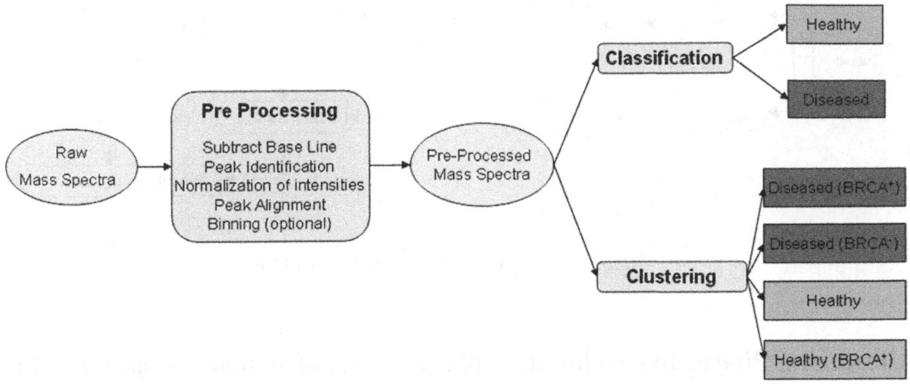

Figure 3. Workflow of Mass Spectrometry Data Mining Analysis

The classification process allows to assign a new samples (i.e. its spectra) to one of the classes identified in a training phase conducted by using known samples. To validate the data analysis component of our framework, we are focusing on analyzing real mass spectrometry data made available by a research group at the U.S. National Cancer Institute (NCI) [1]. Such data, representing mass spectra of different samples taken from healthy and diseased people, are whole spectrum Surface-Enhanced Laser Desorption/Ionization Time of Flight (SELDI-TOF) data produced with several techniques.

Data Preprocessing Phase. As explained in [Wagner et al., 2003] the preprocessing phase of MS data usually involves four steps: (i) *Subtract Base Line*; (ii) *Identification and extraction of peaks*; (iii) *Normalization of Intensities*; (iv) *Alignment of correspondent peaks*. The first step tries to identify the base intensity level (baseline) of each mass spectrum which varies from sample to sample and consequently to subtract this. The underlying hypotheses is that baseline is a variable noise. The second step can be performed by using the data-processing embedded in Mass Spectrometer software or, in case of raw data, we are designing a custom identification algorithm to fit either informatics and biological consideration. The third step enables the comparison of different samples because the absolute peak values of different fraction of spectrum are incomparable. The last step finds a common set of peak locations that will be used for each sample in the different classification schemes. The Clinical Proteomics Program Databank [2] has provided three set of ovarian cancer data that can be used without restriction. Data can be easily modelled with two arrays, the former contains m/z values and the latter intensity values. We are also developing a simple XML Schema to easily wrap and manage such data. *Binning* is a technique to reduce dimension of spectra.

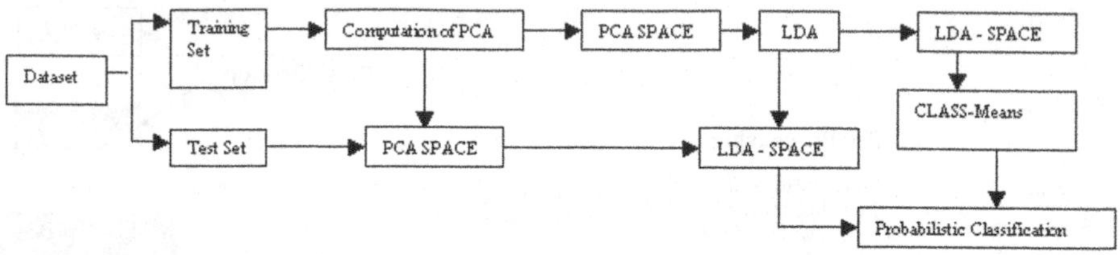

Figure 4. Graphical explanation of Q5

Clustering Phase. In the clustering phase the set of samples is partitioned in clusters. This phase, not yet implemented, could be useful to find novel potentially useful groups of samples [Wagner et al., 2003], or to better organize well known samples in homogeneous clusters. For example, it would be possible that diseased patients could be partitioned with respect to some conditions, or healthy patients could be clustered with respect to the probability to contract a disease. Formally *cluster analysis* tries to determine distinct groups in all data, where members of each group are similar to other members but are different from members of other groups, with respect to a particular distance.

Probabilistic Classification with Q5 Algorithm. The Q5 algorithm [Lilien et al., 2003] is a closed-form solution to the problem of classification of complete mass spectra. Q5 employs a probabilistic classification algorithm built upon dimension-reduced linear discriminant analysis. The classifier computed by Q5 is optimal under this error function with respect to the training set. The Q5 method outperforms previous full-spectrum complex sample spectral classification techniques and can provide clues as to the molecular identities of differentially expressed proteins and peptides. It uses Principal Component Analysis (PCA) [Joliffe, 1986], a well known technique for multivariate analysis. In particular PCA is used to reduce the dimensionality of a data set with little or no information loss as reported in [Lilien et al., 2003].

From a geometrical point of view, each spectrum can be represented as a vector in n-dimensional space. PCA takes the cloud of data points, and rotates it such that the maximum variability is visible. Another way of saying this is that it identifies most important gradients. The first stage in rotating the data cloud is subtracting the mean and dividing by the standard deviation, in this way the centroid of the whole data set is zero. Principal Component Analysis chooses the first PCA axis as that line that goes through the centroid and minimizes the square of the distance of each point to that line. The second PCA axis also goes through centroid and also goes through the maximum variation in the data, but with a certain constraint: *it must be completely uncorrelated.* Formally, given a set of variables $X_1, \ldots, X_n$, PCA produces a new set of variables $Y_1, \ldots, Y_i, \ldots, Y_p$ ($p < N$) in which each of Y_i is a linear combination of $X_1, \ldots, X_n$. PCA ensures that new variables are uncorrelated. Each new variable is a principal component. In this way successive steps can operate on a reduced data set. After PCA, a clustering method performs a discrimination between reduced spectra according to a metric induced in new space obtained.

Although PCA is often used as an unsupervised clustering technique, in Q5 it is used only for dimensionality reduction, whereas Linear Discriminant Analysis (LDA) is used to compute discriminant between classes, taking into account (supervised) the class membership of each sample. Given a system with *n* classes in *k* dimensions it computes *k-1* orthogonal vectors that specify an hyperplane of *k-1* dimensions. Projection of sample points (each spectrum in our experiment) maximizes the between-class scatter (healty-disease) and minimizes the within class scatter. Contrarily to Discriminant Factorial Analysis (DFA), LDA computes the optimal discriminant in a closed form. LDA utilizes class membership of each sample in computation.

The version of Q5 used in our experiment, that works on the whole spectrum, is implemented in *Matlab* script and is freely downloadable [3] under GNU public license. It reads the ovarian cancer data and builds (in case of two class classification) two couples of arrays: (Normal Healthy Intensity, Normal Healthy Mass Charge Ratio), and (Ovarian Cancer Intensity, Ovarian Cancer Mass-Charge Ratio), containing respectively the spectra of healthy and cancerous patients. Next it performs the PCA and LDA analysis to different training and test sets in order to produce the classification. As shown in Fig. 4, a spectral dataset is first partitioned into training set and test set whose relative dimensions can be tuned from user as parameter of Matlab script. These spectra are projected onto PCA basis to create the reduced representation in PCA-SPACE. The spectra in this space are projected onto the LDA discriminant aiming to compute the statistical parameter of classes. Spectra are projected onto PCA basis, then onto LDA discriminant and finally classified. Each sample is assigned to a class using a probability distribution function.

Notes

1. FDA-NCI Clinical Proteomics Program Databank. [http://ncifdaproteomics.com/]
2. [http://clinicalproteomics.steem.com/download-ovar.php]
3. [http://www.cs.dartmouth.edu/~donaldlab/Software/]

References

Aebersold, Ruedi and Mann, Matthias (2003). Mass spectrometry-based proteomics. *Nature*, 422:198–207.

Ball, G., Mian, S., Holding, F., Allibone, R., Lowe, J., Ali, S., Li, G., McCardie, S., Ellis, I., Creaser, C., and Rees, R. (2002). An integrated approach utilizing artificial neural networks and seldi mass spectrometry for the classification of human tumours and rapid identification of potential biomarkers. *Bioinformatics*, 3(18):395–404.

Cannataro, M., Comito, C., Schiavo, F. Lo, and Veltri, P. (2004). Proteus, a grid based problem solving for bioinformatics: Architecture and experiments. *IEEE Computational Intelligence Bulletin*, 3(1):7–18.

Conrads, T.P., Zhou, M., Petricoin, E.F., Liotta, L., and Veenstra, T.D. (2003). Cancer diagnosis using proteomic patterns. *Expert Rev Mol Diagn*, 4(3):411–420.

Cuda, Giovanni, Cannataro, Mario, Quaresima, Barbara, Baudi, Francesco, Casadonte, Rita, Faniello, Maria Concetta, Tagliaferri, Pierosandro, Veltri, Pierangelo, Costanzo, Francesco, and Venuta, Salvatore (2003). Proteomic profiling of inherited breast cancer: Identification of molecular targets for early detection, prognosis and treatment, and related bioinformatics tools. *Lecture Notes in Computer Science*, pages 245–247.

Glish, Gary L. and Vachet, Richard W. (2003). The basic of mass spectrometry in the twenty-first century. *Nature Reviews*, 2:140–150.

Joliffe, I.T. (1986). *Principal Component Analysis*. Springer-Verlag.

Lilien, Ryan H., Farid, Hany, and Donald, Bruce R. (2003). Probabilistic disease classification of expression-dependent proteomic data from mass spectrometry of human serum. *Journal of computational biology*, 10(6):925–946.

Petricoin, E.F., Ardekani, A.M., Hitt, B.A., Levine, P.J., Fusaro, V.A., Steinberg, S.M., Mills, G.B., Simone, C., Fishman, D.A., Kohn, E.C., and Liotta, L.A. (2002). Use of proteomic patterns in serum to identify ovarian cancer. *The Lancet*, 359(9306):572–577.

Wagner, M., Naik, D., and Pothen, A. (2003). Protocols for disease classification from mass spectrometry data. *Proteomics*, 9(3):1692–1698.

FEATURE SELECTION COMBINED WITH RANDOM SUBSPACE ENSEMBLE FOR GENE EXPRESSION BASED DIAGNOSIS OF MALIGNANCIES

Alberto Bertoni, [1] Raffaella Folgieri, [1] Giorgio Valentini, [1]

[1]*DSI, Dipartimento di Scienze dell' Informazione,*
Università degli Studi di Milano,
Via Comelico 39, 20135 Milano, Italia.
bertoni@dsi.unimi.it
folgieri@dico.unimi.it
valentini@dsi.unimi.it

Abstract The bio-molecular diagnosis of malignancies represents a difficult learning task, because of the high dimensionality and low cardinality of the data. Many supervised learning techniques, among them support vector machines, have been experimented, using also feature selection methods to reduce the dimensionality of the data. In alternative to feature selection methods, we proposed to apply random subspace ensembles, reducing the dimensionality of the data by randomly sampling subsets of features and improving accuracy by aggregating the resulting base classifiers. In this paper we experiment the combination of random subspace with feature selection methods, showing preliminary experimental results that seem to confirm the effectiveness of the proposed approach.

Keywords: Molecular diagnosis, ensemble methods, Support Vector Machine, Random Subspace, DNA microarray

1. Introduction

High throughput bio-technologies based on large scale hybridization techniques (e.g. DNA microarray) can provide information for supporting both diagnosis and prognosis of malignancies at bio-molecular level [Alizadeh, A. et al., 2001]. Several supervised methods have been applied to the analysis of cDNA microarrays and high density oligonucleotide chips (see e.g. [S. Dudoit and Speed, 2002]). The high dimensionality and low cardinality of gene

B. Apolloni et al. (eds.), Biological and Artificial Intelligence Environments, 29–35

expression data, together with the high sensitivity required for diagnostic problems, makes the classification of malignant and normal samples very challenging from a machine learning point of view.

An effective approach to this problem is represented by feature selection methods [Guyon et al., 2002], that can be useful both to select the genes more related to malignancies and to enhance the discrimination power between normal and malignant tissues. Recently we proposed an alternative approach [Bertoni et al., 2004] based on random subspace ensembles [Ho, 1998], that is sets of learning machines trained on randomly chosen subspaces of the original input space.

In this paper we propose to integrate the two approaches in order to enhance the accuracy and the reliability of the diagnostic system: at a first stage a subset of genes is selected through a feature selection method, successively subsets of genes randomly drawn from the previously selected genes are used to train an ensemble of learning machines. The ensemble output can be obtained through majority voting or any other aggregation technique. We call this method *Random Subspace on Selected Features* (*RS-SF*).

The proposed combined approach is described in the next section. Some preliminary experimental results are shown in Sect. 3, while in the last section we report conclusions and on-going developments of the present work.

2. Feature selection methods and random subspace ensembles for gene expression data analysis

The major problem in gene expression analysis is the high dimensionality and low cardinality of the data, from which the curse of dimensionality problem arises.

An approach to this problem consists in reducing the dimensionality through feature (gene) selection methods [Golub et al., 1999; Guyon et al., 2002]. Many methods can be applied, ranging from filter methods, wrapper methods, information theory based techniques and "embedded" methods (see e.g. [Guyon and Elisseeff, 2003] for a recent review).

On the other hand we recently experimented a different approach [Bertoni et al., 2004] based on random subspace ensemble methods [Ho, 1998]. For a fixed k, k-subsets of features are selected. according to the uniform distribution. Then the data of the original training set are projected to the selected n-dimensional subspaces and the resulting data sets are used to train an ensemble of learning machines [Ho, 1998].

RS-SF Algorithm

`Input:`

- A data set $\mathcal{D} = \{(\mathbf{x}_j, t_j) | 1 \leq j \leq m\}$, $\mathbf{x}_j \in \mathcal{X} \subset \mathbb{R}^d$, $t_j \in \mathcal{C} = \{1, \ldots, k\}$
- a learning algorithm $\mathcal{L}$
- a feature selection algorithm $\mathcal{F}$
- a number of selected features $n < d$
- a dimension $k < n$ of the random subspace
- number of the base learners I

`Output:`

- Final hypothesis $h_{ran} : \mathcal{X} \rightarrow \mathcal{C}$ computed by the ensemble.

`begin`

$\hat{\mathcal{D}} = \mathcal{F}(\mathcal{D}, \text{n})$

for $i = 1$ to I

begin

$D_i =$ `Subspace_projection`$(\hat{\mathcal{D}}, \text{k})$

$h_i = \mathcal{L}(D_i)$

end

$h_{ran}(\mathbf{x}) = \arg\max_{t \in \mathcal{C}} card(\{i | h_i(\mathbf{x}) = t\})$

`end.`

Figure 1. Random Subspace on Selected Features (*RS-SF*) ensemble method.

In this work we experiment a combination of the two approaches. The role of the gene selection stage consists in eliminating noisy or uninformative genes. Then we can apply random subspace ensembles only with the remaining more discriminant and informative genes, enhancing the accuracy of the resulting base learners though aggregation techniques, while diversity between base learners is maintained by the random choice of the input subspaces.

Fig. 1 summarizes the proposed method. $\mathcal{F}$ denotes a feature selection algorithm, that selects the n most significant features from the original d-dimensional input space. `Subspace_projection` is a randomized procedure that selects, according to the uniform distribution, a k-subset $A = \{\alpha_1, \ldots, \alpha_k\}$ from $\{1, 2, \ldots, n\}$, so defining a projection $P_A : \mathbb{R}^n \rightarrow \mathbb{R}^k$, where $P_A(x_1, \ldots, x_n) = (x_{\alpha_1}, \ldots, x_{\alpha_k})$; then it returns as output the new k-dimensional data set $\{(P_A(\mathbf{x}_j), t_j) | 1 \leq j \leq m\}$, where $\hat{\mathcal{D}} = \{(\mathbf{x}_j), t_j) | 1 \leq j \leq m\}$ is the set of the n-dimensional features selected from the original d-dimensional input space. Every new data set D_i obtained through the iteration of the procedure `Subspace_projection` is given as input to a learning algorithm $\mathcal{L}$ which outputs a classifier h_i. Note that, with abuse of notation, with $h_i(\mathbf{x})$ we ambiguously denote the extension of h_i to the entire $\mathbb{R}^d$ space. All the obtained classifiers are finally aggregated through majority voting.

3. Experiments with the colon adenocarcinoma gene expression data

To evaluate the feasibility of the *RS-SF* ensemble method for the analysis of gene expression data, we considered the colon adenocarcinoma bio-molecular diagnosis problem. The *colon* data set is composed of 62 samples: 40 colon tumor and 22 normal colon tissue samples, with 2000 gene expression data for each sample [Alon, U. et al., 1999].

Main goal of the experiment is the performance comparison of SVMs trained with subsets of genes chosen through a simple but effective feature selection method (Golub's method) [Golub et al., 1999] and *RS-SF* ensembles.

3.1 Experimental setup

Regarding preprocessing of data, we used the same techniques illustrated in [Alon, U. et al., 1999]. Groups of genes have been selected ranking the gene's scores obtained through the Golub's statistics. The selection of the genes has been performed using only training data in order to avoid the selection bias [Ambroise and McLachlan, 2002].

Table 1. Summary of the best results achieved with single SVMs trained on subsets of genes selected through Golub's method (Single *FS-SVM*), *RS-SF* ensembles of SVMs, standard random subspace ensembles (*RS* ensemble), single SVMs without feature selection, and the average error of the base SVMs that compose the ensemble.

	Test Err.	St.dev	Train Err.	St.dev	Sens.	Spec.
RS-SF ensemble	0.0968	0.0697	0.0727	0.0183	0.9250	0.8636
RS ensemble	0.1290	0.0950	0.0000	0.0000	0.9000	0.8182
Single *FS-SVM*	0.1129	0.0950	0.0768	0.0231	0.9250	0.8182
Single *SVM*	0.1774	0.1087	0.0000	0.0000	0.8500	0.7727
Single base *SVM*	0.1776	0.1019	0.0000	0.0000	——	——

We considered different random subspaces of dimensionality from 2 to 2^{n-1}, randomly drawn from each 2^n-dimensional gene space selected from the input space through the Golub's method, while varying n between 5 and 10. According to Skurichina e Duin [Skurichina and Duin, 2002] we applied linear SVMs as base learners. Indeed they showed that random subspace ensembles are effective with linear base learners characterized by a decreasing learning curve (error) with respect to the cardinality n, especially when the dimensionality is much larger than the cardinality. For each ensemble we trained 200 linear SVMs, considering values of the regularization parameter C between 0.01 and 1000.

We computed for both single SVMs and *RS-SF* ensembles the test error and training error, sensibility, specificity and precision through 5-fold cross validation techniques. Regarding software, we developed new C++ classes and applications for random subspace ensembles extending the *NEURObjects* library [Valentini and Masulli, 2002]. For all the experiments, we used the C.I.L.E.A. Avogadro cluster of Xeon double processor workstations [Arlandini, 2004].

3.2 Results

The results show that the best *RS-SF* ensemble outperforms single SVMs trained with a subset of selected genes (Single *FS-SVM*). In fact we obtained respectively a 0.0968 test error in the first case, and 0.1129 for *FS-SVM* (Tab. 1). The test error of *RS-SF* ensemble is consistently equal or lower than single *FS-SVM*, independently of the number of the selected genes, as shown in Fig. 2. In particular the minimum of the test error with 128 selected genes is obtained with 64-dimensional random subspace, while with 512 selected genes with 16-dimensional subspaces. In both considered methods, the sensitivity has the same value from 32 to 128 selected genes, then it decreases for single *FS-SVM*, while becomes constant for *RS-SF* ensembles (Fig. 3). Also the specificity is better for random subspace ensemble combined with feature selection: a maximum is achieved with 128 selected genes, and for number of selected genes larger than 64 *RS-SF* ensembles show better results than single *FS-SVM* (Fig. 3).

The difference between the best *RS-SF* ensemble and single *FS-SVM* is not statistically significant, according to the 5-fold cross validated t-test [Dietterich, 1998] (Tab. 1). On the contrary it becomes significant with standard random subspace ensemble and single SVMs trained without feature selection. Anyway, considering the accuracy in *RS-SF* ensemble and single *FS-SVM* with respect to the number of the selected genes, the difference is significant at 0.05 level in most cases (Fig. 2).

4. Conclusions and developments

The results show the applicability of the combined approach of the random subspace ensemble with feature selection methods, to the analysis of gene expression data. Anyway we need to perform more experiments with other data sets, to confirm, as may be expected, the presented results. The proposed approach doesn't require a specific feature selection method. Regarding this item, we plan to experiment with other feature selection algorithms.

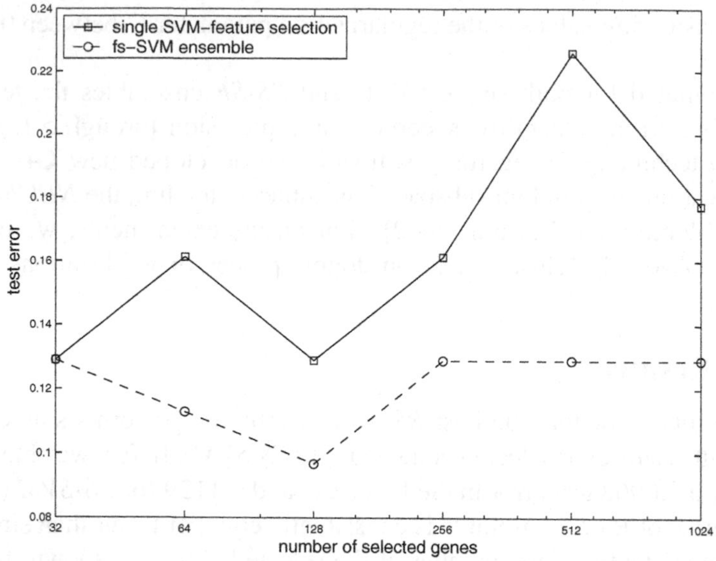

Figure 2. Comparison of the test error with respect to the number of the selected features between *RS-SF* ensembles of SVMs and *FS-SVMs*.

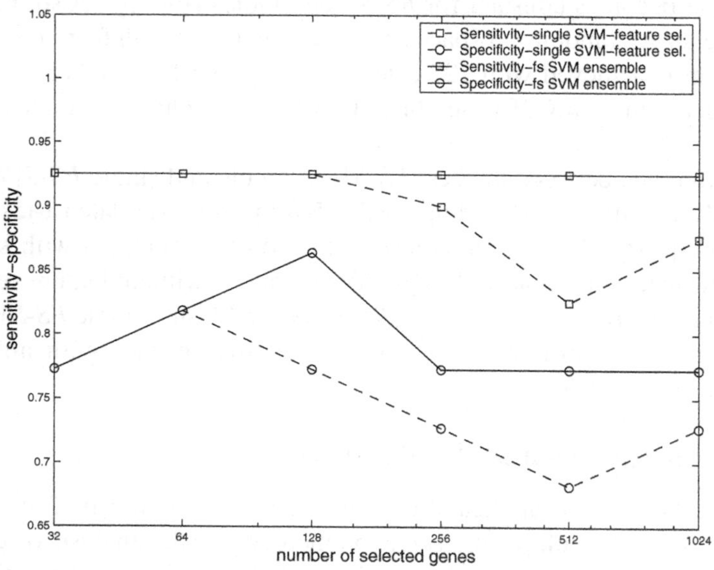

Figure 3. Comparison of sensitivity and specificity with respect to the number of the selected features between *RS-SF* ensembles of SVMs (continuous lines) and *FS-SVMs* (dashed lines).

Acknowledgments

We would like to thank the C.I.L.E.A. for providing *Avogadro* [Arlandini, 2004], the computer Linux cluster used in our experiments.

References

Alizadeh, A. et al. (2001). Towards a novel classification of human malignancies based on gene expression. *J. Pathol.*, 195:41–52.

Alon, U. et al. (1999). Broad patterns of gene expressions revealed by clustering analysis of tumor and normal colon tissues probed by oligonucleotide arrays. *PNAS*, 96:6745–6750.

Ambroise, C. and McLachlan, G. (2002). Selection bias in gene extraction on the basis of microarray gene-expression data. *PNAS*, 99(10):6562–6566.

Arlandini, C. (2004). Avogadro: il CILEA oltre il muro del teraflop. *Bollettino del CILEA*, 91.

Bertoni, A., Folgieri, R., and Valentini, G. (2004). Random subspace ensembles for the biomolecular diagnosis of tumors.

Dietterich, T.G. (1998). Approximate statistical test for comparing supervised classification learning algorithms. *Neural Computation*, (7):1895–1924.

Dudoit, S., Fridlyand, J., and Speed, T. (2002). Comparison of discrimination methods for the classification of tumors using gene expression data. *JASA*, 97(457):77–87.

Golub, T.R. et al. (1999). Molecular Classification of Cancer: Class Discovery and Class Prediction by Gene Expression Monitoring. *Science*, 286:531–537.

Guyon, I. and Elisseeff, A. (2003). An Introduction to Variable and Feature Selection. *Journal of Machine Learning Research*, 3:1157–1182.

Guyon, I., Weston, J., Barnhill, S., and Vapnik, V. (2002). Gene Selection for Cancer Classification using Support Vector Machines. *Machine Learning*, 46(1/3):389–422.

Ho, T.K. (1998). The random subspace method for constructing decision forests. *IEEE Transactions on Pattern Analysis and Machine Intelligence*, 20(8):832–844.

Skurichina, M. and Duin, R.P.W. (2002). Bagging, boosting and the randon subspace method for linear classifiers. *Pattern Analysis and Applications*, 5(2):121–135.

Valentini, G. and Masulli, F. (2002). NEURObjects: an object-oriented library for neural network development. *Neurocomputing*, 48(1–4):623–646.

PRUNING THE NODULE CANDIDATE SET IN POSTERO ANTERIOR CHEST RADIOGRAPHS

Paola Campadelli and Elena Casiraghi
Università degli Studi di Milano,
Dipartimento di Scienze dell'Informazione,
via Comelico 39/41,
20135, Milano
{Campadelli, Casiraghi}@dsi.unimi.it
http://homes.dsi.unimi.it/~campadel/LAIV/index.htm

Abstract In this paper we describe and compare two different methods to reduce the cardinality of the set of candidates nodules, characterized by an high sensitivity ratio, and extracted from PA chest radiographs by a fully automatized method. The methods are a rule based system and a feed-forward neural network trained by back-propagation. Both the systems allow to recognize almost the 75% of false positives without losing any true positives.

Keywords: CAD Systems, Neural Networks, Support Vector Machines

Introduction

In the field of medical diagnosis the chest radiography is by far the most common type of procedure for the initial detection and diagnosis of lung cancer, due to its noninvasivity characteristics, radiation dose and economic considerations. Several studies in the last two decades (see [Austin et al., 1992] and [Forrest and Friedman, 1982]) calculated an average miss rate of 30% for the radiographic detection of early lung nodules by humans. In a large lung cancer screening program 90% of peripheral lung cancers have been found to be visible in radiographs produced earlier than the date of the cancer discovery by the radiologist. This explains why in the last two decades a great deal of research work has been devoted to the development of Computer Aided Diagnostic (CAD) systems aimed to lung nodules detection, and a wide variety of them have been already proposed and reviewed in [van Ginneken et al., 2001]. Most of the methods presented in the literature are based on a two stage processing scheme. At first, the image is processed in order to increase the

B. Apolloni et al. (eds.), Biological and Artificial Intelligence Environments, 37–43

visibility(conspicuity) of the nodules; the regions that may contain nodules are then extracted by means of rule based schemes which exploit the main nodule characteristics, such as the gray level and the circular shape. The second step aims to the selection of the real nodules within the set of the extracted candidates; this is generally done by means of classification methods, which first reduce the number of candidates, usually quite high, and then extract the final ones. The main issue regarding this step is the choice of a proper set of features to describe and represent the data so that the samples belonging to the two classes may easily distinguished. Moreover the main problem of the presented schemes is the high number of false positives; such problem has been faced with two different strategies: either to reduce the number of candidates extracted by the first two steps ([Wu et al., 1994], [Xu et al., 1998], [Yoshida et al., 1995]), or to leave to proper classifiers the task of reduction ([Penedo et al., 1998], [Lin et al., 1996], [Lo et al., 1993], [A. Schilham and Loog, 2003]); in both cases however many true positives are discarded, leaving the problem open.

We developed a fully automatized method using multiscale approaches to segment the lungs (see [Columbano, 2004]) and then enhance the visibility of the nodules in the area detected (see [Campadelli and Casiraghi, 2004]). The multiscale analysis of the image is a fundamental key for both the task of segmentation and nodule detection; in the first case it allows to capture the details of the lung borders which belong to different scales, and in the second case it is used to handle all the possible sizes of the nodules.

This multiscale approach is an additional element with respect to the method presented in the literature and it has proven to be necessary and effective. First of all, it allows to increase the visibility of also the most subtle nodules, facilitating the extraction task which indeed loses very few true positives and creates a set with an high sensitivity ratio. Second, it is employed to extract a set of features which is different from the ones commonly presented in the literature since it captures the properties of the candidates at various scales; in this paper we present our experiments using these features as input to trim the set of candidates initially extracted; to this aim we experimented two different methods and compared their performances: they are a rule based system and a feed-forward neural network trained by back-propagation. Both the systems had similar results.

1. Materials and methods

The method has been tested on a standard database acquired by the Japanese Society of Radiological Technology. It contains 247 radiographs: 154 containing lung nodules and 93 of patients with no disease. The images were digitized with a 0.175 mm pixel size, a matrix size of 2048×2048, and 4096 gray levels.

The diameter of the nodules ranges from 5 to 35 mm. All the nodules in the images have been classified according to the difficulties encountered in their detection by the radiologists. They have been divided in 5 classes ranging from obvious to extremely subtle. The algorithm for the candidate extraction works on images down-sampled to an experimentally set dimension of 256×256 pixels to reduce its computational cost without worsening the performances. The features used as input for nodule classification are instead calculated on the images with 512×512 pixels to have a more detailed representation.

2. Extraction and pruning of the nodule candidate set

The method starts with the segmentation of the images to extract the lung fields (see [Columbano, 2004]) and the enhancement of the conspicuity of the nodules as described in [Campadelli and Casiraghi, 2004]. In [Paola Campadelli and Columbano, 2004] we describe a multiscale method analyzing the *enhanced images* to extract a unique set of candidate regions; it also allows to create an image I_r for different nodule radiuses, $r = 2, .., 12$. The value $I_r(x, y)$, associated to each pixel (x, y), is a measure which represents the pixel as a potential center of a nodule of radius r. The combination of the 11 images I_r is a gray level image $G(x, y)$, obtained by assigning to each pixel in each candidate region the value

$$G(x, y) = \max_{r \in [2,12]} (I_r(x, y)) \tag{1}$$

and then scaling it in the range $[0, 255]$. All the details of the method are described in [Campadelli and Casiraghi, 2004].
With this extraction scheme we get a set of about 32000 regions on the 247 images of the database, with an average of about 130 regions per image and only 5 true positives lost out of 154. The comparison of these results with those presented in the literature and described in [A. Schilham and Loog, 2003] and [Keserci and Hiroyuki, 2002] showed the better performance of our method (see [Campadelli and Casiraghi, 2004]).

To reduce the number of the extracted candidates we searched for a set of rules which could describe the main characteristics of the real nodules, hence allowing us to discard some false positives. To this end we calculated for each region a set of 40 features and studied their distribution. The statistical analysis allowed us to select a set of 12 most representative features, whose combination by means of simple rules, has proved to be effective for a first candidates selection. The created rule based scheme is indeed able to detect and discard more than half false positives. In the following we will describe just the selected features. They are based on the shape and position of the region , the gray level distribution in the original radiograph down-sampled to

the dimension of 512×512 pixels, the values of the gray levels in the image $G(x, y)$, and the set of coefficients $I_r(x, y)$ associated to each pixel for each radius value.
Six features are based on the shape; they are:

- circularity, as defined in [Giger et al., 1988];
- effective radius, that is the radius of the circle with an area equivalent to the one of the region;
- the ratio between the perimeter of the region and the perimeter of the circle with radius of 12 pixels (we are considering $r = 12$ as maximum radius value);
- the ratio between the area of the region and the area of the circle with radius of 12 pixels;
- the ratio between the two dimensions of the minimum bounding box including the region;
- the ratio between the two dimensions of the maximum bounding box including the region;

One feature is based on the gray level distribution of the pixels in the original radiograph down-sampled to the dimension of 512×512 pixels: it is simply the mean of the gray levels of the pixels in each region.
Two features are calculated on the gray level of the pixels in the image $G(x, y)$: they are the mean and the maximum value of the gray level of the pixels.
The position feature has been introduced to eliminate false positives detected on the rib cage boundaries, which are characterized by the fact that they are attached to the lung borders and have an elongated shape. It is calculated considering the external contour of the region and it is the fraction of the number of pixels of the contour which lay outside the lung area with respect to the total number of the pixels in the contour itself.
Two features are calculated as an estimate of the most characteristic radius value to be associated to a generic region X. We use two different methods to get it and hence obtain two values that can be compared. One method first calculates for each pixel (x, y) a most eligible radius $rad(x, y)$. This is done by considering all the $I_r(x, y)$ obtained for that pixel and then calculating:

$$rad(x,y) = Argmax_{r \in [2,12]}(I_r(x,y)) \tag{2}$$

The first radius, R_X^1, associated to X is then $R_X^1 = \max_{(x,y) \in X} rad(x, y)$.
The second method calculates the radius R_X^2 by considering for each different value of r the sum

$$Sum_X(r) = \sum_{(x,y) \in X} I_r(x,y) \tag{3}$$

Again R_X^2 is calculated according to:

$$R_X^2 = Argmax_{r \in [2,12]}(Sum_X(r)) \tag{4}$$

We note that R_X^1 and R_X^2 are very similar in case of true positive elements and significantly different for many false positives; based on this fact we are allowed to recognize some regions as false positives.
The remaining feature is the maximum value of the various $Sum_X(r)$, hence the one associated with R_X^2.

This set of features is the input of a rule based system composed by 12 simple rules: 8 of them basically describe the relationships observed between pairs of features, meanwhile 4 are based on simple tresholding. The system can easily discard 19500 false positives without loosing any true positives, hence reaching a sensitivity ratio equal to 0.97 and a total number of candidates that is about 12000, approximately 50 candidates per image.
Our results can be compared with the ones of the method described in [A. Schilham and Loog, 2003] in which the authors apply a classifier that selects 5028 candidates from the first set composed by 33000 regions, but loosing other 15 true positives in addition to the 20 already lost, for a total of 36 false negatives. Our pruning method is able to discard less false positives but does not loose any nodules. Although the rules chosen are very intuitive and simple they need some thresholds to be experimentally set; therefore they may depend on the images in the database.

3. Employing Neural Network Classifiers for candidates selection

In this section we describe experiments aimed to the use of a feed-forward neural network trained by standard back-propagation to trim the first set of extracted candidates. The advantage of this system with respect to the rule based one is that, once the network is trained, it does not need any threshold to be set. Moreover we expect that learning algorithms working with the global set of features as input, could have better performances since they could learn more complicated relationships than the simple ones of our rule based system.
In the following we describe our experiments aimed to this purpose.
The input of the network is represented by a vector $X = [x_1, ..., x_{12}, x_{13}, x_{14}]$ where $x_1, .., x_{12}$ represent the features previously described, and x_{13}, x_{14} are the spatial coordinates of the center of mass of the nodule; they are expressed in a local coordinate system which has its origin in the center of mass of the lung fields and it is scaled with respect to the width and length of the lung area. We apply to the input vector a preprocessing aimed to data normalization,

followed by a scaling that brings all the values to the range [0.0, 1.0].
One observation to be done is that the two classes to be recognized, *"nodules"* and *"NOT nodules"*, are highly unbalanced (the *"nodules"* are 149, the *"NOT nodules"* are about 32000). Our choice was then to train the neural network in order to recognize and discard the regions whose set of features is totally different from the one of the nodules. To this end we classified the data obtained as *"possible nodules"* and *"NOT nodules"*. This classification was realized considering as *"NOT nodules"* the ones discarded by the rule based system and as *possible nodules* all the others, hence obtaining two classes with about 20000 and 12000 elements. We made experiments using both a training and a validation set. They were formed by randomly choosing from both the classes, the 50% of the elements for the training, and the 10% for the validation. The remaining elements (40% of the total) were used for testing. We used a neural network with 1 hidden layer composed of 8 neurons and an output layer with 2 neurons, and made several experiments changing the parameters of the learning algorithm (the momentum and the learning rate) the maximum number of epochs for the training, the minimum error allowed on the training set, and especially the elements in the input set. During these experiments an input data was classified as belonging to a class when the corresponding output neuron had a value bigger than 0.7. The obtained results are comparable with those of the rule based system: the network does not loose any true positives and in the worst case the number of false positives detected is never less than the 99% of the number recognized by the rule based system.
The final number of candidates obtained by both systems described above is still quite high, and needs a further reduction in order to be useful for clinical purposes. To perform this reduction we experimented neural networks whose input is the sub-image of the candidate itself created by extracting from the original radiograph an area of dimension 400 by 400 centered on the centroid of the candidate region considered. Several experiments have been done using as input down-sampled versions of the sub-images created. We tried with images down-sampled to 40x40, 20x20, 10x10, 8x8 and trained architectures of different complexities. The best results obtained on the test set composed of 11000 false positives samples and 30 true positives allowed to maintain only 1300 false positives but caused the loss of 10 true positives. Since this results are not acceptable we are now looking for other features and different or more complex classifiers, such as Support Vector Machines.

References

A. Schilham, B.Van Ginneken and Loog, M. (2003). Multi-scale nodule detection in chest radiographs. *Proc. MICCAI.*

Austin, J.H.M., Romeny, B.M., and Goldsmith, L.S. (1992). Missed bronchogenic carcinoma: radiographic findings in 27 patients with apotentially resectable lesion evident in retrospect. *Radiology*, 182:115–122.

Campadelli, Paola and Casiraghi, Elena (2004). Nodule detection in postero anterior chest radiographs. *Submitted to MCO2004.*

Columbano, Simon (2004). Analisi di immagini toraciche e relativa segmentazione. *Master Thesis, Universitadegli Studi di Milano.*

Forrest, J. and Friedman, P. (1982). Radiologic errors in patient with lung cancer. *West Journal on Med.*, 134:485–490.

Giger, M., Doi, K., and Mahon, H. Mac (1988). Image feature analisys and computer-aided diagnosis in digital radiography:automated detection of nodules in peripheral lung fields. *Med. Phisycs*, 15:158–166.

Keserci, B. and Hiroyuki, Y. (2002). Computerized detection of pulmonary nodules in chest radiographs based on morphological features and wavelet snake model. *Medical Image Analysis*, pages 431–447.

Lin, J.-S., Lo, S.-C., Freedman, M., and S.Mun (1996). Reduction of false positives in lung nodule detection using a two-level neural classification. *IEEE Trans. Med. Imag.*, 15:206–217.

Lo, S.-C., Freedman, M., Lin, J.-S., and S.Mun (1993). Automatic lung nodule detection using profile matching and backpropagation neural network techniques. *Journal Digital Imaging*, 1:48–54.

Paola Campadelli, Elena Casiraghi and Columbano, Stefano (2004). Lung segmentation and nodule detection in postero anterior chest radiographs. *Accepted to GIRPR2004.*

Penedo, M., Carreira, M., Mosquera, A., and Cabello, D. (1998). Computer aided diagnosis: A neural network based approach to lung nodule detection. *IEEE Trans. Med. Imag.*, 17:872–880.

van Ginneken, B., ter H. Romeny, B.M., and Viergever, M.A. (2001). Computer-aided diagnosis in chest radiography: A survey. *IEEE Trans. On Med. Imag.*, 20:1228–1241.

Wu, Y., Doi, K., Giger, M., Metz, C., and Zhang, W. (1994). Reduction of false positives in computerized detection of lung nodules in chest radiographs using convolution neural network techniques and application for lung nodule detection. *J. Digital Imaging*, 7:196–207.

Xu, X.-W., Katsuragawa, S., Ashizawa, A., MacMahon, H., and Doi, K. (1998). Analisys of image features of histograms of edge gradient for false positive reduction in lung nodule detection in chest radiographs. *Proc SPIE*, 3338:318–326.

Yoshida, H., Xu, X., Doi, K., and Giger, M. (1995). Computer-aided diagnosis (cad) scheme for detecting pulmonary nodules using wavelet transforms. *Proc. SPIE*, 2434:621–626.

PROTEIN STRUCTURE ASSEMBLY FROM KNOWLEDGE OF β-SHEET MOTIFS AND SECONDARY STRUCTURE

Alessio Ceroni, Paolo Frasconi and Alessandro Vullo
Dipartimento di Sistemi e Informatica, Università di Firenze, Italy
{aceroni,p-f,vullo}@dsi.unifi.it

Abstract We develop and test a new hierarchical approach for the prediction of protein structure. An algorithm is described to assemble the 3D fold of a protein starting from its secondary structure and β-sheet topology. Reconstruction is carried out by energy minimization of a reduced protein model, where β-partners are derived from appropriate distance constraints imposed by the knowledge of β-sheet motifs. Additional constraints are imposed in the (ϕ, ψ) torsion space from secondary structure knowledge. Experiments show how the proposed procedure proves to be a reliable and fast predictive approach for a large fraction of proteins of interest. Arrangements of β-sheets are predicted with special recursive neural networks architectures. We first present a unifying framework for description of a large class of contextual recursive models and then show how it is possible to solve the problem at some extent of success.

Keywords: Protein structure prediction, β-sheets prediction, recursive neural networks, protein structure reconstruction.

1. Introduction

Knowledge of the spatial conformation of a protein can help the study of its function. Unfortunately, the number of resolved structures is still limited by the low throughput of available experimental methods. Prediction tools have the potential to bridge the sequence-structure gap, but no reliable and general methods have yet been proposed. Attempts to simplify the problem have been made by trying to predict the contact map of a protein instead of its atomic positions. It has been demonstrated how good protein models can be derived even with noisy contact maps [Vendruscolo et al., 1997]. Unfortunately, prediction of contact maps is still very unreliable and it is not clear whether the type of errors made by the predictor can be corrected by the reconstruction method. In the attempt to train more efficient predictors, a low-detail representation of protein conformation could extract high level relevant information. Prediction of coarse-grained contact maps, i.e. contacts are defined among secondary

B. Apolloni et al. (eds.), Biological and Artificial Intelligence Environments, 45–52

structure segments, has been recently tried [Vullo and Frasconi, 2003], but yet there exists no clear result concerning feasibility of reconstruction using only coarse information.

In this work, we elaborate on efficient and reliable prediction methodologies tailored for a specific class of chains, those that are are mainly characterised by residues in strand conformation. The quality of reconstruction for this kind of proteins can be enhanced by the knowledge of secondary structure and indication of which strands are partners. We focus on contacts defined on β-partners, as the geometry and connectivity of β-strands imposes strong constraints on the overall structure of the protein. In section 2 we propose an efficient procedure to find a structure that matches the aforementioned characteristics of a given protein in its native conformation. In order to fully automate structure prediction, in section 3 we also describe an approach for predicting β-sheet motifs using a powerful class of connectionist models. Finally, in section 4 we describe our experiments and show encouraging results in both directions.

2. Backbone Reconstruction Algorithm

The reconstruction procedure performs energy minimization of a reduced protein model, where knowledge about secondary structure and β-partners in the native conformation is enforced as a set of constraints on candidate solutions. The protein model comprises all backbone heavy atoms plus a single atom for the C_β to represent side chain occupation. Free parameters of this model are the dihedral ϕ and ψ angles. The ω angle is set fixed to 180°, while coordinates of the C_β atom and all bond lengths and angles are set to their average values calculated on the PDB dataset.

Constraints on Protein Structure

Secondary structure information is enforced by constraining the values of the dihedral angles: α-helices (H) and β-strands (E) correspond to two compact regions in the $\phi - \psi$ plot. For every residue in the H and E classes, the distance between its coordinates in the (ϕ, ψ) space and the center of the corresponding region is forced to be lower than a specified threshold:

$$\| (\phi, \psi) - (\phi_s, \psi_s) \| \leq t_s \tag{1}$$

where $s \in \{H, E\}$. For each pair of β-strands we know if they are partners and in this case if they are parallel or anti-parallel. The geometry of two β-partners constrains the distance between hydrogen-bonded residues. Unfortunately, two partner strands can be of different dimensions and we do not want to specify the partnership in terms of connectivity between residues. Let I and J be the sequences of indexes of the residues in two β-strands and I^k and J^k two subsequences of size k. An alignment with parallel orientation is the set

$\{(I_1^k, J_1^k), \ldots, (I_k^k, J_k^k)\}$, while an alignment with anti-parallel orientation is the set $\{(I_1^k, J_k^k), (I_1^k, J_{k-1}^k), \ldots, (I_k^k, J_1^k)\}$. The procedure must test all possible alignments for each pair of strands. For partner strands, given a particular alignment, the distance between every pair of (supposedly) bonded atoms must be in a strict range of values

$$\forall_{i \in 1,k} : d_{min}^b \leq \| \bar{x}(I_i^k) - \bar{x}(J_i^k) \| \leq d_{max}^b \tag{2}$$

and the alignment that violates less constraints contributes to the solution: this enforces the existence of at least one good alignment between partners. For non-partner strands both orientations are tested; given a particular alignment, the distances between paired atoms must be greater than a specified value

$$\forall_{i \in 1,k} : \| \bar{x}(I_i^k) - \bar{x}(J_i^k) \| > d_{min}^{nb}. \tag{3}$$

and the alignment that violates more constraints contributes to the solution; no good alignments must exist between non-partners. Atomic forces impose a lower bound on the distance between two atoms, thus defining an excluded volume for each atom that prevents the protein to collapse in a single point. We introduced these constraints in our procedure by forcing the distances between all pairs of atoms to be higher than a specified threshold:

$$\forall_{i \in 1,k} : \| \bar{x}(I_i^k) - \bar{x}(J_i^k) \| > d_{min}^{nb} \tag{4}$$

Optimization

In order to simplify the optimization task, all the constraints are expressed as quadratic penalty terms:

$$d_{min} \leq d \leq d_{max} \rightarrow \begin{cases} (d - d_{min})^2 & d < d_{min} \\ (d - d_{max})^2 & d > d_{max} \\ 0 & \text{otherwise} \end{cases} \tag{5}$$

Unfortunately, this gives rise to a highly non linear function of the model free parameters. Global optimisation of non-linear cost functions is generally a difficult task, but we adopt here a simple approach consisting in a quasi-newton local optimization procedures (LBFGS [Liu and Nocedal, 1989]) coupled with a multistart strategies. Our non-linear cost function has in general many local minima. To mitigate this problem, we implement a specific protocol during optimization: firstly, we optimise the cost function with only secondary structure constraints, so that β-strands are formed in the backbone; secondly, we add the constraints for β-partners, relaxing the constraints on secondary structure so that a matching conformation is more easily found; finally, we add the constraints on atomic volumes, that could form barriers and prevent parts of the backbone to reach their final positions.

3. Prediction of β-sheet Motifs

As shown in the previous section, our reconstruction procedure needs a bunch of important ingredients: secondary structure, hence the location of β-strands, and the arrangement of β-sheets in the protein must be known. All these information are obtainable either from the PDB files, when the structure is known, or from predictions. Clearly, the former case is of limited interest and it is considered here to analyze upper bound performance of reconstruction. We assume here that secondary structure is known, for instance using one of several successful methods developed for this problem [Jones, 1999; Baldi et al., 1999], and focus on the more difficult task of prediction of β-sheet configurations.

The β-sheets motifs inference problem is modelled as a multi-class classification task. Assume we are given a set $\mathcal{S} = \{s_1, s_2, \ldots, s_n\}$ of strands, each pair of strands (s_i, s_j) defined on $\mathcal{S}$ can be mapped to one of three possible labels: say 0 (no hydrogen bonds between s_i and s_j), -1 (s_i and s_j are antiparallel) and 1 (parallel strands). The connectivity matrix on $\mathcal{S}$ represents the β-sheets motif and is defined as a matrix C whose elements $c_{ij} \in \{0, -1, 1\}$ correspond to the pairs (s_i, s_j). Here we model connectivity matrices as two-dimensional (square) undirected lattices, where nodes correspond to pairs of β-strands and edges connect adjacent pairs. Modelling β-sheets motifs in this way naturally gives rise to complex structured (graphical) representations than simple fixed size attribute-value pairs. The main advantage of using structured data is the possibility to encode intrinsic dependencies among atomic entities allowing powerful learning algorithms to be employed. The approach adopted here for predicting the connectivity matrix resemble those of [Pollastri and Baldi, 2002; G.Pollastri et al., 2003], where contextual Recursive Neural Networks (RNNs) are used to predict contact maps defined at the amino acid or segment level. In the following, we propose a unifying view of contextual RNNs and derive the predictive architecture used for the present case.

RNNs for undirected graphs

A data structure is a graph whose nodes are marked by sets of domain variables, called labels. A skeleton class, denoted by the symbol #, is a set of unlabeled graphs that satisfy some topological conditions. Let $\mathcal{I}$ and $\mathcal{O}$ denote two label spaces: $\mathcal{I}^\#$ (resp. $\mathcal{O}^\#$) refers to the space of data structures with vertex labels in $\mathcal{I}$ (resp. $\mathcal{O}$) and topology #. Recursive models such as RNNs [Frasconi et al., 1998] can be employed to compute functions $\mathcal{T} : \mathcal{I}^\# \rightarrow \mathcal{O}^\#$ which map a structure into another structure of the same form but possibly different labels. In the classical framework, # is contained in the class of bounded DPAGs, i.e DAGs where each vertex has bounded outdegree and whose children are ordered. Recursive models put a causality assumption

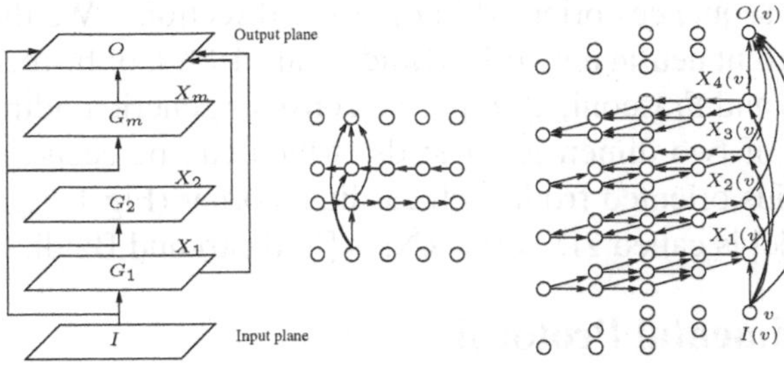

Figure 1. (left): Contextual RNNs, dependencies among input, state and output variables. (center and right): processing of undirected sequences and grids with contextual RNNs (only a subset of connections are shown).

on data processing: structures are processed bottom-up according to a reverse topological order of the nodes. Therefore, the state variables associated to these nodes and then their outputs depend only on the sub-structures induced by their children. The above assumption imposes some restrictions on the amount of contextual information that can be tackled and extensions of these models for dealing with more general undirected structures have been proposed [Baldi et al., 1999; Pollastri and Baldi, 2002; Vullo and Frasconi, 2003].

A more general assumption is considered here: # is contained in the class of bounded-degree undirected graphs. In this case, there is no concept of causality and the computational scheme described in [Frasconi et al., 1998] cannot be directly applied. The strategy consists in splitting graphical processing into a *set* of causal "dynamics", each one computed over a plausible orientation of U. More formally, assume $U = (V, E) \in \mathcal{I}^{\#}$ has one connected component. We identify a set of spanning DAGs $G_1, \ldots, G_m$ with $G_i = (V, E_i)$ such that:

- the undirected version of G_i is U
- $\forall\, v, u \in V\;\, v \neq u\; \exists\, i: \;(v, u) \in E_i^{\star}$ is $E_i^{\star}$ the transitive closure of E_i

and for each G_i, introduce a state variable X_i computed in the usual way. Fig.1 (left) shows a compact description of the set of dependencies among the input, state and output variables. Connections run from vertices of the input structure (layer I) to vertices of the spanning DAGs and from these nodes to nodes of the output structure (layer O). Using weight-sharing, the overall model can be summarized by $m + 1$ distinct neural networks implementing the output function $O(v) = g(X_1(v), \ldots, X_m(v), I(v))$ and m state transition functions $X_i(v) = f_i(X_i(ch_1[v]), \ldots, X_i(ch_k[v]), I(v))$. Learning can proceed by gradient-descent (back-propagation) due to the acyclic nature of the underlying graph. Within this framework, we can easily describe all contextual RNNs architecture developed so far. Fig.1 (center) shows that an undirected sequence is spanned by two sequences oriented in opposite directions. We then obtain bi-directional recurrent neural networks [Baldi et al., 1999], or bi-recursive neural networks [Vullo and Frasconi, 2003] if we consider generic undirected graphs. Our is the case of two-dimensional grids, which can be seen as spanned by four directed grids oriented from each cardinal corner (Fig.1, right). The corresponding model is called 2D DAG-RNNs [Pollastri and Baldi, 2002].

4. Experimental Protocol

The experiments were performed using a representative set of non homologous chains from the Protein Data Bank (PDBSelect, december 2002). For every chain we determined the secondary structure class using the same procedure employed for the CATH database [Orengo et al., 1997]. The final dataset contained only *mainly-β* proteins, for a total of 154 chains whose sequence length is between 30 and 300 residues.

Reconstruction from true and predicted β-sheet motifs

We first tested whether our reconstruction procedure is able to reproduce β-sheet motifs of real protein structures. Accuracy was measured as the proportion of pairs of β-strands correctly assigned as partners or non-partners. The average value obtained was 98.5%, with 74% of test proteins with all β-partners correctly assigned. We then tested whether knowledge of β-sheet motifs is sufficient to reconstruct protein native conformations with good quality. We used two measures of quality: the RMSD calculated on the C_α atoms for all the amino-acids in strands, and the GDT_TS measure adopted in the CASP contest [Zemla et al., 2001]. We obtained an average RMSD value of 7.55 Å, and an average GDT_TS of 29.7. The distribution of those measures in the whole data-set is shown in Fig. 2 (left). We then performed the same test on the β-sheet motifs as predicted from the recursive model (see sec.2). In this case, the average number of correctly assigned β-strands pairs dropped to 75%, since the predictor is likely to produce unrealistic structures. The average value of the RMSD became 16 Å, while the average value of GDT_TS was 24.

Prediction of β-sheet motifs

Together with contextual RNNs for grids, we trained and tested multi-layered feed-forward neural networks (FF-NNs) to predict the class of contact for the (i, j) pair of β-strands. In either cases, input was represented by merging an attribute-value representation for the i-th and j-th strand in the sequence. Segments were described by 23-dimensional feature vectors including the average multiple sequence alignment profile, the relative index of one strand and its normalized start and end amino acid positions. In these experiments, we

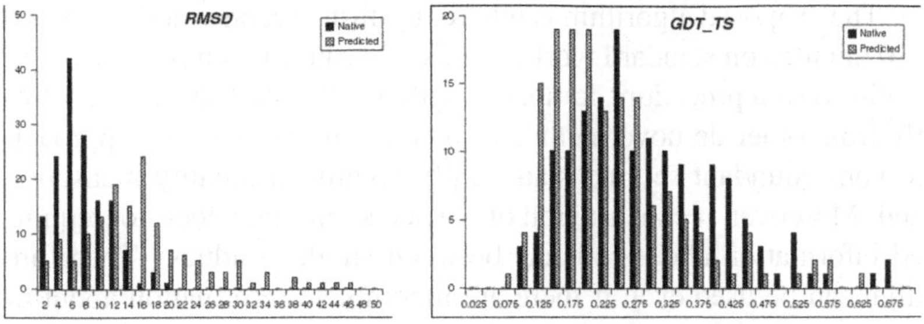

Figure 2. Histograms showing the distribution of RMSD (left) and GDT_TS (right) on the set of reconstructed structures using native and predicted β-sheets topologies.

applied a 5-fold cross validation procedure. In order to control overfitting we applied early-stopping, using for each fold part of the available training data as validation set. After cross validating the two methods, we obtained the results indicated in Table 1. We report several indices together with their 95% confidence intervals: micro-averaged global classification accuracy (Q_3) and accuracy of prediction of anti-parallel (Q_{ap}), parallel (Q_p) and unpaired strands (Q_{nb}). The index Q_3 indicates consistently higher performance than a baseline approach: predicting the class randomly, but with the frequencies observed in the training sets would lead to an expected 72.6% accuracy. It clearly results that contextual RNNs predict anti-parallel and parallel strands consistently better than simple non-recursive nets. The latter model tends to predict the more numerous class in the majority of cases and then it shows better global results (Q_3). A trivial predictor always assigning a pair of strands to the more numerous class (non-contact) would achieve 84.0% but with no use. Finally, the values of Q_{ap} and Q_p give a measure of the difficulty of the problem, the major obstacle being the unbalance among the classes: anti-parallel and parallel pairs represent 13.99% (resp. 1.96%) of the total set of pairs.

Method	Q_3	Q_{ap}	Q_{nb}	Q_p
C-RNNs	80.5±.9	39.1±3.0	89.1±.8	7.1±4.2
FF-NNs	85.1±.8	24.2±2.6	97.2±.4	0.0±.0

Table 1. Experimental comparison of contextual RNNs and feed-forward neural nets for the problem of predicting β-strands pairings.

5. Concluding Remarks

Experimental results demonstrates how the proposed approach is able to build protein models matching the available characteristics of a native conformation. The proposed algorithm is inherently fast – reconstruction takes on average 20 minutes on standard workstations – because it is based on an efficient local optimization procedure combined with a multi-start strategy. By this, differently from other de-novo methods, we were able to test our approach over a large non-redundant set and statistically significant quality measures were obtained. Moreover, reconstruction of β-sheets topology does not require fine-grained information about contacts between single residues. Therefore, our algorithm can be used even if there are incomplete information about the native structure, e.g. during NMR modelling. Unfortunately, the reconstructed structures are quite distant from corresponding native conformations, but we believe the quality of reconstruction could be improved by the addition of different types of contacts between secondary structure elements.

We also explored the case in which nothing is known about strands topology. We built a predictor of partnership between β-strands using recursive neural networks. Reconstruction was then tested using the predicted topology instead of the real one. Unfortunately, the algorithm did not prove to be sufficiently reliable to correct the errors of the predictor, which in turn can be substantially improved with the use of richer input descriptions. This led to a substantial decrease in the quality of reconstruction compared to the previous case. However, we have no knowledge of similar experiments being conducted before, so this can be considered as a first step toward a complete reconstruction procedure based on coarse-grained information alone.

References

Baldi, P., Brunak, S., Frasconi, P., Pollastri, G., and Soda, G. (1999). Exploiting the past and the future in protein secondary structure prediction. *Bioinformatics*, 15(11):937–946.

Frasconi, P., Gori, M., and Sperduti, A. (1998). A general framework for adaptive processing of data structures. *IEEE Transactions on Neural Networks*, 9(5):768–786.

Jones, D.T. (1999). Protein secondary structure prediction based on position-specific scoring matrices. *J.Mol.Biol.*, 292:195–202.

Liu, D.C. and Nocedal, J. (1989). On the limited memory BFGS method for large scale optimization. *Mathematical Programming*, 45:503–528.

Orengo, C.A., Michie, A.D., Jones, S., Jones, D.T., Swindells, M.B., and Thornton, J.M. (1997). CATH - A hierarchic classification of protein domain structures. *Structure*, 5:1093–1108.

Pollastri, G. and Baldi, P. (2002). Prediction of contact maps by recurrent neural network architectures and hidden context propagation from all four cardinal corners. *Bioinformatics*, 18(Supplement 1):S62–S70.

Pollastri, G., Baldi, P., Vullo, A., and Frasconi, P. (2003). Prediction of protein topologies using GIOHMMs and GRNNs. *Advances in Neural Information Processing Systems*, 15.

Vendruscolo, M., Kussel, E., and Domany, E. (1997). Recovery of protein structure from contact maps. *Fold. Des.*, 2:295–306.

Vullo, A. and Frasconi, P. (2003). Prediction of protein coarse contact maps. *J. Bionf. Comp. Biology*, 1(2):411–431.

Zemla, A., Venclovas, C., Moult, J., and Fidelis, K. (2001). Processing and evaluation of predictons in CASP4. *Proteins*, 5:13–21.

ANALYSIS OF OLIGONUCLEOTIDE MICROARRAY IMAGES USING A FUZZY SETS APPROACH IN HLA TYPING

G.B. Ferrara,[1,2] L. Delfino, [2] F. Masulli, [1,3] S. Rovetta, [1,4] R. Sensi[1]

[1] *INFM - Istituto Nazionale per la Fisica della Materia*
Via Dodecaneso 33, 16146 Genova, Italy

[2] *IST - Istituto Nazionale per la Ricerca sul Cancro*
Largo R. Benzi 10, 16132 Genova, Italy

[3] *Dipartimento di Informatica, Universita' di Pisa*
Via F. Buonarroti 2, 56125 Pisa, Italy
masulli@di.unipi.it

[4] *Dipartimento di Informatica e Scienze dell'Informazione*
Universita' di Genova, Via Dodecaneso 35, 16146 Genova, Italy

Abstract The Human Leukocyte Antigen (HLA) region is a part of genome which spans over 4 Mbases of DNA. The HLA system is strongly connected to immunological response and its compatibility between tissues is critical in transplantation. We have developed an application of oligonucleotide microarrays to HLA typing. In this paper we present a method based on a fuzzy system which interactively supports the user in analyzing the hybridization results, speeding-up the decision process moving from raw array data obtained from the scanner to their interpretation (genotyping). The two level procedure starts with evaluation of spot activity, then it estimates probe hybridization levels from activity levels. The method is designed for being readily usable by the biologist, by adopting fuzzy linguistic variables which are familiar to the user and by featuring a standard and complete graphical interface.

Keywords: HLA typing, oligonucleotide microarrays, probe hybridization labelling, fuzzy modeling, fuzzy systems.

Introduction

The HLA system [Klein and Sato, 2000] consists of three regions in the human genome that are strongly connected to immunological response. In transplantation, the match between donor's and receiver's HLA is critical for *histocompatibility* (compatibility between tissues).The number of HLA alleles

B. Apolloni et al. (eds.), Biological and Artificial Intelligence Environments, 53–61

reported in the last decade has risen at a rapid rate. More than 1700 HLA allelic variants have been described to date, and are available from the IMGT/HLA Sequence Database at http://www.ebi.ac.uk/imgt/hla/. Therefore, characterization and identification (*typing*) of HLA is crucial for transplantation, as well as for antigen presentation, autoimmune disease and many others areas of clinical interest [Klein and Sato, 2000].

Among the molecular methodologies, DNA microarray technology can provide a feasible and reliable approach for HLA typing. Oligonucleotide microarrays [Ekins and Chu,1999] make it possible to perform a large quantity (even thousands) of simultaneous experiments. Each experiment corresponds to a given oligonucleotide probe, a DNA strand of 20-30 bases which selectively combines with a complementary sequence in the target RNA sample (this process is termed *hybridization*). The probes are affixed to specific positions (spots) on the surface of a glass substrate, organized as an array. The target is fluorescently labelled, therefore a fluorescence measurement by laser scanning gives information about the amount of RNA hybridized at each *spot*, or specific location on the chip.

The use of microarray technology in HLA typing is promising [Pera et al., 1997; Guo, 1999] but to date not yet widespread. However, the high throughput provided by this method allows the collection and analysis of thousand of single nucleotide polymorphism in parallel [Ekins and Chu,1999; Guo, 1999]. This spot classification task on the basis of the microarray images is complex and can be very time consuming.

In this paper we present a system that interactively supports the user in analyzing the hybridization results, speeding-up the decision process moving from raw array data obtained from the scanner to their interpretation, i.e., genotyping. After a description of our approach to HLA typing with microarray (Sect. 1), we will describe in Sect. 2 the system supporting the measurement of probe hybridization we have developed. In Sect. 3 we discuss a case study for validation of the proposed approach. Discussion and Conclusions are in Sect. 4.

1. HLA typing with microarrays

Our oligonucleotide array approach for HLA typing involves a fluorescently labelled locus specific amplification of genomic DNA followed by hybridization with a panel of probes selected to detect a specific pattern of sequence motifs corresponding to an HLA allele.

The procedure starts with the design of a set of oligonucleotides, of about 15-20 bases, able to discriminate the alleles in high resolution. Each oligonucleotide probe will only anneal to sequences that match it perfectly, a single mismatch being sufficient to prevent hybridization under appropriate conditions

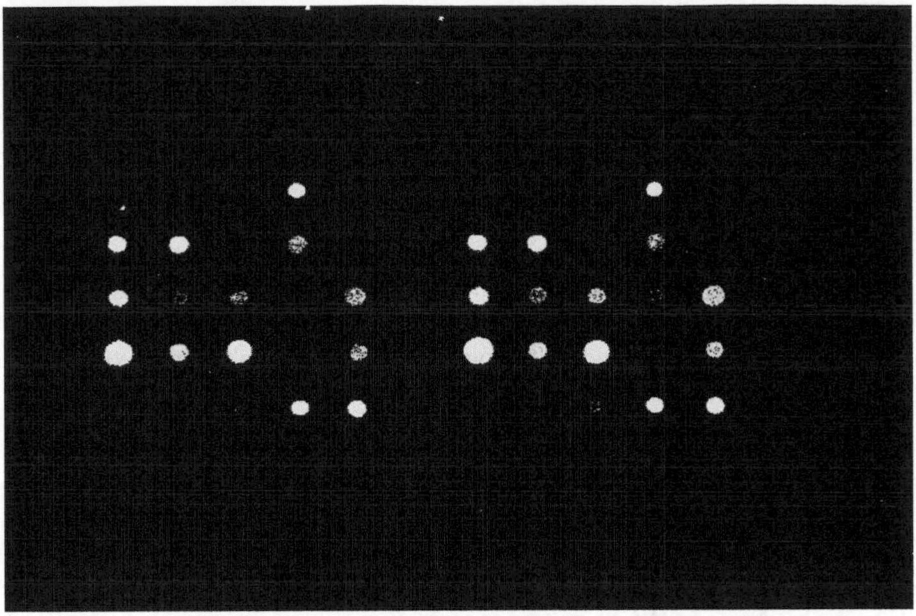

Figure 1. Scanned image of a microarray for HLA typing. The probes are affixed in the central area of the array. One can distinguish spots with positive (lighter ones), intermediate, or negative (darker ones) activities and outliers (noise) spread mostly in the border areas.

[Wallace et al., 1979]. In such as way, to each gene allele to be discriminated we associate a code made up by a list of positive or negative expected hybridization of the ordered set of probes.

Then, oligonucleotide probes are synthesized and spotted on the microarray (chip) using a spot printing robot, and then the microarray is hybridized using the target DNA to be analyzed. After hybridization and stringent washing the slide is scanned using a slide laser scanning system obtaining in such a way the fluorescence image of the microarray.

In Fig. 1 there are the images of two microarrays produced by a Packard-Bell Bioscience Division ScanArray 4000X. In the former image probes are affixed in the central area of the array and their pattern is repeated twice. We can distinguish spots with positive (lighter ones), intermediate, or negative (darker ones) activities and outliers (noise) spread mostly in the border areas. The latter image shows an enlarged detail of another microarray image, with higher presence of outliers.

HLA typing is then obtained by comparing the pattern of hybridization of the ordered set of probes and the codes associated to gene alleles in the probe design step.

The evaluation of probe hybridization is a complex task due to the presence of spots with intermediate activity that must be ascribed either to the choice of probes with too different *melting temperatures* [1] in the probe design step, or to other experimental problems like, e.g., the (partial) probe curling due to the presence of auto-complementary sequences or to the bad anchorage of the probe to the glass. As a consequence, the binary linguistic variable *Probe Hybridization* (with {*Positive*, *Negative*} term set), must be obtained from the the linguistic variable *Spot Activation* that can range in a term set containing *Positive* value, *Negative* value and one or more *Intermediate* values (the last ones usually corresponding to so-called *False Negative/False Positive* spots).

Using the available knowledge about the specific probe and the experimental conditions, *Intermediate* values of *Spot Activity* can be mapped into *Positive/Negative* values of the *Probe Hybridization*. Moreover, one can exploit the redundancies of the microarray (e.g., the repetitions of spots of the same probe, such as in the case in Fig. 1(a)) in order to obtain a more reliable estimation of *Probe Hybridization*.

2. Proposed approach

A typical HLA typing problem can need hundred of probes to be affixed to the microarray that will contain at least a double number of spots. Because of the large throughput typical of microarrays, evaluating probe hybridization by the approach described in Sect. 1 will be very time consuming and complex, computer-assisted analysis is of value in order to provide large-scale allele typing, improve data management, and streamline overall quality control processes.

A direct approach to computer-assisted labelling of *Probe Hybridization* can consist in the definition of a bank of (fuzzy) rules evaluating the probe hybridization on the basis of the image features obtained from the spots. But this approach is not easy, as an expert biologist can discriminate the hybridization level of a probe on the basis of the image produced by the scanner and of the nature of the probe itself, while s/he cannot obtain a reliable classification of spots using only spots' features. As a consequence, a machine learning approach trying to correlate spots' features (inputs) and the *Probe Hybridization* classification made by the biologist (labels) can be more fruitful in supporting the user's labelling task.

The approach we followed to design a system for the support to probe hybridization labelling is based on two sequential interactive steps:

1 A *Spot Labelling Step* modeling the *Spot Activity* of a probe by evaluating the memberships of spots to terms (fuzzy sets) *Positive*, *Negative* and (one or more) *Intermediate*. Moreover, an additional term *Outlier* is considered grouping spots contaminated by noise. To this aim we use a

learning machine that takes as input patterns the values of the spot's sub-image features and as labels the expert biologist's classification based on visual inspection of the spot sub-image.

2 A *Probe Labelling Step* supporting the biologist in the association of *Spot Activity* values to those of *Probe Hybridization. Positive* and *Negative* values of *Spot Activity* are univocally associated to the same terms of *Probe Hybridization*, while *Intermediate* values of *Spot Activity* are associated by the biologist to either *Positive* or *Negative* values of the *Probe Hybridization* on the basis of the available knowledge on the specific probe and on the experimental conditions and exploiting the spot redundancy.

We have developed the system on a 500 MHz Pentium PC in *Sun Java 2*, providing it with an interactive graphical user interface making use of pure *Sun Java Swing* graphical components such as *tables*, *trees*, *menus* and *image panels* (see Fig. 2). In this way, the user has access to a familiar look-and-feel which helps keeping the user training curve smooth.

For each spot we considered its position onto the microarray and the following features computed on the spot's sub-image: average intensity, average background intensity, intensity standard deviation, diameter, circularity, and uniformity. All those data are a sub-set of those produced by the ScanArray Express software equipping the ScanArray 4000X.

The learning machine used in the Spot Labelling step is a network of Fuzzy Basis Functions (FBF) [Mendel, 1995; Wang, 1994; Wang and Mendel, 1992] that is a Mamdani fuzzy logic system [Lee, 1990] with *singleton* fuzzification, *max-product* composition, *product* inference and *height* defuzzification, equivalent to the ANFIS model [Jang, 1993]. A FBF network can learn its parameters from a labelled data set using a gradient descent procedure. A Java implementation is available at http://mlsc.disi.unige.it/HLA/FBF/.

For each class to be modeled we use a FBF network whose task is the discrimination of that class against the remaining others on the basis of the considered spot sub-images features. We use the mean square error (MSE) as a cost function to be minimized by the gradient descent procedure. In this way the FBF network estimates the posterior class conditional probability of any spot [Casalino et al., 1998; Masulli, 1994], that we can consider as the fuzzy membership to the class. We performed model selection on the FBF networks using a K-fold validation method [Amari, 1997; Stone, 1974] that is particularly suitable when only a small data set is available, as in the present case.

Fig. 2 shows an example of interaction in the *Spot Labelling Step*. The user starts by selecting a small set of spots for each *Spot Activity* class: *Positive*, *Medium*, *Negative*, and *Outlier*. In few seconds the FBF networks generalize the classification to all spots in the image. Labels are assigned to spots by

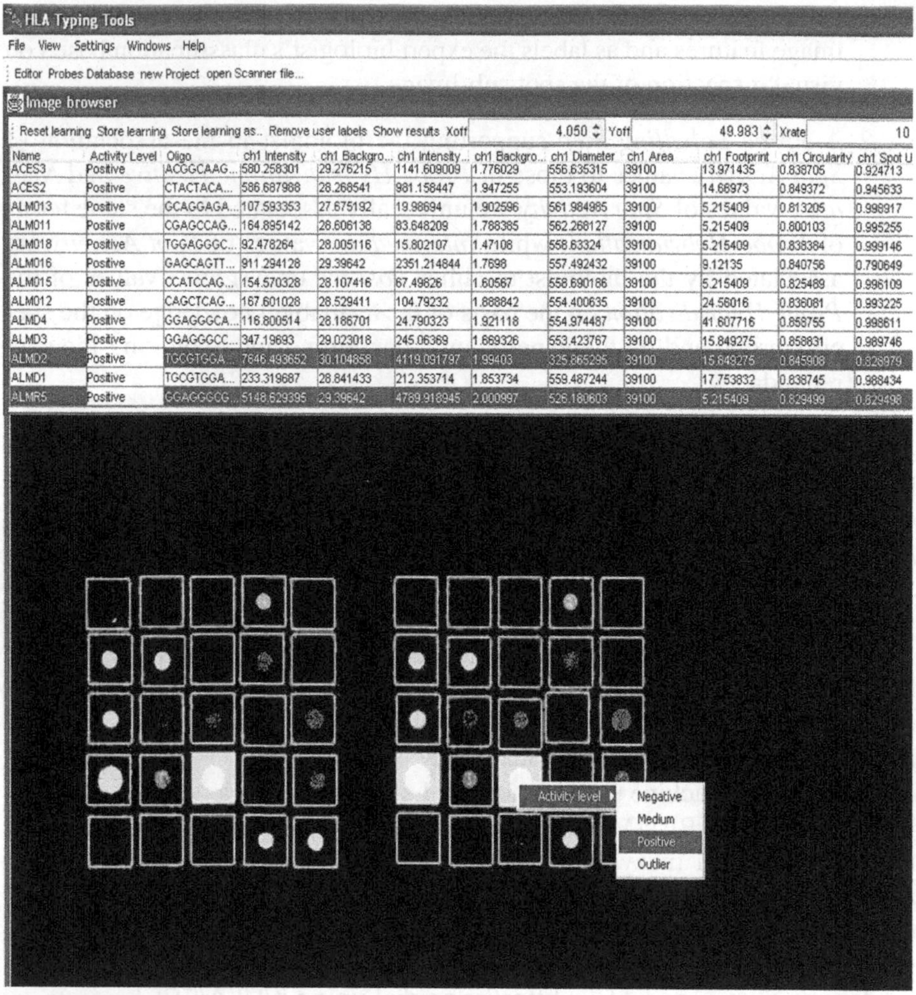

HLA Typing Tools
File View Settings Windows Help
Editor Probes Database new Project open Scanner file...
Image browser
Reset learning Store learning Store learning as.. Remove user labels Show results Xoff 4.050 Yoff 49.983 Xrate 10
Name Activity Level Oligo ch1 Intensity ch1 Backgro... ch1 Intensity... ch1 Backgro... ch1 Diameter ch1 Area ch1 Footprint ch1 Circularity ch1 Spot U
ACES3 Positive ACGGCAAG... 580.258301 29.276215 1141.609009 1.776029 556.635315 39100 13.971435 0.838705 0.924713
ACES2 Positive CTACTACA... 586.687988 28.268541 981.158447 1.947255 553.193604 39100 14.66973 0.849372 0.945633
ALM013 Positive GCAGGAGA... 107.593353 27.675192 19.98694 1.902596 561.984985 39100 5.215409 0.813205 0.998917
ALM011 Positive CGAGCCAG... 164.895142 28.606138 83.648209 1.788385 562.268127 39100 5.215409 0.800103 0.995255
ALM018 Positive TGGAGGGC... 92.478264 28.005116 15.802107 1.47108 558.63324 39100 5.215409 0.838384 0.999146
ALM016 Positive GAGCAGTT... 911.294128 29.39642 2351.214844 1.7698 557.492432 39100 9.12135 0.840756 0.790649
ALM015 Positive CCATCCAG... 154.570328 28.107416 67.49826 1.60567 558.690186 39100 5.215409 0.825489 0.996109
ALM012 Positive CAGCTCAG... 167.601028 28.529411 104.79232 1.888842 554.400635 39100 24.56016 0.836081 0.993225
ALMD4 Positive GGAGGGCA... 116.800514 28.186701 24.790323 1.921118 554.974487 39100 41.607716 0.858755 0.998611
ALMD3 Positive GGAGGGCC... 347.19693 29.023018 245.06369 1.669326 553.423767 39100 15.849275 0.858831 0.989746
ALMD2 Positive TGCGTGGA... 7646.493652 30.104858 4119.091797 1.99403 325.865295 39100 15.849275 0.845908 0.828979
ALMD1 Positive TGCGTGGA... 233.319687 28.841433 212.353714 1.853734 559.487244 39100 17.753832 0.838745 0.988434
ALMR5 Positive GGAGGGCG... 5148.629395 29.39642 4789.918945 2.000997 526.180603 39100 5.215409 0.829499 0.829498
Activity level
Negative
Medium
Positive
Outlier

Figure 2. The interactive user interface. Each row of the table corresponds to a spot and contains the values of its features, and other information, including the class of membership (Positive, Medium, Negative, Outlier, and Reject). On the bottom the squares overimposed to the scanned image represent the positions of spots, and the color of their contours indicate the associated class. The experiment is described in Sect. 3.

using a Winner Take All (WTA) rule that associates the spot to the highest membership class. If the user accepts the classification, the step terminates. Otherwise, the user can either explicitly change the membership class of some spots and terminate the step, or prepare a new sample and retrain. Moreover, every time the user can mark a spot as *Reject*. Rejected spots will not be considered in the *Spot Labelling* and *Probe Labelling Steps*.

Note that many outlier points in the microarray image are implicitly filtered out as they are outside the spots' sub-images. Concerning the outliers belonging to spots' areas, the hosting spot areas are grouped in the class *Outlier* during the previously described interactive learning procedure and, moreover, we add to this class also the spots with low membership to the other classes. The spots assigned to class *Outlier* will not be considered in the subsequent *Probe Labelling Step.*

As already stated, the *Probe Labelling Step* supports the biologist in mapping the *Spot Activity* values already evaluated into the two values of the *Probe Hybridization.* To this aim the biologist exploits the spot redundancy using a choice of operators including maximum, minimum, averaging, and voting, in order to fuse the *Spot Activity* values corresponding to all instances of a given probe, and then he will exploit his knowledge about the probes and the experimental conditions in order to map *Intermediate* values of *Spot Activity* to either *Positive* or *Negative* values of the *Probe Hybridization.*

After the *Probe Labelling Step*, we obtain the typing of the target HLA allele by comparing the ordered list of *Probe Hybridization* levels obtained with the list of alleles' codes produced during probe design.

3. Case study

In this section we describe an experimental validation of our procedure for HLA typing with microarrays and of our system assisting probe hybridization labelling. We used a small number of probes organized in two identical squares of 5×5 spots.

A panel of 20-mer oligonucleotide probes was designed for identifying polymorphic positions located in exon 2 and exon 3 of HLA-A and B loci and in exon 2 of HLA-DRB1 locus. Each probe contained a 5' aminolink for immobilization chemistry and a 12-mer spacer, followed by the 20-mer hybridization sequence. The polymorphic sequence was situated near the center of each hybridization sequence.

Oligonucleotide probes were synthesized and spotted on an array by MWG Biotech Srl. The microarray was hybridized with single strand PCR product amplified from human genomic DNA.

The target DNA was previously HLA typed as A*0216/0301 HLA with an independent approach (high-resolution sequencing with a capillary sequencer, for different HLA loci) and was prepared as follows: double stranded PCR product first generated using locus specific primers and then purified to remove the excess primers. Single stranded DNA molecules were then generated from asymmetric PCR using one 5' Cy5-labelled primer as described in [Wallace et al., 1979].

After hybridization and stringent washing the slide was scanned using a ScanArray 4000XL and the fluorescence image was analysed using the interactive system described in the previous section. We expected to get positive hybridization with six probes (ACES2, ACES3, ALMR5, ALMD2, ALM016, and ALM017) and negative with the others. The analysis with the support of the interactive system (see Fig. 2 for a screen-shot of this analysis) leads to the expected results with few user interactions [2].

4. Discussion and conclusions

We have described a system for assisting the biologist in the analysis of oligonucleotide microarray images for HLA typing [Klein and Sato, 2000]. Because of the large number of probes used in HLA typing computer-assisted analysis is of value in order to provide high-throughput allele typing, improve data management, streamline overall quality control processes. The approach we followed is based on a fuzzy modeling of spot activity and the mapping of spot activity evaluations into the evaluation of the hybridization of related probes.In Sect. 4 we have shown an experimental verification of the system.

On the basis of the promising results obtained with the method described in this paper, we have started the development of a decision-support system for the full processing of HLA typing using the oligonucleotide microarrays technology. Note that the proposed computer-assisted approach increases in relevance while the complexity of the typing task increases and hundred or thousand of spots have to be labelled.

Acknowledgments

Work funded by the Italian National Institute for the Physics of Matter (INFM), the Italian Ministry of Education, University and Research (Prin2002), and Biopattern EU Network of Excellence. The Istituto Scientifico Oncologico (ISO) made available the scientific instrumentation. We thank Cinzia Pera for her support and the anonymous reviewers for their detailed and constructive comments.

Notes

1. The melting temperature of a probe is the optimal temperature for its hybridization and depends on its basis. The quantity of RNA hybridized can increase/decrease if the hybridization experiment has been done at a temperature higher/lower that the probe's melting temperature.

2. On the the web site http:/mlsc.disi.unige.it/HLA/DSS/ there is a detailed description of the interaction with the system.

References

Amari, S., N. Murata, K.-R. Müller, M. Finke, and H. H. Yang. Asymptotic statistical theory of overtraining and cross-validation. *IEEE Transactions on Neural Networks*, 8(5):985–996, September 1997.

Casalino, F., F. Masulli, and A. Sperduti. Rule specialization in networks of fuzzy basis functions. *Intelligent Automation and Soft Computing*, 4:73–82, 1998.

Ekins, R. and F.W. Chu. Microarrays: their origins and applications. *Trends in Biotechnology*, 1999, 17:217-218.

Guo, Z., L. Hood, E.W. Petersdorf. Oligonucleotide arrays for high resolution HLA typing. *Rev Immunogenet*, 1(2):220-230, 1999.

Jang, J.S.R. ANFIS: Adaptive-network-based fuzzy inference system. *IEEE Trans. on Systems, Man, and Cybernetics*, 23:655–684, 1993.

Klein, I. and A. Sato. The HLA system – second of two parts. *New England Journal of Medicine*, 343(11):782–86, 2000.

Lee, C.C. Fuzzy logic in control systems: fuzzy logic controller. I. *IEEE Transactions on Systems, Man and Cybernetics*, 20:404–418, 1990.

Masulli, F. Bayesian classification by feedforward connectionist systems. In F. Masulli, P. G. Morasso, and A. Schenone, editors, *Neural Networks in Biomedicine - Proceedings of the Advanced School of the Italian Biomedical Physics Association - Como (Italy) 1993*, pages 145–162, Singapore, 1994. World Scientific.

Mendel, J.M. Fuzzy logic systems for engineering: A tutorial. *Proceedings of the IEEE*, 83:345–377, 1995.

Pera, C., L. Delfino, A. Morabito, A. Longo, L. Johnston-Dow, C.B. White, M. Colonna, G.B. Ferrara. HLA-A typing. *Tissue Antigens*, 50:372–379, 1997.

Stone, M. Cross-validatory choice and assessment of statistical predictions. *Journal of the Royal Statistical Society, Series B*, 36:111–147, 1974.

Wallace, R.B., J. Shaffer, R.F. Murphy, J. Bonner, T. Hirose, K. Itakura. Hybridization of synthetic oligodeoxyribonucleotides to Φ_χ174 DNA: the effect of a single base pair mismatch. *Nucleic Acid Res*, 6:3543-3557, 1979.

Wang, L. X. *Adaptive Fuzzy Systems and Control*. Prentice Hall, Englewood Cliffs, New Jersey, 1994.

Wang, L. and J.M. Mendel. Fuzzy basis functions, universal approximation, and orthogonal least-squares learning. *IEEE Trans. on Neural Networks*, 5:807–814, 1992.

COMBINATORIAL AND MACHINE LEARNING APPROACHES IN CLUSTERING MICROARRAY DATA

Sergio Pozzi
DISCo, Univ. Milano-Bicocca
sergio.pozzi@disco.unimib.it

Italo Zoppis
DISCo, Univ. Milano-Bicocca
zoppis@disco.unimib.it

Giancarlo Mauri
DISCo, Univ. Milano-Bicocca
giancarlo.mauri@unimib.it

Abstract In this paper we describe the use of a correlation clustering algorithm [Chaitanya, 2004] to group expression level of genes in a microarray dataset. The clustering problem is formalized as a semi-defined optimization program, based on the correlation provided by two quantities, respectively related to an agreement and a disagreement between a pair of genes. We also intend to validate the role of the correlation clustering algorithm by comparing the results with a support vectors clustering approach [Ben-Hur et al., 2001] that is demonstrated to perform well for many applications.

Keywords: Clustering, support vector, consensus, microarray

Introduction

In the last decade the microarray technology [Speed, 2003; Eisen and Brown, 1999] has become a fundamental tool for an increasing number of researchers. The reason for this is the fact that this tool offers biologist the capability to simultaneously analyse the expression level of thousands of genes.

The analysis of such experiments is non trivial because of the large quantity of data and the many degrees of variation introduced at the different stages of each experiment. Common approaches, from the machine learning field,

B. Apolloni et al. (eds.), Biological and Artificial Intelligence Environments, 63–71

attempt to predict functionally significant groups of genes both in an unsupervised and supervised manner. The former approach generally, start with the definition of some measure of distance among patterns: clusters are then obtained with different algorithms as hierarchical clustering [Eisen et al., 1998], [Spellman et al., 1998] or self-organizing map [Tamayo et al., 1999]. In contrast, supervised methods begin with a collection of known classes of genes that are expected to be co-regulated and hence exhibit similar expression profiles: in this case, the analysis is performed on a sample of data in the typical form $\{(\mathbf{x_1}, y_1), (\mathbf{x_2}, y_2), ..., (\mathbf{x_n}, y_n)\}$ where y_i is the label that the system aims to learn and $\mathbf{x_i}$ are the patterns.

Recently, the clustering problem has been modelled as combinatorial optimization problem on graphs [Bansal et al., 2002]. These combinatorial approaches are NP-Hard [Bansal et al., 2002], but efficient polynomial time approximation schemes have been proposed [Chaitanya, 2004; Charikar et al., 2003]. Each of them uses the Williamson and Goemans technique [Goemans and Williamson, 1995] of rounding a relaxed version of the problem. We follow this approach (section 2) to define the problem as a semi-defined optimization program. Here, we analyse 50 patterns of the budding yeast *Saccaromyce Cerevisiae* measured at 17 time step of the cell division cycle. Since we wish to validate our application using a method that is demonstrated to perform well in different contexts, we use an algorithm based on a kernel function as a benchmark [Vapnik, 1998]. In [Schölkopf et al., 2001], [Tax and Duin, 1999] and again in [Ben-Hur et al., 2001] it was suggested how to use such an approach in an unsupervised fashion. This framework briefly reported on in a more detail (in section 2), is also useful for our objective of getting two *consensus* quantities that will form the basis of a measure of performance for both the algorithms. Finally (section 4) we discuss some numerical results and conclude this paper.

1. Support Vectors Clustering

We can represent a microarray as an $n \times m$ matrix $\mathbf{X}$ where each of its m column vectors $(\mathbf{x_1}, \mathbf{x_2}, ..., \mathbf{x_m})$ has n observations of a gene, realized at different stages of an experiment i.e. in our case, at different time steps of the cell-cycle. Similarly to support vectors machine approach, the use of support vectors to cluster these m patterns is obtained by applying a non linear transformation $\Phi : \Gamma \rightarrow \Pi$ from a general input space Γ to some higher dimensional inner product feature space Π. In this space one looks for the smallest sphere of radius R. Hence, given the data matrix X and stated for each $\mathbf{x_i}$ the constraint $||\Phi(\mathbf{x_i}) - \mathbf{a}||^2 \leq R^2 + \xi$ where $\mathbf{a}$ is the centre of the sphere, $||.||$ is the Euclidean norm and $\xi_i \geq 0$ are *slack* variables to allow for outliers [Schölkopf et al., 1999], the problem is solved by introducing the Lagrangian

$$L = R^2 - \sum_j (R^2 + \xi_j - \|\mathbf{\Phi}(\mathbf{x_i}) - \mathbf{a}\|^2)\beta_j - \sum \xi_j \mu_j + C \sum \xi_j \quad (1)$$

in which $\beta_j \geq 0$ and $\mu_j \geq 0$ are Lagrangian multipliers, C is a constant and $C \sum \xi_j$ is a penality term. Setting the derivative of L to zero, with respect to R, ξ_j and $\mathbf{a}$, results to

$$\sum_j \beta_j = 1 \qquad \mathbf{a} = \sum_j \beta_j \Phi(x_j) \qquad \beta_j = C - \mu_j \quad (2)$$

The KKT conditions [Fletcher, 1987] are $\xi_j \mu_j = 0$ and $(R^2 + \xi_j - \|\phi(\mathbf{x_j}) - \mathbf{a}\|^2)\beta_j = 0$. From the above expressions one can eliminate in (1) the variables R, $\mathbf{a}$ and μ_j, turning the lagrangian into the dual form

$$W = \sum_j \beta_j K(\mathbf{x_j}, \mathbf{x_j}) - \sum_{i,j} \beta_i \beta_j K(\mathbf{x_i}, \mathbf{x_j}) \quad (3)$$

The solution is finally obtained by optimizing this final expression. We follow this approach by using the Gaussian kernel $K(\mathbf{x_i}, \mathbf{x_j}) = e^{-q\|\mathbf{x_i} - \mathbf{x_j}\|^2}$ with the width parameter q. Note that thanks to Eqs. (2) one can handle three different sets of vectors, respectively:

- Bounded Support Vectors (BSV) which lie outside the boundaries. These points have $\xi_i > 0$ and $\beta_i > 0$. They therefore have, from KKT conditions, $\mu_i = 0$ and $\beta_i = C$. One can also note that, when $C > 1$ no BSVs exist due to the constraint (2).

- Support Vectors (SV) which lie on cluster boundaries. A point $\mathbf{x_i}$ with $\xi_i = 0$ is mapped to the inside or to the surface of the features space sphere. If its $0 < \beta_i < C$ then, from KKT conditions, the image $\mathbf{\Phi}(\mathbf{x_i})$ lies on the surface of the feature space sphere.

- The set of all other points that lie inside the boundary.

Cluster assignment

The definition of the kernel and Eqs. (2) allow us to write the distance $R^2(\mathbf{x})$ of each point's image in the feature space as

$$R^2(\mathbf{x}) = K(\mathbf{x}, \mathbf{x}) - 2\sum_j \beta_j K(\mathbf{x_j}, \mathbf{x}) + \sum_{i,j} \beta_i \beta_j K(\mathbf{x_i}, \mathbf{x_j}) \quad (4)$$

Since the radius of the sphere is $R = R(\mathbf{x_i})$, where $\mathbf{x_i}$ is a support vector, the contour that enclose points in data space is the set $\{\mathbf{x_i} | R(\mathbf{x_i}) = R\}$. The function $\mathbf{\Phi}(\mathbf{x})$ is unknown, we therefore cannot seek points belonging to different cluster by its inverse. One can, however, apply the following geometrical approach: given a pair of inputs belonging to different clusters, any path that connects them (for instance, a segment) must exit from the sphere in the feature space. Such a path contains a point $\mathbf{y}$ with $R(\mathbf{y}) > R$. Therefore, one can define an $m \times m$ matrix $\mathbf{A}$ whose component $a_{i,j}$, for $1 \leq i \leq m$ and $1 \leq j \leq m$, is defined as follows

$$a_{i,j} = \begin{cases} 1 & \text{if, for all } \mathbf{y} \text{ on the line segment connecting } \mathbf{x_i} \text{ and } \mathbf{x_j},\ R(\mathbf{y}) \leq R \\ 0 & \text{otherwise} \end{cases}$$

Clusters are then obtained from the connected components of $\mathbf{A}$.

2. Correlation Clustering Problem

The Correlation Clustering Problem was been introduced in [Bansal et al., 2002]. An instance of the problem can be represented as a graph $G = (V, E)$, where each edge is labelled either as "+" (this means that the vertices of the edge are similar) or "-" (the vertices of the edge are different). The intention is to cluster the nodes of the graph so that the "+" edges lie within the clusters and the "-" edges lie between clusters. More precisely, we want to maximize *agreements*: the number of "+" edges within clusters and "-" edges between them. This combinatorial optimization problem has been proven to be NP-Hard [Bansal et al., 2002]. Instead of dealing with qualitative edges ("+", "-") we want to deal with quantitative instances in which each edge e has two positive weights: $w_{in}(e) \geq 0$ and $w_{out}(e) \geq 0$. The weights $w_{in}(e)$ and $w_{out}(e)$ represent the gain of agreement if the vertices of edge e are respectively clustered together or not. Let $\mathbf{e}_i \in R^n$ be the vector with 1 in the ith coordinate and 0 elsewhere and let $\mathbf{x}_i \in R^n$ be a variable vector in the n dimensional Euclidean space, the correlation clustering problem can now be stated more formally as follows:

$$\max_{\mathbf{x}_i \in \{\mathbf{e}_1, \ldots, \mathbf{e}_n\}} \sum_{e=(i,j)} \left(w_{in}(e)\, \mathbf{x}_i \cdot \mathbf{x}_j + w_{out}(e)\, (1 - \mathbf{x}_i \cdot \mathbf{x}_j) \right) \tag{5}$$

Assigning $\mathbf{x}_u$ to the vector $\mathbf{e}_v$, means that the vertex u has been put in cluster v so that the above sum equals the weight of agreement for a given clustering. The above formulation is an integer quadratic combinatorial optimization problem and, as previously stated, it has been proved to be NP-Hard [Bansal et al., 2002]. Because of the hardness, attention has shifted to approximation schemes.

Approximation Algorithm

For the correlation clustering problem, one of the approximation algorithm that achieves the best performance is based on the Williamson and Goemans approximation scheme [Goemans and Williamson, 1995]. This scheme consists of solving a continuos relaxation instance of the original problem in polynomial time. Then a solutin for the original problem is found by means of a probabilistic rounding procedure. For the correlation clustering problem the continuous relaxation is the following:

$$\begin{aligned} \max_{\mathbf{x}_i \in R^n} \sum_{e=(i,j)} & \left(w_{in}(e)\, \mathbf{x}_i \cdot \mathbf{x}_j + w_{out}(e)\,(1 - \mathbf{x}_i \cdot \mathbf{x}_j) \right) \\ & \mathbf{x}_v \cdot \mathbf{x}_v = 1 \qquad \forall v \\ & \mathbf{x}_u \cdot \mathbf{x}_u \geq 0 \qquad \forall u, v, u \neq v \end{aligned} \tag{6}$$

This is a semi-definite quadratic programming problem and can be efficiently solved in polynomial time using an interior point algorithm [Alizadeh and al., 2000]. To obtain an integer solution the following stochastic procedure is used [Chaitanya, 2004]: two hyperplanes passing through the origin are choosing independently and uniformly at random. These hyperplanes partition the R^n space into four regions. These regions are interpreted as clusters. Each of the $\mathbf{x}_i$ vector is assigned to a cluster, depending on the region it belongs to. The probability $p_{in}(\theta)$ that two vertices lie in the same cluster depends only on the angle between them: $\mathbf{x}_i \cdot \mathbf{x}_j = cos\theta$. It can clearly be seen that $p_{in}(\theta) = (1 - \frac{\theta}{\pi})^2$. The following lemma has been proven in [Chaitanya, 2004]:

LEMMA 2.1 *For any* $\theta \in [0, \frac{\pi}{2}]$, $p_{in}(\theta) \geq 0.75 cos\theta$ *and* $p_{out}(\theta) \geq 0.75\,(1 - cos\theta)$.

The following theorem gives the expected performance guarantee to the rounding procedure described above. It is easely proved by means of lemma 2.1.

THEOREM 2.2 *The above rounding procedure delivers a solution of expected value of at least* $0.75OPT$.

3. Numerical Results

In this preliminary work, our intent is mainly that of comparing the machine learing and correlation clustering approaches. For this reason, even though the time complexity of both approaches is polynomial, the number of genes involved is limited to 50. For the same reason, since the correlation clustering algorithm does not explicitly take into account the outliers, we decided to avoid outliers also in the support vector clustering approach ($C = 1$). This choice clearly prevents to fully exploit the Support Vector abilities of clustering in a

noisy environment as suggested in [Ben-Hur et al., 2001]. Our analysis is conducted on 50 patterns of the budding yeast *Saccaromyce Cerevisiae* taken at 17 different stages of the cell division cycle. In agreement with [Chen et al., 1999], we filtered out both patterns whose expression levels were below a detection threshold (≤ 200) and patterns expressed but without significant variation over time, for instance, maximum and average expression level satisfy $(\text{MAX} - \text{AVG})/\text{AVG} \leq 0.1$. In order to reduce the dimension of a pattern, we computed the principal components on the above 50 extracted points by transforming each of them into a two dimensional space given by the first two principal components. In our experiments these two components account for about 96% of the total variance.
In our experiments the value of parameter C, as defined above, is always set to 1. We computed the support vectors with a value of $q = 10^{-7}$, allowing us to obtain 4 clusters as shown in Figure 1. In this preliminary comparison work, this choice is motivated in order to maintain the same number of clusters in both approaches. Nontheless the limit of 4 clusters is not mandatory and it can be avoided in future work: in [Chaitanya, 2004] the author has shown a 0.7666 approximation algorithm for an arbitrary number of clusters. This algorithm uses a rounding scheme on the solution of a relaxated instance, similar to the 4 cluster case adopted here. Moreover the limit on the number of clusters is quite unnatural for the support vector approach: in [Ben-Hur et al., 2001], the authors suggest to apply an iterative approach starting from small q values and then increasing the q parameter to obtain more clusters.

Agreement, Disagreement Measure

In order to define an instance of the problem for the correlation clustering approximation algorithm, we must provide a pair of weights $w_{in}(e)$ and $w_{out}(e)$ for each pair of nodes relative to an edge e. We propose, now, a measure of agreement between nodes on the basis of the support vectors machine metric. In section 1, we decided whether or not to include each pair of nodes in the same cluster on the basis of the mapping in feature space sphere: if the path in feature space is entirely inside the sphere, we included the nodes in the same cluster. For a pair of nodes for which the linear path between them is mapped outside the sphere, we have choosen to assign a w_{out} weight equals to 1. A w_{in} weight equals to 1, can be assign for a pair of nodes whose linear path is mapped, in feature space, entirely inside the sphere. For each pair of genes, the agreement and disagreement matrices in this way were passed to correlation clustering algorithm and the resulted clusters is shown in Figure 2.

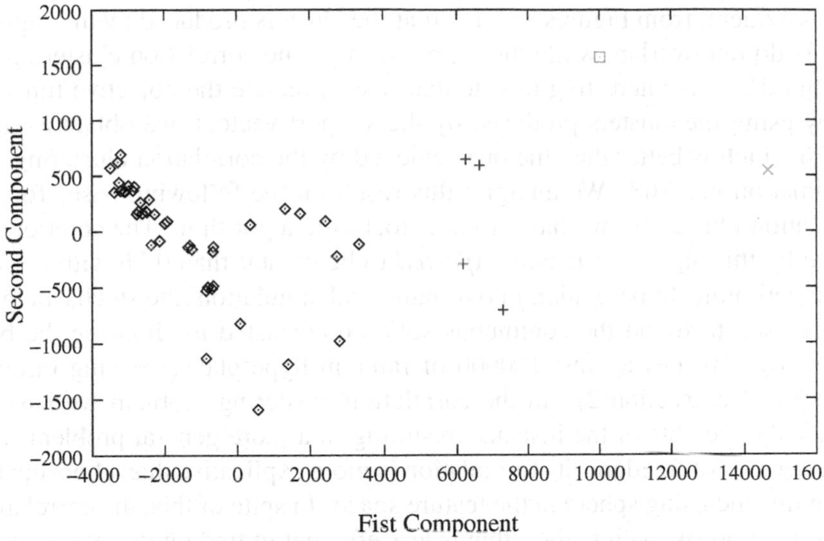

Figure 1. Support Vector Machines Clustering.

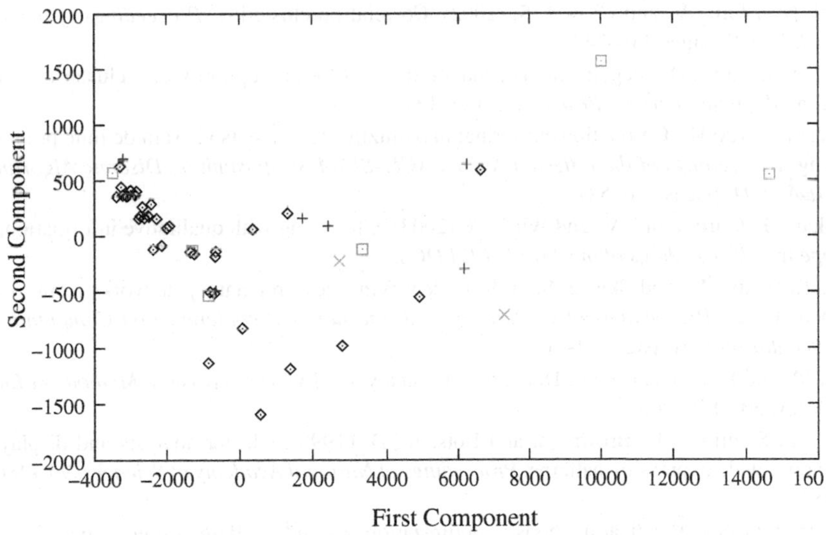

Figure 2. Correlation Clustering.

4. Conclusions

It is evident, from Figures 1 and 2, that the clusters produced by the support vectors do not overlap, while those produced by the correlation clustering algorithm do. It is interesting to note that if we evaluate the objective function (5) by using the clusters produced by the support vectors, we obtain a value of 875 which is better than the one achieved by the correlation clustering approximation i.e. 768. We interpret this result on the following base: for the correlation clustering, we have used a stochastic algorithm. The solution returned by this algorithm is only *expected* to be greater than 0.75 with respect to the optimum. In particular, in our numerical simulation, the stochastic procedure used to round the continuous solution consisted in choosing the best pair of hyperplanes against 100000 of random hyperplanes passing through the origin (see section 2). In the correlation clustering problem we have to specify the weights of the instance, resulting in a more general problem with more degrees of freedom. Its formulation is more explicative than choosing the minimum enclosing sphere in the feature space. In spite of this, the correlation clustering approximation algorithm is less efficient in finding its solution than the support vectors clustering approach.

References

Alizadeh, F. (1991). Interior-point methods in semidefinite programming with applications to combinatorial optimization. *SIAM Journal on Optimization*, 5:13–51.

Bansal, N., Blum, A., and Chawla, S. (2002). Correlation clustering. *Proceedings of the 43rd IEEE FOCS*, pages 238–247.

Ben-Hur, A., Horn, D., Siegelmann, H., and Vapnik, V. (2001). Support vector clustering. *Journal of Machine Learning Research*, 2:125–137.

Chaitanya, S. (2004). Correlation clustering: maximizing agreements via semidefinite programming. *Proceedings of the Fifteenth Annual ACM-SIAM Symposium on Discrete Algorithms SODA 2004*, pages 526–527.

Charikar, M., Guruswami, V., and Wirth, A. (2003). Clustering with qualitative information. *To appear in Proceedings of the 44rd IEEE FOCS.*

Chen, T., Filkov, V., and Skiena, S. (1999). Identifying gene regulatory networks from experimental data. *Proceedings of the third annual international conference on Computational molecular biology*, pages 94–103.

Eisen, M. and Brown, P. (1999). Dna arrays for analysis of gene expression. *Methods in Enzymology*, 303:179–205.

Eisen, M., Spellman, P., Brown, P., and Botstein, D. (1998). Cluster analysis and display of genome-wide expression patterns. *Proceedings of National Academy of Sciences*, 95:14863–14868.

Fletcher, R. (1987). Practical methods of optimization, second ed. *Willey-Intersciences.*

Goemans, M. and Williamson, D. P. (1995). Improved approximation algorithms for maximum cut and satisfiability problems. *Journal of the ACM*, 42:1115–1145.

Schölkopf, B., Platt, J., Shave-Taylor, J., Smola, J., and Williamson, R. (2001). Estimating the support of a high-dimensional distribution. *Proceeding of the annual conference on Neural Information Systems*, 913:1443–1472.

Schölkopf, B., Smola, A., and Muller, K. (1999). Advances in kernel method - support vector learning. *MIT Press*.

Speed, T. (2003). Statistical analysis of gene expression microarray data. *Chapman Hall*.

Spellman, P., Sherlock, G., Zhang, M., Iyer, V., Anders, K., Eisen, M., Brown, P., Botstein, D., and Futcher, B. (1998). Comprehensive identification of cell cycle-regulated genes of the yeast saccharomyces cerevisiae by microarray hybridization. *Molecular Biology of the Cell*, 9:3273–3297.

Tamayo, P., Slonim, D., Mesirov, J., Zhu, Q., Kitareewan, S., Dmitrovsky, E., Lander, E., and Golub, T. (1999). Interpreting patterns of gene expression with self-organizing maps. *Proceedings of National Academy of Sciences*, 96:2907–2912.

Tax, D. and Duin, R. (1999). Support vector domain description. *Pattern Recognition Letters*, 20:1991–1999.

Vapnik, V. (1998). Statistical learning theory. *Willey*.

GENE EXPRESSION DATA MODELING AND VALIDATION OF GENE SELECTION METHODS

Francesca Ruffino[1]

[1]*Dipartimento di Scienze dell'Informazione, Università di Milano, Milano, Italy*
ruffino@dsi.unimi.it

Abstract Several gene selection methods have been proposed to identify sets of genes related to a particular disease or to a particular functional status of the tissue. An open problem with gene selection methods consists in evaluating their performance; since we usually know only a smell subset of the genes involved in the onset of a status, and many times no relevant genes are known "a priori". We propose an artificial system, based on modeling gene expression signatures, to generate synthetic gene expression data for validating gene selection methods. Comparison between gene selection methods using data generated through the artificial model are performed and preliminary results are reported.

Keywords: DNA-microarray, Gene selection.

1. Introduction

DNA experiments provide parallel measurements of the gene expression of the level of the entire genome of an organism [Lockhart and Winzeler, 2000].

The dataset obtained through several microarray experiments can be represented by a table with m rows and n columns: each of its rows is associated with an examined tissue and each column corresponds to one of the considered genes. To specify a particular state for each tissue, a final column must be added to the table. Typically $m \sim 100$, while $n \sim 10000$.

When analyzing this table to retrieve a model for diagnosis, we have two different targets: besides finding a method that recognizes the state pertaining to a specific tissue (*discrimination*) [S. Dudoit and Speed, 2002] , we wish to determine the genes involved in this prediction (*gene selection*) [Guyon and Elisseeff, 2003] . The quality of the discrimination task can be simply estimated through a measure of accuracy, obtained by proper methods (hold-out,

B. Apolloni et al. (eds.), Biological and Artificial Intelligence Environments, 73–79

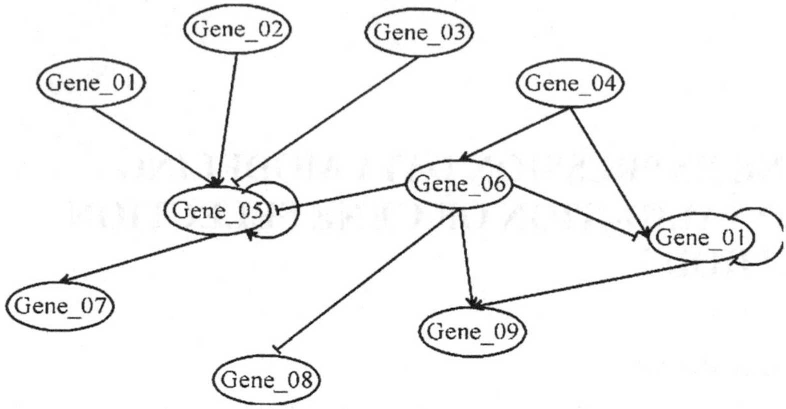

Figure 1. An example of a gene regulating network.

cross validation, etc.). On the contrary, it is very difficult to evaluate the results of the gene selection process, since the genes really involved in the onset of a state are actually unknown.

A possible way of validating gene selection could be to analyze the performance of the considered method on a diagnosis problem where significant genes are known. Unfortunately, at the present no problem of this kind is available. An alternative approach consists in building an artificial model, starting from proper biological motivations, that generates data having the same statistical characteristics of gene expression levels produced by microarray experiments.

A model of this kind not only allows the quality of gene selection methods to be evaluated but it even gives general information about the structure of the classification problem involving microarray analysis.

To this aim it is necessary to build the artificial model starting from biological motivations and to have a statistical rule that measures similarity between artificial and real data.

2. Biological motivations and Measures of similarity

As proposed by Repsilber [Repsilber and Kim, 2003] , the behavior of a biological system can be described through regulatory networks that represent the interaction between different genes (Fig.1).

The nodes and the edges of these networks are ruled by dynamic equations that involve the concentration of products encoded by genes and consequently the gene expression levels. Each concentration is expressed through a real variable that changes with time and can determine the transition of the system from a state to another.

When the organism is in a particular state some concentrations are lower than a given threshold (specific for each gene), while others exceed a proper value. Thus, if we select a definite state, we can say that a gene is in the active state, if its expression level has a value consistent (lower or greater than a specific threshold) with that state. With this definition each gene can be described by a binary variable, assuming value 1 if the gene is active and 0 otherwise.

Also the presence of the considered state can be expressed through a Boolean variable, which takes the value 1, if the tissue is in that state, and 0 otherwise. Consequently, the whole biological system can be described by a Boolean function f with n inputs. Each of the m available microarray experiments corresponds to a particular entry of the truth table for the function f; it is formed by an input-output pair (x, y), where x is a vector of n binary values associated with the examined genes and y is a binary value asserting if the corresponding tissue is in the considered state or not.

According to this setting, a technique to generate artificial data for validating gene selection methods consists in building a proper Boolean function f, whose truth table entries share the same statistical characteristics of gene expression levels produced by microarray experiments. Then, the quality of the gene selection method is measured by the percentage of significant genes retrieved. Although each Boolean function can be described by a logical expression containing only AND, OR and NOT operations, in our case it is more convenient to obtain f in a different way. In fact, it can be observed that in biological systems genes can be assembled into groups of expression signatures, i.e. subsets of coordinately expressed genes related to specific biological functions [Alizadeh and al., 2000] . These groups of genes are, in some sense, equivalent with respect to the state determination. Thus, the Boolean function f can be viewed as a combination of several groups of genes. Each group is considered active if a sufficiently large number of its genes is active. Then, the function f assumes value 1 if the number of active groups exceeds a given threshold.

A proper algorithm for constructing Boolean functions with these characteristics has been implemented. It is able to generate data resembling those produced by several microarray experiments for diagnostic purpose. In these cases two or more different states are analyzed and the algorithm constructs a specific Boolean function (adopting the above approach) for each state. Then, to allow the application of the gene selection method, a set of input-output pairs is produced for each Boolean function built.

The algorithm includes several parameters that can be tuned to achieve a good agreement between the resulting collection of input-output pairs and the dataset produced by microarray experiments for a specific problem.

The similarity between a model and a specific real case can be analyze using a statistical technique. In particular standard tests could be used, but, since few data are available, strong constraints (often not verified in practice) on the behavior of the distribution have to be imposed (e.g. normality). Alternatively, one can think of using one or more discrimination methods for validating the model in a statistical way. For example, a comparison between the collection of input-output pairs produced by the artificial model and the dataset produced by microarray experiments can be performed by looking at the accuracy values scored by a discriminant method for different numbers of considered genes.

3. Preliminary results

In this contribution, Leukemia and Colon datasets described in [Golub and al., 1999; Guyon and al., 2002] have been considered and two proper artificial models have been generated by constructing a specific Boolean function for each class of the two datasets examined. Figures 2 and 3 show the accuracy values obtained through the leave-one-out approach by applying Recursive Feature Elimination (SVM-RFE) method described in [Guyon and al., 2002] and the technique proposed by Golub [Golub and al., 1999] to leukemia and artificial leukemia datasets. As one can note, the agreement between the success rate curves is excellent in both situations.

In analogous way Figures 4 and 5 show the results obtained by applying the same methods to colon and artificial colon datasets: even if there is less agreement between the success rate curves, trend is quite similar especially with Golub's method (Fig.5).

In artificial leukemia dataset genes involved in the onset of AML and ALL are 71. If we denote with R the vector composed by the first 71 genes, ordered in decreasing relevance value, obtained by using the SVM-RFE method and with G the analogous vector obtained with Golub method, we can note that the percentage of relevant genes in R and in G is 25% and 61%, respectively.

In artificial colon dataset relevant genes, involved in the groups constituting the two functions, are 58 in total. SVM-RFE identified 29% of the genes correlated with the discrimination between tumoural and normal samples, while Golub's method recognized 45%.

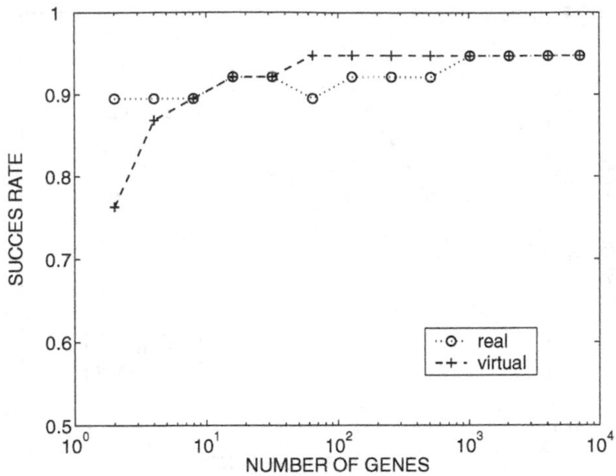

Figure 2. Accuracy values obtained using a SVM-RFE through the leave-one-out approach for the Leukemia dataset and for the dataset produced by the proposed artificial model, when varying the number of considered genes.

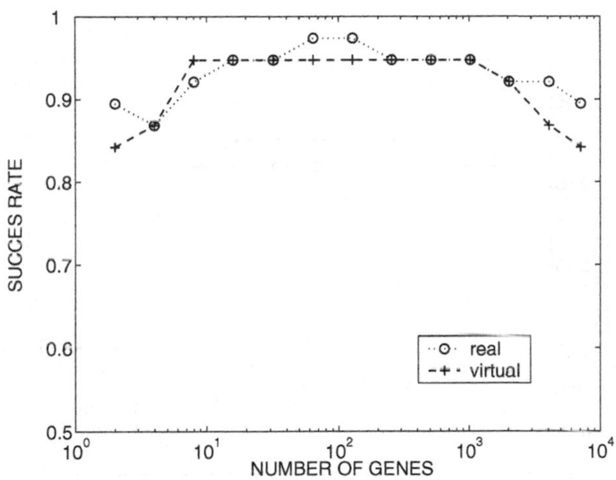

Figure 3. Accuracy values obtained using Golub's method through the leave-one-out approach for the Leukemia dataset and for the dataset produced by the proposed artificial model, when varying the number of considered genes.

4. Conclusions

We proposed an artificial model for validating gene selection methods. Preliminary experimental results, using two different gene selection methods and two dataset seem to confirm the feasibility of the model. Nevertheless we plan

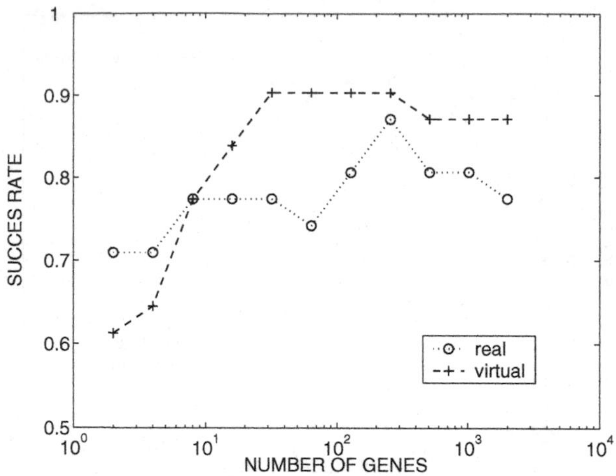

Figure 4. Accuracy values obtained using SVM-RFE through the leave-one-out approach for the Colon dataset and for the dataset produced by the proposed artificial model, when varying the number of considered genes.

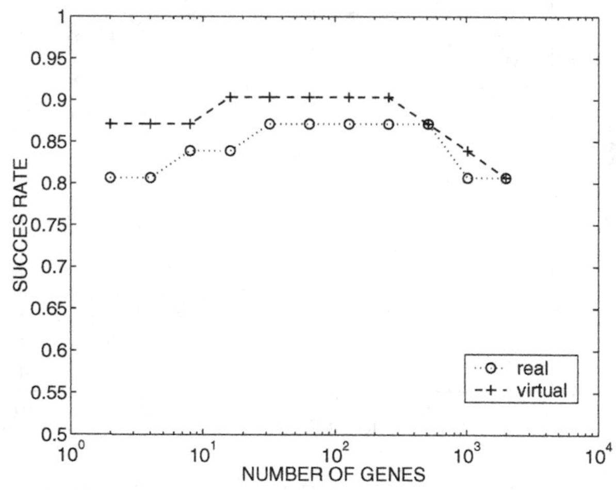

Figure 5. Accuracy values obtained using Golub's method through the leave-one-out approach for the Colon dataset and for the dataset produced by the proposed artificial model, when varying the number of considered genes.

to put more datasets to test in order to get more inputs into the effectiveness of our approach.

References

Alizadeh, A. and al. (2000). Distinct types of diffuse large b-cell lymphoma identified by gene expression profiling. *Nature*, 403:503–511.

Dudoit, S., J. Fridlyand and Speed, T. (2002). Comparison of discrimination methods for the classification of tumors using gene expression data. *JASA*, 97(457):77–87.

Golub, T. R. and al. (1999). Molecular classification of cancer: Class discovery and class prediction by gene expression monitoring. *Science*, 286:531–537.

Guyon, I. and al. (2002). Gene selection for cancer classification using support vectors machines. *Machine Learning*, 46:389–422.

Guyon, I. and Elisseeff, A. (2003). An introduction to variable and feature selection. *Jurnal of Machine Learning Research*, 3:1157–1182.

Lockhart, D. J. and Winzeler, E. A. (2000). Genomics, gene expression and DNA arrays. *Nature*, 405:827–836.

Repsilber, D. and Kim, J. T. (2003). Developing and testing methods for microarray data analysis using an artificial life framework. *Advances in Artificial Life*, pages 686–695.

MINING YEAST GENE MICROARRAY DATA WITH LATENT VARIABLE MODELS

Antonino Staiano[1*], Roberto Tagliaferri[1,3], Lara De Vinco[1], Angelo Ciaramella[1], Giancarlo Raiconi[1], Giuseppe Longo[2,3], Gennaro Miele[2,3], Roberto Amato[2], Carmine Del Mondo[2], Ciro Donalek[2,3], Gianpiero Mangano[2,3], Diego Di Bernardo[4]

[1]*Department of Mathematichs and Informatics, University of Salerno, Via Ponte don Melillo, I-84084, Fisciano (SA), Italy*

[2]*Department of Physical Sciences, University of Napoli Federico II, via Cinthia 6, Napoli, Italy*

[3]*INFN - Italian Institure of Nuclear Physics Unit of Naples, via Cinthia 6, Italy*

[4]*Telethon Institute for Genetics and Medicine, Via Pietro Castellino 111 I-80131 Napoli, Italy*

Abstract Gene-expression microarrays make it possible to simultaneously measure the rate at which a cell or tissue is expressing each of its thousands of genes. One can use these comprehensive snapshots of biological activity to infer regulatory pathways in cells, identify novel targets for drug design, and improve diagnosis, prognosis, and treatment planning for those suffering from disease. However, the amount of data this new technology produces is more than one can manually analyze. Hence, the need for automated analysis of microarray data offers an opportunity for machine learning to have a significant impact on biology and medicine. Probabilistic Principal Surfaces defines a unified theoretical framework for nonlinear latent variable models embracing the Generative Topographic Mapping as a special case. This article describes the use of PPS for the analysis of yeast gene expression levels from microarray chips showing its effectiveness for high-D data visualization and clustering.

Keywords: Probabilistic Principal Surfaces, Visualization, Clustering, Data Mining, Yeast Genes

1. Introduction

Data mining techniques, by this time, have spread abroad across several scientific research fields, all sharing a common peculiarity: the availability of enormous amount of data. Despite the presence of these massive data sets, the

*Contact author: Staiano Antonino, DMI, Università di Salerno, Via Ponte don Melillo, I-84084, Fisciano (Sa), Italy. Email: astaiano@unisa.it

B. Apolloni et al. (eds.), Biological and Artificial Intelligence Environments, 81–89

key for the success of whatever applied scientific research, is to properly exploit this information to derive new knowledge leading to new discovers and progress enhancement. Data mining is now a research field which brings together several scientists of different backgrounds (i.e. statisticians, computer scientists and expert of the domains) who continuously add their contribute for developing new tools aiding the humans for the interpretation and the exploitation of scientific information. Genetics and medicine are examples of scientific fields which are living a revolutionary era thanks to the technological and methodological progress. As an example one can think of gene-expression microarrays, whose development started in the second half of the 1990's, which are having a powerful impact on molecular biology. In fact, although the ability to measure transcription of a single gene is not new, the ability to measure at once the transcription of all genes in an organism is new and the amount of data that biologists need to examine is overwhelming. The advent of microarray technologies for large-scale transcriptional profiling is leading to new methods of diagnosis and treatment for any number of diseases. However, it is become increasingly clear that simply generating the data is not enough; one must be able to extract from it meaningful information about the system being studied.

1.1 Gene-expression microarray and machine learning techniques

Statistical techniques and other classical methods of data analysis alone, are not sufficiently adequate to cope with this sudden increase in the data volume and especially in the data complexity. Therefore, in the last decade numerous works have been focused on the development of machine learning methodologies suited for the analysis of genetic data. Just to mention a few, support vector machines have been used for functional classification of genes [Brown et al., 2000], clustering techniques are used for grouping similar expression patterns across a number of experiments of all the genes of the yeast Saccharomyces cerevisiae [Spellman et al., 1998], and Neural networks have been employed both for clustering and visualization of gene microarray data [Tamayo et al., 1999; Toronen et al., 1999]. In this paper we discuss a unified nonlinear latent variable model which embraces Generative Topographic Mapping [Bishop et al., 1998] as a special case, i.e, Probabilistic Principal Surfaces [Chang and Ghosh, 2001; Staiano, 2003], as an effective high-D data visualization and clustering tool for mining yeast gene microarray data.

2. From GTM to PPS: a unified latent variable model

2.1 Generative Topographic Mapping

The *GTM* defines a non-linear, parametric mapping $\mathbf{y}(\mathbf{x}; \mathbf{W})$ from a Q-dimensional latent space ($\mathbf{x} \in \mathbb{R}^Q$) to a D-dimensional data space ($\mathbf{t} \in \mathbb{R}^D$), where normally $Q < D$. The mapping $\mathbf{y}(\mathbf{x}; \mathbf{W})$ (defined continuous and differentiable) maps every point in the latent space to a point into the data space (see Fig. 1). Since the latent space is Q-dimensional, these points will be confined to a Q-dimensional manifold non-linearly embedded into the D-dimensional data space. GTM builds a constrained mixture of Gaussians (all of them share the same variance and priors are all fixed to $\frac{1}{M}$)

$$p(\mathbf{t}|\mathbf{W}, \beta) = \frac{1}{M} \sum_{m=1}^{M} p(\mathbf{t}|\mathbf{x}_m, \mathbf{W}, \beta), \tag{1}$$

and each component has the form:

$$p(\mathbf{t}|\mathbf{x}, \mathbf{W}, \beta) = \left(\frac{\beta}{2\pi}\right)^{\frac{D}{2}} exp\left\{-\frac{\beta}{2}\sum_{d=1}^{D}(t_d - y_d(\mathbf{x}, \mathbf{W}))^2\right\}, \tag{2}$$

where $\mathbf{t}$ is a point in the data space and β^{-1} denotes the noise variance.

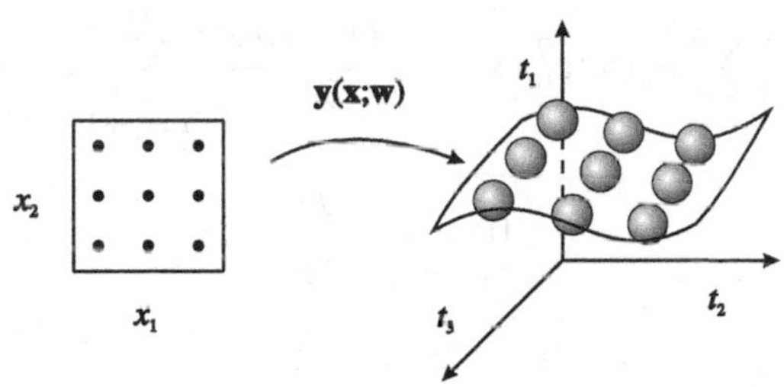

Figure 1. Each node $\mathbf{x}_m$ is mapped into a corresponding point $\mathbf{y}(\mathbf{x}_m; \mathbf{w})$ in data space, and forms the center of a corresponding Gaussian distribution

The parameters $\mathbf{W}$ and β of the mixture are computed by means of the Expectation-Maximization algorithm used for optimizing the model log-likelihood function with respect to $\mathbf{W}$ and β themselves. The form of the mapping $\mathbf{y}(\mathbf{x}; \mathbf{w})$ is defined as a generalized linear regression model

$$\mathbf{y}(\mathbf{x}; \mathbf{w}) = \mathbf{W}\phi(\mathbf{x}) \tag{3}$$

where the elements of $\phi(\mathbf{x})$ consist of L fixed basis functions $\{\phi_l(\mathbf{x})\}_{l=1}^{L}$, and $\mathbf{W}$ is a $D \times L$ matrix.

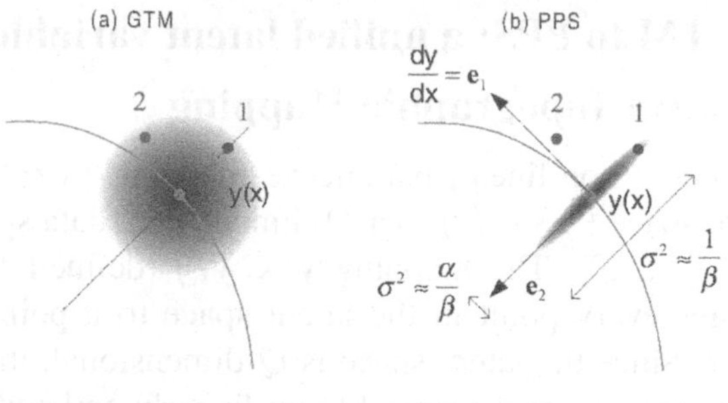

Figure 2. Under a spherical Gaussian model of the *GTM*, points 1 and 2 have equal influences on the center node $y(\mathbf{x})$ (a) *PPS* have an oriented covariance matrix so point 1 is probabilistically closer to the center node $y(\mathbf{x})$ than point 2 (b)

2.2 Probabilistic Principal Surfaces

The *PPS* generalizes the GTM model by building a unified model and shares the same formulation as the GTM, except for an oriented covariance structure for the Gaussian mixture in $\mathbb{R}^D$. This means that data points projecting near a principal surface node (i.e., a Gaussian center of the mixture) have higher influences on that node than points projecting far away from it. This is illustrated in Fig. 2.

Therefore, each node $\mathbf{y}(\mathbf{x};\mathbf{w})$, $\mathbf{x} \in \{\mathbf{x}_m\}_{m=1}^{M}$, has covariance

$$\mathbf{\Sigma}(\mathbf{x}) = \frac{\alpha}{\beta}\sum_{q=1}^{Q}\mathbf{e}_q(\mathbf{x})\mathbf{e}_q^T(\mathbf{x}) + \frac{(D-\alpha Q)}{\beta(D-Q)}\sum_{d=Q+1}^{D}\mathbf{e}_d(\mathbf{x})\mathbf{e}_d^T(\mathbf{x}), \qquad (4)$$

$$0 < \alpha < \frac{D}{Q}$$

where

- $\{\mathbf{e}_q(\mathbf{x})\}_{q=1}^{Q}$ is the set of orthonormal vectors tangential to the manifold at $\mathbf{y}(\mathbf{x};\mathbf{w})$,
- $\{\mathbf{e}_d(\mathbf{x})\}_{d=Q+1}^{D}$ is the set of orthonormal vectors orthogonal to the manifold in $\mathbf{y}(\mathbf{x};\mathbf{w})$.

The complete set of orthonormal vectors $\{\mathbf{e}_d(\mathbf{x})\}_{d=1}^{D}$ spans $\mathbb{R}^D$. The parameter α is a clamping factor and determines the orientation of the covariance matrix. The unified *PPS* model reduces to GTM for $\alpha = 1$ and to the manifold-aligned GTM for $\alpha > 1$

$$\mathbf{\Sigma}(\mathbf{x}) = \begin{cases} 0 < \alpha < 1 & \perp \text{ to the manifold} \\ \alpha = 1 & I_D \text{ or spherical} \\ 1 < \alpha < D/Q & \parallel \text{ to the manifold.} \end{cases}$$

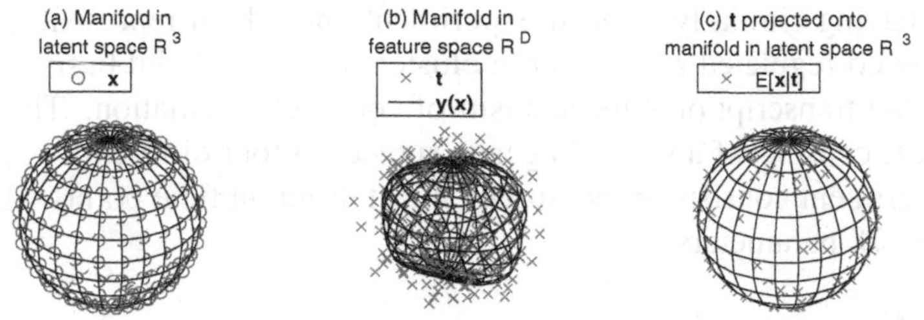

Figure 3. (a) The spherical manifold in $\mathbb{R}^3$ latent space. (b) The spherical manifold in $\mathbb{R}^3$ data space. (c) Projection of data points $\mathbf{t}$ onto the latent spherical manifold

The EM algorithm can be used to estimate the PPS parameters $\mathbf{W}$ and β, while the clamping factor is fixed by the user and is assumed to be constant during the EM iterations. If we choose a $3D$ latent space, then a spherical manifold can be constructed using a PPS with nodes $\{\mathbf{x}_m\}_{m=1}^{M}$ arranged regularly on the surface of a sphere in $\mathbb{R}^3$ latent space, with the latent basis functions evenly distributed on the sphere at a lower density. After a PPS model is fitted to the data, the data themselves are projected into the latent space as points onto a sphere (Fig. 3).

The latent manifold coordinates $\hat{\mathbf{x}}_n$ of each data point $\mathbf{t}_n$ are computed as

$$\hat{\mathbf{x}}_n \equiv \langle \mathbf{x}|\mathbf{t}_n \rangle = \int \mathbf{x}p(\mathbf{x}|\mathbf{t})d\mathbf{x} = \sum_{m=1}^{M} r_{mn}\mathbf{x}_m$$

where r_{mn} are the latent variable responsibilities defined as

$$r_{mn} = p(\mathbf{x}_m|\mathbf{t}_n) = \frac{p(\mathbf{t}_n|\mathbf{x}_m)P(\mathbf{x}_m)}{\sum_{m'=1}^{M} p(\mathbf{t}_n|\mathbf{x}_{m'})P(\mathbf{x}_{m'})} = \frac{p(\mathbf{t}_n|\mathbf{x}_m)}{\sum_{m'=1}^{M} p(\mathbf{t}_n|\mathbf{x}_{m'})}.$$

These coordinates lie within a unit sphere. Spherical PPS is particularly well suited to capture the sparsity and periphery of data in large input spaces which are due to the curse of dimensionality. In [Staiano, 2003; Staiano et al., 2004] a data mining framework PPS-based with advanced visualization methods was proposed to accomplish a number of activities from high-D data visualization to clustering.

3. Experimental Results

We started from the work of Spellman and his colleagues described in [Spellman et al., 1998] which provides a comprehensive catalog of yeast genes whose transcript levels vary periodically within the cell cycle. In order to produce the catalogue, samples from yeast cultures synchronized with different experiments were used. In [Spellman et al., 1998] a type of agglomerative hierarchical clustering [Eisen et al., 1998] was used in order to identify clusters of genes behaving similarly in each experiment and which represent groups of apparently co-regulated genes. These clusters provide a solid basis for understanding the transcriptional mechanism of cell cycle regulation. The data set used by us, consists of a set 6125 genes subject to four different experiments. Each experiment consists of measurements at different time points which correspond to 73 parameters.

3.1 Preprocessing

In order to make this data set more tractable by PPS, we applied a preprocessing phase in which through the use of a nonlinear PCA [Tagliaferri et al., 1999] we reduced each experiment to 8 measurements and eliminated the genes whose experiments had to much missing data. Hence, the used data set consists of 5425 genes and 32 features. Furthermore, since, in general, microarray data is noisy, it is necessary to resort to some kind of cleaning procedure, to identify those genes affected from noise process involved in the generation of data from microarrays. At this aim, we decided to train a PPS with a high number of latent variables, so that each one is responsible of a limited number of data points, afterward, we apply a clustering procedure on the nodes of the manifold in the data space. So doing, a number of identified clusters containing genes with low variance (i.e. genes whose transcript levels show a poor periodic behavior) have been thrown away. At completion of this phase the number of genes to examine was fixed to 2761.

3.2 PPS and yeast gene data: results

We used a PPS with 266 latent variables and 40 latent basis functions and a clamping factor α set to 0.5. After the completion of the training phase we projected the data in latent space and computed the responsibility for each latent variable as shown in Fig. 4. On the basis of probability density function visualized in figure 4 we decided to compute 30 clusters through an hierarchical clustering procedure. For each cluster we plotted the prototype trend with respect to the 32 features, as it can be seen in figure 5, which highlights the periodic behavior of each gene belonging to the cluster.

4. Conclusions

Although this work is at a first stage, Fig. 6 shows interesting trends. Before discussing the table, we wish to stress that the two clustering procedures were completely different: Spellman in fact clustered the gene properties using a priori knowledge on their characteristics and thus he worked with only 209 genes to cluster, while our algorithm made use of statistical properties of the data with no a priori knowledge. In spite of this, some remarkable patterns may be detected: Spellman's clusters number 1 falls near entirely in our

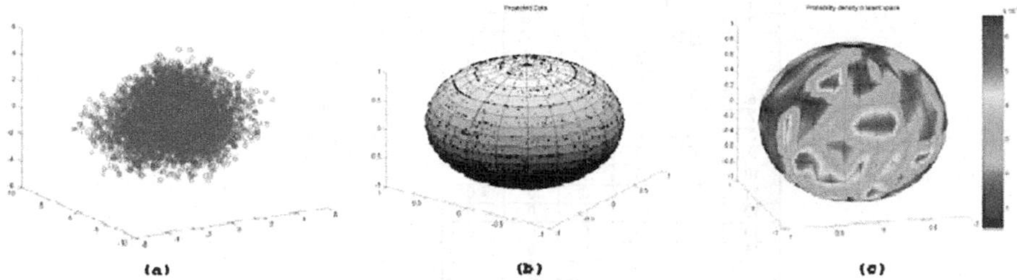

Figure 4. Yeast Gene Data Set: (a) $3D$ PCA projection (b) Data point projections in the latent space (c) Data probability density in the latent space

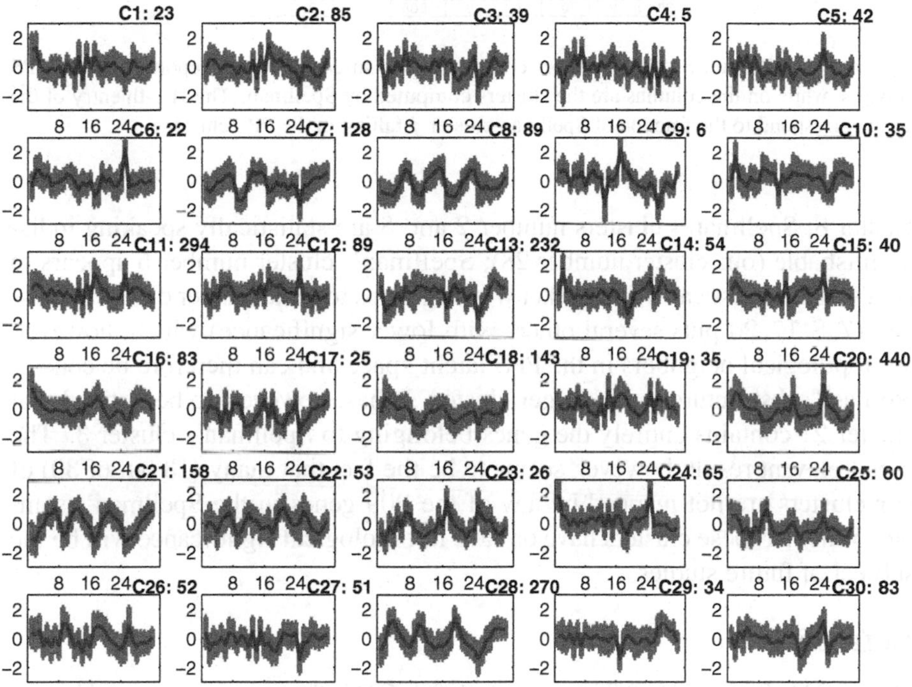

Figure 5. Cluster prototype periodic behaviors and error bars (3σ) showing the standard deviation of genes from the prototypes for a fixed cluster On the top of each subplot the cluster number and the number of genes within each cluster is reported

	1	2	3	4	5	6	7	8
1	0	0	0	0	0	0	0	0
2	0	0	0	10	0	0	0	0
3	3.4483	0	0	0	0	0	0	0
4	0	0	0	0	0	0	0	0
5	0	0	0	20	0	0	0	0
6	0	0	0	0	0	0	0	0
7	0	0	0	0	10.345	0	0	3.7037
8	***89.655***	0	0	0	20.69	0	4.5455	0
9	0	0	0	0	0	0	0	0
10	0	0	0	0	0	0	0	0
11	0	0	0	0	0	0	0	0
12	0	0	0	0	0	0	0	0
13	0	0	0	0	0	0	0	0
14	0	0	0	0	0	0	0	0
15	0	0	0	0	0	0	0	0
16	0	0	0	***50***	0	0	0	0
17	0	0	0	10	***31.034***	0	0	0
18	0	0	0	10	3.4483	0	0	0
19	0	0	0	0	0	0	0	0
20	0	0	0	0	13.793	7.6923	0	0
21	6.8966	2.5	***100***	0	0	23.077	0	0
22	0	0	0	0	0	***69.231***	0	0
23	0	0	0	0	3.4483	0	0	0
24	0	0	0	0	0	0	0	0
25	0	0	0	0	10.345	0	***90.909***	0
26	0	0	0	0	0	0	4.5455	0
27	0	0	0	0	0	0	0	0
28	0	***97.5***	0	0	0	0	0	***96.296***
29	0	0	0	0	0	0	0	0
30	0	0	0	0	6.8966	0	0	0

Figure 6. PPS and Spellman cluster comparisons. On each row are reported the 30 PPS clusters, while on the columns are the clusters computed by Spellman. The A_{ij}-th entry of the table correspond to the fraction of Spellman cluster j falling in the PPS cluster i

cluster 8; Spellman's clusters number 2 and 8 are statistically speaking indistinguishable (our cluster number 28); Spellman's cluster number 5 appears to be a sort of statistical waste basket which groups together rather different clusters $(7, 8, 17, 20$ plus several others with lower significance) which, however, are topological neighbors in the PPS latent space and can therefore be considered as "substructures" of a larger cluster. It has, however, to be noticed that cluster 21 contains entirely the genes belonging to Spellman's cluster 3. The most relevant result, however, seems to be the fact that many (13 out of 30) of our clusters are not mapped by any of the 209 genes in the Spellman's sample. Whether these clusters have or have not biological significance will be the subject of future studies.

References

Bishop, C.M., Svensen, M., Williams, C.K.I. (1998). GTM: The generative topographic mapping. Neural Computation.

Brown, M., Grundy, W., Lin, D., Cristianini, N., Sugnet, C., Furey, T., Ares, M. Jr., Haussler, D. (2000). Knowledge-based Analysis of Microarray Gene Expression Data by Using Support Vector Machines. Proceedings of the National Academy of Science USA, 97 (1), 262–267.

Chang, K., Ghosh, J. (2001). A unified model for probabilistic principal surfaces. IEEE Transactions on Pattern Analysis and Machine Intelligence, 23, (1).

Eisen, M.B., Spellman, P.T., Brown, P.O., Botstein, D. (1998). Cluster analysis and display of genome-wide expression patterns. PNAS, 95:14863–14868

Spellman, P.T., Sherlock, G., Zhang, M.Q., Iyer, V.R., Anders, K., Eisen, M.B., Brown, P.O., Botstein, D., Futcher, B. (1998). Comprehensive identification of cell cycle-regulated genes of the yeast saccharomyces cerevisiae by microarray hybridization. Molecular Biology of the Cell, 9:3273–3297.

Staiano, A. (2003). Unsupervised Neural Networks for the Extraction of Scientific Information from Astronomical Data. PhD thesis, Università di Salerno, Italy.

Staiano, A., Tagliaferri, R., De Vinco, L., Longo, G. (2004). High-D Data Visualization Methods via Probabilistic Principal Surfaces for Data Mining Applications. In Chang, S.K. (Ed) Multimedia Databases and Image Communication, Salerno. Series on Software Engineering and Knowledge Engineering - World Scientific - in press.

Tagliaferri, R., Ciaramella, A., Milano, L., Barone, F., Longo, G. (1999).Spectral analysis of stellar light curves by means of neural networks. Astronomy and Astrophysics Supplement Series, 137:391–405.

Tamayo, P., Slonim, D., Mesirov, J., Zhu, Q., Kitareewan, S., Dmitrovsky, E., Lander, E.S., Golub, T.R. (1999). Interpreting patterns of gene expression with self-organizing maps: Methods and application to hematopoietic differentiation. PNAS, 96:2907–2912.

Toronen, P., Kolehmainen, M., Wong, G., Castren, E. (1999). Analysis of gene expression data using self-organizing maps. FEBS Letters 451:142–146.

RECENT APPLICATIONS OF NEURAL NETWORKS IN BIOINFORMATICS

Matthew J. Wood[1], Jonathan D. Hirst[1]

[1] *School of Chemistry, University of Nottingham, University Park, Nottingham, UK*

Abstract In the post-genomic era, bioinformatics methods play a central role in understanding vast amounts of biological data. Due to their ability to find arbitrarily complex patterns within these data, neural networks play a unique, exciting and pivotal role in areas as diverse as protein structure and function prediction. This paper presents a critical overview of recent advances in bioinformatics which have utilised neural network methods.

Keywords: Bioinformatics, neural networks, structure prediction, function prediction, cascade-correlation.

1. Introduction

Like their biological counterparts, neural networks consists of simple functional units that receive and process signals from other units. The ability of neural networks to learn arbitrarily complex functions from large amounts of data, without the need for predetermined models, makes them an ideal tool to aid in the solving biological problems such as protein structure prediction. The application of neural networks to bioinformatics is becoming established. There are a number of reviews of earlier work in the field [Hirst and Sternberg, 1992; Rost and Sander, 1993]. Bioinformatics encompasses a large number of disciplines, many of which are beyond the scope of this paper. Here we appraise state of the art applications of neural networks in the field of protein folding prediction, focusing on studies published in the last 18 months.

The prediction of protein three dimensional structure from sequence is one of the most important, unsolved problems in molecular biology. Following the completion of several high profile genome projects, the amino acid sequence for each gene in a mapped organism's genome is available. From only this information, organisms are capable of producing all the proteins necessary to sustain life. The genomic DNA sequence is translated into RNA, which is transcribed into a series of peptide-bonded amino acids. This polypeptide chain of amino acids folds and undergoes further modification to become a functioning

B. Apolloni et al. (eds.), Biological and Artificial Intelligence Environments, 91–97

protein. Since a protein's function is determined by its full three-dimensional structure, the resolution of this structure is of vital importance in understanding how a protein achieves its function, how this function may be altered in a disease state and how that disease state may be alleviated. However, structural determination techniques, such as X-ray crystallography and nuclear magnetic resonance are costly, relatively slow and are not suitable for all proteins. Thus, computational methods that predict a protein's structure from sequence information have enjoyed a great deal of attention in the past 50 years.

Contained within the final, three dimensional structure of a functioning protein are a structural motifs ranging from broad secondary structural elements which span a number of amino acid residues, to more subtle bonding states involving a pair of, or even single, amino acids. The role of artificial neural networks in attempting to predict these structural motifs, whatever their size, from sequence information alone is broad. A number of sequence representations are commonly used and range from an orthogonal encoding featuring 20 numbers which describe the amino acid type of a single residue, to larger, more complex input values comprising information on multiple residues, often incorporating evolutionary information. Indeed, the use of neural networks in bioinformatics is so wide reaching, that the networks themselves have recently been used to derive new sequence representations from known structures, for use in the prediction of unknown structures [Lin et al., 2002].

2. Protein structure prediction

Recent applications include the prediction of various structural features from a range of sequence representations [Ahmad et al., 2003; Sheperd et al., 2003; Jones and Ward, 2003; Chou and Cai, 2003]. The prediction of one such feature, protein surface accessibility, has benefited greatly from the application of neural networks. Until recently, the most successful previous methods [Naderi-Manesh et al., 2001] utilised information theory, but limited predictions to an accessible surface state. Like many other structure prediction methods, a major motivation for the prediction of solvent accessibility is that the derived information may be used to aid the development of other methods attempting to predict full three-dimensional protein structure from amino acid sequence. Whilst capable of correctly allocating 70-75% of residues to a surface accessibility state, the categorical nature of previous methods actually reduced the amount of information available to methods built upon it, when compared to available structural data. In an attempt to overcome this inherent problem, multilayer, feed-forward neural networks were employed to predict real number surface accessibility values from a 21 bit sequence representation [Ahmad et al., 2003]. The results were encouraging, with reported mean absolute errors of 18 to 19.5%, representing a significant improvement in the field.

Along with increases in the accuracy of structure prediction from sequence, neural networks have also been responsible for large improvements in other recent bioinformatics methods that aim to enhance the understanding of protein folding by examining the known structure of proteins. Using graph theory, DomainParser [Xu et al., 2000] accurately predicts structural domains (believed to be one of the fundamental units of protein folding) within a protein. Whilst reasonably accurate, one of the major drawbacks of DomainParser is that its predictive ability is far lower when the number of structural domains present in a protein is not known *a priori*. In an attempt to overcome this drawback [Guo et al., 2003], neural networks have been used to predict the number of structural domains from protein structure. The neural network performance is good, correctly predicting between 85.1% and 87.6% of protein structural domains. This information is then used to boost the DomainParser performance, increasing its predictive ability from 74.5% to 81.9% accuracy. Whilst structure from sequence modelling (discussed above), and structural domain decomposition are very different problems, the use of neural networks has made recent, significant contributions to both long standing research fields.

3. Secondary structure prediction

The accurate prediction of protein secondary structure is both a useful tool for bench biologists and a good starting point for those attempting to model three dimensional protein structure [Rost and Sander, 1994]. The secondary structure of a protein is characterised by a number of regularly occurring structural elements, including α-helix, β-sheet, and a number of irregularly occurring elements, such as random coils and tight turns [Kaur and Raghava, 2004]. First used in 1988 [Qian and Sejnowski, 1988], neural networks have played a pivotal role in protein secondary structure prediction. Indeed, neural networks remain at the heart of many of these types of methods, including the current most successful method, PSIPRED [Jones, 1999]. Despite a huge amount of interest in this area [Rost and Sander, 1994; Cuff and Barton, 2000], there has been little increase in predictive power of neural network methods in the past 5 years. Whilst a large number of different algorithms have been applied to this problem (including bidirectional recurrent networks [Baldi et al., 2000], back-propagating feed-forward networks [Jones, 1999] and cascade-correlation networks [Wood and Hirst, 2004]). Reported improvements can largely be attributed to novel sequence and structure representations, rather than any algorithmic improvement.

Attention has also been focused on the type of algorithm best suited to bioinformatic problems, such as protein secondary structure prediction. A recent study [Wood and Hirst, 2004] compared the learning speed and predictive accuracy of the commonly used back-propagation neural network, with the cascade-correlation learning architecture [Fahlman and Lebiere, 1990]. Using position-specific-scoring-matrices [Altschul et al., 1997] from multiple alignments, a constructive cascade-correlation network and a pre-defined back-propagation network were trained to predict secondary structure. A position-specific-scoring-matrix is a 20 by n matrix (where n is the number of residues in a protein sequence), which contains information about the possibility of a residue substitution at a particular point in the sequence. These matrices have been used extensively in protein structure prediction work [Jones, 1999; Rost and Sander, 1994] as they include information on the evolutionary stability of a particular residue in a particular position, and long-range interactions of residues. The scoring matrices for each residue in the dataset were combined with the scoring matrices for seven residues towards the N and C termini of the protein. This window of 15 residues was presented to the two types of neural network, which both attained a high degree of predictive accuracy. However, the cascade-correlation algorithm learnt to predict structure in a shorter time. Whilst there was no increase in predictive accuracy, the speed increase shown means that the cascade-correlation network is better suited to handle the larger databases that are frequently experienced in all fields of bioinformatics.

Along with regular secondary structure prediction, neural networks also feature prominently in recent methods to predict non-regular protein secondary structure. Using homology information, and neural network derived secondary structure predictions as inputs to the main network, α-turn, β-turn and γ-turn secondary structure can be correctly allocated 78%, 75.5% and 74.0% of the time, respectively [Kaur and Raghava, 2004; Kaur and Raghava, 2003a; Kaur and Raghava, 2003b]. Other non-regular secondary structures, hairpins and diverging turns have also been predicted using neural networks trained on homology information and predicted secondary structure prediction, reaching 75.9% and 73.9% accuracy respectively [Kuhn et al., 2004].

4. Protein Function Prediction

Another particularly active area of bioinformatics research is that of protein function prediction. Many believe that this area holds the key to a more complete understanding of protein folding and the opportunity to better develop novel, targeted drug therapies. As structure is so closely related to function, it can be argued that the progress in the prediction of protein structure also aids in this area. Neural networks have been used as a tool to predict a number of protein function information [Nair and Rost, 2003; Cia et al., 2002; Yang and Chou, 2004; Ofran and Rost, 2003; Keil et al., 2004]. The prediction of ligand binding sites is of particular interest, as success in this area would facilitate the accurate location of enzyme active sites, the site of biological catalysis and a common therapeutic target. A recent study [Gutteridge et al., 2003] not only reported a novel, neural network based method for predicting enzyme active targets, but also highlighted the tight integration between neural network based bioinformatics tools that is becoming common. The method uses structural parameters, such as those predicted by neural networks above, as inputs to neural networks in order to identify residues with a high probability of being part of an active site. Clustering algorithms then search the neural network results to produce a prediction. The active site is correctly predicted in 69% of test cases.

Whilst this method is trained on data from known protein structures, these data could have been augmented with a larger number of predicted values from proteins of unknown structure. Indeed, this kind of integration, with new methods using neural network values directly, is commonly seen in a number of recent bioinformatic studies [Kaur and Raghava, 2004; Kuhn et al., 2004; Guermeur et al., 2004; Bindewald et al., 2003].

5. Conclusions

Bioinformatics covers a wide range of topics and neural networks have been employed to some extent in many of them. However, due to the nature of the complex network of units, scoring functions and weights, whilst neural networks are often a useful and successful tool in bioinformatics, they are often not able to provide biological insight in their own right, in the way that other machine learning tools can achieve. They are often seen as a 'black box', with an associated inability to explain their model. That said, recent attempts at gaining this important information from neural networks have been relatively successful. One recent study [Browne et al., 2004] attempted to use the connecting weights from a trained neural network to produce a decision tree, which could then be used to search for novel biological information in existing databases, with an assumed additional intuition. Preliminary results are encouraging, and further research may allow neural networks to not only model and make predictions on data, but also provide biological insight based on those predictions.

Neural network development has far reaching implications, and it is clear that research into bioinformatics has benefited greatly both in the past, and in recent years from a neural networks' ability to map arbitrarily complex functions, without the need for predetermined models. Whilst the lack of intrinsic biological insight could be seen as a hindrance to their application in this field, the wide range of successful recent applications including protein structure and function prediction shows this not to be the case, and that neural network usage is as healthy as ever in the bioinformatics field.

6. Acknowledgements

We thank the "Computational Intelligence for Biopattern Analysis in Support of e-healthcare" supported by the EU 6th Framework Network of Excellent (contract number: IST e-health 508803) for funding. We also thank the BBSRC for a PhD studentship.

References

Ahmad, S., Gromiha, M. M., and Sarai, A. (2003). Real value prediction of solvent accessibility from amino acid sequence. *Proteins: Structure, Function and Genetics*, 50:629–635.

Altschul, S. F., Madden, T. L., Schaffer, A. A., Zhang, Z., Miller, W., and Lipman, D. J. (1997). Gapped blast and psi-blast: a new generation of protein database search programs. *Nucleic Acids Res.*, 25:3389–3402.

Baldi, P., Brunak, S., Frasconi, P., Pallastri, G., and Soda, S. (2000). *Bidirectional Dynamics for Protein Secondary Structure Prediction in Sequence Learning: Paradigms, Algorithms, and Applications, R.Sun and C.L. Giles*. Springer.

Bindewald, E., Cestaro, A., Heiler, M., and Tosatto, S. C. E. (2003). Manifold: protein fold recognition based on secondary structure, sequence similarity and enzyme classification. *Protein Science*, 16:785–789.

Browne, A., Hudson, B., Whitley, D., Ford, M., and Picton, P. (2004). Biological data mining with neural networks: implementation and applications of a flexible decision tree extration algorithm to genomic problem domains. *Neurocomputing*, 57:275–293.

Chou, K-C. and Cai, Y-D. (2003). Predicting protein quaternary structure by pseudo amino acid composition. *Proteins: Structure, Function and Genetics*, 53:282–289.

Cia, Y-D, Liu, X-J, and Chou, K-C (2002). Artificial neural network model for predicting protein subcellular location. *Computers and Chemistry*, 26:179–182.

Cuff, C. A. and Barton, G. J. (2000). Application of multiple sequence alignment profiles to improve protein secondary structure prediction. *Proteins: Structure, Function and Genetics*, 40:502–511.

Fahlman, S. E. and Lebiere, C. (1990). *The Cascade-correlation Learning Architecture, Advances in Neural Information Processing Systems 2*. Kaufmann Publishers, Los Altos, CA.

Guermeur, Y., Pollastri, G., Elisseeff, A., Zelus, D., Paugam-Moisy, H., and Baldi, P. (2004). Combining protein secondary structure prediction models with ensemble methods of optimal complexity. *Neurocomputing*, 56:305–327.

Guo, J., Dong, X., Dongsup, K., and Ying, X. (2003). Improving the performance of domain-parser for structural domain partition using neural network. *Nucleic Acids Res.*, 31:944–952.

Gutteridge, A., Bartlett, G. J., and Thornton, J. M. (2003). Using a neural network and spatial clustering to predict the location of active sites in enzymes. *J. Mol. Biol.*, 330:719–734.

Hirst, J. D. and Sternberg, M. J. E. (1992). Prediction of structural and functional features of protein and nucleic-acid sequences by artificial neural networks. *Biochemistry*, 31:7211–7218.

Jones, D. T. (1999). Protein secondary structure prediction based on position-specific scoring matrices. *J. Mol. Biol.*, 292:195–202.

Jones, D. T. and Ward, J. J. (2003). Prediction of disordered regions in proteins from position specific scoring matrices. *Proteins: Structure, Function and Genetics*, 53:573–578.

Kaur, H. and Raghava, G. P. S. (2003a). A neural-network based method for prediction of gamma-turns in proteins from multiple sequence alignment. *Protein Science*, 12:923–929.

Kaur, H. and Raghava, G. P. S. (2003b). Prediction of beta-turns in proteins from multiple alignment using neural network. *Protein Science*, 12:627–634.

Kaur, H. and Raghava, G. P. S. (2004). Prediction of alpha-turns in proteins using PSI-BLAST profiles and secondary structure information. *Proteins: Structure, Function and Genetics*, 55:83–90.

Keil, M., Exner, T., and Brickmann, J. (2004). Pattern recognition strategies for molecular surfaces III. binding site prediction with a neural network. *Journal of Computational Chemistry*, 25:779–789.

Kuhn, M., Meiler, J., and Baker, D. (2004). Strand-loop-strand motifs: Prediction of hairpins and diverging turns in proteins. *Proteins: Structure, Function and Genetics*, 54:282–288.

Lin, K., May, A. C. W., and Taylor, W. R. (2002). Amino acid encoding schemes from protein structure alignments: Multi-dimensional vectors to describe residue types. *J. Theor. Biol.*, 216:361–365.

Naderi-Manesh, H., Sadgehi, M., Arab, S., and Movahedi, A. A Moosavi (2001). Prediction of protein surface accessibility with information theory. *Proteins: Structure, Function and Genetics*, 42:452–459.

Nair, R. and Rost, B. (2003). Better prediction of sub-cellular localization by combining evolutionary and structural informatioin. *Proteins: Structure, Function and Genetics*, 53:917–930.

Ofran, Y. and Rost, B. (2003). Predicted protein-protein interaction sites from local sequence information. *FEBS Letters*, 544:236–239.

Qian, N. and Sejnowski, T. J. (1988). Predicting the secondary structure of globular proteins using neural network models. *J. Mol. Biol.*, 202:865–884.

Rost, B. and Sander, C. (1993). Progress in protein-structure prediction. *Trends Biochem Sci*, 18:120–123.

Rost, B. and Sander, C. (1994). Combining evolutionary information and neural networks to predict protein secondary structure. *Proteins: Structure, Function and Genetics*, 19:55–72.

Sheperd, A. J., Gorse, D., and Thornton, J. M. (2003). Novel approach to the recognition of protein architecture from sequence using fourier analysis and neural networks. *Proteins: Structure, Function and Genetics*, 50:290–302.

Wood, M. J. and Hirst, J. D. (2004). Predicting protein secondary structure by cascade-correlation neural networks. *Bioinformatics*, 20:419–420.

Xu, Y., Xu, D., and Gabow, H. N. (2000). Protein domain decomposition using a graph-theoretic approach. *Bioinformatics*, 16:1091–1104.

Yang, Z. R. and Chou, K-C. (2004). Predicting the linkage sites in glycoproteins using bio-basis function neural network. *Bioinformatics*, 20:903–908.

AN ALGORITHM FOR REDUCING THE NUMBER OF SUPPORT VECTORS

Davide Anguita, Sandro Ridella and Fabio Rivieccio
Dept. of Biophysical and Electronic Engineering,
University of Genova, Genova, Italy.
{anguita,ridella,rivieccio}@dibe.unige.it

Abstract According to the Support Vector Machine algorithm, the task of classification depends on a subset of the original data-set, which is the set of Support Vectors (SVs). They are the only information needed to compute the discriminating function between the classes and, therefore, to classify new data. Since both the computational complexity and the memory requirements of the algorithm depend on the number of SVs, this property is very appealing from the point of view of hardware implementations. For this reason, many researchers have proposed new methods to reduce the number of SVs, even at the expenses of a larger error rate. We propose in this work a method which aims at finding a single point per each class, called archetype, which allows to reconstruct the classifier found by the SVM algorithm, without suffering any classification rate loss. The method is also extended to the case of non-linear classification by finding an approximation of the archetypes in the input space, which maintain the ability to classify the data with a moderate increase of the error rate.

Keywords: Archetypes, Support Vectors, Compression

1. Introduction

One of the drawbacks of the SVM [Cortes and Vapnik, 1995] is that the number of Support Vectors (SVs) can be a large fraction of the training set. This is inconvenient both from a cognitive point of view, because a large number of archetypes is difficult to interpret, and for computational reasons, because the number of operations needed by the SVM for performing the feed-forward phase grows linearly with the number of SVs. Some proposals have recently appeared in the literature, which try to lower the number of SVs ([[Downs et al., 2001; Schölkopf et al., 1998]]).

This work proposes a new method that identifies only *one* archetype for each class resulting, in general, in a very large information compression. Despite this achievement, no information loss is suffered when a linear discriminating

B. Apolloni et al. (eds.), Biological and Artificial Intelligence Environments, 99–105

function is adopted, while some loss exists in the nonlinear case, albeit it can be lowered by increasing the number of archetypes.

In the following section, we briefly revise the SVM and propose a method to extract the archetypes, which exemplify the two classes, in the linear case. In the same section we show how our method can be extended to the nonlinear case, that is when the SVM makes use of kernels for mapping the data from the input to the feature space, and describe a method for (approximately) mapping the archetypes back in the input space. In the section 3 we describe some experimental results on both linear and nonlinear classification cases. Some final considerations end the work.

2. Archetypes Extraction

Let us consider a two–class labelled data-set $\{(\boldsymbol{x}_i, y_i), i = 1 \dots n\}$, where $\boldsymbol{x}_i \in \Re^m$ and $y_i = \pm 1$.

The hyperplane constructed by the SVM is expressed in terms of a linear combination of the patterns of the training set [Cortes and Vapnik, 1995]:

$$f(\boldsymbol{x}) = \text{sign}\left(\boldsymbol{w} \cdot \boldsymbol{x} + b\right) = \text{sign}\left(\sum_{i=1}^{n} \alpha_i y_i \boldsymbol{x}_i \cdot \boldsymbol{x} + b\right) \tag{1}$$

where the coefficients are obtained by solving a constrained quadratic programming problem [Cortes and Vapnik, 1995].

We define the archetypes $\boldsymbol{a}^+$ and $\boldsymbol{a}^-$ (one for each class) as the points lying on the axis normal to the hyperplane and as close as possible to the mass centers of the two classes $(\boldsymbol{c}^+, \boldsymbol{c}^-)$, as depicted in Fig. 1. Note that the archetypes plus their distance from the hyperplane embed the entire information of the SVM after learning and, at the same time, provide some average information about the position of the patterns in the input space.

The archetypes can be found by minimizing

$$\min_{a_l^+, a_l^-} \frac{1}{m} \sum_{l=1}^{m} \left[\left(a_l^+ - c_l^+\right)^2 + \left(a_l^- - c_l^-\right)^2\right] \tag{2}$$

subject to

$$\boldsymbol{w} = \mu\left(\boldsymbol{a}^+ - \boldsymbol{a}^-\right) \tag{3}$$

where μ is a positive value. Eq. (2) minimizes the squared distance of the two archetypes from the two centers of gravity, while the constraint forces them to lie on a straight line perpendicular to the separating hyperplane.

Due to the lack of space we directly state the final form for the two archetypes:

$$\boldsymbol{a}^{\pm} = \frac{1}{2} \sum_{i=1}^{n} \gamma_i^{\pm} \boldsymbol{x}_i \tag{4}$$

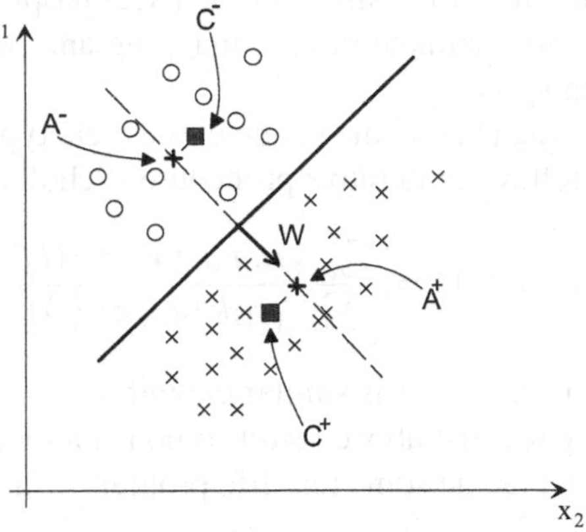

Figure 1. The archetypes ($\boldsymbol{a}^+$, $\boldsymbol{a}^-$) with respect to the optimal separating hyperplane (solid line) and the centers of gravity of the two classes ($\boldsymbol{c}^+$, $\boldsymbol{c}^-$).

where $\gamma_i^\pm$ is defined as

$$\gamma_i^\pm = \frac{n + y_i\,(n^- - n^+)}{2n^+n^-} \pm \chi\frac{\alpha_i y_i}{\|\boldsymbol{w}\|^2} \tag{5}$$

and χ equals:

$$\chi = \frac{1}{n^+}\sum_{\substack{i,j=1\\ y_i=+1}}^{n} y_j\alpha_j\boldsymbol{x}_i\cdot\boldsymbol{x}_j - \frac{1}{n^-}\sum_{\substack{i,j=1\\ y_i=-1}}^{n} y_j\alpha_j\boldsymbol{x}_i\cdot\boldsymbol{x}_j \tag{6}$$

If we let d be, for example, the distance of $\boldsymbol{a}^-$ from the separating hyperplane, then:

$$d = \frac{|\boldsymbol{w}\cdot\boldsymbol{a}^- + b|}{\|\boldsymbol{w}\|} \tag{7}$$

and we can rewrite eq.(1) as:

$$f(\boldsymbol{x}) = \operatorname{sign}\left((\boldsymbol{a}^+ - \boldsymbol{a}^-)\cdot\boldsymbol{x} - (\boldsymbol{a}^+ - \boldsymbol{a}^-)\cdot\boldsymbol{a}^- - d\|\boldsymbol{a}^+ - \boldsymbol{a}^-\|\right) \tag{8}$$

The results obtained above can be extended to the feature space by considering the mapping $\boldsymbol{x}\to\boldsymbol{\Phi}(\boldsymbol{x})$.

However, the archetypes lie in the feature space and, in general, will not have a corresponding representation in the input space. This is a severe drawback for at least two reasons: (1) the nonlinear mapping $\boldsymbol{\Phi}(\cdot)$ is usually unknown and (2) the lack of a corresponding archetype in the input space vanishes the effort of extracting information from a single representative sample of the entire class.

We suggest to use a result by Smola et al. [Schölkopf et al., 1998], which allows to perform an approximate inverse mapping and build an image of the archetype in the input space.

In the case of a gaussian kernel the image of the archetypes in the input space can be found by the following iterative procedure [Schölkopf et al., 1998]:

$$\boldsymbol{z}^{\pm}(t+1) = \frac{\sum_{i=1}^{n} \gamma_i \boldsymbol{x}_i k\left(\boldsymbol{x}_i, \boldsymbol{z}^{\pm}(t)\right)}{\sum_{i=1}^{n} \gamma_i k\left(\boldsymbol{x}_i, \boldsymbol{z}^{\pm}(t)\right)} \tag{9}$$

which can be stopped when z^{t+1} is similar enough to z^t.

We extend in this paper the above result to non stationary kernels [Genton, 2001], which can better tackle some real-life problems, such as the polynomial one:

$$k\left(\boldsymbol{x}, \boldsymbol{z}\right) = \left(\boldsymbol{x} \cdot \boldsymbol{z} + 1\right)^r \tag{10}$$

for which the following iterative procedure can be derived:

$$\boldsymbol{z}^{\pm}(t+1) = \frac{\sum_{i=1}^{n} \gamma_i \boldsymbol{x}_i \left(\boldsymbol{x}_i \cdot \boldsymbol{z}^{\pm}(t) + 1\right)^{r-1}}{\sum_{i=1}^{n} \gamma_i \left(\boldsymbol{x}_i \cdot \boldsymbol{z}^{\pm}(t) + 1\right)^{r}} \left(\boldsymbol{z}^{\pm}(t) \cdot \boldsymbol{z}^{\pm}(t) + 1\right) \tag{11}$$

3. Experimental results

We selected two data-sets for our experiments, which allows us to show some of the interesting characteristics of archetypes. The first data-set (FACE) has been used for gender recognition [O'Toole, 1988] and consists of photos of male and female faces, in gray levels.

This data-set contains a total of 90 images of male (44) and female (46) faces. Each photo is in grayscale (256 levels) and is composed of 60×60 pixels. Note that each image shows only the face of the subject: no extra information (e.g. hair, neck, ears) is present and none of the subjects shows characteristic signs other than the natural ones.

We performed an experiment with the FACE data-set, to check if the archetypes retain the same kind of information as the SVs do. In fact, each SV, being also a training pattern, is an actual face, while the centers of gravity of each class are simply the average of all male or female faces. The dimensionality of the input space is very high, so we do not need to switch to the feature space to find a linear separation.

The found archetypes appear as faces, as reported in Fig. 2. This result is valuable both because it shows that the input space has some structure and because a point t belonging to the segment connecting the archetypes:

$$t(\lambda) = (1 - \lambda) \cdot a^{+} + \lambda \cdot a^{-} \quad (12)$$

can be reviewed as a step of the morph, here above parameterized by λ, from the archetypal male to the archetypal female. This can be interesting from a cognitive point of view as the point $t(\lambda)$ bears a mix of the interesting features of the two archetypes [Johnstone et al., 2001].

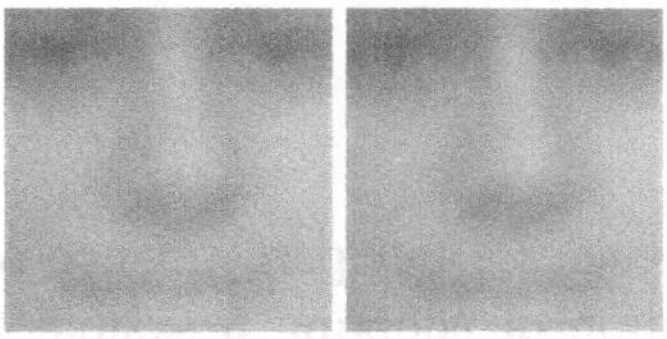

Figure 2. Female (left) and male (right) archetypes.

The second one (IRIS) is the well-known Fisher's Iris data-set [Duda and Hart, 1973].

The full IRIS data-set consists of a 150 patterns of 5 measurements made on Iris flowers belonging to 3 different classes: Setosa, Versicolor and Virginica. We select two classes (Setosa and Virginica) and two features in order to be able to plot the results.

An interesting feature of the approximate archetypes is that their position reveal, in some way, the complexity of the separator: to show this relation, we focus on the non–linearly separable classes Versicolor and Virginica. Let us consider a Gaussian kernel with several values of σ^2. It is well-known that as σ^2 decreases, the complexity (i.e. the Vapnik-Chervonenkis (VC) dimension) of the SVM classifier goes toward infinity. It is expected, therefore, that, for large values of σ^2, the separator behaves almost like the linear one, while it differs greatly from it when small values are selected. Fig.(3) shows the archetypes, found by the procedure described in Section 2, for different values of the σ^2 parameter. As the complexity of the separator increases, the approximate archetypes approach the one derived by the linear separator.

The table Tab.1 is displayed for the sake of comparison between standard SVM classification and archetypes classification. Tab.1 shows the different requirements in number of operations needed to accomplish the classification task on new data-points in the SVM case or selecting the class to which the closest archetype belongs. The notable difference is due to the different scalings between the methods: $O(n_{SV} \cdot n_i)$ for SVM and $O(n_i)$ for the other case.

Also, in view of an hardware implementation, the memory space in Kilobytes required by the two algorithms is shown (we suppose to store double precision values). The storage space is also subject to a scaling similar to the above illustrated. The above results confirm the idea that when additional

Table 1. Comparison of the estimated number of operations for the classification task and of the estimated required storage space in Kilobytes for the considered data-sets.

	Required Operations		**Req. Storage Space in KB**	
Datasets	SVM	Archetypes	SVM	Archetypes
FACE60	367251	14400	1434.80	56.30
IRIS	60	8	0.30	0.03

constraints are present, besides a fair performance requirement, one should carefully consider the option of adopting a system which relies on a compressed SV information against a partial loss in the generalization capability.

4. Conclusions

In this work, a method to extract two archetypes from a two–class data-set and a linear separation is presented, allowing a considerable information compression with respect both to the original data-set and to a classification through support vectors. The method can be extended to non–linear kernel–based discriminating functions by approximating the true archetypes in the feature space with two points in the input space. The experimental results show the consistency of the method and the possible use of the obtained archetypes for a very fast (albeit less accurate) nearest–neighbor classification.

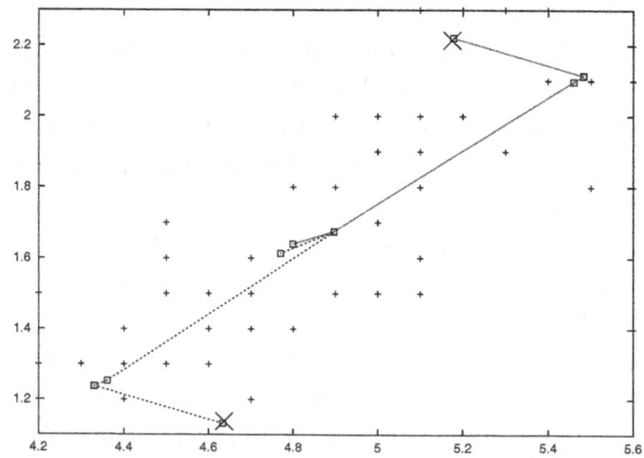

Figure 3. Iris Virginica VS Versicolor. The paths of the approximate archetypes (boxes) for increasing σ^2 are shown. Large crosses indicates the archetypes in the linear case.

References

Cortes, C., Vapnik, V.N. *Support Vector Networks*, Machine Learning Vol. 20, pp. 1–25, 1995.

Downs, T., Gates, K.E., Masters, A. *Exact simplification of support vector solutions* Journal of Machine Learning Research, Vol. 2, pp. 293–297, December 2001.

Duda, R.O., Hart, P.E. *Pattern Classification and Scene Analysis* John Wiley & Sons, see page 218, 1973.

Genton, M.G. *Classes of Kernels for Machine Learning: A Statistics Perspective*, Journal of Machine Learning Research, Vol. 2, pp. 299–312, 2001.

Johnstone, V.S., Hagel, R., Franklin, M., Fink, B., Grammer, K. *Male facial attractiveness evidence for hormone-mediated adaptive design.* Evolution and Human Behavior, Vol.22 pp. 251–267, 2001.

O'Toole, A.J., Millward, R.B. and Anderson, J.A., *A physical system approach to recognition memory for spatially transformed faces* Neural Networks, Vol. 1, pp. 179–199, 1988.

Schölkopf, B., Burges, C.J.C., Smola, A.J. *Advances in kernel methods: support vector learning* MIT Press, 1998.

Schölkopf, B., Knirsch, P., Smola, A. and Burges, C. *Fast approximation of support vector kernel expansions, and an interpretation of clustering as approximation in feature spaces* In P. Levi, M. Schanz, R.-J. Ahlers, and F. May, editors, Mustererkennung 1998 — 20. DAGM-Symposium, Informatik aktuell, pp. 124–132, Berlin, Springer, 1998.

GENETIC DESIGN OF LINEAR BLOCK ERROR-CORRECTING CODES

Alan Barbieri, Stefano Cagnoni, and Giulio Colavolpe
Università di Parma
Dipartimento di Ingegneria dell'Informazione
Parco Area delle Scienze 181/A
43100 Parma - ITALY
barbieri@tlc.unipr.it, cagnoni@ce.unipr.it, giulio@unipr.it

Abstract

In this paper we describe a new method, based on a genetic algorithm, for generating good (in terms of minimum distance) linear block error-correcting codes. We offer a detailed description of the algorithm, with particular regard to the genetic operators (selection, mutation and crossover) which have been specifically adapted to the problem. Preliminary experimental results indicate that the method can be very effective, especially in terms of fast production of good sub-optimal codes.

Keywords: Genetic algorithms, error-correcting codes, linear block codes, minimum distance, distance spectrum.

1. Introduction

In the technical literature, the problem of finding good error-correcting codes has been tackled by many authors using different algorithms and techniques. As an example, a linear programming-based approach has been recently used in [Ferrari and Chugg, 2003] to optimize the distance spectrum of linear block codes whereas in [Farkaš and Brühl, 1994; Farkaš and Herrera-Garcia, 2001] a search algorithm based on the McCluskey theorem [McCluskey, 1959] has been presented.

The search space for the problem of finding good codes is too large for many of the standard search algorithms. In such cases, genetic algorithms can be very effective in finding good solutions in a relatively short time.

A genetic approach to code generation was followed in [Dontas and Jong, 1990]. In this case, however, the target was to find the entire codebook. That

B. Apolloni et al. (eds.), Biological and Artificial Intelligence Environments, 107–116

requirement makes such an approach useful, in practice, only for codes whose parameters are no larger than few units.

Genetic algorithms have previously been used also for other purposes related to coding theory: for instance, as in [Maini et al., 1994; Cardoso and Arantes, 1999], they have been applied to soft-decoding problems.

To partially limit problem complexity, in the approach described in this paper, a genetic algorithm is used to search a space restricted to the sub-class of linear codes, by generating the columns of their generator matrix. The algorithm maximizes a fitness function that takes into account not only the minimum distance of the code, which is the main quality factor for a linear code, but also the distance spectrum distribution. Doing so, once a certain distance is reached, for which several codes can be found, the algorithm goes on searching according to that secondary quality factor.

In [Brouwer and Verhoeff, 1993] a table of minimum-distance bounds for binary linear codes has been presented, while in [Hill and Traynor, 1990] the authors demonstrate that some codes do not exist at all, thus obtaining some new minimum-distance bounds. These bounds may be used as references in evaluating the effectiveness of new search algorithms.

2. Theory of linear block codes

In this section, we introduce some definitions and theoretical results regarding error-correcting codes, with particular attention to linear block codes.

Suppose one wants to transmit a sequence of k binary symbols (word), collected for convenience in a row vector $\mathbf{u}$ of k elements, over a channel affected by additive white Gaussian noise. At the receiver end, due to the channel noise, a corrupted word will be detected. We will denote this corrupted sequence of bits by $\mathbf{u} + \mathbf{e}$, where the sum is modulo 2 and $\mathbf{e}$ represents a sequence of bits whose Hamming weight (i.e., the number of its non-zero elements) is the number of corrupted bits.

A binary error-correcting code can be used to reduce the probability of word errors. The coding operation consists of the following transformation:

$$\mathbf{c} = \Gamma(\mathbf{u}) \tag{1}$$

where $\mathbf{c}$ is the codeword, represented by an n-bit row vector, with $n > k$, that is transmitted on the channel in place of $\mathbf{u}$. This transformation defines a codebook $\mathcal{C}$ of 2^k codewords, taken from a set of 2^n possible words. It is worth noting that there is a tradeoff between the correction capability of a code and the redundancy introduced due to the insertion of new bits in the transmitted word. An important parameter which takes into account this tradeoff is the *rate* of the code, defined as

$$R = \frac{k}{n}, \; 0 < R < 1 \tag{2}$$

which is stricly related to code efficiency—the higher the value of R (which implies low redundancy), the lower the correction code capability.

An important parameter which determines the asymptotic performance of a block code for low error probabilities is the code *minimum distance*. It is defined as the Hamming distance between the two nearest codewords, i.e.,

$$d_{min} = \min\{d(\mathbf{c}_i, \mathbf{c}_j) | \mathbf{c}_i \neq \mathbf{c}_j \in \mathcal{C}\} \tag{3}$$

where $d(\mathbf{c}_i, \mathbf{c}_j)$ represents the Hamming distance between codewords $\mathbf{c}_i$ and $\mathbf{c}_j$ and is defined as the number of elements in which these two codeword differ. An upper bound on the word error probability, the so-called *union bound*, may be obtained from knowledge of the *distance spectrum* of the code. For each $l \in \{0, 1, \ldots n\}$, let us define a_l as the average number of codewords at distance l from a given codeword, i.e.,

$$a_l = \frac{1}{2^k} \left| \{(i,j) | d(\mathbf{c}_i, \mathbf{c}_j) = l\} \right| \tag{4}$$

where $|\cdot|$ represents the cardinality of the corresponding set. We define $\mathbf{a} = (a_0, a_1, \ldots, a_n)$ as the distance spectrum of the code [Proakis, 2001], with $a_0 + a_1 + \ldots + a_n = 2^k$. With this definition, the minimum distance is the first $k > 0$ such that $a_k > 0$. It is worth noting that, for fixed values of k and n, codes with greater d_{min} are asymptotically better. However, the word error probability is related to the entire spectrum, and not only to the minimum distance. Furthermore, we define the weight spectrum for the code as

$$w_l = \left| \{i | w(\mathbf{c}_i) = l\} \right| \tag{5}$$

where $w(\cdot)$ stands for the Hamming weight.

Finally, a code is said to be *systematic* if, for every possible $\mathbf{u}$, the corresponding codeword is $\mathbf{c} = [\mathbf{u}|\mathbf{p}]$, where $\mathbf{p}$ is a $(n-k)$-bit row vector containing the so-called parity bits (the redundancy bits).

A code is said to be linear if both the following conditions hold

$$\begin{aligned} &\mathbf{0} \in \mathcal{C} \\ &\forall \mathbf{c}_1, \mathbf{c}_2 \in \mathcal{C}, \mathbf{c}_1 + \mathbf{c}_2 \in \mathcal{C}\,. \end{aligned} \tag{6}$$

In this case, Γ is a linear transformation and eq. (1) becomes $\mathbf{c} = \mathbf{u}\mathbf{G}$, where $\mathbf{G}$ is a $k \times n$ binary matrix, called *generator matrix*. It is easy to show that, for given values of k and n, there are 2^{kn} possible codes, which is a huge space for a search algorithm. An important result of coding theory is that a linear block code maintains the same distance spectrum (and hence the same performance), if we apply linear operators to the generator matrix. Therefore, by applying suitable transformations, we can obtain an equivalent systematic code from a non-systematic one. For this reason, we can reduce the complexity of our search by considering only systematic codes, whose generator matrices $\mathbf{G}$ can be written as

$$\mathbf{G} = [\mathbf{I}_k | \mathbf{P}^t] \tag{7}$$

where $\mathbf{I}_k$ is the identity matrix of size k, $\mathbf{P}$ (of dimension $(n-k) \times k$) is called *parity matrix*, and $(\cdot)^t$ denotes matrix transposition. In this case, defining the code *parity check matrix* as

$$\mathbf{H} = [\mathbf{P} | \mathbf{I}_{n-k}] \tag{8}$$

we find that

$$\mathbf{c} \in \mathcal{C} \Leftrightarrow \mathbf{c}\mathbf{H}^t = \mathbf{0}\,. \tag{9}$$

Therefore the parity check matrix helps in verifying if a given word is a valid codeword.

It is straightforward to verify that, for a linear code, the distance spectrum and the Hamming weight spectrum correspond, that is,

$$\begin{aligned} a_l &= \frac{1}{2^k} \left|\{(i,j) | d(\mathbf{c}_i, \mathbf{c}_j) = l\}\right| \\ &= \left|\{i | w(\mathbf{c}_i) = d(\mathbf{c}_i, \mathbf{0}) = l\}\right| . \end{aligned} \tag{10}$$

Therefore, if a code has a given d_{min}, that implies that there exists at least a codeword with Hamming weight d_{min} and, equivalently, that there is a set of d_{min} columns of matrix $\mathbf{H}$ which sum to the all-zero column.

In [McCluskey, 1959] a simple theorem, that relates the minimum distance and the parity check matrix, is presented.

McCluskey Theorem: P is a parity check matrix for a code of minimum distance d_{min} if and only if

1 the weight of each column of P is greater than or equal to $d_{min} - 1$;

2 the weight of the sum (modulo 2) of k columns is greater than or equal to $d_{min} - k$.

A proof of this theorem can be found in [McCluskey, 1959]. As we will see in the next sections, the genetic algorithm under consideration is essentially based on the result provided by this theorem.

3. Genetic algorithm

In this section we present a general overview of the proposed genetic algorithm. The algorithm is aimed at finding good codes, i.e., codes with given k and n, and maximum d_{min}. When new maximum-distance codes are found, their parity matrix and distance spectrums are saved. In our implementation, we co-evolve more than one fixed-size population at one time.

Each individual is encoded as the $(n-k) \times k$ bits of the parity matrix $\mathbf{P}$.

We used a classical genetic algorithm, with some adaptations to the problem under consideration, which will be discussed in details later. Each iteration of the algorithm for a single population of size M consists of the following steps:

1 *selection*;

2 *column sorting*: This phase is peculiar to the problem under consideration and is propaedeutic to crossover. The columns of every individual are sorted from best to worst, according to a criterion which will be specified in the following;

3 *crossover*: for every couple of consecutive individuals (within the random population ordering induced by selection), crossover is performed with fixed probability;

4 *mutation*: a bit is flipped with fixed probability;

5 *check for population degeneration*: the genetic diversity of the population is checked to verify whether the number of genes having equal values in the great majority of individuals has reached a fixed critical threshold.

Population is initialized with randomly generated individuals.

It may be advantageous to co-evolve more than one population at the same time, to increase diversity. Every population has different parameters and evolves independently of the others for most of the time. When a population degenerates, it is crossed over with another one by swapping some of its individuals, randomly chosen, with individuals, randomly chosen, belonging to the latter. As a further method to avoid population degeneration, before population crossover, a fixed portion of the individuals, randomly selected, are replaced with randomly generated ones.

Two populations may be crossed over, with given probability (randomly-generated before the first iteration) even if they have not degenerated.

The fitness function and the genetic operators are more precisely defined as follows.

Fitness : let $\mathcal{C}$ be an individual with distance spectrum $\mathbf{a} = (a_0, a_1, \ldots, a_n)$ and minimum distance d_{min}; fitness is defined as:

$$f(\mathcal{C}) = d_{min} + 1 - \sum_{i=d_{min}}^{n} a_i 2^{-k(i-d_{min}+1)} . \tag{11}$$

The integer part of the fitness value is the minimum distance, while the fractional part is related with the distance spectrum. Exact evaluation of d_{min} and of the distance spectrum is a computationally demanding problem: in [Dumer et al., 2003] authors prove that it is impossible to find algorithms that approximate d_{min} in polynomial time. For this reason, fitness evaluation is the most time-consuming task of our genetic algorithm.

Selection : for each population, we use a classical tournament-based elitistic scheme, whose number of participants is randomly generated (within a user-defined interval) when the population is initialized.

Crossover : during initialization, a crossover rate R is also randomly generated (within a user-defined interval) for each population. Crossover is always made between consecutive individuals up to the $(R \cdot M)^{th}$ individual in the population. The order in which individuals are sorted is the order in which tournaments, for which each individual is a winner, have been performed on randomly selected individuals. Therefore, using a deterministic scheme on the ordered population to perform crossover has no biasing effect on the search.

Crossover is performed by picking a random integer C between 1 and the number of columns N_c in an individual, and then swap the columns from $C+1$ to N_c of the two individuals undergoing crossover.

Before crossover is performed, however, the columns making up an individual are sorted from best to worst. The "quality" of a column is related to the number of groups of linearly-dependent columns which include it: the better the column, the lower the number of groups of linearly-dependent columns in which it appears. This sorting operation is aimed at increasing the probability that the new individuals generated by crossover have a high fitness. As convergence occurs, the best individuals tend to be similar to one another, which means that it is quite likely that the best columns be the same in many individuals.

With no ordering, the best columns would be in random positions within the generator matrices and could become dominant characters of the individuals.

That means that it would be very likely to find them repeated more than once within the same individual, with obvious disrupting effects on column quality (the worst column one can think of is one which appears twice or even more frequently in the same matrix, according to the above-reported quality criterion). On the contrary, a crossover between two ordered individuals makes it unlikely to produce matrices having sets of identical columns. The fact that, doing so, the swapped columns are always bad-quality columns is less relevant, since the quality criterion is local to a single matrix, and a column which is bad for a matrix may be good for another one, while having two identical columns in the same matrix always affects fitness negatively.

Mutation : for every bit of every code, a weighted coin toss decides whether that bit must be flipped; the mutation parameter is randomly generated before the first iteration with values belonging to a given interval. This parameter is adaptive and is adjusted according to the following rule: if, at a certain iteration, the best fitness of the population does not change, mutation rate increases as $p_{new} = p_{old}^{\beta}$, where $\beta < 1$ is a parameter that is randomly generated at initialization; otherwise, if the best fitness has increased, $p_{new} = p_0$. This behaviour should prevent convergence on local maxima and, in addition to tournament selection, premature convergence from occurring.

4. Results

In this section, we show results of several runs of the genetic algorithm. We have used two different kinds of code: (34,15,9) and (21,11,6), where the notation (n, k, d_{min}) indicates a $n \times k$ code with upper bound on the minimum distance d_{min} (see [Brouwer and Verhoeff, 1993]).

We cannot repeat out experiments with other existing algorithms, because the algorithm presented in [Farkaš and Brühl, 1994] was not completely detailed, while the genetic one in [Dontas and Jong, 1990] uses a different approach to generate codes, i.e., it generates the entire codebook instead of the generator matrix, thus it was not possible (for computational reasons) to apply it to the considered test cases. However, in the case of the $(34, 15, 9)$ code, the algorithm in [Farkaš and Brühl, 1994] (that is based on classical techniques) had been already tested by its authors and some results are reported in [Farkaš and Herrera-Garcia, 2001].

n	a	b	best fitness	codes found
1	35	730	8.999603	1
2	28	463	8.999573	1
3	5	1309	8.999359	1
4	28	403	8.999664	2
5	34	2039	8.999481	1
6	27	295	8.999573	1
7	42	304	8.999451	2
8	22	1716	8.999237	1
9	25	250	8.999359	2
10	19	143	8.999390	1

n	a	b	best fitness	codes found
1	39	104	6.936035	1
2	62	62	6.935547	1
3	34	34	6.933594	1
4	N.A.	55	5.995583	1
5	172	172	6.935059	1

Table 1. Convergence and best code found in each run for the (34,15) and the (21,11) code: n is the experiment, a the iteration when the first code with d_{min}=8 and 6 respectively has been found and b the iteration when the best-fitness code has been found. The last column reports the number of codes with best fitness that have been found in each run.

Experiments with (34,15,9) codes

We have performed ten experiments, each with different random initialization and with the following parameters: 4 populations composed by 100 individuals. Each run has been stopped after 2500 iterations. The first part of Table 1 presents some results regarding convergence, for all ten experiments. The best fitness was 8.999664 and was reached in the fourth experiment, on the 403rd iteration. Two different codes corresponding to this fitness have been found, but we cannot report here their parity matrices due to space limitations. It is worth noting that the best codes found have $d_{min} = 8$, while the upper bound of the (34,15) code is $d_{min} = 9$ [1]. However, it should be also noticed that only very few codes with $d_{min} = 9$ have been reported in literature [Farkaš and Herrera-Garcia, 2001], and that a population of 100, as we used in our preliminary tests for time restrictions, is probably by far too small to explore such a huge space really effectively.

Experiments with (21,11,6) codes

In this case, we ran a total of 5 experiments, with 3 populations of 200 individuals and a maximum of 1000 iterations. The second part of Table 1 reports the iteration at which each run reached convergence (i.e., the best fitness). As can be noticed, in this case the algorithm has been able to reach the theoretical bound on the minimum distance ($d_{min} = 6$) for the considered code in all experiments but one.

5. Discussion

The search space to be explored in generating linear error-correcting block codes is extremely challenging, first of all for its size, but also for the disrupting effects that a single bit flip may have on code quality. In defining the fitness, by considering not only the code minimum distance by itself, but also the distance spectrum, we managed to shape the fitness landscape in order to make it smoother and richer of information that could point to good solutions.

Although very preliminary, results reported in the previous section show that genetic algorithms may be an interesting way to find good linear block error-correcting codes.

In particular, this approach is able to produce good sub-optimal codes in very few iterations. It is worth noticing how, in the most complex case, the first appearance of a code having the minimum distance finally reached by the algorithm has always occurred within the first 42 iterations.

As regards computation efficiency, about 3 hours of computation time are required to run 1000 iterations of the algorithm applied to the (34,15) code, with four populations of size 100, on a 2.6 GHz-Pentium class PC.

Future developments of our research will be aimed, in first place, at exploring how a large increase in population size can improve results and at improving effectiveness of the search strategy by further adapting the genetic operators to the challenges posed by the problem under consideration.

Notes

1. It is still a matter of discussion whether it could be possible to find a solution with $d_{min} = 10$. Up to now, no one could find it, nor could anybody demonstrate that it cannot exist.

References

Brouwer, A. E. and Verhoeff, T. (1993). An updated table of minimum-distance bounds for binary linear codes. *IEEE Transactions on Information Theory*, 39(2).

Cardoso, F. A. C. M. and Arantes, D. S. (1999). Genetic decoding of linear block codes. *Proceedings of the 1999 Congress on Evolutionary Computation*, 3.

Dontas, K. and Jong, K. De (1990). Discovery of maximal distance codes using genetic algorithms. In *Proceedings of the 2nd International IEEE Conference on tools for Artificial Intelligence*, pages 805–811.

Dumer, I., Micciancio, D., and Sudan, M. (2003). Hardness of approximating the minimum distance of a linear code. *IEEE Transactions on Information Theory*, 49(1):22–37.

Farkaš, P. and Brühl, K. (1994). Three best binary linear block codes of minimum distance fifteen. *IEEE Trans. Inform. Theory*, 40:949–951.

Farkaš, P. and Herrera-Garcia, S. (2001). Three new optimal [34,15,9] codes. *ElectronicsLetters.com (web journal).*

Ferrari, G. and Chugg, K. M. (2003). Linear programming-based optimization of the distance spectrum of linear block codes. *IEEE Transactions on Information Theory*, 49(7).

Hill, R. and Traynor, K. L. (1990). The nonexistence of certain binary linear codes. *IEEE Trans. Inform. Theory*, 36:917–922.

Maini, H., Mehrotra, K., Mohan, C., and Ranka, S. (1994). Soft decision decoding of linear block codes using genetic algorithms. *Proceedings of the IEEE International 1994 Symposium on Information Theory.*

McCluskey, E. J. (1959). Error-correcting codes–a linear programming approach. *Bell System Tech. J.*, 38:1485–1512.

Proakis, J. G. (2001). *Digital Communications*. McGraw-Hill, New York, 4th edition.

NEURAL HARDWARE BASED ON KERNEL METHODS FOR INDUSTRIAL AND SCIENTIFIC APPLICATIONS

Andrea Boni
DIT, University of Trento
Via Sommarive, 14, 38050 Trento Italy
andrea.boni@unitn.it

Ignazio Lazzizzera
Dept. of Physics, University of Trento, Via Sommarive 14, 38050, Trento, Italy
ignazio.lazzizzera@unitn.it

Alessandro Zorat
DIT, University of Trento
Via Sommarive, 14, 38050 Trento Italy
alessandro.zorat@unitn.it

Abstract This paper describes the design of a digital architecture suitable for the classification of large quantities of measurement data by means of a method based on the Support Vector Machines (SVMs). The proposed approach can be applied for solving general inverse modeling problems and for processing complex measurement data requiring real-time processing, possibly in a distributed mode over a number of physically small and geographically separated 'computational nodes'. A problem of nonlinear channel equalization and a classification task from high energy physics are presented as discussed as two case studies for which the ability of achieving real-time processing is of paramount importance. The performance of such architectures is then analyzed in terms of its speed of execution, occupancy of the hardware modules available in a Virtex II FPGA chip, and classification error.

Keywords: Support Vector Machines, High Energy Physics, Digital Architectures, FPGA

Introduction

Several data analysis problems require the processing of large amounts of data in streaming in from a number of data acquisition devices. As it is often

B. Apolloni et al. (eds.), Biological and Artificial Intelligence Environments, 117–123

the case in this context, the computation has to be performed at a rate that is at least as fast as the incoming data rate, thus resulting in a real-time constraint that can pose a challenge even for the powerful general-purpose computers available today. In order to satisfy the real-time constraint, a common solution is that of employing hardware-based devices that can handle the incoming stream of data by performing the required operations directly in hardware, possibly in a multistage arrangement. A classic approach to data analysis is to determine an appropriate algorithm that will perform the desired analysis and code it in a suitable language. However, in many applications, for example data classification, the algorithm that is required to process the incoming data is not known, even though one has some examples of the desired output. In such cases, an approach that has gained the attention of the scientific community in recent years is that of letting the machine use these known examples to learn a suitable algorithm that can be used to process the data stream. This technique has been used toward the solution of problems from a wide range of application area, including fault recognition, digital signal processing, pattern recognition, and many others. In its generality, the technique entails the devising of an algorithm that learns a typically non-linear unknown relationship on the basis of a set of input/output measurements Z. A well known example of this technique are the Artificial Neural Networks (ANNs) which have been applied with various degrees of success. The critics of the ANN-based algorithms point out that the learning process can get stuck in a local minimum during its iterative search for an optimal configuration. While many solutions have been proposed and implemented to overcame this problem, in principle there is no guarantee that the ANN-based algorithm converges toward an optimal solution and hence alternative approaches have been proposed. Recently, the Kernel-Based Methods (KBMs) [B.Schölkopf, et al., 2002] has been proposed as a new paradigm of learning by examples. KBMs are based on the Statistical Learning Theory (SLT), formulated by Vapnik and Chervonenkis in the '70s [Vapnik, 1998]. The SLT basis provides a solid theoretical background that guarantees some desirable properties of their underlying algorithms. An example of KBMs are the well known Support Vector Machines (SVMs) for which the search for an optimal non-linear relations between inputs and outputs is transformed in the solution of a constrained quadratic optimization problem, which Ű by its own nature Ű can have exactly one solution. Hence, the process cannot get stuck in local minima and the solution found is guaranteed to be the one corresponding to the optimal configuration. The outcome of the SVM-based algorithm is a vector of parameters that are used to estimate the class of new inputs during the so called forward phase. In many applications, the classification of new input data during the forward phase has to be completed very quickly to keep up with the stream of data coming in. Also, in several contexts, the input data are collected by a number of sensors and transducers that must satisfy hard constraints for example regarding physical dimension, power consumption, cost, or geographical distribution. Examples include the distributed sensor networks used to monitor some environment, or the data produced by the myriad of sensors in a high-energy physics experiment. In the context of applications outlined above, a standard general purpose computer might be hard pressed to meet the various requirements since it might not yield the required computational performance to operate in real time, or it cannot satisfy the low power and cost. An alternative approach can be that of resorting to a hardware implementation of the corresponding KBM. The realization of fast KBMs through a hardware implementation has become an important area of research: after the first preliminary studies several analog and digital implementations of KBMs for both learning and forward phases have been proposed [Anguita, et al., 2003], [Genov, et al., 2003]. This paper presents the digital implementation on of an SVM on a Field Programmable Gate Array (FPGA) hardware system to achieve real-time execution during the forward phase. By using an FPGA implementation, fast prototyping could be achieved and the resulting circuits could be functionally tested through simulation and their speed performance evaluated very quickly. Once these preliminary tests were carried out satisfactorily, the FPGA hardware was configured so that it realized the corresponding circuits and the testing could be performed directly on the hardware implementation. (A third phase could be carried out later on to transform the resulting FPGA circuits in a silicon chip, which could be advisable when for a full-fledged production run.) As a case study, two different applications were analyzed and their performance was derived: a telecommunication problem, such as a channel equalization, characterized by few parameters, and a scientific application, such as a tagging problem of High Energy Physics (HEP) experiments, where a big amount of measures must be processed in real time. Section II briefly describes the problem formulation, while section III describes the compared architectures and their performance. The two case studies are introduced and analyzed in the section IV, followed by some conclusions.

1. Problem Formulation

A general inverse modeling problem is defined as follows: a discrete signal $u(n)$ acting as the input of a non linear discrete system, having unknown dynamics, must be estimated on the basis of the signal $x(n)$ observed at the output of the system itself. As the unknown system can introduce a correlation on the signals, several output samples are observed in order to provide an input signal estimate $\hat{u}\,(n-D)$, where D represents the intrinsic delay of the estimator. In particular, such an estimate is given on the basis of the r-dimensional feature vector: $\underline{x}_n^{(r)} = [x\,(n)\,, x\,(n-1)\,, \ldots, x\,(n-r+1)]^T$. In order to build such an estimator KBMs use a set Z of input/output samples called the training set:

$Z = \left\{\underline{x}_i^{(r)}, u_i\right\}_{i=1}^{N}$. This is also the case of a general measurement system, where a set of measures each one composed by an r-attributes vector must be classified according to a given rule. Thus, our problem can be defined in the following way: given a set of measures Z obtained by an unknown measurement system, provide its 'best' relationship, from a generalization point of view. The SLT establishes the conditions under which such a relationship is the best [Vapnik, 1998]. SVMs are a special kind of KBMs, and their final function is:

$$\hat{u}(n-D) = \sum_{i \in SV} \alpha_i u_i K\left(\underline{x}_i^{(r)}, x_n^{(r)}\right) + b \qquad (1)$$

where $SV = \{i : \alpha_i \neq 0, i = 1, \ldots, N\}$ is the indexes set of the Support Vectors (SVs), that is the only input measures important for the classification. The parameters α_i and b are found after the resolution of a constrained quadratic optimization problem [B.Schölkopf, et al., 2002], whilst $K()$ is a kernel function, for example a Gaussian kernel [B.Schölkopf, et al., 2002].

2. System Architecture

To implement eq. 1, several FPGA based architectures were designed and tested using a Xilinx Virtex XC2V1000 embedded on a MEMEC Board (see Figure 1). The advantage of this approach consists of the flexibility offered by the high level description of the design in the VHDL language which allowed one to quickly and easily change the implementation parameters in order to fit the specifics of the application to be solved and to experiment with different architectural approaches. In particular, several versions were designed, comparing the effects of using a special purpose module based on the CORDIC algorithm [Andraka, 1998] for its exact computation of the exponential function and that of the much simpler module based on small lookup table (LUT) that traded simplicity and compactness for a much coarser approximation of the calculations of the exponential functions needed by the Gaussian Kernel.

3. Two case study

The first case study used to assess the performance of the proposed hardware architecture is a typical equalization problem [Anguita, et al., 2003], characterized by few training data (N = 32, 64, 128 were used), and where the non linear effects of the channel are modeled as a FIR filter (see [Boni, et al., 2004] for the details). The model defined in [Anguita, et al., 2003] was adopted, using a two-feature input vector $\underline{x}_i^{(r)}$, and an output $u_i \in \{+1, -1\}$. Input values had a S/N ratio of 7 dB, so the signal was quite 'clean' for this application. After the initial training, about 6000 samples were used for the test and evaluation of the resulting SVM. Feature data were encoded as 16 bit fixed point

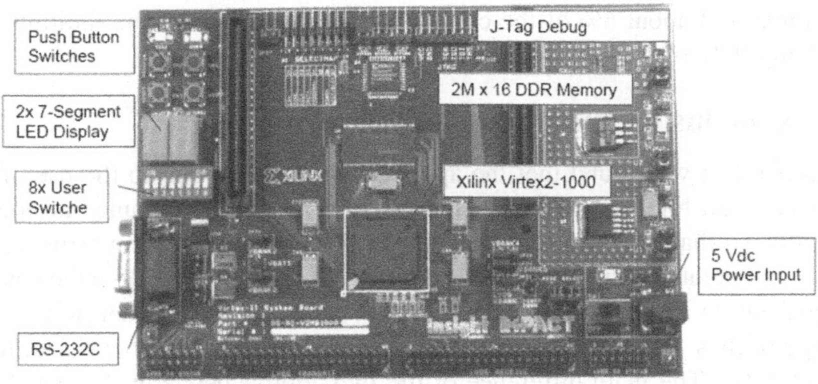

Figure 1. The Virtex–II V2MB1000 development board.

numbers; in the CORDIC-based approach, only the most significant 12 bits were used for the calculation and in the LUT, the same 12 bits were used to select the appropriate entry of the 4096x16 bit table.

Of all the computation slices available in the Virtex II, only about 8% were used for the CORDIC approach; also, 8% of the built-in multipliers available in the Virtex II and 8% of its internal RAM blocks were used for the computation of the inner products and the storage of intermediate values and constants, respectively. The LUT approach apparently is much more thrifty, since only 5% computational slices were needed and only 5% of the multipliers were used. However, 40% of available internal RAM block were needed for storing of the LUT itself. This leads to an unbalanced design, since the storage requirements quickly use up all the available resources.

The second application is an HEP class of experiments for top/anti-top ($t\bar{t}$) quark couples detection; data is composed by a two-classes set of samples organized as follows: a first half, used for training comes from the 'RUN I' experiments at the Collider Detector at Fermilab (CDF), and the other class comes from a simulation of the $t\bar{t}$ generation event; a real time hardware that was designed to fast tag the generation events and neglect the real-world background events [Amerio, et al., 2004]. Each sample is composed by $r = 8$ measurements representing the main characteristics of the experiment. $N = 4190$ samples were used for the training, while the remaining 4000 samples were used to measure the classification error. Once again, feature data was encoded in 16 bit integers; both in the CORDIC and in the LUT approaches, the most significant 14 bits were used in the calculation and for addressing the 16K x 16 bit LUT. In this case, the CORDIC approach required about 10% of the available slices and 8% of the available multipliers, while the ROM blocks for internal storage consumed about 20% of the available resources. The LUT approach required about 6% of the computational slices, 5% of the multipliers and a hefty 95% of the RAM blocks for the LUT.

4. Conclusion and discussion

In general, it was found that the approximation errors due to the use of a LUT were well tolerated by the adaptability of the SVM tolerance to noise and errors, so that their performance in terms of the classification error were roughly comparable with those obtained by the CORDIC method: in the channel equalization application, the classification error was of he order of 4% for both approaches, while for the HEP experiment classification error was of the order of 24%. The main difference of the two approaches is in the speed at which FPGA chip could be clocked: The simulation of the resulting architectures on the FPGA indicated that for the CORDIC-based approach a maximum clock rate of 60-70 MHz should be achievable, while for the LUT-based approach, a 90 MHz operation was possible. This is due Ű in part - to the more complex CORDIC algorithm which requires more slices on the FPGA chip and places them far apart, in turn causing the distribution of signals within the FPGA chip to be routed along relatively long lines which cannot be switched very fast. On the development board we used in our actual experiments on the hardware, one can select between a 50 and a 100 MHz clock. The CORDIC solution could only be run at the slower setting, while the LUT solution could run at the maximum speed, confirming the results from the simulations. Classification error percentage, speed performance, and slice occupancy for computational parts indicate the LUT-based solution as preferable. The main drawback of that approach is the very high cost required to store the LUT itself, a cost that is overwhelming in the HEP case study, where 95% of the resources are used to store a 16KByte LUT. As pointed out earlier, the LUT approach seems to be 'unbalanced' in resource usage and this has lead to the investigation of alternative approaches. Current efforts are directed toward an implementation of the system that moves the LUT to external memory which is available on the MEMEC development board. The internal RAM blocks of the Virtex II FPGA will be used to create a cache memory that will store pertinent portions of the LUT the support vectors $\underline{x}_i$, the products $\alpha_i u_i$ $(i \in SV)$ that are currently being used. This will add the complexity and the times required to access the memory, but it will lead to a much more scalable design since larger LUTs and more numerous support vectors can be accommodated. In addition, investigations have been started to put the unused portion of the slices and the multipliers to good use. The idea is to make multiple copies of the architecture described above, so that several input data can be processed in parallel. Given that all inputs (x_n) in the forward phase will have to be processed by computing the kernels and the products ai ui, a common cache internal to the FPGA should suffice. Further research and experimentation are needed to confirm the validity of this approach.

References

Amerio S., Anguita D., Lazzizzera I., Ridella S., Rivieccio F. and Zunino R. (2004). Model Selection in Top Quark Tagging with a Support Vector Classifier. Proceedings of IEEE International Joint Conference on Neural Networks, Budapest.

Andraka R. (1998). A survey of CORDIC algorithms for FPGAs. FPGA '98. Proceedings of the 1998 ACM/SIGDA sixth international symposium on Field programmable gate arrays. Feb. 22-24, Monterey, CA., 191-200.

Anguita, D., Boni, A., and Ridella, S. (2003). A Digital Architecture for Support Vector Machines: Theory, algorithm and FPGA Implementation. IEEE Trans. on Neural Networks. **14** 5 993-1009.

Boni, A., Pianegiani, F., Petri, D. (2004). Inverse Modeling with SVMs-Based Dynamically Reconfigurable Systems. IEEE Instrumentation on Measurement Tech. Conf. Como, Italy, 18-20.

Genov, R. and Cauwenberghs G. (2003). Kerneltron: Support Vector Machine in Silicon. IEEE Trans. on Neural Networks, **14**5 1426-1434.

Schölkopf, B. and Smola, A. (2002). Learning with Kernels. The MIT Press.

Vapnik, V.N. (1998). Statistical Learning Theory. John Wiley, NY, USA.

STATISTICAL LEARNING FOR PARTON IDENTIFICATION

D. Cauz, M. Giordani, G. Pauletta, M. Rossi, and L.Santi
Dipartimento di Fisica, Universita di Udine e I.N.F.N. di Udine
Via delle Scienze 208,
33100 Udine, Italia

Abstract The application of methods of statistical learning to the identification of the partons from which hadronic jets originate is investigated using simulated jets in the CDF detector with the ultimate objective of applying them at the trigger level. Using only jet-related properties, it appears to be raltively easy to distinguish between jets originating from gluons and those originating from quarks in an energy-independent manner. Distinguishing between quark flavours is more difficult and will require inclusion of other variables.

Keywords: HEP, Parton Identification, Multi-Layer Perceptron

1. Introduction

With the exception of the recently discovered top (t) quark, partons fragment into hadron showers immediately after production and what information one can have concerning the partons must be deduced from the properties of the corresponding hadron showers, which are measured by tracking devices and calorimeters. Whereas the charge and the kinematical parameters can be measured with reasonable accuracy, the nature of the parton is not easily determined because all partons hadronize in a similar manner.

A method of parton identification (PID) would add useful information to many analyses. For example, it would greatly facilitate the separation of the top quark signal from the background because the top quark decays (because of its great mass) into lighter quarks and leptons. A method of rejecting soft gluon radiation would therefore be extremely useful. The ability to distinguish between bottom (b) quarks and lighter quarks would be even more useful because t decay is distinguished by the production of a b quark. This is also the situation for the separation of signals corresponding to a number of as yet undetected particles (e.g. the Higgs) which are at the focus of current and future research.

B. Apolloni et al. (eds.), Biological and Artificial Intelligence Environments, 125–132

The work reported here focusses on discriminating between quarks and gluons on the basis of the characteristics of the jets of particles into which they immediately dissociate. By quarks (q) we mean all quarks produced in naturally occuring proportions, which implies they are practically all light quarks. However, it is our ambition to identify the heavier b quarks (b) Existing means of identifying b's depend principally on tracking.

On the basis of our previous work [Bianchin, 1992a]-[Badgett, 1992], we begin by defining feature space in terms of a number of parameters which depend on the energy distribution and the charge distribution around the jet axis. We refer the reader to the above references for a detailed description of these parameters.[1]

Briefly, they are:

- nchar: both charged and neutral particles contribute to the jet energy deposited in the calorimeter. nchar is the number of charged tracks in the jet.
- Pt02: the sum of transverse momenta of tracks contained in a the cone closest (radius 0.2) to the jet axis.
- Pt04: the sum of transverse momenta of tracks contained in a the conical shell between 0.2 and 0.4.
- Pt07: the sum of transverse momenta of tracks contained in a the conical shell between 0.4 and 0.7.
- EEMOM: a measure of the width of the jets transverse energy distribution in pseudorapidity η (which is a measure of the polar angle).
- PPMOM: a measure of the width of the jets transverse energy distribution in azimuthal angle ϕ.
- PTL: the transverse momentum Pt of the leading(i.e. the one with the largest Pt) in the jet.
- RADL: the distance from the jet axis of the leading particle.

The total jet transverse energy also features indirectly in the variables 2,3,4 and 7. These are divided by ETJ so as to reduce the classifier dependence on the total transverse energy. Feature space is therefore defined by f1-f8 corresponding, respectively, to: $NCHAR$, $Pt02/ETJ$, $Pt04/ETJ$, $Pt07/ETJ$, $EEMOM$, $PPMOM$, PTL/ETJ, and $RADL$. Collisions in the CDF detector are simulated using successive monte carlo (MC) simulations. To begin

[1] The association of the acronym PID with parton identification is an extension of what is usually understood by the acronym (i.e. particle identification).

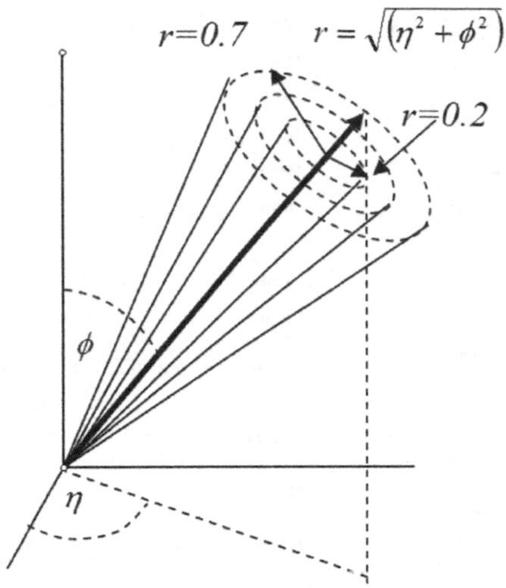

Figure 1. An illustration of how a jet is segmented to evaluate its features

with, physics generators [Sjostrand, 2001], [Corcella, 2000] simulate the collisions. Based on current physics theories, the interactions between partons in the colliding beams generate outgoing partons which are then hadronized. A second MC then propagates the resulting particles through a detailed simulation of the CDF detector. The simulated event data is then reduced using the standard CDF production software and analyzed to extract our features f1-f8 for each of the two classes (e.g. quarks and gluons) which are tagged accordingly (e.g. +1 and -1, respectively). Data sample of 20000 jets each were generated for each of three ETJ thresholds: $ETJ > 20GeV$ (jet-20 samples), $ETJ > 50GeV$ (jet-50 samples) and $ETJ > 90GeV$ (jet-90 samples)

The best possible discriminating power obtainable in our feature space is determined using a Bayesian classifier. This also serves as a benchmark for evaluating the performance of practical classifier algorithms such as multi-layer perceptrons (MLP), support vector machines (SVM) [Cortes, 1995] and the reactive tabu search (RTS), specifically designed for hardware application [Battiti, 1994].

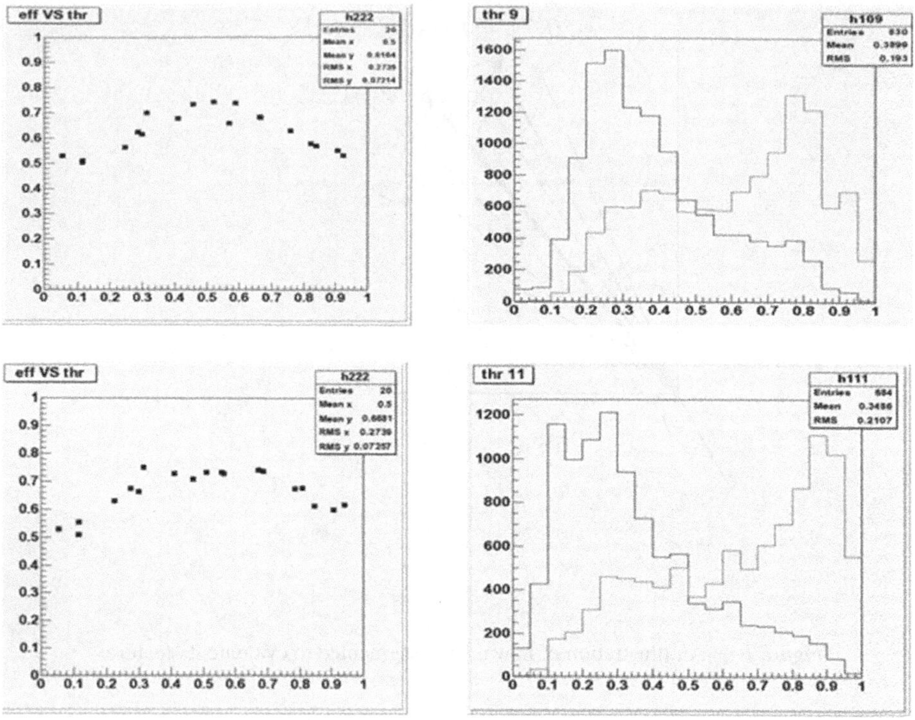

Figure 2. The results of the Bayesian classifier for 20000 jets with $ETJ > 20GeV$ (top two inserts) and $ETJ > 90GeV$ (bottom two inserts). Efficiency (vertical axis), as defined for the MLP in the text, is plotted as a function of classifier threshold on the left hand side. Frequency (vertical axis) is plotted agains Bayesian probability on the right

2. Classification

Discriminating power

Given a tagged data set obtains the best possible separation of the two components simply by dividing up the feature space into progressively smaller cells and calculating the Bayesian probability that an pattern which occupies that cell is of one species or the other. The best a classifier can do is to reproduce the Bayesian probability distribution. Given the inevitable limitation in statistics, the results obtained by the Bayesian classifier depend on how one goes about subdividing parameter space and on the minimum number of events required per cell.

The results of the Bayesian classifier for a tagged sample of 20000 jets (1/2 quarks and 1/2 gluons in each) is shown in Fig. 2.

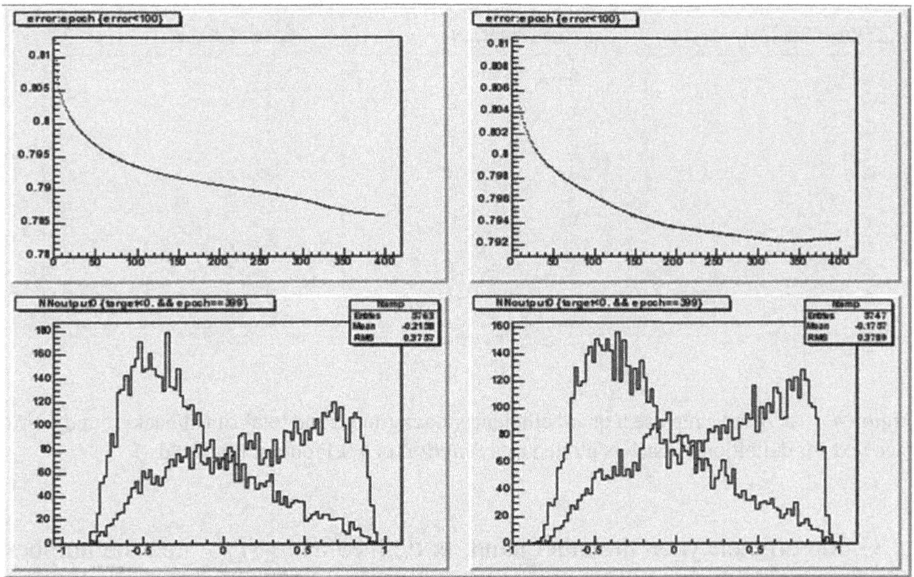

Figure 3. MLP results with the $qg - 20$ data set. (a) shows how the MLP error function for the training sample is reduced as a function of epoch number. (b) shows the corresponding value of the error function for the test sample. Overlearning is seen to set in around epoch 380. (c) and (d) show the MLP output distributions for each species of each sample.

The MLP

A MLP comprising 8 input nodes, 6 hidden nodes and 1 output node was trained using the first 10000 jets of each data set. Conventional sigmoids were used for transfer functions and a backpropagation algorithm for training. The output error as a function of epoch (1 epoch corresponds to a cycle through the entire data sample) for both training and test data samples is shown in the upper inserts of fig. 3 for a jet 20 sample of undiscriminated quarks (i.e. mostly light quarks). The output distributions for both training and test samples are shown in the bottom two inserts of the same figure. These should be compared to the results of the Bayesian classifier shown in fig. 2 (after transforming the Bayesian classifier output range for (0,1) to (-1, +1)).The MLP is seen to reproduce the results of the MLP within the differences due to limited statistics.

Three measures of the goodness of classification for the MLP are shown in Fig. 3. Each is plotted as a function of a classification threshold value of the MLP output above which quarks (gluons) are considered correctly (incorrectly) classified and below which quarks (gluons) are considered uncorrectly classified. Quark efficiency is defined as $q > /qtot$, i.e. the number of quarks above threshold as a fraction of the total number of quarks in the sample.

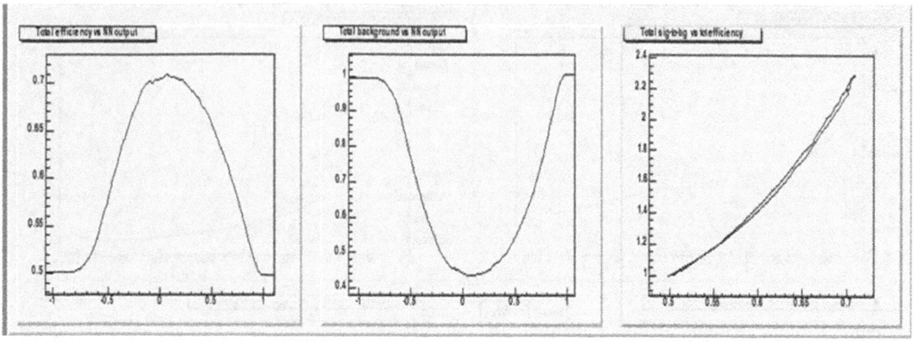

Figure 4. a, b and c represent quark efficiency, background and total signal/background ratios (see text for definitions). Each is plotted as a function of MLP output threshold

Gluon efficiency, on the other hand, is defined as $g_{<}/g_{tot}$, i.e., the number of gluons below threshold a a fraction of the total number of gluons. Total efficiency is defined as $(q_{>} + g_{<})$ as a fraction of the total $(q_{tot} + g_{tot})$ number of events.

Background fractions are calculated by substituting the number of incorrectly classified events for the correctly classified ones (i.e. $g_{>}$ for $q_{>}$ and $q_{<}$ for $g_{<}$) in the above expressions for efficiency. The signal to background ratios are the ratios of correctly classified events to incorrectly classified ones, i.e. $q_{>}/g_{>}$ for quarks, $g_{<}/q_{<}$ and $(q_{<} + g_{>})/total$. See Fig. 4.

Similar results are obtained for quark/gluon jets generated with higher lower transverse energy bounds ($qg - 50$ and $qg - 90$). In each case the MLP easily achieves the maximum possible discrimination efficiency as represented by the Bayesian classifier.

SVM methods will not therefore be able to improve on classification efficiency in this feature space. Preliminary results confirm this expectation. What they will be able to do, is to furnish what is seriously lacking from the MLP, i.e. a reliable estimate of the generalization error.

Any improvement in classification efficiency must come from a corresponding improvement in the definition of the features used for classification. We are currentlly working in this direction and preliminary results show that our present simulated quark sample may be contaminated by final-state gluon radiation. This is suggested by the hump in the quark distribution at lower (< 1) output values. Preliminary SVM results support this hypothesis. Further improvement must be obtained by incrementing feature space.

Separating b-quarks from gluons and other quark flavours was also attempted in the same feature space. It was found that b-quarks could more easily be separated from gluons at higher values of transverse energy (see Fig. 5) than was

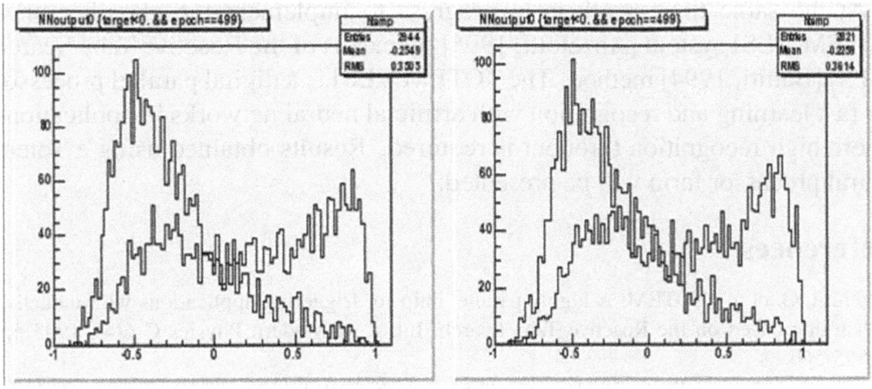

Figure 5. MLP output for b-quarks and gluon jets (bg-90)

expected while it was very difficult to distinguish between b-quarks and the lighter species (see Fig. 6). It appears from these results that incrementing feature space is essential. Inclusion of new tracking variables is being investigated.

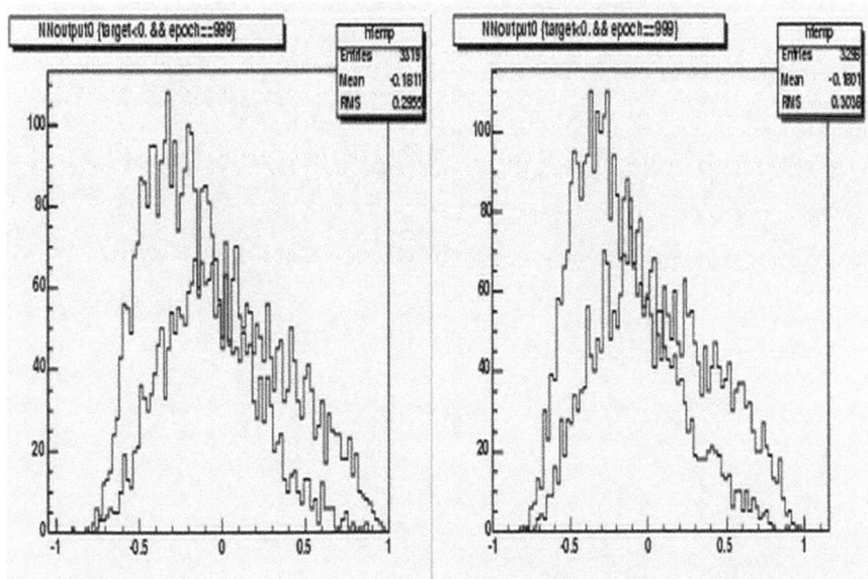

Figure 6. MLP output for b-quarks and light quark jets (bq-90)

At the same time, work is in progress to implement the classifier on a TOTEM VLSI system [Anzelotti, 1995] by means of the Reactive Tabu Search (RTS) [Battiti, 1994] method. The TOTEM VLSI is a digital parallel processor for fast learning and recognition with artificial neural networks in applications where high recognition throuput is required. Results obtained using a Totem neural processor farm will be presented.

References

Anzelotti, G. et al., TOTEM: A highly parallel chip for triggering applications with inductive learning based on the Reactive Tabu Search, Int. J. of Modern Physics C 6(4), 1995 pp. 555-560.

Battiti, R. and Tecchiolli, G. The Reactive Tabu Search. ORSA Journal of Computing, Vol 6 n. 2, 1994 pp. 126-140.

Badgett, W. et al., Neural networks at the Tevatron, AIHENP2, Agelonde France 1992, Ed. D. Perret Gallix , World Scientific 1992.

Bianchin, S. et al., in Classification of jets from pp-bar collisions at Tevatron energies, AI-HENP2, Agelonde France 1992, Ed. D. Perret Gallix , World Scientific 1992.

Bianchin, S. et al, Int. J. of Neural Systems, Vol. 3 (Supp 1992).

Corcella, G. et al HERWIG6: An Event Generator for Hadron Emission Reactions With Interfering Gluons, hep-ph/0011363, Cavendish-HEP-99/03, CERN-TH/2000-284.

Cortes, C. and Vapnik, V. Support Vector Networks in Machine Learning, 20, 1995, pp. 1; K.-R. Müller, S. Mika, G. Rätsch, K. Tsuda, and B. Schölkopf. An introduction to kernel-based learning algorithms, IEEE Neural Networks, 12(2):181-201.

Sjostrand, T. Lonnblad, L. Mrenna, S. PYTHIA 6.2: Physics and Manual, LU-TP-01-21, Aug 2001, hep-ph/0108264.

TIME-VARYING SIGNALS CLASSIFICATION USING A LIQUID STATE MACHINE

Antonio Chella[1,2] and Riccardo Rizzo[2]

[1] *DINFO, Viale delle Scienze 90128, Palermo, Italy*

[2] *C.N.R. – ICAR, Viale delle Scienze 90128, Palermo, Italy*

Abstract The liquid state machine is a novel computation paradigm based on the transient dynamics of recurrent neural circuitry. In this paper it is shown that this systems can be used to recognize complex stimuli composed by non-periodic signals and to classify them in a very short time. Even if the network is trained over a segment of the signal the classification task is completed in a time interval significantly shorter than the time-window used for the training. Stimuli composed by many complex signals are recognized and classified even if some signals are absent.

Keywords: Liquid State Machine, classification, Spiking Neurons

1. Introduction

Reaction times of biological systems are usually very short, so short that there is not time to integrating or averaging over a long–time window; a stream of input signals is usually processed in few *m secs*, a time interval that allows to generate a small number of neural spikes. Neural microcircuits, small networks of spiking neurons, are usually identified as the new generation of neural networks; the dynamic of this systems is complex and difficult to constrain and manipulate so that one of the approach is to take a weighted sum of the activity of the neurons using a suitable read-out circuit. In [Joshi and Maass., 2004] this activity is defined as *liquid state* $x(t)$ and models the impact that a neuron of the circuit may have on the membrane potential of a generic read-out neuron.

In [Maass and Natschlager, 2002] a new computational model, called the Liquid State Machine (LSM), that exploits the liquid state as a resource for a real time computing system was presented. The LSM is constituted by two separated subsystems: the liquid, that is used to obtain a very complex time-varying vector state, and the readout function: a memoryless subsystem

B. Apolloni et al. (eds.), Biological and Artificial Intelligence Environments, 133–139

(usually a simple perceptron or a set of neurons without connection loops) that is used to extract information from the liquid. The LSM is capable to process time-varying inputs without stable states, but using the perturbed state of the liquid that, at any moment, is the result of the present and past inputs.

The plasticity of the microcircuits is not exploited in LSM, as said in [Joshi and Maass., 2004], all the plasticity and adaptation is implemented in read-out circuits trained to produce the desired output.

2. The Neuron Model

The liquid dynamics is an important issue or the implementation of the LSM: the liquid should have two very important features:

1 a complex but not chaotic dynamics because virtually it should contain the transition functions of many finite state machines;

2 the separation property that allows to separate the states due to two different input signals.

Both properties were introduced in [Maass and Natschlager, 2002]: while the second one is clearly stated and defined, the first one is introduced when the liquid fading memory and the need of dynamic synapses is discussed. The dynamic of the liquid is also in relationship with the length of the neural connections. To obtain this equilibrium between a complex dynamics and a not chaotic response it is necessary to pay a special attention to the neuron model: a rich model is needed to obtain a complex dynamics but a low computational complexity is necessary for an efficient simulation.

On the two opposite sides are the simple Integrate & Fire model (I&F model) and the Hodgkin-Huxley model: both of them used in LSM simulations [Maass and Natschlager, 2002], [Kaminski and Wojcik, 2004]. The Hodgkin-Huxley model is a complex model constituted by 4 differential equations and tens of biophysically meaningful parameters, it is complete but very expensive to simulate and it is not a suitable choice especially if it is necessary to simulate a large array of neurons as in a LSM.

In [Izhikevich, 2004] some of the models of spiking neurons are compared in order to evaluate their applicability to a large-scale simulation. A simple model capable to exhibit a very complex behavior is presented in [Izhikevich, 2003]. This model is simple to implement and, using only 4 parameters, is capable to reproduce many firing patterns, as the bursting, continuous spiking with frequency adaptation, and chattering. This model was used in our simulation.

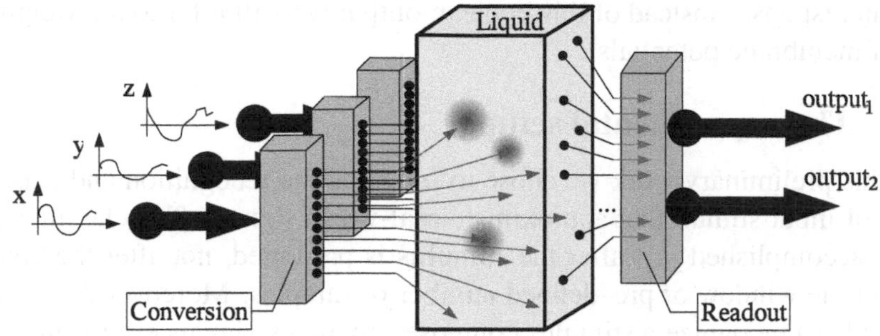

Figure 1. A representation of the Liquid State Machine: on the left side the conversion subsystem, one for each input signal connected to the liquid using 10 lines; on the right the readout subsystem and the output lines.

3. The System Implementation

The liquid is a set of neurons organized in a three-dimensional structure, in our implementation the liquid is made by a set of $25 \times 10 \times 4$ neurons connected using the same random pattern explained in [Maass and Natschlager, 2002]. The probability of a sinaptic connection from neuron a to neuron b is defined by a Gaussian probability distribution with an average value of 4 (the smaller dimension of the structure of the liquid) and variance $\lambda = 8$ that controls the average distance between neurons synaptically connected. The weight of connections are randomly chosen with a mean value of $w_e = 1$ if the connection is excitatory and $w_i = -2$ if the connection is inhibitory and in a way that 80% of the connections are excitatory and 20% inibitory, according to [Izhikevich, 2003]. The four parameters of the neural model are randomly varied in order to obtain different spiking patterns.

In our system a converter was added in order to bring a time function in input to the liquid (see fig. 1). The time-varying inputs signals are converted in impulse trains using the mechanism described in [Bothe et al., 2002] and a set of ten Class 1 excitable neurons: values of the input waves are converted in a set of 10 impulse trains that are applied to the liquid. Each converter uses 5 impulses to transform a single value of the input signal.

Each impulse train is connected to the liquid using the same connection schema used to build the connections among the neurons in order to obtain an activation area when an input impulse is present. This situation is represented on the left of fig. 1 by the blurred circle areas on the surface of the liquid.

The output is constituted by the liquid state: the set of all membrane potentials. The readout neurons are modeled as a set of perceptrons that take the contributions of all the liquid neurons filtered with a membrane time constant of 20 msec, the filter output is weighted and applied to a threshold to obtain a boolean response. Instead of this boolean output we will refer to the weighted sum of membrane potentials.

4. The experimental setup

In this preliminary work we chose to focus on the recognition and classification of input stimuli that approximate real-world signals. The classification task is accomplished just after the stimulus is presented, not after the end of a fixed time window or pre–defined number of samples. Moreover the system is capable to recognize a stimulus composed by many signals even if just few of them are presented. All the stimuli taken into account are constituted by two or three time-varying signals that are non periodic, generated convolving a Gaussian kernel with a set of random impulses. The first experiment is focused to the recognition speed of stimuli composed by two signals and to highlight that the status of the liquid can be maintained even if just a part of the stimulus is presented. The second experiment is aimed to verify that the liquid is capable to recognize a complex stimulus from a part of it and to evaluate the output to ambiguous stimulus.

First Experiment

The first task to accomplish is to recognize the two couples of input waves (two stimuli), when presented to the liquid inputs. Two output perceptrons are trained to recognize the input stimuli: the first perceptron is trained to recognize the input stimulus $x_1 - y_1$, the second perceptron is trained to recognize the input stimulus $x_2 - y_2$. After a successfully training of the output perceptron the liquid is capable to recognize the signal from just a part of them. To do that the input is constituted by the couple $x_1 - y_1$ during the first half of the time interval (125 msec), and then switched to $x_2 - y_2$ during the second part of the time interval. An example of the response of the liquid is plotted in fig. 2, the values plotted are the weighted sum of the states of the liquid using the set of weights of the first perceptron. The average time needed to recognize the signal is about 7 *msec* so that there is not time to complete the signal. The efficacy of the classification task measured as the sum of the square classification error is not a function of the distance of the two stimuli (measured, as defined in [Maass and Natschlager, 2002], as the L^2 norm of the difference of the two couple of signals), results not shown here.

The next task is aimed to understand if the response of the liquid can be maintained even if the input of the liquid is not complete. This is obtained submitting to the liquid the couple $x_1 - y_1$ during the first half of the time interval and $x_1 - 0$ during the second interval. Fig. 3 shows that the input in the second half of the time interval is difficult to recognize and the output is oscillatory. The output of the system is above the threshold for some time

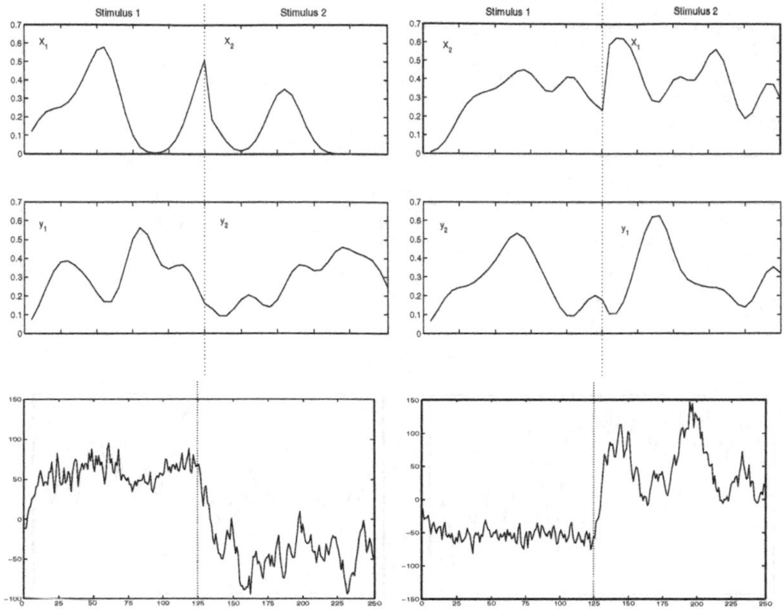

Figure 2. (Upper left) the input sequence $x_1 - y_1, x_2 - y_2$; (lower left) output of the system (weighted sum of the membrane potential of all neurons); (upper right) the input sequence $x_2 - y_2, x_1 - y_1$; (lower right) the output signal

and then goes below the threshold after some oscillations. This is due to the memory of the liquid that maintains for some time the effect of the last input.

The last task is constituted by the signal $x_2 - 0$ for the first half of the time window and $x_1 - y_1$ for the second half of the time window. In the first part of the input the liquid maintains a response below the threshold, but the output goes above the threshold when the next stimulus is recognized. The precedent state of the liquid allow to obtain a response just above the recognition threshold.

Second Experiment

In the second experiment the goal is to understand if the system is capable to classify a stimulus if only a part of it is available or if two stimuli are very similar.

The two stimuli are built using the five signals and labeled x_1, y_1, z_1, x_2, z_2; the two stimuli are constituted by the signal combinations $x_1 - y_1 - z_1$, and $x_2 - y_1 - z_2$, where y_1 is the common part. The output perceptron can be successfully trained and the system correctly classify the two stimuli (results not shown). Left side of fig. 4 shows what happens if the stimuli $x_1 - y_1 - 0$

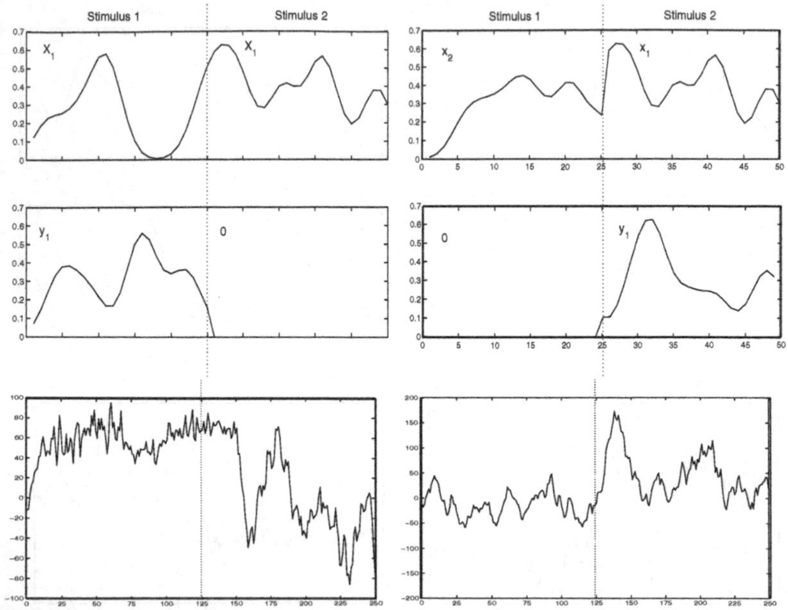

Figure 3. (Upper left) the input sequence $x_1 - y_1, x_1 - 0$; (lower left)output of the system (weighted sum of the membrane potential of all neurons); (upper right) the input sequence $x_2 - 0, x_1 - y_1$ (lower right) the output signal.

is presented to the system. The liquid maintains an output over the recognition threshold even is the stimulus is not complete.

The right side of figure 4 shows what happens if the input is just the common part of the input stimuli (the signal y_1), the liquid state is oscillating between two states corresponding to the two different input stimuli.

5. Conclusions and Future Works

Liquid State Machines are an interesting paradigm suitable or computing in real time systems, and in this work it was demonstrated that LSM can be used to classify time varying-signal. Although the tasks proposed are similar to a real world situation were input signals are not periodic and need to be quickly recognized even if not completed, it it necessary to understand what kind of limitations the liquid has. Another problem is related to the readout system, because many of the performances of the system depends on it.

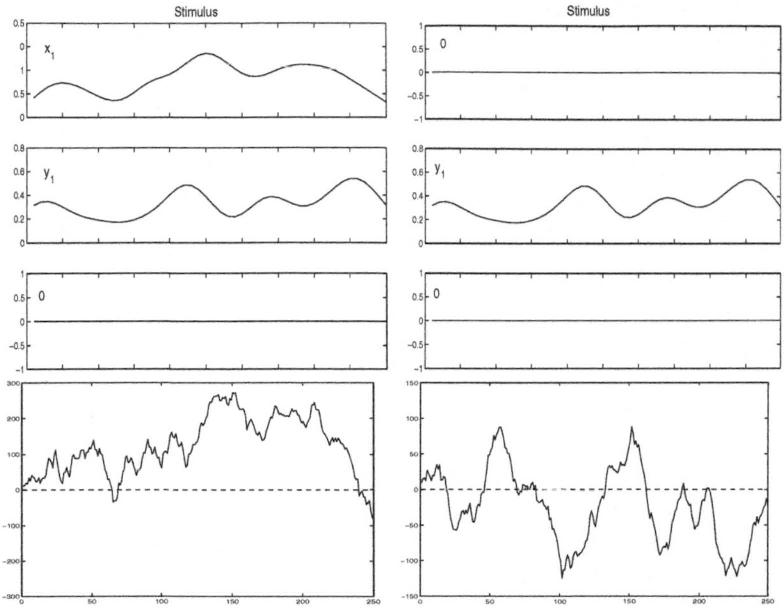

Figure 4. (Upper left) the composition of signals $x_1 - y_1 - 0$; (lower left) the output of the liquid; (upper right) the input stimuli compose by $0 - y_1 - 0$;(lower right) the system output.

References

Bothe, S. M., La Poutre, H. A., and Kok, J. N. (2002). Unsupervised clustering with spiking neurons by sparse temporal coding and multi-layer rbf networks. *IEEE Transaction on Neural Networks*, vol. 13(n.2):426–435.

Izhikevich, E. M. (2003). Simple model of spiking neurons. *IEEE Transaction on Neural Networks*, vol.14(n. 6):1569–1572.

Izhikevich, E. M (2004). Which model to use for cortical spiking neurons? *IEEE Transaction on Neural Networks*, 15(5):1063–1070.

Joshi, P. and Maass., W. (2004). Movement generation and control with generic neural microcircuits. In Ijspeert, A. J., Mange, D., Murata, M., and Nishio, S., editors, *Proc. of the First International Workshop on Biologically Inspired Approaches to Advanced Information Technology*, pages 16–31, Lausanne. Bio-Adit.

Kaminski, W. A. and Wojcik, G. M. (2004). Liquid state machine built of hodgkin-huxley neurons. *Informatica*, 15(1):39–44.

Maass, W. and Natschlager, T. (2002). Real–time computating without stable states: A new framework for neural computation based on pertubations. *Neural Computation*, 14:2531–2560.

FPGA BASED STATISTICAL DATA MINING PROCESSOR

Eros Pasero, Walter Moniaci, Tassilo Mendl

Polytechnic of Turin,Neuronica Laboratory, INFN sez. di Torino, Corso Duca degli Abruzzi 24,10129 Torino,Italy

Abstract: The goal of this project is to realize an enhanced data mining system which performs intelligent processing on data received from sensorial agents in a very flexible manner with reusability prospective. The project is implemented through a "digital core" constituted of a FPGA, a microcontroller and several memory blocks which co-operate to the computation. The FPGA is programmed in VHDL to implement the data mining process. The data mining system is composed of a sophisticated statistical non parametric part and a recurrent artificial neural network. The core was written in a recursive manner to permit the reconfigurability of the network and its reusability to all the systems which can be modeled through a similar system.

Keywords: data mining; fpga; neural network; Parzen method.

1. Introduction

The target is a platform for fast data processing, which can be easily reused for other applications by changing only some parameters and reprogramming the FPGA. All other function for the control and the management of the data-path, external interfaces and control unit features will be done by the micro-processor. However, for performance reasons it might be necessary to perform some of these functions although by a FPGA. Since, the core of the system is adaptable, various sensors can be connected and different environment conditions can be analyzed. Concurring sensors will allow the system to collect and log a huge amount of data. This renders

B. Apolloni et al. (eds.), Biological and Artificial Intelligence Environments, 141–148

it necessary to perform real-time advanced processing in order to structure and synthesize the information.

2. Algorithm description

The information embedded in environmental data is not just the sum of information coming out of each sensor but also correlations between data can be relevant for a specific target. For this purpose we developed a generic data mining processes that comprises the following principal phases:

1. Characterizing sampling methods
2. Focusing on a limited number of meaningful quantities
3. Searching and organizing data links between the variables
4. Clustering variables in separate classes.
5. Analyzing cross-correlations between qualitative and quantitative variables.
6. Computing multivariate inferences on heterogeneous populations

For the exploration and modeling of data suitable statistical methods have to be used. Among the available ones, a methodology to inference the distribution of data without any a-prior knowledge on the noise seems to be the best solution.

We chose a combination of a statistical non parametric algorithm and a neural network. For the statistical algorithm we use the Parzen method.

With the Parzen method cross correlation among the probability density functions of each parameter can be evaluated and groups of data in the database can be selected, which fit best to the current environmental data. These groups can then be used to evaluate the environmental conditions.

This analysis will also provide inferences that can be used for reliable short term forecasting (nowcasting) if the amount of available data is sufficient. As mentioned the Parzen method selects groups of data in the database, which fit best to the current environmental data. Therefore, this data can also be used to predict future evolution of the data in a short period. In our case the predicting part is realized through a recurrent neural network, considering the timing evolution of these parameters and the previous forecasts made by it. The neural network MLP (Multi Layer Perceptron) is implemented on a Xilinx FPGA with appropriate memory blocks. The memory is used to store the parameters of the neural network: weights, number of inputs, number of neurons and activation functions.

Anyhow, it is necessary to have characteristic conditions and their evolution in the historical database in order to provide a reliable prevision.

Therefore, we provide also a synthetic database to the processing, which contains those conditions.

3. Parzen method

The neural system we use to nowcast the future environmental conditions must consider hundredths of thousands of data sampled and stored during last years. The reliability of the prediction is based on the highest quantity of data. The neural network uses this "knowledge" to estimate the trend of the interested parameters in the future. But it should be useless to train the network using the whole data set. This set must be analyzed to extract only the most significant information which can be used to forecasts. Our approach is based on a statistical non parametric method that we developed for this purpose. It must choose the best "predictors" for each parameter that must be predicted. We define the entropy of the parameters in the following way:

$$e(x) = -\int_{-\infty}^{+\infty} \log(p(x))\, p(x)\, dx \quad (1)$$

In this formula *p(x)* is the Probability Density Function (PDF) of a random variable *x*. *e(x)* is an index of dispersion that lies in the range]-∞,+∞[. Let Z be the vector of all the possible predictors that can be used to foresee the variable *y* (predictand). Now let X1 and X2 be two particular subsets of predictors taken from Z. The number of elements in X1 and X2 has to be the same. In order to establish the best set of predictors between X1 and X2 we calculated the following entropy difference:

$$\begin{aligned} d(X,y) &= e(X,y) - e(X) = \\ &= -\int \log P(X,y)\, P(X,y)\, dX dy + \\ &+ \int \log P(X)\, P(X)\, dX \end{aligned} \quad (2)$$

where p(X,y) is the joint PDF of X and y and p(X) is the PDF of X (the predictors). Both PDFs are unknown and therefore it's impossible to evaluate the integrals in (2). We circumvented this problem by estimating the unknown PDFs through the Parzen method [E.Parzen,1962]. This method estimates the unknown probability density functions making a sum of Gauss kernels, each one centered on a record of the database. The formula is the following:

$$P_X^*(X;\mathbf{D},\Lambda)=\frac{1}{n}\sum_{i=1}^{n}\prod_{j=1}^{m}\frac{1}{\sqrt{2\pi\lambda_j^2}}\exp\left[-\frac{(x_j-x_{ij})^2}{2\lambda_j^2}\right] \quad (3)$$

where,

- $\mathbf{D} = \{\mathbf{X}_1, \ldots\ldots\mathbf{X}_n\}$: it' s the data vector
- n: database dimension (number of records)
- xi,xij: these are the j-th component of X and X_i
- Λ: standard deviation vector, $\Lambda = (\lambda 1, \ldots, \lambda m)$

Each standard deviation in Λ regulates the resolution of the estimator along the corresponding dimension. In its turn this allows us to estimate d(X1,y) and d(X2,y). The best between X1 and X2 is the one that gives rise to the smallest entropy difference. The sets X_i are the same data of the database but delayed in time.

4. The neural system

When the statistical procedure, described before, has chosen the best predictors an artificial neural network is requested to predict future values. Feed forward neural networks have been successfully used to solve problems that require the computation of a static function i.e. a function whose output depends only upon the current input, and not on any previous inputs. In the real world however, one encounters many problems which cannot be solved by learning a static function because the function being computed changes with each input received. Thus, any system that seeks to predict the future evolution of phenomena must have some notion of how the past inputs affect the processing of the present input, as well as a way of storing the past inputs. In other words such a system must have a memory of the past input and a way to use that memory to process the current input.

In order to take in account the time evolution of a generic environmental variable we chose the recurrent neural network architecture as shown in the following picture.

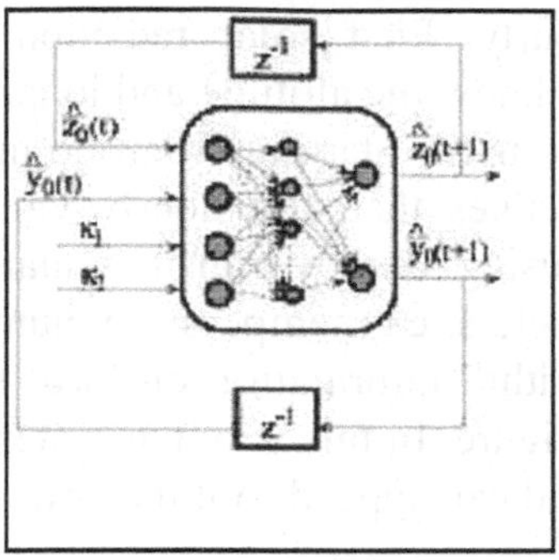

Figure 1. Neural System

From the previous figure we can see that, for the forecast at the instant *t+1*, the network uses the previous network outputs, at the instant *t*, together with the inputs *k1* and *k2* chosen using the Parzen method. In particular we used a RNN [Pineda,1987] with three layers:

- Input layer
- Hidden layer (5 neurons)
- Output layer (1 neuron)

We chose the *backpropagation rule* [P.Werbos,1974] *to* calculate de derivative of the cost function with respect to the weights and, consequently, to reduce the difference between the network output and the real value (*target*). For the optimization of the free parameters of the network (*weights*) we used the Levenberg – Marquardt algorithm [D.Marquardt,1963], that dynamically mixes Gauss – Newton and gradient descent iterations.

5. Synthetic database

In order to make the system at once working it's necessary to have a large database with which training the neural system. And so when we use the system in a new place we have to wait a long time to collect the necessary data. To avoid this problem we have thought to create a synthetic database able to represent the meteorological characteristics of the place the system is installed in. For each place the following parameters are calculated:

- Air temperature [°C]
- Relative humidity [%]
- Precipitation [mm]
- Atmospheric pressure [hPa]
- Solar radiation [W/m^2]
- Wind velocity and direction [m/s], [°N]

The sampling is hourly. First solar radiation is simulated; for this purpose it's necessary to know the altitude and longitude of the place. Other additional parameters are used. Starting from the monthly global radiation values, first the daily values than the hourly values [Graham,1990] are generated stochastically using Markov transition matrices [Aguiar,1988].

Then the other parameters, e.g. temperature, humidity, wind are derived from these. In this algorithm information on local effects is considered as shown in the following figure. In this way the system can run at once using this synthetic database and can append to it the new acquired data.

Terrain	Features
Open	Open site, open terrain, north facing incline, no raised skyline. Applies to most sites.
Depression	Depression or very flat valley floor, in which cold air collects, particularly in the Jura and the Alps.
Sea/lake	Shore of sea or larger lake (up to 1 km from the shore).
City	Centre of larger city (over 100'000 inhabitants).
Valley	Valley floor in mountainous valley at higher altitudes. Valley floor inclined (flat valleys are often treated as depressions).
Valley Central Alps	Floor of large central Alpine valley (e.g. Alpine regions of Valais).
Foehn valley	Valley floor of foehn valley (regions with warm descending air currents).
Valley Alpine foothills	Valley floor in northern Alpine foothills.

Figure 2. Features for different terrain types

6. System overview

However, the statistical algorithm is complex and therefore slow. The most promising solution for this problem is to use parallel processing which cannot be performed by a simple microcontroller, but can be implemented very efficient in an FPGA [Omondi,2002],[Bade,1994].

In a first step we evaluated the algorithm for performance using simulation on a standard PC. This simulation has been done using Matlab, because it provides proper libraries for statistical processing.

We implemented for this purpose the sensor interfacing on an 8 bit microcontroller, which transfers the measured data to a PC. The PC performs then the data processing (which will be done later on by the FPGA), and returns the result of the analysis (in our case a prevision of the future values of the parameters) backwards to the microcontroller in order to display both the measured values and the analysis result on a display. Currently we are working on implementing the algorithm on the FPGA.

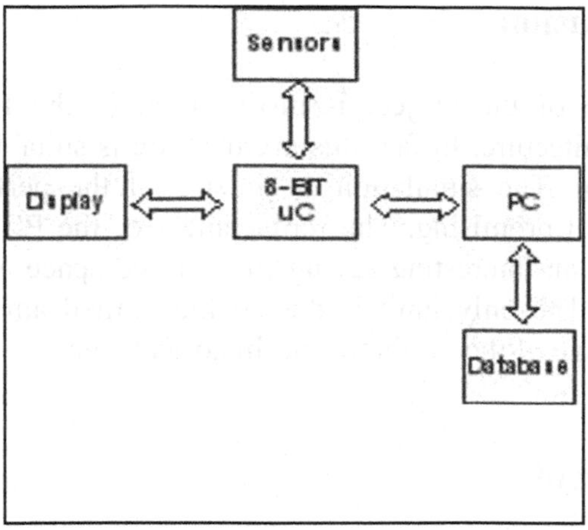

Figure 3. System connected to a PC

A hardware realization on an FPGA seems to be best suited to build that highly parallel distributed computing system. However, the operating modes management and the interface management to the sensors and the display will still be implemented with the microcontroller, because it allows for faster modifications.

In contrast, the Parzen method and the neural network require a lot of computation, which can be performed by parallel processing, which is the domain of FPGAs. Therefore, we evaluated a modular structure of the statistical processing with respect to the paradigm of parallel processing. We establish for this purpose locally distributed processing

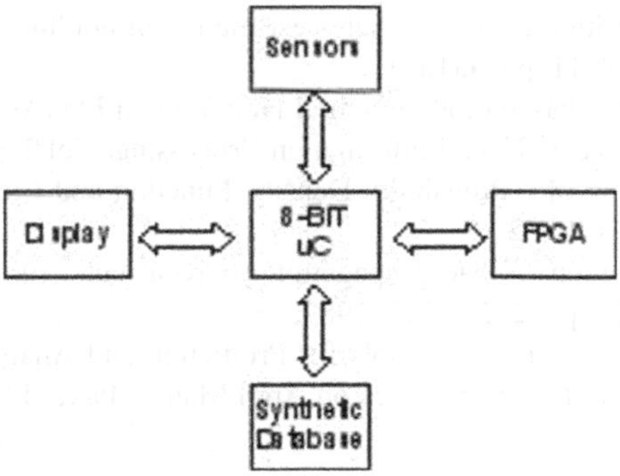

Figure 4. System connected to a FPGA

units and a single control unit. These processing units are implemented on the FPGA (using a high-level description language like VHDL up to the FPGA synthesis). During the final design of the building blocks performance for speed and power consumption has to be further studied and optimized.

7. Conclusion

The relevance of the project is most of all in the flexibility of the implemented architecture. In fact this architecture is suitable for every data driven application. The simulation at the PC of the performance of the system is just well promising. The replacement of the PC with the FPGA will provide both an interesting saving of cost and space and an enormous gain in velocity. The only limit is due to the limited amount of memory available for storage of the synthetic and historical data.

Acknowledgment

This work was partly funded by MIUR research project n.2002095532_002_ and by INFN group V, project Haptic.

References

Aguiar, R. and M. Collares-Pereira (1988): A simple procedure for generating sequences of daily radiation values using a library of markov transition matrices. *Solar Energy*, Vol.40, No.3, pp.269-279.

Bade, S.L. and B.L. Hutchings (1994): FPGA-Based Stochastic Neural Networks-Implementation. IEEE Workshop on FPGAs for Custom Computing Machines, pages 189-198.

Graham, V. and K. Hollands (1990): A method to generate synthetic hourly solar radiation globally. *Solar Energy*, Vol.44, No.6, pp.333-341.

Marquardt, D. "An algorithm for least-squares estimation of nonlinear parameters," *SIAM J. Appl. Math.*, 1963, Vol. 11, pp. 431ñ441.

Omondi, A.R. and J.C.Rajapakse (2002): Neural Networks in FPGAs. Proceedings of the 9th International Conference on Neural Information Processing, Vol.2, pp.954-959.

Parzen, E. "On Estimation of a Probability Density Function and Mode". Ann. Math. Stat., Vol.33 , pp. 1065 -1076, 1962.

Pineda, F.J., "Generalization of backpropagation to recurrent neural networks," *Physical Review Letters,* Vol. 18, pp. 2229-2232, 1987.

Werbos, P. "Beyond regression: New Tools for Prediction and Analysis in the Behavioural Sciences". Ph.D. dissertation, Committee on Appl.Math., Harvard Univ., Cambridge, MA, Nov. 1974.

NEURAL CLASSIFICATION OF HEP EXPERIMENTAL DATA

Salvatore Vitabile[1], Giovanni Pilato[1], Giorgio Vassallo[2], S.M. Siniscalchi[2], Antonio Gentile[1,2] and Filippo Sorbello[1,2]

[1] *ICAR-CNR, Istituto di Calcolo e Reti ad Alte Prestazioni*
Consiglio Nazionale delle Ricerche, Palermo, Italy.
{vitabile,pilato} @pa.icar.cnr.it

[2] *DINFO, Dipartimento di Ingegneria Informatica*
Università di Palermo, Italy.
siniscalchi@csai.unipa.lt, {gvassallo, gentile, sorbello} @unipa.it

Abstract High Energy Physics (HEP) experiments require discrimination of a few interesting events among a huge number of background events generated during an experiment. Hierarchical triggering hardware architectures are needed to perform this tasks in real-time. In this paper three neural network models are studied as possible candidate for such systems. A modified Multi-Layer Perceptron (MLP) architecture and a EαNet architecture are compared against a traditional MLP. Test error below 25% is archived by all architectures in two different simulation strategies. EαNet performance are 1 to 2% better on test error with respect to the other two architectures using the smaller network topology. The design of a digital implementation of the proposed neural network is also outlined.

Keywords: Neural Networks, Intelligent Data Analysis, Embedded Neural Networks.

1. Introduction

High Energy Physics (HEP) experiments generate huge amounts of data that require classification and event discrimination. As example, a run on the Collider Detector at Fermilab generates a dataset of events characterized by the generation of top/anti-top quark couples.
The top/anti-top quark couples was discovered at the Fermilab Tevatron in 1995. This was either the culmination of the nearly two decades of intense research at particle accelerators around the world, or the major triumph for the Standard Model of particle physics since it predicted the top quark existence. In HEP experiments, along with interesting events, background noise is generated by the collision, which occurs in a very small time lapse. Different

B. Apolloni et al. (eds.), Biological and Artificial Intelligence Environments, 149–155

backgrounds have very different kinematic properties, so HEP data classification is a very complex tasks.
Neural networks have been applied in HEP experiments as function approximators to obtain a functional form which describes some distribution [Beri et al., 2000], [Bhat and Bhat, 2000], or for event classification, combining information from different variables [Hays and Kotwal, 2002], [Tuttle et al., 2001], [Ciobanu et al., 1999]. On the other hand, neural based high speed triggering devices, normally organized in a hierarchy, are then required to discriminate useful data from background noise [Fent et al., 1996], [Janauschek et al., 1999].
The research described in this paper is aimed at developing a neural architecture capable of real-time processing of these massive amounts of data. The paper will be articulated in two separate parts. In the first part, the analysis of the reference application domain as well as the issues related to the neural models testing and selection are addressed. In the second part of the paper, the digital design, for FPGA implementation of the neural architectures developed in the previous part is outlined.

2. Background

Notoriously, data sets used in typical neural network applications are characterized by large cardinality and unknown statistical distribution. There is in fact no guarantee that input-output pairs be statistically significant when considered under neural network testing, which makes the traditional test-set validation procedure potentially incorrect.
The authors have previously introduced three "quality factors" to give a measure, without using the test set, of the generalization capability of a feed-forward neural network. Based on the properties of these quality indexes, the E-αNet architecture has been developed and successfully employed in several application contexts [Gaglio et al., 2000], [Pilato et al., 2001].
In other application arenas, the authors have developed a simulation environment for a Multi-Layer Perceptron (MLP) design showing large performance ratings in terms of both recognition rate and classification speed. This design uses sinusoidal shaped activation functions for hidden layer neurons and linear functions for output layer neurons. Successful applications of the design have been reported in the area of handwritten character recognition [Sorbello et al., 1999] and road sign recognition [Vitabile et al., 2002], [Vitabile et al., 2004].
In what follows, a brief description of both E-αNet architecture and the "sinusoidal" MLP is reported.

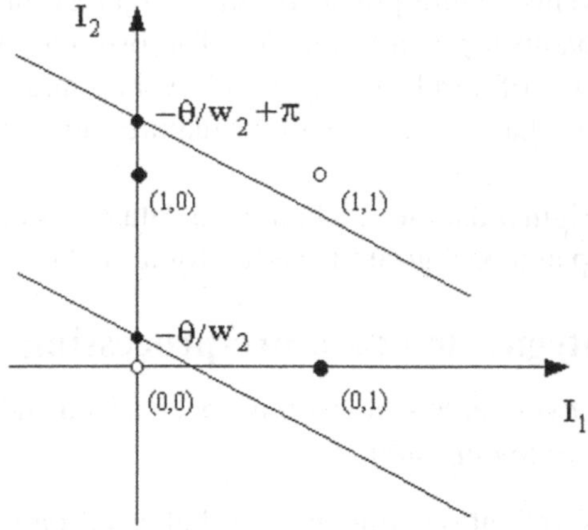

Figure 1. The XOR problem: separation boundary of the two classes obtained using the sinusoidal function.

The EαNet Neural Network

The EαNet is a feed forward neural architecture capable to learn the activation function of its hidden units during the training phase. These networks are characterized by low quality factors when compared to traditional feed-forward networks with sigmoidal activation functions. Network learning capability has been obtained through the combination of Powell modified Conjugate Gradient Descent (CGD) [Powell, 1968] and the Hermite regression formula. Hidden layer activation functions are based on the first R Hermite orthonormal functions where R is *a priori* chosen before the learning process.

The "sinusoidal" Multi-Layer Perceptron

In the classification task, the choice of the activation functions for the hidden and the output layers has an important role. The Multi-Layer Perceptron (MLP) architecture employed in this research uses sinusoidal activation function for the hidden layer. This choice guarantees a better separation of classes, with a small number of hidden units as illustrated for the XOR problem in Figure 1. At the output layer, a linear activation function is used as it improves both learning speed and the recognition rate when compared with sigmoidal function [Sorbello et al., 1999]. Powell modified Conjugate Gradient Descent (CGD) [Powell, 1968] is also used as learning strategy.

3. Experimental Results

A data-set generated from a MonteCarlo simulation is used for the definition of a system capable of detecting specific events, discriminating them from

the backgrounds events. More precisely, the sought events are related to the production of a top/anti-top quark couple. The original synthetic data-set is composed by a series of 11448 background events, and a total of 4213 top events. Each event is characterized by eight features and a label specifying the class of the event.
Starting from the original data sets, a balanced data-set is created to contain an equal number of top and background events, for a total of 8380 patterns.

Simulation strategies and data pre-processing

Several neural network architectures have been tested and their performances evaluated using the following strategies:

- 10-fold cross validation strategy: ten balanced data sets are generated each with 838 patterns (419 background patterns and 419 quark patterns). Ten different training/testing sessions were run, using 9 sets for training and one set for testing.

- 2-fold cross validation strategy: two balanced data sets are generated each with 4190 patterns (2095 background patterns and 2095 quark patterns). Two different training/testing sessions were run, using 1 sets for training and one for testing.

In addition, each generated training set was normalized using the following formula:

$$z = \frac{x - \mu}{\sigma} \tag{1}$$

where z is the new normalized value, x is the original value, μ is the training set mean value and σ is the training set standard deviation.
The corresponding test sets were normalized similarly using the μ and σ values of the corresponding training set.
The overall training and test error is calculated as the average value across all train and test sessions, respectively.

Simulation results

Several simulations were executed to compare the performance of the following neural architectures:

- a traditional MLP with a sigmoidal activation function in both hidden and output layers;

- a sinusoidal MLP with sinusoidal activation function in the hidden layer, and linear activation function in the output layer;

- a EαNet architecture;

Table 1. Neural networks architecture results with the 10-fold strategy.

Neural Architecture	Topology	Training Error (%)	Test Error (%)
Traditional MLP	8-30-2	22.68	23.48
Sinusoidal MLP	8-25-2	22.82	23.27
EαNet	8-20-2	18.61	22.32

Table 2. Neural networks architecture results with the 2-fold strategy.

Neural Architecture	Topology	Training Error (%)	Test Error (%)
Traditional MLP	8-30-2	19.47	24.89
Sinusoidal MLP	8-25-2	20.53	24.15
EαNet	8-20-2	17.76	22.43

In Table 1 and in Table 2 are reported the obtained results for the 10-fold and 2-fold strategy, respectively.

4. Digital Implementation of a feed-forward neural network

The digital MLP design was developed and tested using an algorithmic-like hardware programming language: the Handel-C language. Handel-C allows structure design description, how it is decomposed into sub-designs, and how those sub-designs are interconnected. Secondly, design description is done using a familiar programming language form (Handel-C uses an ANSI C similar syntax with the addition of inherent parallelism). Thirdly, being described using an hardware description language, a digital design can be simulated before being manufactured, so that designers can quickly compare alternatives and test for correctness without the delay and expense of hardware devices. Finally, the output from Handel-C is a file that is used to create the configuration data for FPGAs, allowing digital design implementation on these logic programmable devices.
The architectural design aims to the best compromise between several constraints, such as high modularity of design, high density of neurons on device, high recognition rate and speed. Taking these constraints into account (i) data input acts in a serial way; (ii) data processing acts in parallel among the neurons and serially within each neuron; (iii) second layer processing is pipelined with first layer processing.
The proposed architecture is composed of two layers of neurons and is shown in Figure 2 . The Winners Take All (WTA) circuit selects, among a set of m

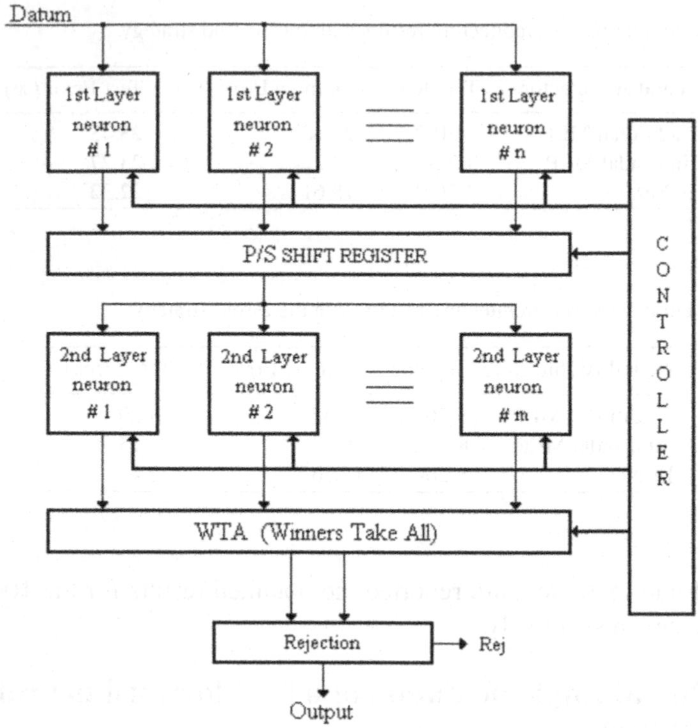

Figure 2. Functional scheme of the whole digital architecture. The n and m values was fixed to 20 and 2, respectively.

numbers of p bits, the two greatest activation level units. The time required to perform the selection does not depend on m and varies linearly with $2 * p$. If the classification is *weak* (i.e. the difference between the winning and the second classified unit is less than a prefixed threshold), a rejection circuit rejects the item to guarantee a better classification rate.
First experimental trials have shown that network performance and area usage on FPGA are optimized when using sinusoidal activation function. Exploiting its periodicity, the activation function is implemented at each neuron with a small look-up table and a small accumulator, with no carry bit.

5. Conclusions

Three neural architectures have been evaluated in this paper for HEP experiments. Architecture generalization capability was tested using a data-set generated from a Montecarlo simulation. As pointed out in several papers, HEP data classification is a very complex tasks since different background events can have very different kinematic properties. Simulation results prove that the

EαNet architecture shows a better behavior with a smaller hidden layer on both 10-fold and 2-fold strategies. Future works will be aimed to implementation and testing of neural architectures on FPGA devices.

References

Beri, S.B., Bhat, P., Kaur, R., and Prosper, H. (2000). Top quark mass measurements using neural networks. *Proc. of VII International Workshop on Advanced Computing and Analysis Techniques in Physics Research.*

Bhat, C. and Bhat, P. (2000). Using ensembles of neural networks in hep analysis. *Proc. of VII International Workshop on Advanced Computing and Analysis Techniques in Physics Research.*

Ciobanu, C., Hughes, R., and Winer, B. (1999). Using neural networks to identify single top. *CDF Note CDF/ANAL/TOP/GROUP/5370.*

Fent, J., Froechtenicht, W., .Gaede, F, H.Getta, D.Goldner, and A.Gruber (1996). The realization of a second level neural network trigger for the h1 experiment at hera. *Proc. of Fifth International Workshop On Software Engineering, Artificial Intelligence, Neural Nets, Genetic Algorithms, Symbolic Algebra, Automatic Calculation.*

Gaglio, S., Pilato, G., Sorbello, F., and Vassallo, G. (2000). Using the hermite regression formula to design a neural architecture with automatic learning of the hidden activation functions. *Lecture Notes in Artificial Intelligence, Springer-Verlag*, 1792:226–237.

Hays, C. and Kotwal, A.V. (2002). Using a neural network for electron identification. *CDF Note CDF/DOC/ELECTRON/CDFR/5810.*

Janauschek, L., Dichtl, J., Eberl, M., Enzenberger, M., and Fent, J. (1999). Artificial neural networks as a second level trigger at the h1 experiment at hera performance analysis and physics results. *Proc. of Sixth International Workshop On Software Engineering, Artificial Intelligence, Neural Nets, Genetic Algorithms, Symbolic Algebra, Automatic Calculation.*

Pilato, G., Sorbello, F., and Vassallo, G. (2001). An innovative way to measure the quality of a neural network without the use of the test set. *International Journal of Artificial Computational Intelligence*, 5:31–36.

Powell, M.J.D. (1968). Restart procedures for the conjugate gradient method. *Mathematical Programming*, 12:241–254.

Sorbello, F., Gioiello, G.A.M., and Vitabile, S. (1999). Handwritten character recognition using a mlp. *L.C. Jain and B. Lazzerini Eds., Knowledge-Based Intelligent Techniques in Character Recognition, CRC Press*, pages 91–119.

Tuttle, J.P., Hays, C., and Kotwal, A.V. (2001). Neural networks for electron and photon identification. *CDF Note CDF/DOC/ELECTRON/CDFR/5791.*

Vitabile, S., Gentile, A., and Sorbello, F. (2002). A neural network based automatic road signs recognizer. *Proc. of IEEE World Congress on Computational Intelligence - International Joint Conference on Neural Networks*, 3:2315–2320.

Vitabile, S., Gentile, A., and Sorbello, F. (2004). Real-time road signs recognition on a simd architecture. *WSEAS Transactions on Circuits and Systems*, 3:664–669.

THE RANDOM NEURAL NETWORK MODEL FOR THE ON-LINE MULTICAST PROBLEM

Giovanni Aiello,[1] Salvatore Gaglio,[1,2] Giuseppe Lo Re,[1,2] Pietro Storniolo,[2] and Alfonso Urso,[2]

[1]*DINFO, Dipartimento di Ingegneria Informatica*
University of Palermo, Italy.
aiello.giovi@virgilio.it, {lore,gaglio}@unipa.it

[2]*ICAR-CNR, Istituto di Calcolo e Reti ad Alte Prestazioni,*
Consiglio Nazionale delle Ricerche, Palermo, Italy.
{storniolo,urso}@pa.icar.cnr.it

Abstract In this paper we propose the adoption of the Random Neural Network Model for the solution of the dynamic version of the Steiner Tree Problem in Networks (SPN). The Random Neural Network (RNN) is adopted as a heuristic capable of improving solutions achieved by previously proposed dynamic algorithms. We adapt the RNN model in order to map the network characteristics during a multicast transmission. The proposed methodology is validated by means of extensive experiments.

Keywords: Dynamic Multicasting, Random Neural Network Model

Introduction

Multimedia networking applications such as distance education, remote collaboration, video-on-demand services and teleconferencing will become wide-spread, relying on the ability of the network to provide multicast services effectively and efficiently. The multicast transmission refers to the capability of sending the same data towards multiple destinations. A distribution tree connecting source and destinations must be selected on the graph, which represents the network topology. Two different criteria can be adopted for the optimization of the multicast tree. The first exploits the concept of the shortest path and it is known as *"shortest path tree"*. The shortest path [Dijkstra, 1959] can be defined as the *"minimum cost path"* that connects two hosts in the network. Another criterion of optimization consists of minimizing the cost of the overall tree. This is equivalent to find the optimal Steiner Tree and it is universally referred as the Steiner Tree Problem in Networks *(SPN)*. This problem

B. Apolloni et al. (eds.), Biological and Artificial Intelligence Environments, 157–164

has been proved to be NP-Complete in its decisional version. However, there exist several heuristics [Winter, 1987] that allow to determine sub-optimal solutions in polynomial time. The literature presents, also, some post-processing techniques [Di Fatta and Lo Re, 1999], which are capable of improving previously determined solutions. A further classification of the multicast problem consists of the following two categories: *static multicast problem*, in which the destination subset is fixed, and the best Steiner tree has to be determined; *dynamic multicast problem*, in which the destination subset can dynamically change because of join or delete requests. In this paper, we deal with the Dynamic Multicast and we try to minimize the spanning tree cost during the overall session. We present the *"Real Time Random Neural Network" (RTRNN)* heuristic, a post-processing technique, which improves multicast trees in the dynamic case. It is based on the Random Neural Network (RNN) [Gelenbe, 1989], which its authors successfully applied to the static case of the SPN [Gelenbe et al., 1997]. RNNs find their applications in many NP-complete problems, such as the Traveling Salesman Problem [Gelenbe et al., 1993], function approximations [Gelenbe et al., 1999], cognitive packet networks [Kokak et al., 2003], etc., and their good capability of reinforcement learning has been demonstrated [Kokak et al., 2003].

In this paper, we show that the Random Neural Network model is applicable to the dynamic multicast problem, and we compare *RTRNN* with three well known dynamic heuristics: *Greedy Heuristic (GH)* [Waxman, 1988], *Weighted Greedy Heuristic (WGH)* [Waxman, 1988], and *Virtual Trunk Dynamic Multicast (VTDM)* [Lin and Lai, 1998]. The remainder of this paper is structured as follows: in the next section we introduce the Random Neural Network model, and in section 2 we describe the application of the RNN to the dynamic multicast problem. Section 3 is devoted to the experimental results.

1. The Random Neural Network Model

In the *Random Neural Network* model neurons are characterized by a state or potential k such that $k_i \geq 0, \forall i \in S$, where S represents the set of neurons that constitute the network. The neuron potential depends on the potentials of other neurons through the exchange of $spikes$. $Spikes$ are unitary amplitude signals that have the effect of increasing or decreasing the potentials of neurons in which they arrive. Spikes can be classified as: *excitatory spikes* represented by $+1$, and *inhibitory spikes* represented by -1. Excitatory spikes increase the potential of the target neurons, activating them, if disabled. Inhibitory spikes decrease the potential of their target neurons; null potential means that neuron is disabled, and an inhibitory spike does not produce any effect. A neuron with positive potential can randomly fire either excitatory or inhibitory spikes. The interfering rate r_i, for sending signals to other neurons or outside the network, is exponentially distributed. When the neuron i fires, the spike will arrive at neuron j with a probability p_{ij}^{+} if the spike is excitatory, and with a probability p_{ij}^{-} if the spike is inhibitory. Furthermore, a neuron i can fire spikes outside the network with a probability d_i. The probability assignment is constrained by the following equation:

$$d_i + \sum_j [p_{ij}^{+} + p_{ij}^{-}] = 1 \tag{1}$$

We define the rate, at which neuron i sends excitatory spikes to the neuron j, as $w_{ij}^{+} = r_i p_{ij}^{+}$, and the rate, at which the neuron i sends inhibitory spikes to the neuron j, as $w_{ij}^{-} = r_i p_{ij}^{-}$. The following two parameters describe the RNN model:

$$p(k,t) = Pr[K(t) = K], \quad q_i(t) = Pr[k_i(t) > 0] \tag{2}$$

where $K(t) = (k_1(t), k_2(t), \ldots, k_n(t))$ represents the vector of the network state, and k is a fixed value of the network potential. Equations 2 represent, respectively, the distribution of probability of the network state and the marginal probability that neuron i is excited at t instant. In our heuristic we adopt the last parameter to select the neuron which is a potential Steiner vertex candidate. The time-dependent behavior of the model is represented by an infinite system of Chapman-Kolmogorov equations for discrete state space and continuous Markovian systems. Let t fixed, the stationary probability distribution associated with the model is the quantity produced in the following equations:

$$p(K) = \lim_{t\to\infty} Prob[K(t) = K], \quad q_i = \lim_{t\to\infty} Pr[k_i(t) > 0] \tag{3}$$

If the neuron i is stable[4], the q_i quantity is given by:

$$q_i = \frac{\lambda_i^{+}}{r_i + \lambda_i^{-}} \tag{4}$$

where λ_i^{+} and λ_i^{-} represent respectively the excitatory spikes and the inhibitory spikes that neuron i receives from others neurons and from outside the network. Their formalization is shown in the following equations:

$$\lambda_i^{+} = \sum_{j=1}^{n} q_j r_j p_{ji}^{+} + \Lambda_i\ , \quad \lambda_i^{-} = \sum_{j=1}^{n} q_j r_j p_{ji}^{-} + \lambda_i \tag{5}$$

where Λ_i is the rate of exogenous excitatory signals that arrive at neuron i, λ_i represents the rate of inhibitory spikes that neuron i receives from outside the network. Both Λ_i and λ_i arrive at neuron i with a rate that satisfies the Poisson distribution with average value $1/r_i$.

2. Random Neural Networks for dynamic SPN

The Steiner Tree Problem can be defined as the one of finding the minimum cost tree, which spans the nodes belonging to a given subset of all the graph nodes. It can be considered as a problem of optimum interconnection, within the scope of an assigned topology. The dynamic version of the multicast problem consists of finding a sequence of optimal trees, after the execution of a sequence of operations representing node insertions or deletions. Operations are coded in a two component-vector $(node, action)$ that represents the history of multicast session. The problem of updating a multicast tree after each insertion or deletion during the same session is known as *"The on-line multicast problem"*. In this paper we assume that each session starts with the source node only. Starting from a sequence representing the multicast session in the form (n, a) where $n \in V$ is a node belonging to the network and $a \in \{0,1\}$ is the action such as insertion or deletion, the On-Line Multicast Problem can be defined as follows:

Given:

1 An indirect, connected graph $G = (V, E, c)$ where E is a set of edges and $c : E \rightarrow R^+$ is a weight function mapping edges in R^+, the "weight" can be defined as the cost of the link,

2 A set of multicast nodes $Z \subseteq V$,

3 A vector of requests $R = \{r_1, r_2, \ldots, r_n\}$ where $r_i \in R$ is a pair (n_i, a_i).

4 A multicast tree $T(V', E')$ where $V' \subseteq V$ and $E' \subseteq E$.

Find: The sequence of trees $T_1, T_2, \ldots, T_m$ such that nodes-member of each tree T_i are obtained from T modified by requests $r_1, r_2, \ldots, r_m$, and their cost (sum of weights of edges) is minimum between all the possible combinations of T_i.

The goal of our algorithm is the efficient updating of a multicast tree after each real time insertion or deletion of other multicast nodes. In order to apply the RNN to dynamic multicast, we associate a physical meaning to the involved variables. A mapping of a computer network on a RNN can be carried out as follows:

1 a neuron represents a node of the real network;

2 the weight of the edge connecting neurons i and j depends on the rate used by neuron i to send excitatory spikes to neuron j and it is calculated, as in [5], according to the following equations:

$$w_{ij}^{+} = \frac{A'}{A_{ij}}\ if\ A_{ij} \neq \infty, \quad w_{ij}^{-} = 0\ if\ A_{ij} = \infty \tag{6}$$

where A' is the network link average cost, A_{ij} is the cost of link connecting node i to node j. If $A_{ij} = \infty$, the link $< i, j >$ does not exist. Therefore, since w_{ij}^{+} is inversely proportional to the cost of the link, it may be viewed as the link capability of transporting multicast packets;

3 parameter w_{ij}^{-} may be simply viewed as a flag indicating the existence in the network of a link connecting node i to node j. Consequently, w_{ij}^{-} is computed as follows:

$$w_{ij}^{-} = 0\ if\ A_{ij} \neq \infty, \quad w_{ij}^{-} = 1\ if\ A_{ij} = \infty \tag{7}$$

4 the k_i potential of the i neuron is constant: this means that the random neural network is analyzed in steady state;

5 the marginal probability distribution q_i may be associated to the goodness of neuron i to be a potential Steiner vertex candidate, and it is calculated according to:

$$q_i = \frac{\sum_j q_j \cdot w_{ij}^{+} + \Lambda_i}{r_i + \sum_j q_j \cdot w_{ij}^{-} + \lambda_i} = \frac{pckts\_entering\_neuron\_i}{pckts\_unreachable\_neuron\_i} \tag{8}$$

From the equation 8 it emerges that with a fixed numerator, the probability that neuron i will be chosen as potential Steiner vertex candidate is inversely proportional to the the number of multicast packets that do not enter the i neuron. The q_i value depends on the current tree topology. If a neuron is a multicast node, it must receive all multicast packets and therefore $q_i = 1$, which, according to [Gelenbe, 1989], means neuron instability.

Let X be the set of Steiner vertices of T, Z the set of multicast nodes, and Y the set of vertices used for the neural network configuration, the algorithm works as follows: initially, it builds a tree using one of the existing heuristics (Greedy Heuristic, Weighted Greedy Heuristic or Virtual Trunk Dynamic Multicast); then, $RTRNN$ is applied and, if during its execution, an insertion request is received by node i, (meaning that node i must receive all multicast packets) q_i is set to 1. Afterwards node i will be inserted into the Y set; $RTRNN$ will take this into account at the next iteration, and it will find a new tree called $T_{RNNtemp}$, which will become the updated tree after the request will be satisfied. In order to calculate $T_{RNNtemp}$, a further temporary tree, T_{NEW} is created, primarily, to connect the i node to the tree, by means of the shortest path between them; then all q_j s.t. $j \notin Y$ are calculated, in order to choose the neuron k corresponding to the largest q_k. Such a node will be appended to Y as *best Steiner vertex candidate.* If during the $RTRNN$ execution a disconnect request is received by the node j, it will be labeled as *"not for Z"*, the tree will be pruned and, if node j is not a leaf node, node j will be labeled as *Steiner vertex.* Afterwards, node j will be deleted from the Y set, and q_j will be set to 0 in order to compute all q_k s.t. $k \notin Y$ and to choose the neuron s with the largest q_s. At the end of requests $RTRNN$ is guaranteed to find a tree better than the one found by the basic heuristic.

3. Experimental results

In order to validate our algorithm, simulations are carried out in which it is supposed that sessions begin just with the source node; afterwards, sessions continue with the insertion or the deletion of the nodes that request either to join or to leave the multicast group. For our simulations, a set of requests equal to the 20% of the number network's nodes is generated. Furthermore, whenever the cost of the tree exceeds a fixed bound, an experimental measure to compare the three heuristics with their improved-version is carried out. In the dynamic case, because we did not know the optimal costs, we compare the costs achieved by the RTRNN with the costs obtained by the Stirring algorithm [Di Fatta and Lo Re, 1999].

The cumulative cost competitiveness graphs for both Steinlib [Voss et al.,] and BRITE networks [Medina et al.,], are shown in figures 1 and 2. The Steinlib graphs represent a well known testbed in the literature, whilst BRITE networks are internet like graphs. The competitiveness, shown in the charts, represents the ratio between the cost produced by the heuristic and the optimal cost. By optimal cost we mean the real best solution for the static case and the best found solution for the dynamic case. Figure 1 shows the relevant improvement produced by $RTRNN$ when applied to GH, WGH and $VTDM$. Both $GH + RTRNN$ and $WGH + RTRNN$ find always a Steiner tree such that $C_{Heur}/C_{Opt} \leq 1.105$.

Figure 2 shows that $RTRNN$ applied to $BRITE$ networks outperforms the behavior obtained on Steinlib graphs; the $GH + RTRNN$ curve converges at 100% for competitiveness values not much greater than 1.08. Likewise, $RTRNN$ is able to improve considerably in real time the sequence of multicast trees found by $VTDM$.

Figure 2 also shows that $RTRNN$ obtains a better improvement when applied to WGH. Finally, although WGH presents a behavior worse than GH on Internet-like networks, RTRNN+WGH has a better behavior than $RTRNN+GH$. $RTRNN$, therefore, improves WGH more than GH, and finds multicast

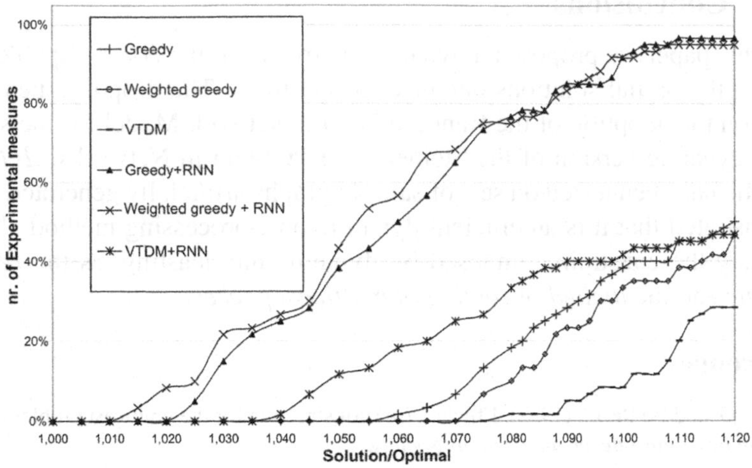

Figure 1. Cumulative Competitiveness for Steinlib Networks.

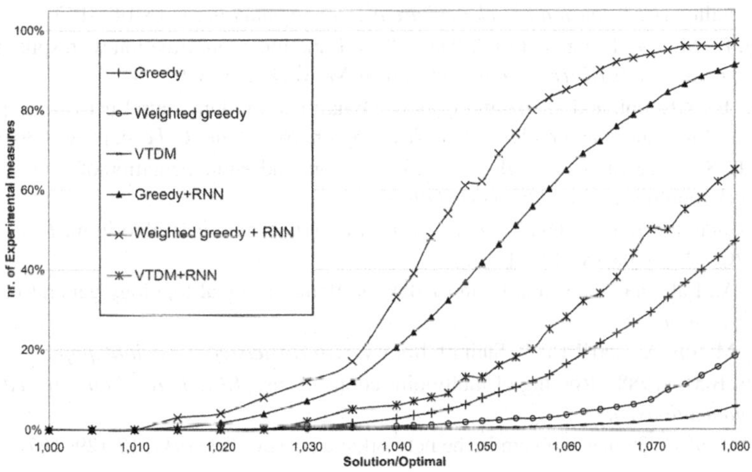

Figure 2. Cumulative Competitiveness for BRITE Networks.

trees with cost distant from the optimum less than 8%. Another $RTRNN$ feature is due to the limited tree topology changes involved after each operation. This constitutes an advantage because a limited re-routing of packets is required. Namely, the tree topology changes, on average, after each operation are limited between 1.5% and 3.5%, satisfying the constraint imposed by dynamic multicasting.

4. Conclusions

In this paper we proposed a dynamic heuristic for the SPN capable of improving the partial solutions obtained in real time. The proposed heuristic is based on the adoption of the Random Neural Network Model for the solution of the dynamic version of the Steiner Tree Problem in Networks. $RTRNN$ heuristic has been tested on sets of sample graphs artificially generated and we demonstrated that it is an efficient dynamic post-processing method able also to satisfy the constraints imposed by dynamic multicasting, as the *real time dynamic* and the *limited re-routing of multicast packets*.

References

Di Fatta, G. and Lo Re, G. (1999). Efficient tree construction for the multicast problem. *Journal of the Brazilian Telecommunications Society,*.

Dijkstra, E.W. (1959). A note on two problems in connections with graphs. *Numerische Mathemat.*, 1:269–271.

Gelenbe, E. (1989). Random neural networks with negative and positive signals and product form solution. *Neural computation*, 7:502–511.

Gelenbe, E., Ghanwani, A., and Srini-Vasonr, V. (1997). Improved neural heuristics for multicast routing. *IEEE Journal on selected areas in communications*, 15:147–155.

Gelenbe, E., Mao, Z. Hong, and Li, Y. Da (1999). Function approximation with spiked random neural networks. *IEEE Transaction on Neural Networks,*, 10:3–9.

Gelenbe, E., V.Koubi, and F.Pekergin (1993). Dynamical random neural network approach to the travelling salesman problem. *Proc. IEEE Symp. Syst. Man, Cybern*, pages 630–635.

Kokak, T., Seeber, J., and Terzioglu, H. (2003). Design and implementation of a random neural network rounting engine. *Illinois GALab*.

Lin, H. Chun and Lai, S.Chuan (1998). Vtdm a dynamic multicast algorithm. *Proc. of IEEE INFOCOM '98*, pages 1426–1432.

Medina, A., Lakhina, A., Malta, I., and J.Bayers. Brite universal topology generator. *www.cs-pub.bu.edu/brite*.

Voss, S., Martin, A., and T.Koch. Steinlib library. *elib.zib.de/steinlib/steinlib.php*.

Waxman, B.M. (1988). Routing of multipoint connections. *IEEE Journal on selected areas in communications*, 6.

Winter, P. (1987). Steiner problem in the networks: a survey. *Networks*, 17:129–167.

ERAF: A R PACKAGE FOR REGRESSION AND FORECASTING

M. Filippone,[1] F. Masulli, [1,2] S. Rovetta[1,3]

[1] *INFM - Istituto Nazionale per la Fisica della Materia*
Via Dodecaneso 33, 16146 Genova, Italy

[2] *Dipartimento di Informatica, Universita' di Pisa*
Via F. Buonarroti 2, 56125 Pisa, Italy

masulli@di.unipi.it

[3] *Dipartimento di Informatica e Scienze dell'Informazione*
Universita' di Genova, Via Dodecaneso 35, 16146 Genova, Italy

Abstract We present a package for R language containing a set of tools for regression using ensembles of learning machines and for time series forecasting. The package contains implementations of Bagging and Adaboost for regression, and algorithms for computing mutual information, autocorrelation and false nearest neighbors.

Keywords: R package, statistical computing, time series, Bagging, Adaboost, Takens-Mane theorem, mutual information, autocorrelation, false nearest neighbors.

Introduction

R [Ihaka and Gentleman, 1996] is a programming language and environment for statistical computing similar to the S language and environment which was developed at Bell Laboratories [Becker, 1984; Venables and Ripley, 2002]. It is an interpreted language, providing a large set of tools optimized for a very wide range of problems. It is based on objects such as vectors, matrices, and more complex structures (data frames, lists). There are many operators acting directly on these objects, which make any computation fast and expressed in a straightforward way. These properties, its GNU license [1] and a generic resemblance to Matlab (which shares with R the presence of matrices and vectors as native objects), have boosted its diffusion in the statistical and machine learning communities.

Among the available tools there are also packages for multilayer perceptrons, for support vector machines, for multivariate optimization. Moreover,

B. Apolloni et al. (eds.), Biological and Artificial Intelligence Environments, 165–173

the language features all standard programming constructs (conditional instructions, loops) and a very handy 2D and 3D graphics drawing capability.

Being an interpreted language, interactive development and use of programs is possible. The peculiar conventions adopted make it a straightforward task, since they allow even very complicated constructs to be expressed compactly. However, there is the drawback of low speed. Although the tools have been optimized, each statement still has to be interpreted. For instance, executing 10^8 trivial cycles in C requires about fifty times less than the corresponding R code. Therefore, it is possible to call external C, C++, or Fortran routines from within an R program. This is useful when parts of the code are computation-intensive and difficult to optimize in R. Moreover, recently a R to C compiler has been released (see `http://hipersoft.cs.rice.edu/rcc/`).

In this paper we present an overview of a ERAF, an R package containing a set of algorithms implementing Ensembles for Regression and for time series Analysis and Forecasting we have implemented [2].

In next section we illustrate some learning machines and some ensemble methods that that can be used in regression tasks. In Sect. 2 we show a set of procedures for time series analysis that permit to transform a forecasting problem in a regression problem.In Sect. 3 we present an experimental test case. Conclusions are in Sect. 4.

1. Ensembles for regression

Base learners and ensembles

In R many learning machines (base learners) are available as components of standard packages, including:

- *Multilayer perceptrons* (MLP) are implemented in R through the function *nnet* of the package *nnet* contributed by Venables and Ripley [Ripley, 1996; Venables and Ripley, 2002]. The following parameters can be set: type of architecture (multilayer or single layer perceptron), number of hidden layer units $nnhl$, decay parameter λ for weight decay, stopping criterion (on cost threshold and/or on maximum number of iterations); initialization values for weights, and activation function for output units.

- *Support vector machines* (SVM) [Cortes and Vapnik, 1995] are implemented in R through the function *svm* of package *e1071*. The implementation is the porting of Chang and Lin code [Chang and Lin, 2001; Chang and Lin, 2002]. The adjustable parameters are: kernel type (linear, polynomial, Gaussian), kernel parameters (γ for Gaussian kernel, p and b_0 for polynomial kernel), regularization parameter C, and ε in Vapnik's loss function.

Due the large number of parameters to be set in both *nnet* and *svm*, we included in ERAF package two meta-learners allowing the user to to evaluate the test set error (root mean square), while scanning the parameters, in order to speeding-up the model selection procedure.

The generalization of a learning machine (or base learner) using a finite data set has been studied in the frameworks of the notions of margin [Vapnik, 1998] and of classical bias-variance decomposition of the error [Geman et al., 1992], that recently have been shown to be equivalent [Domingos, 2000].

Ensemble methods [Valentini and Masulli, 2002] aggregate the output of many base learners and can increase generalization on the same data set, as they can boost margins, reduce variance, and also bias. The overall effectiveness of a learning machine depends on the specific characteristics of the base learners (more details are, e.g., in [Valentini and Dietterich, 2003]).

In ERAF package we implemented the Bagging [Breiman, 1996] and the Adaboost [Freund and Schapire, 1996] algorithms that are two powerful ensemble methods based on data set re-sampling that have been extensively studied in classification task. The implementations we have enclosed in ERAF package are tailored for regression tasks.

Bagging

Bagging (Bootstrap AGGregatING) [Breiman, 1996] makes a bootstrapping on a dataset consisting in creating new data sets by sampling with replacement from the original data, with equal probabilities for each data item. The basic algorithm creates a model for each new data set and then combining the different estimations thus obtained, by an averaging operation. More formally, starting from the original dataset $\mathcal{L} = \{(\mathbf{x}_1, y_1), \cdots, (\mathbf{x}_l, y_l)\}$ we build p new training sets $\mathcal{L}_k$ with $k = 1, \cdots, p$ sampling from $\mathcal{L}$ with replacement. A model $f_k(\mathbf{x}, \mathcal{L}_k)$ is identified from each new dataset, then the predictive model is built as

$$f(\mathbf{x}, \mathcal{L}) = \frac{1}{p} \sum_{i=1}^{p} f_k(\mathbf{x}, \mathcal{L}_k) \tag{1}$$

Adaboost

Adaboost [Freund and Schapire, 1996] stands for ADAptive BOOSTing, meaning that the procedure is adaptive with respect to the level of complexity of the training set. The implemented algorithm for regression follows [Drucker, 1997].

The algorithm starts by assigning a probability $p_i^{(1)} = 1/l$ to be sampled to each of the l data items belonging to the set $\mathcal{L} = \{(\mathbf{x}_1, y_1), \cdots, (\mathbf{x}_l, y_l)\}$. A training set $\mathcal{L}_1$ is generated by sampling with replacement from the original set $l^{(1)}$ examples, and the first learner is trained. We obtain $f^{(1)}$ which gives the output $\hat{y}_i^{(1)}$ for each $\mathbf{x}_i \in \mathcal{L}$. Then we compute the loss $L_i^{(1)}$ selectable among the following:

$$L_i^{(1)} = \frac{|\hat{y}_i^{(1)} - y_i|}{D}; \qquad L_i^{(1)} = \left(\frac{|\hat{y}_i^{(1)} - y_i|}{D}\right)^2; \qquad L_i^{(1)} = 1 - e^{-\frac{|\hat{y}_i^{(1)} - y_i|}{D}} \tag{2}$$

where D is a normalization constant such that $L_i \in [0, 1]$, i.e.,

$$D = \max_i |\hat{y}_i^{(1)} - y_i|. \tag{3}$$

Then we compute $\bar{L}^{(1)} = \sum_{i=1}^{l^{(1)}} L_i^{(1)} p_i^{(1)}$, i.e., the average of the $L_i^{(1)}$ weighted on $p_i^{(1)}$, and $\beta^{(1)} = \frac{\bar{L}^{(1)}}{1-\bar{L}^{(1)}}$, a quantity whose value is inversely related to the quality of learning as measured on $\mathcal{L}$: Now the sampling probabilities are updated as follows:

$$p_i^{(1)} = p_i^{(1)} \left(\beta^{(1)}\right)^{1-L_i^{(1)}} \tag{4}$$

and of course they are normalized to 1. With this procedure we can assign a larger sampling probability to the examples featuring the larger error. It is iterated until a value of T is reached such that $\bar{L}^{(T)}$ is larger than 0.5 or a selected number of iterations is reached.

The ensemble thus obtained yields a output on a given $\mathbf{x}_i$ which is computed as the median of the $\hat{y}_i^{(t)}$ weighted with the corresponding $\beta^{(t)}$. (The median is used to give robustness to the method.) We consider $\hat{y}_i^{(t)}$ and the corresponding $\beta^{(t)}$ of all T machines which took part to the procedure. They are renamed so that $\hat{y}_i^{(1)} < \hat{y}_i^{(2)} < \cdots < \hat{y}_i^{(T)}$, keeping intact the association between a $\hat{y}_i^{(t)}$ and $\beta^{(t)}$. Then $\log \frac{1}{\beta^{(t)}}$ is summed over t until

$$\sum_t \log \frac{1}{\beta^{(t)}} \geq \frac{1}{2} \sum_t \log \frac{1}{\beta^{(t)}} \tag{5}$$

If t^* is the minimum value of t such that (5) holds, the output $\hat{y}_i$ is that made by machine t^*, that is, $\hat{y}_i = \hat{y}_i^{(t^*)}$.

2. Time series analysis and forecasting

From forecasting to regression

The forecasting problem requires modeling an unknown system, which is assumed to generate the observed time series. Given a time series of n elements $(s_1, s_2, \cdots, s_n)$ obtained by sampling an observed variable of the system, the Takens-Mane [Takens, 1981; Mane, 1981] theorem guarantees that its dynamics can be reconstructed in the space of vectors

$$\mathbf{y}_i = (s_i, s_{i+T}, \cdots, s_{i+(d-1)T}) \tag{6}$$

T and d must be selected appropriately for the dynamics to be correctly reconstructed. Therefore we have implemented the mutual information, autocorrelation, and nearest neighbors algorithms[Abarbanel, 1996] as T can be estimated as the the first minimum of mutual information or as the first zero crossing of autocorrelation, and then we can estimate d using, e.g, false nearest neighbors algorithm [Abarbanel, 1996]. ERAF package includes also two local learners for forecasting, as proposed in [Abarbanel, 1996].

Mutual information

The algorithm for computing *mutual information* implements the following formula [Abarbanel, 1996]:

$$I(T) = \sum_{s_i, s_{i+T}} P(s_i, s_{i+T}) \log_2 \left(\frac{P(s_i, s_{i+T})}{P(s_i)P(s_{i+T})} \right) \tag{7}$$

The interval (a, b) is split into in k contiguous subintervals (typically hundreds) $A = (u, v) = \Delta_1 \cup \Delta_2 \cup \Delta_3 \cup \cdots \cup \Delta_k$, with $\Delta_1 = \left(u, u + \frac{v-u}{k}\right)$, and $\Delta_j = \left[u + (j-1)\frac{v-u}{k}, u + j\frac{v-u}{k}\right)$, $j = 2, \cdots, k$.

To obtaining $P(s_i)$ we count how many s_i belong to each subinterval, then divide by N. $P(s_i)$ is therefore an object of type $\{P_i\}_{i=1,k}$. To obtain the joint probability we build a $k \times k$ matrix J. Element $J_{i,j}$ counts how many pairs (s_i, s_{i+T}) are such that $s_i \in \Delta_i$ and $s_{i+T} \in \Delta_j$i (this quantity is then divided by the number of pairs $N - 1$). Therefore mutual information is computed as:

$$I(T) = \sum_{i=1}^{k} \sum_{j=1}^{k} J_{i,j} \log_2 \left(\frac{J_{i,j}}{P_i P_j} \right) \tag{8}$$

where the summation is limited to $P_i P_j \neq 0$.

Autocorrelation

The *autocorrelation* is defined as:

$$C(T) = \sum_i (s_i - \bar{s})(s_{i+T} - \bar{s}) \tag{9}$$

where $\bar{s} = \frac{1}{N} \sum_{i=1}^{N} s_i$ is the average of s [Abarbanel, 1996]. The algorithm is written in C.

False nearest neighbors

The *false nearest neighbors* algorithm [Abarbanel, 1996] allows us to estimate the embedding dimension of dynamical system. After choosing T corresponding to the first minimum of mutual information or to the first zero crossing of autocorrelation, we consider an element $\mathbf{y}(k) = (s_k, \cdots, s_{k+(d-1)T})$ and we search the vector $\mathbf{y}^{NN}(k) = \mathbf{y}(u) = (s_u, \cdots, s_{u+(d-1)T})$ closest to it. To assess whether the vectors $\mathbf{y}(k)$ and nearest neighbor $\mathbf{y}^{NN}(k)$ are close or far in passing from the current space to the space obtained by adding the next coordinate, we check for one of the following two conditions [Abarbanel, 1996]:

$$\frac{|s_{k+dT} - s_{u+dT}|}{\sqrt{\sum_{m=1}^{d} \left(s(k+(m-1)T) - s(u-(m-1)T)\right)^2}} > 15 \tag{10}$$

$$\frac{|s(k+dT) - s(u+dT)|}{\frac{1}{N}\sum_{k=1}^{N}(s(k) - \bar{s})^2} > 2 \tag{11}$$

If one of them is fulfilled, we consider $\mathbf{y}^{NN}(k)$ as a false neighbor of $\mathbf{y}(k)$ We repeat the procedure for all vectors $\mathbf{y}(k)$ and compute the percentage of false neighbors. The computation is made starting from $d = 1$ up to a selected maximum value of d. The algorithm for searching the vector $\mathbf{y}^{NN}(k)$ is written in C and optimized following [Nene and Nayar, 1997] and is quite well performing in terms of speed. Selection of T and data processing are made by a procedure written in R.

3. Case study

In this section we present some results concerning the test of ensemble methods on a time series forecasting problem. In particular we compare their performance with those of base learners.
The time series chosen is the well known Lorenz [Abarbanel, 1996] chaotic series obtained sampling the x variable, solution of this differential equations system:

$$\begin{cases} \dot{x} = \sigma(y - x) & \sigma = 16 \\ \dot{y} = -xz + rx - y & b = 4 \\ \dot{z} = xy - bz & r = 45.92 \end{cases} \tag{12}$$

Using a short time sampling (e.g. $\tau_s = 10^{-2}$) the forecasting problem is easy and all considered learning machines (MLP, SVM and their bagged and boosted versions) obtained similar good generalization results. In this paper we present an experiment where we strongly sub-sampled the series x ($\tau_s = 0.2$) obtaining the series of 1000 values shown in figure 1.

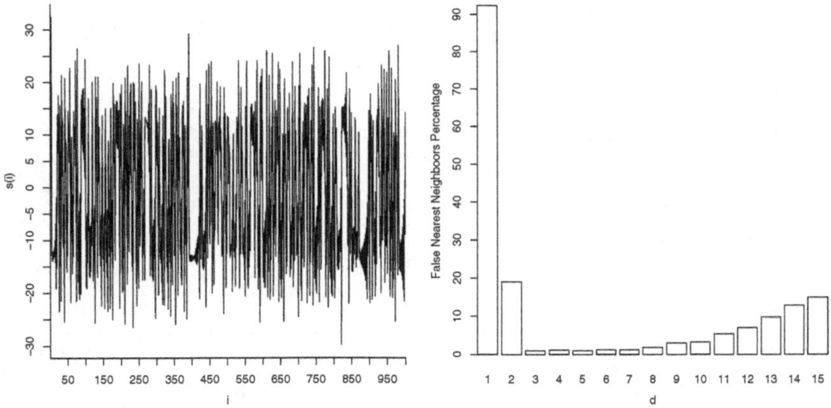

(a) (b)

Figure 1. (a) The Lorenz time series (b) False nearest neighbors vs embedding dimension

	MLP	SVM	Bagging MLP	Bagging SVM	Adaboost MLP	Adaboost SVM
$rmse$	2.13	2.76	2.42	2.89	**2.02**	3.02

Table 1. Results on the Lorenz time series.

The problem was to forecast the last 200 values using the first 800 for training. We used the mutual information minimum to estimate the time lag between two sample to use in the construction of the time-delayed coordinates vectors: we obtained $T = 1$. These vectors are used in the false nearest neighbors algorithm to estimate the embedding dimension: we found $d = 4$.

Using this value of d we trained many MLP and SVM in order to find the best set of parameters that leads to the minimum of the root mean square error ($rmse$) on the test set. All the necessary software is made available by the the EASY package.

Then we built ensemble methods with base learners with the best set of parameters. All the ensembles were made up by 100 base learners using training sets of the same dimension of the original training set. The best set of parameters for this problem were $\gamma = 5$, $C = 5$ and $\varepsilon = 0.005$ for SVM using Gaussian kernel and $nnhl = 36$ and $\lambda = 0.1$ for MLP (see Sect. 1). All the results are shown in table 1. In figure 2 we can see the differences between the regression lines for the best MLP and Adaboost with MLP.

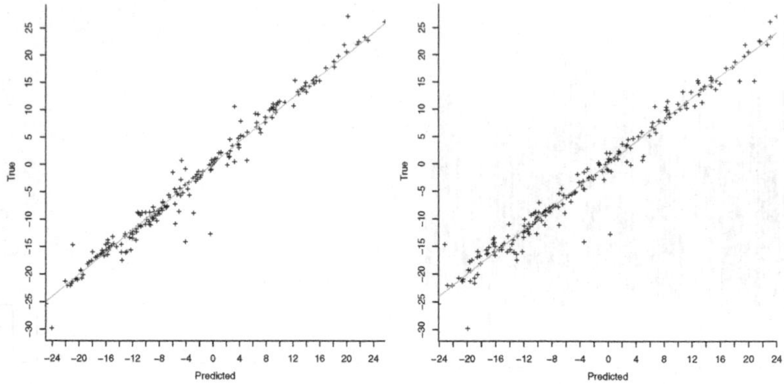

(a) (b)

Figure 2. (a) Regression line for Adaboost with MLP (b) Regression line for MLP

4. Conclusions

The procedures contained in the ERAF package we have described in this paper allow the R programmer to face regression and time series forecasting problems using state of the art methods. In particular, ERAF makes available:

- Bagging and Adaboost meta-learners that can improve the generalization results in regression tasks of base learners, such as multi-layer perceptron and support vector machines, already available in R;
- Tools for calculating mutual information, autocorrelation and false nearest neighbors allowing the user to turn a forecasting problem into a regression problem, on the basis of the embedding theorem and related prescriptions;

We are extending the ERAF package in order to make available local forecasters [Abarbanel, 1996], and the procedures for Singular-Spectrum Analysis [Vautard and Ghil, 1989; Vautard et al., 1992] able to extract trends from the time series.

Acknowledgments

Work funded by the Italian National Institute for the Physics of Matter (INFM), and the Italian Ministry of Education, University and Research (MIUR).

Notes

1. The R language is available at `http://www.r-project.org/` for the most common computer platforms (Windows, Linux, Mac OS).
2. The package is available at `http://mlsc.disi.unige.it/R`.

References

Abarbanel, H.D.I. *Analysis of Observed Chaotic Data.* Springer, New York, 1996.

Becker, R.A. and Chambers, J.M. *Design of the S System for Data Analysis.* Comm. A.C.M., 27:5 pp. 486-495, 1984.

Breiman, L. Bagging predictors. *Machine Learning*, 24:123–140, 1996.

Chang, C.C. and Lin, C.J. *Training ν-support vector classifiers: Theory and algorithms.* Neural Computation, 13(9):2119-2147, 2001.

Chang, C.C. and Lin, C.J. *Training ν-support vector regression: Theory and algorithms.* Neural Computation, 14(8):1959-1977, 2002.

Cortes, C. and Vapnik, V. Support Vector Networks. *Machine Learning*, 20:273–297, 1995.

Domingos, P. A Unified Bias-Variance Decomposition for Zero-One and Squared Loss In Proceedings of the Seventeenth National Conference on Artificial Intelligence, pages 564-569, Austin, TX, AAAI Press, 2000.

Drucker, H. Improving regressors using boosting techniques. In D. H. Fisher, editor, *Proceedings of the Fourteenth International Conference on Machine Learning*, pages 107–115. Morgan Kaufmann, 1997.

Freund, Y. and Schapire, R.E. *Experiments with a New Boosting Algorithm.*. Proceedings of the Thirteenth Conference, ed: L. Saitta, Morgan Kaufmann, pp. 148-156, 1996.

Geman, S., Bienenstock, E. and Doursat, R. *Neural networks and the bias-variance dilemma.*. Neural Computation, 4(1):1-58, 1992.

Ihaka, R. and Gentleman, R. *R: A language for data analysis and graphics.* Journal of Computational and Graphical Statistics, 5(3):299-314, 1996.

Mane, R. On the dimension of the compact invariant sets of certain non-linear maps. In D.A Rand and L. S. Young, editors, *Dynamical Systems and Turbulence, Lecture Notes in Mathematics*, vol. 898 p. 230–242, 1981. Springer-Verlag, Berlin.

Nene, S.A. and Nayar, S.K. *A simple algorithm for nearest neighbor search in high dimensions.* IEEE Transactions on Pattern Analysis and Machine Intelligence, 19:989-1003, 1997.

Ripley, B.D. *Pattern Recognition and Neural Networks.* Cambridge, 1996.

Takens, F. Detecting strange attractors in turbulence. In D.A. Rand and L.-S. Young, editors, *Dynamical Systems and Turbulence, Lecture Notes in Mathematics*, vol. 898, pp. 366–381, 1981. Springer-Verlag, Berlin.

Vautard, R. and Ghil, M. Singular-spectrum analysis in nonlinear dynamics, with applications to paleoclimatic time series. *Physica D*, 35:395–424, 1989.

Vautard, R., You, P., and Ghil, M. Singular-spectrum analysis: A toolkit for short, noisy chaotic signals. *Physica D*, 58:95–126, 1992.

Valentini, G. and Masulli, F. Ensembles of Learning Machines, in M. Marinaro and R. Tagliaferri, editors, Neural Nets WIRN Vietri-02, Series Lecture Notes in Computer Sciences, Springer-Verlag, Heidelberg (Germany), vol. 2486, pp.3-19, 2002

Valentini, G. and Dietterich, T.G. Bias-variance analysis of Support Vector Machines for the development of SVM-based ensemble methods Journal of Machine Learning Research (in press).

Vapnik, V.N. *Statistical Learning Theory* . Wiley, New York, 1998.

Venables, W.N. and Ripley, B.D. *Modern Applied Statistics with S.* Springer, 2002.

NOVEL PHEROMONE UPDATING STRATEGY FOR SPEEDING UP ACO APPLIED TO VRP

Tommaso Loreto
INFOCOM Dept., Facolta' di Ingegneria, Universita' di Roma "La Sapienza"
t.loreto@fastwebnet.it

Giuseppe Martinelli
INFOCOM Dept., Facolta' di Ingegneria, Universita' di Roma "La Sapienza"
martin@infocom.uniroma1.it

Abstract Ant Colony Optimization (ACO) algorithms are based on the imitation of how ants of a colony find the shortest path between the nest and the food. This result is achieved by stigmergetic information, i.e. ants deposit a chemical substance (the pheromone) on the path they follow and their movement is guided by the amount of pheromone.

The imitation of this simple mechanism is the core of any ACO algorithm. In the present contribution we propose a new pheromone updating technique with the aim of speeding up the resulting algorithm for rendering it suited to a real-time implementation.

The ACO algorithms are very dependent on the specific application of interest. In this contribution the Vehicle Routing Problem is considered and the proposed algorithm is compared with 3 classic pheromone updating methods with respect to known benchmarks.

Keywords: Swarm Intelligence, Ant Colony Optimizer, Combinatorial Optimization, Metaheuristic Algorithms, Vehicle Routing Problem

1. Introduction

Stigmergetic information was first introduced in biology to indicate indirect communication mediated by modifications of the environment that can be observed in several social insects with particular evidence in the case of ant colonies. The communication among ants is achieved by means of pheromone trails. A moving ant lays some pheromone on the ground, thus marking the path by a trail of this substance. While an isolated ant moves at random, successive ants can detect the pheromone and decide with high probability

B. Apolloni et al. (eds.), Biological and Artificial Intelligence Environments, 175–182

to follow the marked path, thus reinforcing the trail with its own pheromone. The emerging autocatalytic collective behavior, tempered by pheromone evaporation, is characterized by a positive feedback: [Dorigo et al., 2000; Dorigo, 2001].

The Ant Colony Optimization (ACO) metaheuristic is obtained by imitating the behavior of real ants. The artificial ants introduced for this purpose are simple agents with some further capability with respect to real ants. In particular, they have some memory, they are not completely blind and live in an environment where time is discrete.

The artificial ant colony moves on a graph directly associated with the problem to be solved. The path an ant follows defines a solution of the problem. The choice of a branch of the path is based on a mechanism which uses a suitable probability depending both on the pheromone laid on it and on some specific property of the problem. The mechanism should balance between the exploitation of the experience gathered by the ants of the colony and the exploration of unvisited or relatively unexplored search space regions. This balance is achieved through the management of the pheromone deposit by part of the ants of the colony. Consequently, ACO algorithms are iterative and usually consists of three main steps:

1 Generation of solutions by the ants of the colony according to private and pheromone information;

2 Application of a local tuning to the ant solutions;

3 Update of the pheromone information.

This last step is the more significant and influential. For this reason, the ACO algorithms proposed in the technical literature mainly differ for pheromone management. In the present paper we suggest a simplified method for carrying out this step. Since the convenience of an ACO algorithm strongly depends on the specific performance required to the solution of the problem to be solved, it is necessary to relate the proposed procedure to a specific problem. In the following we will focus our attention on a very important application, the Vehicle Routing Problem (VRP).

The VRP is a well known combinatorial optimization problem, extensively studied in the technical literature. It involves the construction of a set of vehicle tours starting and ending at a single depot and satisfying the demands of a set of customers, where neither vehicle capacities nor maximum tour lengths are violated. The performance of the solution of the VRP is measured by the total tour length L. Therefore, L should be minimized. The VRP belongs to the class of $\mathcal{NP}$-hard problems. Hence no efficient exact solution methods are possible, and the existing solution approaches are of heuristic nature. Recently the focus of research on this problem was on the use of meta-heuristics, such as ACO.

In the technical literature several procedures are proposed for solving the VRP and optimal results concerning benchmarks are available. In the present paper we exploit the pheromone updating with the purpose of obtaining an algorithm with low computational burden yielding results close to the optimal ones. The final goal is to speed up the resulting ACO algorithm for real-time implementation even if that result is obtained at the cost of a slightly reduced absolute accuracy.

2. Classical Pheromone Updating Algorithms and the Novel Proposed Procedure

There are 3 classical techniques for pheromone management:

1 the Rank based Ant System (ASrank): [Bullnheimer et al., 1999];

2 the Max-Min Ant System (MMAS): [Stützle et al., 2000];

3 the Ant Colony System (ACS): [Dorigo, 1997].

They will be shortly described in the following in order to understand the successive proposed procedure.

Rank based Ant System Pheromone is updated following two concepts borrowed from Genetic Algorithms, namely ranking and elitism to deal with the tradeoff between exploration and exploitation. In correspondence to the current iteration, it is necessary to consider the solutions obtained up to it by the ants of the colony. The ants are then ranked on the basis of the quality of their solutions. The elite is constituted by the best E ants. The updating formula for the (ij) branch depends on how it is involved in the paths found by the elitists:

- the branch is included in the path corresponding to the best solution scoring a value of the objective function equal to L_{best}. In this case the pheromone updating is:

$$\tau_{ij} = \rho\tau_{ij} + \frac{E}{L_{\text{best}}} \tag{1}$$

where $(0 < \rho < 1)$ is the trail persistence.

- The branch is included in some of the paths found by the elitists. In this case the pheromone updating is based both on the paths of the set P where it is present and on the value of the objective function L_r scored by the corresponding ant:

$$\tau_{ij} = \rho\tau_{ij} + \sum_{r \in P} \frac{E - r}{L_r} \ . \tag{2}$$

- The branch is not included in the paths found by the elitists:

$$\tau_{ij} = \rho\tau_{ij} \ . \tag{3}$$

Max-Min Ant System In this case only the global best solution found during the execution of the algorithm is reinforced. Namely, the branch (ij) belonging to the corresponding path is updated by (1) with $E = 1$. All other branches are subject to evaporation. Since this procedure may lead to extensive exploitation and insufficient exploration, some simultaneous controls are added. More specifically upper and lower bounds, τ_{up} and τ_{lo} , on the pheromone values are introduced to avoid stagnation caused by large differences between the pheromone values. By tuning the difference between the upper and lower bound the tradeoff between exploration and exploitation can be modelled. Due to the pheromone evaporation some values might decrease below τ_{lo}. In this case its value is increased to τ_{lo}. The initialization of the pheromone is set to a value greater than τ_{up} .This favors exploration in the early iterations of the algorithm as the pheromone only gradually evaporates, and reinforcement of good solution elements has a rather small impact. Over time some pheromone values will tend to the upper bound, while most will tend to the lower bound and the search turns from exploration to exploitation.

Ant Colony System As in the Max-Min Ant System, only the best solution found up to the current iteration is reinforced. However, to avoid extensive exploitation of the best solution, evaporation is also restricted to the elements of this best solution, while all other branches are left unchanged. Moreover, a successive mechanism of evaporation is added in order to force exploration by rendering the branches belonging to the said solution less attractive. Therefore, in the successive iterations the choice of these branches will not be the most attractive option and alternative choices will be made. This evaporation is done as follows:

$$\tau_{ij} = \rho\tau_{ij} + (1 - \rho)\tau_{\text{lo}} \tag{4}$$

where τ_{lo} is the lower pheromone value to be used and (4) guarantees that pheromone values are bounded below by this value as in the case of the Max-Min Ant System.

Proposed Pheromone Updating Algorithm

The proposed method is a modification of ACS, taken into consideration for its simple approach. ACS is potentially suited to obtain the speeding up of the desired ACO algorithm. Observing the evolution of the ACS best solution over time, we remark that two such successive solutions share several branches of the associated paths.

Such property is not completely exploited in ACS, since the enhancement of the pheromone level is carried out only for the branches belonging to the current best solution path. Our proposed method, instead, fully exploits the said property by enhancing the pheromone level also on the branches of paths "close" to that best solution.

Moreover, in order to improve the balance between exploitation and exploration, the pheromone is decreased on those branches belonging to solutions distant from the best found one. This operation is equivalent to a selective further pheromone evaporation. The proposed algorithm is therefore as follows, with reference to the k-th ant of the colony:

if $L^k < (1 + \Theta)L_{\text{best}}$ then

$$\tau_{pq} = \alpha\tau_{pq} + \frac{(1 - \alpha)}{L^k - L_{\text{best}}}, \quad \forall\,(pq) \in L^k \tag{5}$$

else, if $L^k \gg L_{\text{best}}$

$$\tau_{pq} = \beta\tau_{pq}, \quad \forall\,(pq) \in L^k \tag{6}$$

where $(0 < \alpha, \beta < 1)$ and L^k is the cost of the solution found by the k-th ant; the update in (5) is performed if $L^k \neq L_{\text{best}}$ and $L^k \neq L^{k-1}$. The update in (6) represents the above said further evaporation applied to the branches belonging to very high cost solutions.

Since Θ may be viewed as a threshold on the solution's cost, the modified algorithm will be denoted in the following as Thresholded Ant Colony System (t-ACS). The resulting algorithm is, in fact, a modified version of ACS.

3. Simulation Results

In this section we compare the performance of the proposed algorithm against the 3 other versions described in the preceding section. All the algorithms were implemented in Matlab 6.5 and were tested on a set of 5 classic VRP benchmarks ([Christofides et al., 1979]), ranging from 50 to 200 cities. For each problem were executed 5 runs in constant time (max 720 seconds each). The 5-trial mean results for each problem are then averaged to provide a single-valued performance index. The common parameters' values were kept the same during each run. Simulations were executed on a Pentium IV 2.4 GHz 1Gb RAM Windows 2000 PC.

Table 1. Performance comparison of 4 ACO variants for the VRP

	ASrank	*MMAS*	*ACS*	*t-ACS*
$L\%$	90.01	88.36	89.46	**91.95**
$\sigma_{L\%}$	0.94	1.31	1.24	0.80
$\underline{T}$ (sec)	541.46	639.34	656.49	**536.44**
mean.iter	32.52	73.52	12.92	8.88

Table 1 shows simulation results in terms of absolute accuracy obtained by each algorithm in relation to the mean optimal solutions L_k^*, $k = 1 \ldots 5$ reported in the technical literature relatively to the 5 considered benchmarks. Namely, $L\%$ is obtained by averaging on the said benchmarks the mean best solutions obtained over 5 trials for each algorithm, as follows:

$$L\% = 100\frac{\underline{L}}{\underline{L}^{(\mathrm{alg})}}\,; \quad \underline{L}^{(\mathrm{alg})} = \frac{1}{25}\sum_{k=1}^{5}\sum_{i=1}^{5} L_{ik}^{(\mathrm{alg})}\,; \quad \underline{L} = \sum_{k=1}^{5} L_k^* \tag{7}$$

where $L_{ik}^{(\mathrm{alg})}$ is the tour length obtained by each algorithm (ASrank, MMAS, ACS and t-ACS) for each trial i in each benchmark k.

$\sigma_{L\%}$ is the standard deviation of $L\%$ over the set of benchmarks taken into account.

In the same table there are also shown the mean CPU time $\underline{T}$ and the mean number of colony iterations (mean.iter) needed to achieve the best solution.

Table 2. Performance of 3 ACO variants in relation to t-ACS

	ASrank	*MMAS*	*ACS*
$L\%_{\mathrm{RPD}}$	2.11 %	3.90 %	2.70 %
$\underline{T}_{\mathrm{RPD}}$	+0.94 %	+19.18 %	+22.38 %

Table 2 shows mean Relative Percentage Difference (RPD) of the best solution found and mean RPD of the CPU times (for each algorithm j) in relation to t-ACS' performance, i.e.:

$$L\%_{\mathrm{RPD}} = 100\frac{L\%_{(\mathrm{t-ACS})} - L\%_{(j)}}{L\%_{(\mathrm{t-ACS})}}, \quad \underline{T}_{\mathrm{RPD}} = 100\frac{\underline{T}_{(j)} - \underline{T}_{(\mathrm{t-ACS})}}{\underline{T}_{(\mathrm{t-ACS})}}. \tag{8}$$

The two above tables evidence the optimal performance of the proposed algorithm in the given running time (720 sec) with respect to ACS and MMAS. We note that the imposed convergence time limitation penalizes MMAS for its slow converging behavior, also if it is potentially superior to the other algorithms in terms of final accuracy.

Our method also outperforms ASrank in terms of CPU time required for attaining the best solution. The gain amounts to about 1% due to a large reduction in the mean number of iterations.

4. Conclusions

In the present contribution we investigated the problem of speeding up ACO algorithms by modifying the pheromone updating strategy. The performance of the proposed method is analyzed with respect to the important VRP application.

The results obtained so far are encouraging, although they are very preliminary. In particular, the consideration of large problem instances is necessary in order to evaluate the convenience of our approach, also in comparison with different approaches to speeding-up ACO algorithms based on parallel implementation as in [Stützle, 1998].

References

Bullnheimer, B., Hartl, R.F., Strauss, C.: A new rank based version of the ant system: a computational study. Central European Journal of Operations Research (1999) 25–38

Christofides, N., Mingozzi, A., Toth, P.: The Vehicle Routing Problem. In et al., N.C., ed.: Combinatorial Optimization. Wiley, Chichester (1979)

Dorigo, M., Gambardella, L.M.: Ant Colony System: A cooperative learning approach to the traveling salesman problem. IEEE Transactions on Evolutionary Computation **1** (1997) 53–66

Dorigo, M., Bonabeau, E., Theraulaz, G.: Ant algorithm and stigmergy. Future Generation Computer Systems (2000) 851–871

Dorigo, M., Stützle, T.: The ant colony optimization metaheuristic: algorithms, applications and advances. In Glover, F., Kochenberger, G., eds.: Metaheuristic Handbook, International Series in Operations Research and Management Science. Kluwer (2001) 1–42

Stützle, T.: Parallelization strategies for ant colony optimization. In A. E. Eiben et al. eds.: PPSN-V, Springer-Verlag (1998) 722–731

Stützle, T., Hoos, H.H.: MAX-MIN Ant System. Journal of Future Generation Computer Systems **16** (2000) 889–914

INDUCING COMMUNICATION PROTOCOLS FROM CONVERSATIONS IN A MULTI AGENT SYSTEM

N. Nailah Binti Abdullah, M. Liquire and S.A. Cerri
Lirmm-University Montpellier II, 161 Rue Ada, Montpellier Cedex 5, France

Abstract This paper demonstrates some issues in agent interaction on the Web, which is the center point of supporting the needs of fully-realized learning GRID in the future. Of particular importance is the conversation support., with its core element, communication protocols. We propose to construct communication protocols through learning of performatives of ACL messages based on the FIPA-ACL messages. The work involves two steps: 1) converting real conversations into a markup agent communication language and then 2) inducing communication protocols based on these set of converted conversations.

Keywords: Agent communication languages, multi agent system, evolutionary computation, machine learning, GRID

1. Introduction

Real World Scenario. We unfold an important domain. [Clancey, 2003] presented a scenario of research collaborators, scientist who engage in a joint project. The author studies the collaboration between scientist at Haughton Crater in the High Canadian Artic. They have A working with B on Devon Island, where these people bring additional research capabilities to an effort. Each may be specialized in using particular instrument, or doing a particular kind of analysis. Joint research is defined as collaborators negotiating goals-such as (i.e. who will do what, how capabilities and efforts will leverage off of one another). They enter into normally an informal contract, or may write a research proposal to define roles and responsibilities. During this work, collaborators sustain other commitments and participation. Collaborating scientists must negotiate because it is assumed that they retain their individual interests and their contributions will serve multiple, personal purposes. Because of the interests and intelligent capabilities of professional participants, successful collaboration requires negotiation of objectives, methods, roles and schedules [Clancey, 2003]. Handling thousands of large jobs for a big complex like NASA or SDSC computer centers led the managers to create control software and a network to connect scientists to a remote system leading to the GRID.

B. Apolloni et al. (eds.), Biological and Artificial Intelligence Environments, 183–189

GRID computing refers to computing in a distributed networked environment where computing and data resources are located throughout a network [Jiang and Cybenko, 2004]. Certain services must be identified during the course of collaboration to fulfill the needs of the collaborators and in turn maximizing what the GRID can provide [Jiang and Cybenko, 2004]. Knowing exactly what to provide to the collaborators as services is not a simple task, as computer users themselves do not potentially know what sort of services the computer systems can provide. One suggestion is to learn dynamically the sort of services that the learning GRID may provide [Cerri et al., 2004]. This can be initially achieved through tracking the conversational process [Clancey, 2003]; among the collaborators and/or among the communicating agents.

A successful GRID is an incorporation of an Multi-Agent Systems (MAS) which organizes the collaboration between the participants. An MAS can support distributed collaborative problem solving that is required by the GRID by agent collections that dynamically organize themselves having diversified capabilities and needs. Thus, enabling scientists to generate, analyze, share and discuss their insights, experiments and results in an effective manner on the GRID.

During the course of collaboration, interaction emerges and challenges of specifying and implementing agent communication protocols emerges as well [Paurobally and Cunningham, 2002]. The communication protocol aspects between the artificial agents↔artificial agents and human↔artificial agents needs to be defined to give a guideline on *how agents should communicate with each other* and *to accommodate the kinds of exceptions* that arise in MAS.

Our proposed work focuses on two main aspect: 1) *learning agents' conversations* and 2) *construction of communication protocols inductively.*

2. Agents conversations in a society with social protocols

Agent programs are designed to autonomously collaborate with each other in order to satisfy both their internal goals and the shared external demands generated by virtue of their participation in agent societies [Draa and Dignum, 2002]. The balance between collaboration and fulfilling it's own goals is made by each agent individually and depending on the situation. Due to this autonomy of the agents the collaboration needs a sophisticated system of agent communication. An assumption is made that an Agent Communication Language (ACL) can best handle the issues of communication between agents.

As part of its program code, every agent must implement tractable decision procedures that *allow the agent to be able to select and produce ACL messages* that are appropriate to its intentions [Draa and Dignum, 2002]. By engaging in pre-planned or stereotypical conversations, much of the search space of

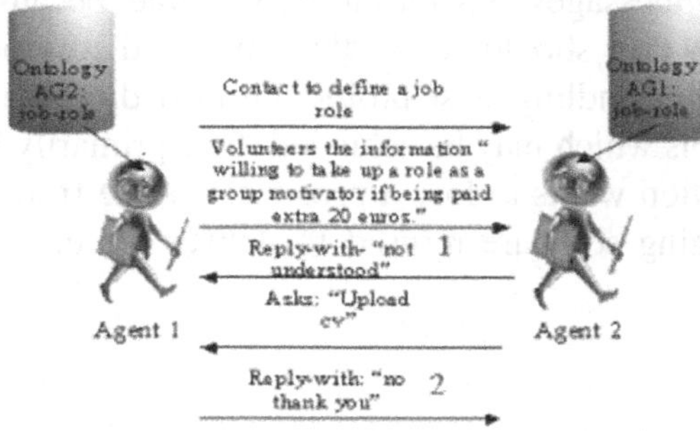

Figure 1. Web services for a collaboration between work groups.

possible agent responses can be eliminated, while still being consistent with the ACL semantics.

When agents join in one or more roles in an environment, they acquire the commitments that go with their individual and social roles. The commitments of a role are restrictions on how agents playing that role must act and, in particular, communicate. *Such requirements requires communication protocols to ensure a non-dysfunctional system.* Current initiative to construct protocols are normally being predefined. It is very unlikely, that all protocols and their exceptions can be predefined without a formal definition and a centralized language when concerning a collaborative environment.

Agents communicating with each other on a certain task

MAS Scenario. Agent1 contacts Agent2 about defining job roles in a research group. For protocol, they agree to use a modified Agent Communication Language, in which each message contains one of a half-dozen standard performatives to identify the intent of message, and message contents follow a standard define-your- role ontology. The client requested something which was not defined in the standard-performatives and thus conversation during this particular context has terminate as if nothing took place and was replied with a performative "not- understood". Situation has been modified from [Hanson et al., 2002]. Readers please refer to Figure 1. One of the messages would have probably been:

(volunteers[1] :sender AG1; :receiver AG2 :content (role (AG1, group- motivator) ← meeting-group (x) = = true))

The performative volunteers does not exactly fit the standard performatives such as inform, request and propose as defined in the FIPA-ACL [Abdullah et al., 2004].

This unexpected messages may turn to be valuable, because they may contain clues as to how they should be handled. We need a proper assignment of function. One way in handling these problem is providing adaptability in communication protocols which may be achieved if we primarily learn the conversations. No institution wants to lose a prospect service from their employees because its messaging software refused to deliver the employees's idiosyncratic offer.

Sample Data

We use real dialogues between people chatting online and in shops. Refer to [Abdullah et al., 2004] for the complete sample data. Real chat conversations were converted using equational fragment of first order logics (contains function symbols,predicates and equality) to convert into a markup FIPA-ACL. The conversion steps can be found in [Abdullah et al., 2004]. We will use these sample data as some of the input to the learning algorithm for inducing protocols.

Sample Chat 1: Ordering a pizza through the phone

1. Lorenzo: " Hi there. How can I help you?"
ask (L, J, want (J, anything))
(request-whenever
:sender L
:receiver J
:content (give (J, anything))
:reply-with re2)

2. John : "Well, do you deliver? "
ask (J, L, deliver (item))
(request
:sender J
:receiver L
:content (deliver (item))
:in-reply-to re2)

Communication protocols

Step Number	Agent Performing Action	Action	Resulting Negotiation State
			-negotiating
1	Agent Lorenzo from Lorenzo's pizza	Initial-offer medium pizza, two toppings, 7.00 euros, free delivery	Offered (lorenzo) medium pizza, two toppings, 7.00 euros, free delivery
2	Agent John for client John	John.agree medium pizza, two toppings, 7.00 euros, free delivery	Agreed (john) Agreement : Lorenzo delivers a medium pizza, two toppings for 7.00 euros to John.

Scenario 2.3. John buying a pizza from Lorenzo's Pizzeria.

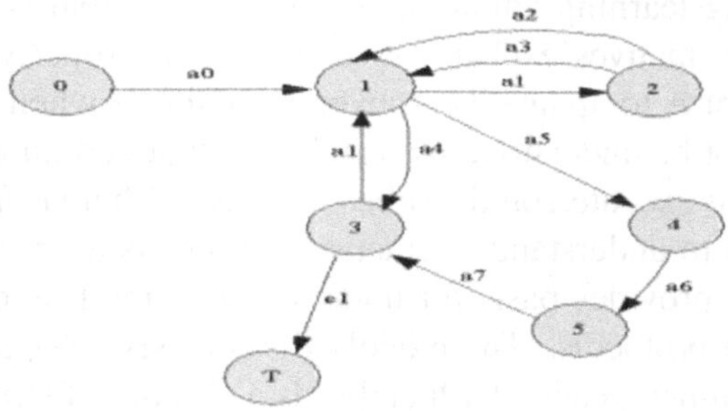

Figure 2. A markup model of a finite state automaton for the demonstration of communication protocol for scenario in Scenario 2.3.

Refer to Figure 2. This is a markup model of a possible finite state automaton used for inducing communication protocols [Abdullah et al., 2004]. This model is not complete, we have to take into account if Agent John cancels the order when the pizza did not arrive in 45 minutes or change the type of toppings he had ordered. There are probably many other possible events that may occur even in a simple example such as buying a pizza and many possible modifications to be made to Figure 2. So many possible ways to handle situations and exceptions.

3. Requirements of an agent communication protocols

Protocols generally require: 1) precise format for valid messages (a syntax); 2) procedure rules for data exchange (grammar); and 3) vocabulary of valid messages that can be exchanged, with their meaning (semantics) [Holzman, 1991]. The grammar of the protocol must be logically consistent and complete; under all possible circumstances the rules should be prescribe in terms what is allowed and what is forbidden in order to maximize the best performance in collaboration acts. Important needs of an agent communication protocols; which are in our opinion are: 1) Consistent 2) Interactive; 3) Adaptive; 4) Capable of solving state of conflicts between protocols (i.e. shifting and firing protocols) and at the same time; 6) Explanatory. Please refer to [Abdullah et al., 2004] for comparions of the current state of the art of communication protocols.

4. The proposed learning model

We consider these properties for the learning model; 1) feedback properties (i.e. neural networks); 2) adaptiveness and merging (i.e. genetic algorithms) and 3) representation language (i.e. galois lattice). The set of inputs to the learning algorithm will be the set of performative exchanges. During the first stage of simulating learning among these agents, the goal is to study the interactions of performatives exchanges. A feedback property in the learning model allows agent A to update its' conversational rule when some performatives sent could not be understood by agent B or that certain action that agent A wants agent B to execute could not be executed. Whereas adaptiveness and merging is crucial to understand interactions of agents at the population level (i.e. domain) and provides basis for understanding the role of performatives in communication protocols. The model will consists a population of agents in a virtual environment, each of which holds a number of structure that allow them to generate sentences (i.e. performatives) as well as analyze other agents' performatives.

The set of output of these agents should be a set of possible communication protocols. The environment itself would need constraints, so that the communication will terminate if it does not converge or when value of communication decreases (i.e. negative).

5. Conclusions

We begin our study by analyzing real conversations on the Web. We suggest that conversation support is vital in any interactive environment that employs different artificial agents and each interacting to fulfill their own goals. In particular, we discuss issues that normally arises during interaction between a service and a client agent. Although, some communication protocols have been established for these purpose, none however focuses in improving the conversations itself among these agents.Communication protocols are generally to ensure that the agents abides to a certain "rule" during communication, however little attention is given to unexpected messages. As a consequence, the core issue of finding out why certain malfunction interaction goes unstudied. We have suggested to use an evolutionary computational method as well as machine learning technique that initially learns the conversational examples of interacting agents through different steps of generations. Experimentation will be done in the near future once the tools are made available. Later, we shall hope that these findings provide us as a mean to construct communication protocols inductively.

References

Abdullah, N.N., Cerri, S.A., and M., Liquiere (2004). Grid services as learning agents: Steps towards induction of communication protocols. *Proceedings of the Workshop of GRID Learning Services ITS 2004*. To Appear.

Cerri, S.A., M., Eisenstadt, and C., Jonquet (2004). Dynamics learning agents and enhanced presence on the grid. *3-rd International LeGE-WG Workshop: Grid Infrastructure to support future technology enhanced Learning*. Berlin.

Clancey, W.J. (2003). Agent interaction with human systems in complex environments: Requirements for automating the function of capcom in apollo 17. *AAAI Spring Symposium on Human Interaction with Autonomous Systems in Complex Environments.* Stanford.

Draa, B.C. and Dignum, F. (2002). Computational intelligence. *Trends in Agent Communication Language*, 5. Blackwerll Publisher.

Hanson, J.E., P., Nandi, and Levine, D.W. (2002). Conversation-enabled web services for agents and e-business. *Proceedings of the International Conference on Internet Computing (IC-02)*, pages 791–796. CSREA Press.

Holzman, G.J. (1991). *Design and Validation of Computer Protocols.* Prentice-Hall.

Jiang, G. and Cybenko, G. (2004). Functional validation in grid computing. *Autonomous Agents and Multi-Agent Systems*, 8:119–130. Kluwer Academic Publishers.

Paurobally, S. and Cunningham, J. (2002). *Achieving Common Interaction Protocols in Open Agents Environments.* AAMAS, Melbourne, Australia.

WORDNET AND SEMIDISCRETE DECOMPOSITION FOR SUB-SYMBOLIC REPRESENTATION OF WORDS

Giovanni Pilato[1], Giorgio Vassallo[2], and Salvatore Gaglio[1,2]

[1] *ICAR-CNR, Istituto di Calcolo e Reti ad Alte Prestazioni Consiglio Nazionale delle Ricerche, Palermo, Italy.*
pilato@pa.icar.cnr.it

[2] *DINFO, Dipartimento di Ingegneria Informatica University of Palermo, Italy.*
{gvassallo, gaglio} @unipa.it

Abstract A methodology for sub-symbolic semantic encoding of words is presented. The methodology uses the standard, semantically highly-structured WordNet lexical database and the SemiDiscrete matrix Decomposition to obtain a vector representation with low memory requirements in a semantic *n*-space. The application of the proposed algorithm over all the WordNet words would lead to a useful tool for the sub-symbolic processing of texts.

Keywords: SemiDiscrete Decomposition, Sub-symbolic encoding of words, Statistical Natural Language Processing

Introduction

The sub-symbolic approach to natural language processing has gained considerable attention over the last years [Bellegarda, 2000; Hofmann, 2000; Honkela et al., 1995; Siivola, 2000; Siolas and d'Alche Buc, 2000; Yang and Lee, 2000]. The simplest method to associate uncorrelated codes to words is to assign a unit vector for each token. However this method is not manageable when a large number of words has to be considered, therefore Honkela et al. [Honkela et al., 1995] used a SOM Network for creating word category maps describing relations of words based on their contexts. In more recent years a framework has been developed, called Latent Semantic Analysis (LSA)[Landauer et al., 1998]: according to this technique, text data is represented as a words-by-documents co-occurrence matrix, then the SVD decomposition is used to generate a semantic space where words and documents can be mapped. Another framework, similar to LSA, for developing high dimensional vector representations of words based on a co-occurrence analysis of large samples

B. Apolloni et al. (eds.), Biological and Artificial Intelligence Environments, 191–198

of written texts, is the Hyperspace Analogue to Language [Burgess and Lund, 2000] method, while a different methodology, called *Random Indexing* has been developed by Sahlgren [Sahlgren et al., 2002] for constructing context vectors representing the distributional profiles of words. Other approaches can be found in [Siolas and d'Alche Buc, 2000; Widdows et al., 2002; Yang and Lee, 2000].

All the aforementioned techniques extract and represent the meaning of words by statistical computations applied to a large corpus of raw texts; however, in various applications of the human language technology, it is commonly used WordNet[Miller et al., 1990], a lexical database which represents the largest publicly available lexical resource where lexical information is organized in terms of word meanings in a semantic net.

In this paper it is presented a methodology for a "standard" sub-symbolic semantic encoding of words. It exploits both the well-founded, standard, structure of WordNet[Miller et al., 1990] instead of an arbitrary text corpus, and the LSA paradigm to generate a semantic space where each WordNet word can be represented as a vector. The idea is an evolution of what presented in [Vassallo et al., 2003]: it exploits the LSA paradigm to generate a semantic space, in which all WordNet words can be mapped. The proposed technique differs from other similar works cited above because *a)* the Tanimoto measure is used to calculate the meaning similarity between words; *b)* the LSA paradigm is applied to a standard lexical database (WordNet) instead of a free text corpus; *c)* because WordNet is very large, the SemiDiscrete Decomposition technique (SDD) [Kolda and O'Leary., 2000] has been chosen for its low memory requirements, instead of the classical SVD matrix decomposition used in LSA. For the same reason, all words have been grouped according to the WordNet lexicographers' files classification criteria: these groups have been called "*lexical sets*". As a consequence the vector representing a word is composed of two parts, called "*lexical part*" and "*semantic part*". While the lexical part is built in a prearranged way, the semantic part instead is calculated using the information yielded by the WordNet lexical database [Miller et al., 1990] and the Semi Discrete Matrix Decomposition algorithm [Kolda and O'Leary., 2000]. Preliminary experimental results, obtained processing the "*noun.motive*" WordNet lexical set are also reported: the harmonic mean of precision and recall [Sebastiani, 2002] yielded is an interesting 0.82.

1. Theoretical Background

WordNet

WordNet is a lexical database that organizes lexical information in terms of word meanings in a semantic net [Miller et al., 1990]. Nouns, verbs, adjectives and adverbs are settled into synonymous sets, which are further arranged into a

set of 45 "*lexicographers' files*" by syntactic category and other organizational criteria.
The term "*word*" is generally used to relate both to the orthographic expression and its associated meaning. In WordNet the term "*word form*" is used for referring to the physical utterance or inscription and "*word meaning*" for referring to the associated lexicalised concept. In WordNet, a word meaning is represented by listing the word forms that can be used to express it: this set of synonyms is called "*synset*". A short gloss is usually connected to a synset to specify the associated concept. In order to discern the different meanings of a word form, WordNet associates an integer, called "*sense number*", to each word form [Miller et al., 1990]. In this paper, for simplicity, the term "*word*" indicates the word form associated with its sense number. Therefore, one word form with different sense numbers represents different "*words*".

Latent Semantic Analysis and Semidiscrete Matrix Decomposition

Latent Semantic Analysis (LSA) [Landauer et al., 1998] is a paradigm to extract and represent the meaning of words by statistical computations applied to a large corpus of texts. LSA is based on the *vector space method*: a text collection is represented as a matrix $\vec{A}$ where rows are associated to words, while columns are associated to documents or other contexts. The content of the (i,j)-th cell of $\vec{A}$ is a function of the i-th word frequency in the j-th text; then the matrix $\vec{A}$ is replaced with a low-rank approximation generated by the truncated singular-value decomposition (SVD) technique [Landauer et al., 1998].
Kolda et al. proposed to use another decomposition technique, called SemiDiscrete Decomposition (SDD) [Kolda and O'Leary., 2000] which approximates the matrix $\vec{A}$ as a weighted sum of external products formed by vectors with entries constrained to be in the set $S = \{-1; 0; 1\}$. The SDD decomposes an $m \times n$ matrix $\vec{A}$ as $\vec{A} \approx \vec{X}\vec{D}\vec{Z}^T$, where each column of $\vec{X}$ is an m-vector with entries from the set $S = \{-1; 0; 1\}$, each row of $\vec{Z}$ is a n-vector with entries from the set S, while $\vec{D}$ is a diagonal matrix with positive scalar elements. The SDD-based LSA works as well as the SVD-based LSA, requiring approximately less than one twentieth of the storage [Kolda and O'Leary., 2000].

2. The Proposed Solution

The aim of the work is to encode each word of the well founded and structured WordNet lexical database as a sequence of n numbers, representing a vector in a n-space, so that semantically near words will be also close points in this n-dimensional space that will therefore constitute a semantic space.
Since words composing a synset represent the same meaning, they will be encoded as the same n-vector, which is called here "*synset vector*". Then the goal

turns to how to encode all the single synsets of WordNet.
Because WordNet is a huge semantic net, we have decided to build the synset vector as composed of two parts: the first one is called "*lexical part*" and indicates the lexical information, while the second one, called "*semantic part*", indicates the semantic information. The lexical part is constituted by n_1 elements, while the semantic part by n_2 components. Then a synset will be represented as a point in a space of $n = n_1 + n_2$ dimensionality. The whole process is illustrated in figure 1 and it will be explained in the following paragraphs.

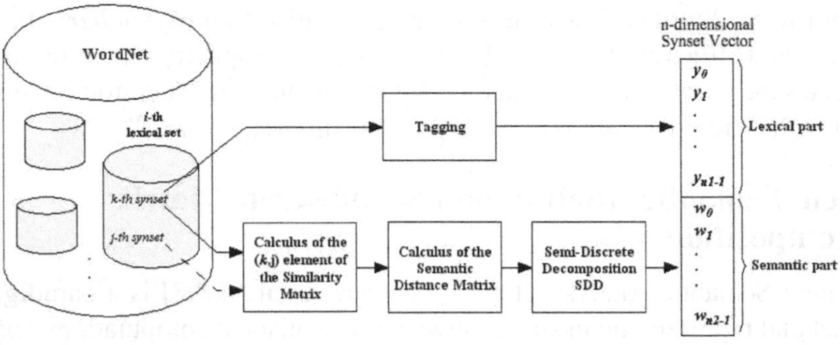

Figure 1. Procedure of encoding the *k*-th synset of the *i*-th lexical set

The "Lexical" Part

All the synsets contained in WordNet have been grouped according to the classification criteria adopted by lexicographers who concurred to the creation of WordNet. Accordingly, we call the resultant groups of synsets "*lexical sets*". The dimension n_1 of the lexical part is 45, corresponding to the number of lexical sets; therefore, if a synset belongs to the *i*-th lexical set, the corresponding lexical part will be tagged by a 1 in the *i*-th position and by 0 in the rest of the lexical part.

The "Semantic" Part

To build the semantic part of a synset vector, it has been introduced a set of word forms, called "*descriptive set*", which goal is to describe the meaning of a synset. Descriptive sets play a key role in the whole process. The descriptive set of a synset is constructed by using the information in the WordNet semantic net, i.e.

- all the word forms of the synset itself;
- the word forms of the syntactic category of nouns and adjectives in the gloss of the synset (example sentences are not considered);

- the word forms of the direct hypernym synset.

Because several uninflected words can be found in the gloss, each noun and adjective of the gloss has been transformed in its base form using the JWNL (Java WordNet Library) morphological processor [Didion, 2002].
In order to calculate the semantic part, we introduce:*a)* a semantic similarity measure between sets to calculate the similarity matrix; *b)* a distance measure to transform the similarity matrix into a distance matrix; *c)* a matrix decomposition algorithm to recover the latent semantic information from the distance matrix. In the following, the descriptive set of the *k*-th synset belonging to the *i*-th lexical set will be indicated by $S_i(k)$, the number of synsets belonging to the *i*-th lexical set will be indicated by M_i, whereas the n_2-vector corresponding to the semantic part of the *k*-th synset of the *i*-th lexical set will be indicated by $w^i(k)$.

Calculus of the Semantic Similarity and Distance Matrix. To express the semantic similarity between synsets (represented by descriptive sets), it has been used the Tanimoto measure [Sloan Jr and Tanimoto, 1979] which is a measure of similarity between sets. According to this measurement, the semantic similarity between the synsets *k* and *j* belonging to the *i*-th lexical set is defined as:

$$sim_i(k,j) \equiv \frac{|S_i(k) \cap S_i(j)|}{|S_i(k) \cup S_i(j)|} \tag{1}$$

It is usual that descriptive sets of synsets with different meaning occasionally present some word forms in common. This leads to a value of $sim_i(k,j)$ greater than zero; for this reason the similarity has been filtered so that:

$$sim_i^{\vartheta}(k,j) = \begin{cases} sim_i(k,j) & \textit{if } sim_i(k,j) \geq \vartheta \\ 0 & \textit{otherwise} \end{cases} \tag{2}$$

where the value of the parameter ϑ is experimentally determined.
The filtered value $sim_i^{\vartheta}(k,j)$ will be the general element (k,j) of the *"similarity matrix"*. Starting by $sim_i^{\vartheta}(k,j)$, it is possible to define a *"semantic distance"* between the k-th and j-th synsets belonging to the i-th lexical set as:

$$\delta_i^{\vartheta}(k,j) = 1 - sim_i^{\vartheta}(k,j) \tag{3}$$

The value $\delta_i^{\vartheta}(k,j)$ represents the *(k,j)* element of the *"semantic distance matrix"* $\vec{\Delta}_i^{\vartheta}$ associated to the *i*-th lexical set:

$$\vec{\Delta}_i^{\vartheta} \equiv \left[\delta_i^{\vartheta}(k,j)\right] \tag{4}$$

where *k* and *j* are ranging from 1 to M_i, therefore $dim\left(\vec{\Delta}_i^{\vartheta}\right) = M_i$. Furthermore the matrix $\vec{\Delta}_i^{\vartheta}$ is square, symmetric, with a null diagonal and its elements are ranging in the interval $[0,1]$.

Semantic Distance Matrix Decomposition. In order to calculate the semantic parts $\vec{w}^i(k)$, it has been applied the semi-discrete decomposition algorithm (SDD) to the semantic distance matrix. Experimental results proved that it is necessary to pre-process the distance matrix before decomposing it. The pre-processing is based on a non linear mapping of the range of the distance matrix elements' values from $[0, 1]$ to $[1, e^{\alpha}]$, using the formula[Vassallo et al., 2003]:

$$a_i^{\vartheta}(k, j) \equiv e^{\alpha \cdot \delta_i^{\vartheta}(k,j)} \tag{5}$$

where α is a parameter to be experimentally determined, and $\delta_i^{\vartheta}(k, j)$ is the element (k, j) of the matrix $\vec{\Delta}_i^{\vartheta}$ (see formula (3)). The value $a_i^{\vartheta}(k, j)$ determines the element (k, j) of the new semantic distance symmetric matrix $\vec{A}_i^{\vartheta}$ for the synsets belonging to the *i*-th lexical set.
The SDD decomposes each $\vec{A}_i^{\vartheta}$ into three matrices:

$$\vec{A}_i^{\vartheta} = \vec{X}_{i,h}^{\vartheta} \vec{D}_{i,h}^{\vartheta} \vec{Z}_{i,h}^{\vartheta T} \tag{6}$$

The semantic parts $\vec{w}^i(k)$ of the synsets belonging to the *i*-th lexical set are given by the rows of the matrix $\vec{X}_{i,h}^{\vartheta}$, and the dimension n_2 of the vectors $\vec{w}^i(k)$ is determined by the number of elements generated by the SDD, that is $n_2 = h$.

3. Experimental Results

In order to examine the semantic part of the synset vector, to each synset *k* of the *i*-th lexical set it has been associated the set of its hypernyms and hyponyms belonging to the same lexical set. This set has been called "*reference correlation set*". We made this choice to test both the preservation of information (the direct hypernym is part of the descriptive set) and the "generalization" capability of the technique (an hyponym is a word whose meaning contains the entire meaning of another word).

Evaluation procedure

The synset vectors are calculated and for each synset, the scalar products are sorted in increasing order. We use a threshold to select a significant set of correlated synsets. This set of synsets will be called in the following "*calculated correlation set*".
The effectiveness of the encoding is determined evaluating the correspondence between the reference and the calculated correlation sets. On this purpose, it has been used the harmonic mean f of precision π and recall ρ computed as macroaveraging (i.e. all the correlation sets count the same) according to the

following formulas[Sebastiani, 2002]:

$$\pi = \frac{\sum_{i=1}^{C} \frac{TP_i}{TP_i+FP_i}}{C}, \rho = \frac{\sum_{i=1}^{C} \frac{TP_i}{TP_i+FN_i}}{C}, f = \frac{2\pi\rho}{\pi+\rho} \quad (7)$$

where C is the number of correlation sets, the precision π_i is the percentage of synsets deemed to belong to the *i*-th reference correlation set that in fact belong to it and the recall ρ_i is the percentage of synsets belonging to the *i*-th correlation set that are in fact deemed to belong to it; TP_i, FP_i and FN_i refer respectively to the sets of true positives (i.e. the set of the calculated relevant synsets), false positives (i.e. the set of the calculated non-relevant synsets) and false negatives (i.e. the set of the non-calculated relevant synsets) of the *i*-th correlation set.

Analysis of the "*noun.motive*" lexical set

To show the efficiency of the encoding technique, the preliminary results obtained with the *noun.motive* lexical set, which is the same lexical set used in [Vassallo et al., 2003], are here reported. The 16-th lexical set *noun.motive* holds the synsets belonging to the syntactic category of nouns regarding "*the reason for the action or that which gives purpose and direction to behavior*", according to the WordNet lexical database.
Experimental trials prove that $\vartheta = 0.9$ (formula(2)), $\alpha = 5$ (formula(5)) and a number of $n_2 = h = 100$ (formula(6)) is a good choice for the generation of the semantic part.
The application of the encoding evaluation methodology presented in the previous paragraph to the *noun.motive* lexical set gave a value of precision π of 0.74, a value of recall ρ of 0.92, and consequently the value of the harmonic mean of precision and recall yielded is 0.82.

4. Conclusion and Future Work

A methodology which exploits the WordNet semantic net and the SDD technique for sub-symbolic semantic encoding of words has been illustrated. First preliminary results are interesting: future work will regard more evaluation results and comparison with other methods. The proposed technique will lead to a useful tool for the sub-symbolic processing of texts using, for example, neural networks for tasks of classification, organization and automated search in non structured repositories of texts.

5. Acknowledgments

Authors would thank Alessandro Puglisi, Andrea Maggio and Engineering Ingegneria Informatica S.p.A. for their contribution to this research.

References

Bellegarda, J.R. (2000). Exploiting latent semantic information in statistical language modeling. *Proceedings of the IEEE*, 88:1279–1296.

Burgess, C. and Lund, K. (2000). The dynamics of meaning in memory. *Cognitive dynamics: Conceptual and Representational Change in Humans and Machines.E. Dietrich and A. Markman, Hillsdale, N.J, Lawrence Erlbaum Associates.*

Didion, J. (2002). Jwnl (java wordnet library). *http://www.sourceforge.net.*

Hofmann, T. (2000). Learning the similarity of documents: An information-geometric approach to document retrieval and categorization. *Advances in Neural Information Processing Systems, S.A. Solla, T.K. Leen and K.R. Muller (eds*, pages 914–920.

Honkela, T., Pulkki, V., and Kohonen., T. (1995). Contextual relations of words in grimm tales, analyzed by self-organizing map. *Proceedings of International Conference on Artificial Neural Networks, ICANN-95.*, pages 3–7.

Kolda, T.G. and O'Leary., D.P. (2000). Computation and uses of the semidiscrete matrix decomposition. *Trans. Math. Software.*

Landauer, T.K., Foltz, P.W., and Laham., D. (1998). Introduction to latent semantic analysis. *Discourse Processes*, 25:259–284.

Miller, G.A., Beckwidth, R., Fellbaum, C., Gross, D., and Miller, K.J. (1990). Introduction to wordnet: An on-line lexical database. *International Journal of Lexicography*, 3:235–244.

Sahlgren, M., Karlgren, J., Cöster, R., and Järvinen, T. (2002). Sics at clef 2002: Automatic query expansion using random indexing. *The CLEF 2002 Workshop, September 19-20, 2002 , Rome, Italy.*

Sebastiani, F. (2002). Machine learning in automated text categorization. *ACM Computing Surveys*, 34:1.

Siivola, V. (2000). Language modeling based on neural clustering of words. *IDIAP-Com 02, Martigny, Switzerland.*

Siolas, G. and d'Alche Buc, F. (2000). Support vector machines based on a semantic kernel for text categorization. *Proceedings of the IEEE-INNS-ENNS International Joint Conference on Neural Networks, IJCNN*, 5:205–209.

Sloan Jr, K.R. and Tanimoto, S.L. (1979). Progressive refinement of raster images. *IEEE Transactions on Computers*, 28:871–874.

Vassallo, G., Pilato, G., Maggio, A., Puglisi, A., and Gaglio, S. (2003). Sub-symbolic encoding of words. *Proc. of 8-th Congress of AI*IA, Lecture Notes in Artificial Intelligence*, 2829:449–461.

Widdows, D., Cederberg, S., and Dorow, B. (2002). Visualisation techniques for analysing meaning. *Fifth International Conference on Text, Speech and Dialogue, Brno, Czech Republic*, pages 107–115.

Yang, H. and Lee, C. (2000). Automatic category generation for text documents by self-organizing maps. *Proc. of IEEE-INNS-ENNS International Joint Conference on Neural Networks*, 3:581–586.

THE HOPFIELD AND KOHONEN NETWORKS: AN *IN VIVO* TEST

Rita Pizzi[1], Andrea Fantasia[1], Danilo Rossetti[1], Giovanni Cino[1], Fabrizio Gelain[2] and Angelo Vescovi[2]

[1] *Department of Information Technologies, University of Milan, via Bramante 65 –26013 Crema (CR) Italy , e-mail pizzi@dti.unimi.it - [2] Stem Cells Research Institute DIBIT San Raffaele , via Olgettina 58 – 20132 Milano Italy*

Abstract: In the frame of a collaboration between Department of Information technology of the University of Milan and Stem Cells Research Institute of the DIBIT- San Raffaele, Milan, learning methods are under study following known models of the Artificial Neural Networks on human neural stem cells cultured on MEA (Multielectrode Arrays) support. The MEAs are constituted by a glass support where a set of tungsten electrodes are inserted to form a lattice structured by our group following the artificial Hopfield and Kohonen models. In such a way it is possible to electrically stimulate the neurons and to record their reaction, opening the possibility to verify *in vivo* learning models of the Artificial neural Networks. Neurons are stimulated with digital patterns constituted by bursts of different voltages at the input electrodes, and the electrical output generated by the neurons is analyzed with advanced methods in order to highlight organized answers by the natural neural network. The experiments performed up to now show how neurons react selectively to different patterns and show similar reactions in front of the presentation of identical or similar patterns. These results suggest the possibility of using the learning capabilities of these hybrid networks in different application fields, in particular in bionic applications.

Keywords: Neural Networks, Stem Cells, Learning, Microelectrode Arrays.

B. Apolloni et al. (eds.), Biological and Artificial Intelligence Environments, 199–207

1. Introduction

During the last decade several experiments have been performed on the interfacing between electronic devices and biological neurons, in order to develop useful tools for the neurophysiological research and to build the technological bases for future bioelectronic prostheses, bionic robots and biological computers.

As microelectrodes implanted directly into brain give rise to infections, scientist are experimenting the direct attachment of neurons to conductive material.

Important results have been achieved by groups of the Max Planck Institute [Fromherz et al., 1991] , the Georgia Tech [Lindner and Ditto, 1996] , the Northwestern and Genoa University [Reger et al., 2000] and the Caltech [DeMarse et al., 2002] .

Aim of our group is to develop architectures based on Artificial Neural Networks (following in particular the Hopfield and Kohonen models) using human neurons adhering to a glass support endowed with microelectrodes (MEA).

The MEAs are connected to a PC by means of a standard acquisition card and custom hardware that allow both to stimulate the neurons and to record the voltages generated by the neurons, allowing to monitorize the electrical activity of the neural network after the pattern stimulation.

In such a way we are able to investigate the learning capabilities of networks of biological neurons and the possible technological applications of such hybrid architectures.

2. Materials and Methods

The problem of the adhesion between neurons and electrodes is crucial: materials have to be biocompatible and neurons must adhere firmly to the MEA electrodes in order to obtain the maximum local conductivity.

Our MEAs are glass disks with 90 nickel-tungsten electrodes whose diameter is around 10 μ . The mean distance between electrodes is 70 μ (Fig. 1). In such a way we should have approximately one neuron for each electrode. The MEA is connected to the PC via an USB acquisition card (IOTech Personal DAQ/56).

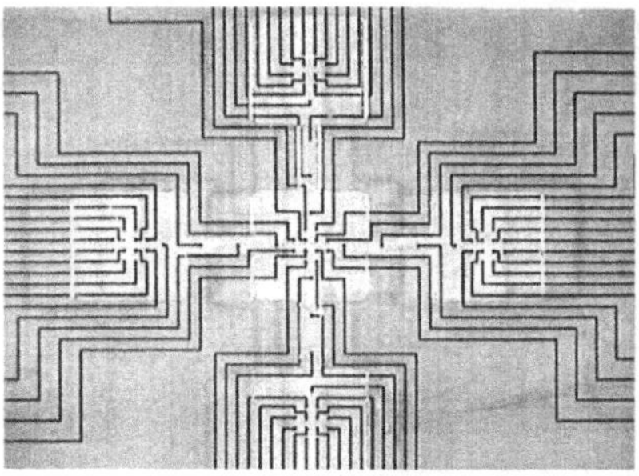

Figure 1. MEA's structure

Our neurons are adult cells cultured by indifferentiated stem cells [Vescovi et al., 1999] .

In our experiments the electrodes have been connected following two theoretical models:

- A Kohonen Self-organizing Map [Kohonen, 1990], composed by an input layer and a competitive layer connected following the standard architecture. In the Kohonen models, as known, the classification capability is carried out by means a competition between neurons.
- A Hopfield Network [Hopfield, 1984] , where the set of input electrodes coincides with the set of output electrodes. In the theoretical model, learning takes place when the network stabilizes in an equilibrium configuration and memories are placed in the local minima of the energy landscape.

The choice of these models is due both to their architecture, easy to implement on MEAs, and to their resemblance to neurophisiological structures, often highlighted by their authors [Kohonen, 1990], [Hopfield, 1984].

The next step was to realize two hybrid networks able to discriminate simple patterns. A software simulation showed that the minimum configurations able to recognize two different patterns , "zero" and "one", pure or affected by noise, formed each one by 8 bits, were

1) a Kohonen networks with 8 input neurons and 3 output neurons and
2) a Hopfield networks with 8 input/output neurons .

These networks have been implemented on the MEAs, culturing the stem cells on the connection sites and structuring the networks correctly by means of hardware connections (Fig.2).

The input patterns are converted into suitable electrical stimuli (similar to the biological action potentials at 40 Hz) by a custom hardware device. The output signals are also sampled at 40 Hz. These choices have been made on the basis of neurophysiological considerations. In fact several studies seem to confirm that signals related to the most advanced CNS activities (perception, cognition, conscience) synchronize around 40 Hz [Menon and Freeman, 1996] .

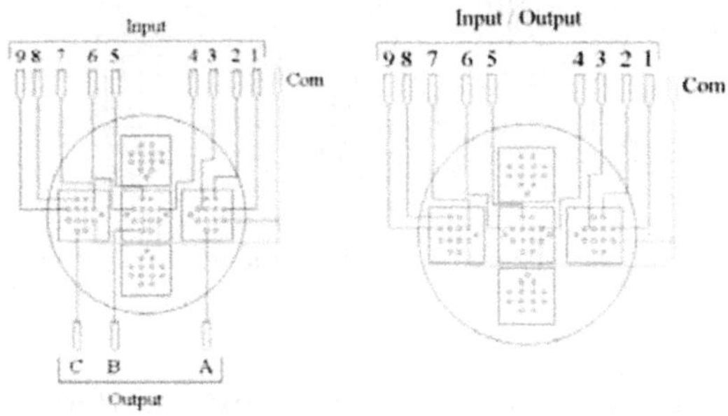

Figure 2. Kohonen (left) and Hopfield (right) architecture on MEA

In order to be sure that the recorded signals were actually coming from the electrical neural activity, we compared the reaction of a MEA containing only culture liquid with the electrical activities of the MEA with living cells (Fig. 3) .

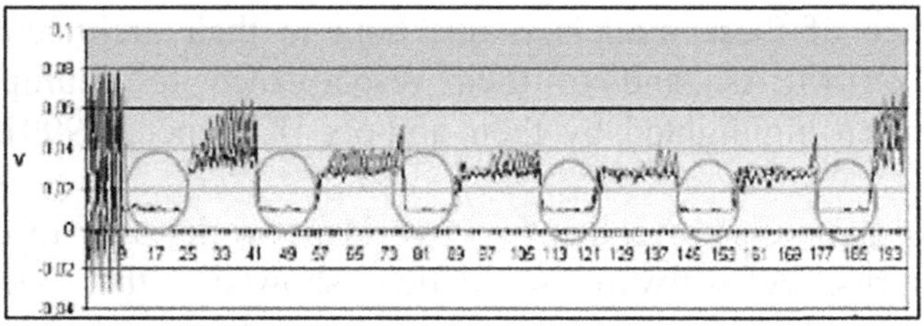

Figure 3. Electrical signals from neurons

It is evident that the neurons reply to a “zero” pattern, formed by the highest voltage (all the 8 electrodes “on”), emitting the lowest voltage (green circles in figure), whereas the culture liquid, as expected by a conductive medium, answers to the “zero” pattern with a high voltage (Fig. 4).

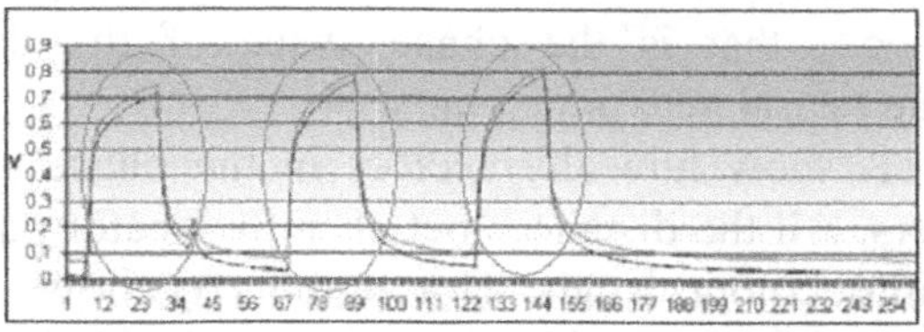

Figure 4. Electrical signals from the culture liquid

Fig. 5 shows the reaction of the Kohonen network after the stimulation with "zero" patterns pure or affected by noise (green circles) and with "one" patterns pure or affected by noise (red circles) . Similar effects have been shown even by the Hopfield network.

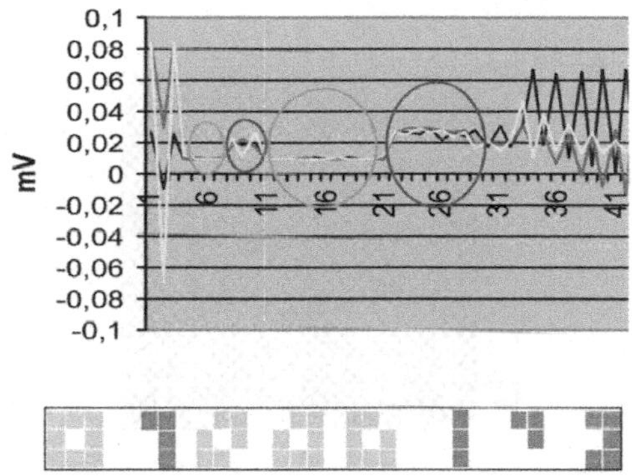

Figure 5. Electrical signals from neurons stimulated with different patterns: "zero" (green circles) and "one" (red circles)

A training phase has been carried out on the networks by stimulating them repeatedly with all the patterns, pure and affected by noise.

At the end of the experiments we recorded the neural activities in order to ascertain the presence of "permanent" learning. Differently from the culture liquid, that shows the same kind of behavior before and after the stimulations, the MEAs with neurons show significant differences in their electrical activities.

The recorded activities have been analyzed by means of Recurrence Quantification Analysis (RQA) [Zbilut and Webber, 1992] .

Such non-linear analysis tool elaborates the signal time series in a multi-dimensional space , that is the phase space of the dynamical system represented by the neural network signals.

Recurrent Plots show how the vectors in the phase space are near or distant each others. All the distances between the vector pairs are calculated and translated into colour bands. Hot colours (yellow, red, orange) are associated to short distances, cold colours (blue, black) show long distances. Signals repeating fixed distances between vectors are organized, signals with random distances are not.

In this way we obtain uniform colour distribution of random signals, whereas deterministic and self-similar signals show structured plots with wide colour bands.

Our RQA analysis of the neural activity lead to interesting results: after the training, signals coming from the reply to similar patterns form similar Recurrent Plots. In the following figures we can see the self-organization of a single output channel (corresponding to a specific electrode/neuron) before stimulation, during training and after training as a reply of a specific pattern.

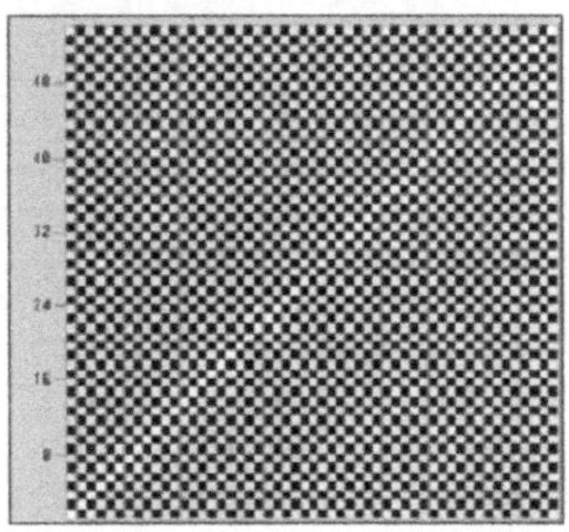

Figure 6a. RQA plot of a Kohonen output channel before stimulation

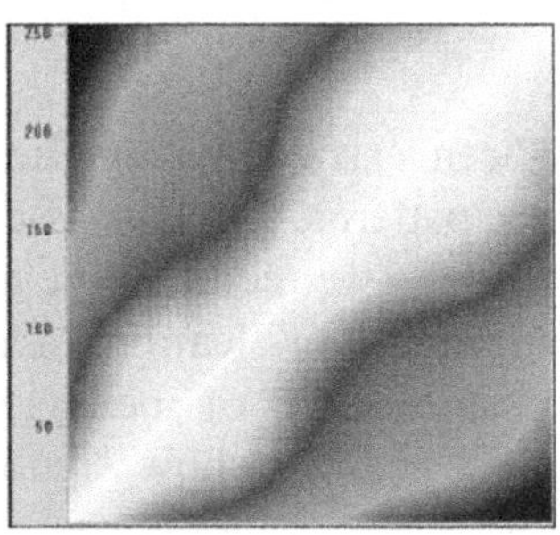

Figure 6b. RQA plot of a Kohonen output channel after training

Fig. 6a shows a Kohonen output channel before stimulation. The plot is not structured and show lack of self-organization

The training phase generates a change in the plots structure. The plot of the same channel after the training phase (fig. 6b) shows wide uniform colour bands corresponding to high self-organization. The band width grows in time during the training.

Fig. 7a shows the answer after stimulation with "zero " pattern and Fig. 7b shows the same output after stimulation with "one" pattern. The plots show that the network behaves differently depending on the stimulation pattern.

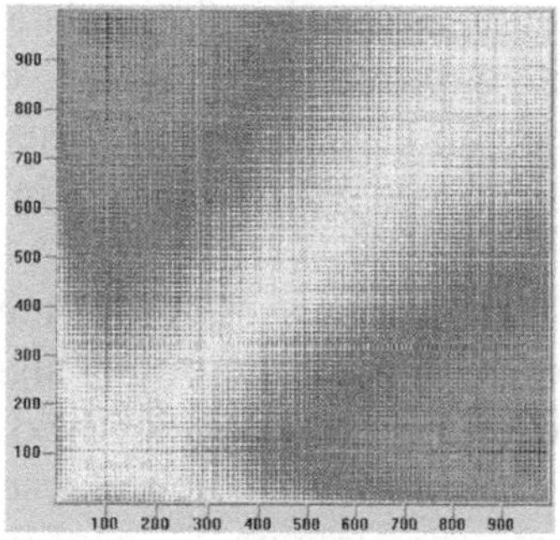

Figure 7a. RQA plot after stimulation with "zero" pattern

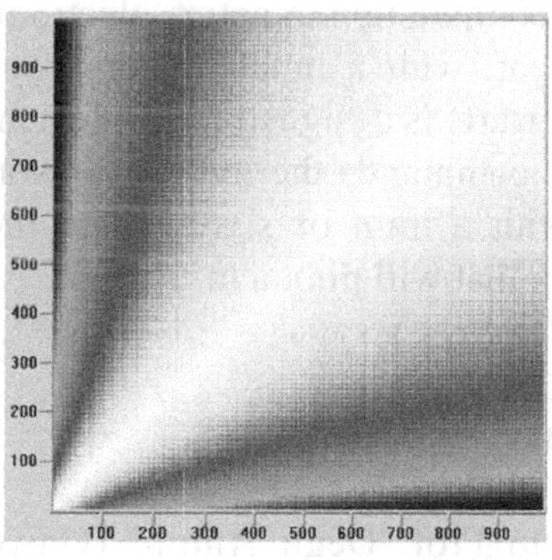

Figure7b. RQA plot after stimulation with "one" pattern

We applied the same procedure to the output signals coming from the Hopfield network, obtaining the same kind of reactions.

3. Discussion and Conclusions

After a qualitative analysis of the output signals we can reasonably affirm that stimulation with organized electrical patterns modifies the system and improves the system information suggesting a kind of learning and memorization.

The neural networks show, after a training stage constituted by iterated stimulation with different patterns, an organized behavior and the capability of reacting selectively to different patterns.

Besides, similar patterns make the neurons react in similar manner.

Thus the neurons show a form of selective coding, highlighting a strong and lasting self-organization as a reply of stimulation.

In the future we will improve both the cell culture on MEA and the measuring and interfacing tools and the analysis methods. We will also increase the connections between MEAs and PC in order to implement more complex networks.

At the moment we are carrying on experiments with more complex patterns and new kinds of analysis of the output signals. In particular, we are using the ITSOM Artificial neural network [Pizzi et al., 2002] in order to codify the output and to discriminate the neural response.

Our first results are encouraging , confirming the possibility of discriminating different patterns by means of different binary strings, coming out from the artificial network that elaborates the biological signal output. In this way it will be possible to use the neural replies in several ways, from robotics to biological computation to neuro-electronic prostheses.

Our new experiment, with a much faster acquisition card and a more advanced custom hardware, is designed to implement a real actuator. We will stimulate with simple commands the hybrid network system, the biological network will reply with a train of signals that the artificial network will codify in binary string that will pilot a minirobot.

Acknowledgements

We are indebted to Prof. Degli Antoni (University of Milan) for his precious suggestions and encouragement , and with ST Microelectronics for the financial support.

References

DeMarse, T.B., Wagenaar, D.A., Potter, S.M. (2002), The neurally-controlled artificial animal: a neural-computer interface between cultured neural networks and a robotic body, SFN 2002, Orlando, Florida .

Fromherz, P. , Schaden, H. , Vetter, T. (1991), *Neuroscience*,129:77-80 .

Hopfield, J.J. (1984), Neural Networks and Physical Systems with Emergent Collective Computational Abilities, Proc. Nat. Acad. Sci USA, 81.

Kohonen, T. (1990), *Self-Organisation and Association Memory*, Springer Verlag .

Lindner, J. F., Ditto, W. (1996), Exploring the nonlinear dynamics of a physiologically viable model neuron, AIP Conf. Proc. 375(1): 709 .

Menon, V., Freeman, W.J. (1996), Spatio-temporal Correlations in Human Gamma Band Electrocorticograms, *Electroenc. and Clin.. Neurophys*. 98, 89-102 .

Pizzi, R., de Curtis, M., Dickson, C. (2002), Evidence of Chaotic Attractors in Cortical Fast Oscillations Tested by an Artificial Neural Network, in: *Advances in Soft Computing*, J. Kacprzyk ed., Physica Verlag .

Reger, B., Fleming, K.M., Sanguineti, V., Simon Alford, S., Mussa Ivaldi, F.A. (2000), Connecting Brains to Robots: The Development of a Hybrid System for the Study of Learning in Neural Tissues, Artificial Life VII, Portland, Oregon .

Vescovi., A.L., Parati, E.A., Gritti, A. , Poulin, P. , Ferrario, M. , Wanke, E. , Frölichsthal-Schoeller, P. , Cova, L. , Arcellana-Panlilio, M. , Colombo, A. , and Galli, R. (1999), Isolation and cloning of multipotential stem cells from the embryonic human CNS and establishment of transplantable human neural stem cell lines by epigenetic stimulation. , *Exp. Neurol*. 156: 71-83 .

Zbilut, J.P., Webber, C.L. (1992), "Embeddings and delays as derived from quantification of recurrent plots", *Phys. Lett.* 171.

SUPPORT VECTOR REGRESSION WITH A GENERALIZED QUADRATIC LOSS

Filippo Portera and Alessandro Sperduti
Dipartimento di Matematica Pura ed Applicata
Università di Padova, Padova, Italy
{portera,sperduti} @math.unipd.it

Abstract The standard SVR formulation for real-valued function approximation on multidimensional spaces is based on the ϵ-insensitive loss function, where errors are considered not correlated. Due to this, local information in the feature space which can be useful to improve the prediction model is disregarded. In this paper we address this problem by defining a generalized quadratic loss where the co-occurrence of errors is weighted according to a kernel similarity measure in the feature space. We show that the resulting dual problem can be expressed as a hard margin SVR in a different feature space when the co-occurrence error matrix is invertible. We compare our approach against a standard SVR on two regression tasks. Experimental results seem to show an improvement in the performance.

Keywords: Regression, Support Vector Machines, Loss Functions, Kernel Methods.

1. Introduction

Statistical Learning Theory [Vapnik, 1998] provides a very effective framework for classification and regression tasks involving numerical features. Support Vectors Machines are directly derived from this framework and they work by solving a constrained quadratic problem where the convex objective function to minimize is given by the combination of a loss function with a regularization term (the norm of the weights). While the regularization term is directly linked, through a theorem, to the VC-dimension of the hypothesis space, and thus fully justified, the loss function is usually (heuristically) chosen on the basis of the task at hand. For example, when considering binary classification tasks, the ideal loss would be the 0-1 loss, which however cannot directly be plugged into the objective function because it is not convex. Thus, convex upper bounds to the 0-1 loss are used, e.g., the Hinge loss or the quadratic loss. In general, however, the used loss does not exploit the correlation that the input patterns may exhibit. A first attempt to exploit this type of information for

B. Apolloni et al. (eds.), Biological and Artificial Intelligence Environments, 209–216

classification tasks has been presented in [Portera and Sperduti, 2004], where a family of generalized quadratic loss is defined. The basic idea is to first of all take into consideration the correlation between input patterns (eventually corrected by the targets of the involved examples), which can be coded as cross-coefficients of pairs of errors in a fully quadratic form, and then to modulate the strength of these cross-coefficients through a new hyperparameter. The "right" value of this new hyperparameter is then chosen by a search in the hyperparameters space (eventually involving a validation set) of the machine so to optimize the final performance [Zhang and Oles, 2001]. The experimental results presented in [Portera and Sperduti, 2004] seem to indicate a systematic improvement in the performance.

In this paper, we show that the same idea and advantages can be extended to real-valued function regression. Specifically, we suggest to use a loss function that weights every error associated to two patterns proportionally to the pattern similarity. This can be done by modifying the primal objective function of the SVR model with a loss that is a quadratic expression of the slack variables, weighting couples of errors by a pattern similarity measure based on a kernel function. In addition, signed slack variables are used so that given two distinct patterns, the modified SVR solution will penalize couple of errors (of similar patterns) that are both due to an overestimate (or underestimate) of the target values versus couple of errors (of similar patterns) that are due to an overestimate of one of the target values and an underestimate of the other target value. This method should bias the learning towards solutions where the local concentration of errors of the same type (either underestimate or overestimate) is discouraged.

We show that using this generalized quadratic loss function in a Support Vector Regression method, the resulting dual problem can be expressed as a hard margin SVR in a new feature space which is related to the original feature space via the inverse of the similarity matrix and the target information. Thus, in order to get a well-formed dual formulation we need to work with a similarity matrix which is invertible.

We compare our approach against a standard SVR with ϵ-insensitive loss on a couple of regression tasks. The experimental results seem to show an improvement in the performance.

2. SVR definition for a generalized quadratic loss

Suppose that l inputs $(\vec{x}_1, y_1), \ldots, (\vec{x}_l, y_l)$ are given, where $\mathbf{x_i} \in \mathbb{R}^{\mathbf{d}}$ are the input patterns, and $y_i \in \mathcal{R}$ are the related target values of our supervised regression problem. The standard SVR model for 2-norm ϵ-insensitive loss function [Cristianini and Shawe-Taylor, 2000], that we denote QSVR, is:

$$\begin{aligned} &\min_{\vec{w},b,\vec{\xi},\vec{\xi^*}} ||\vec{w}||^2 + c(\vec{\xi}'\vec{\xi} + \vec{\xi^*}'\vec{\xi^*}) \\ \text{s.t.:} & \\ &\vec{w}\cdot\vec{x}_i + b - y_i \leq \epsilon + \xi_i, \qquad i = 1,\ldots,l \\ &y_i - \vec{w}\cdot\vec{x}_i + b \leq \epsilon + \xi_i^*, \qquad i = 1,\ldots,l \end{aligned} \tag{1}$$

where $\vec{w}$ and b are the parameters of the linear regressor $\vec{w}\vec{x} + b$, ξ_i is the slack variable associated to an over-estimate of the linear regressor over input $\vec{x}_i$ and ξ_i^* is the slack variable associated to an under-estimate on the same pattern; ϵ determines the size of the approximation tube and c is the constant that controls the tradeoff between the empirical error as measured by the loss function and the regularization term. Note that non negativity constraints over $\vec{\xi}$ and $\vec{\xi^*}$ components are redundant. The solution of (1) can be expressed in general using a kernel function $K(\vec{x},\vec{y})$ with $f(\vec{x}) = \frac{1}{2}\sum_{i=1}^{l}(\alpha_i^{*+} - \alpha_i{}^+)K(\vec{x}_i,\vec{x}) + b^+$ where $\vec{\alpha^{*+}}$, $\vec{\alpha^+}$ is the dual optimal solution and an optimal bias value b^+ can be derived from the KKT conditions.

To weight the co-occurrence of errors corresponding to close patterns we adopted the following formulation :

$$\begin{aligned} &\min_{\vec{w},b,\vec{\xi},\vec{\xi^*}} ||\vec{w}||^2 + c(\vec{\xi} - \vec{\xi^*})'S(\vec{\xi} - \vec{\xi^*})) \\ \text{s.t.:} & \\ &\vec{w}\cdot\vec{x}_i + b - y_i \leq \epsilon + \xi_i, \qquad i = 1,\ldots,l \\ &y_i - \vec{w}\cdot\vec{x}_i - b \leq \epsilon + \xi_i^*, \qquad i = 1,\ldots,l \end{aligned} \tag{2}$$

where S is a positive definite matrix. Defining $\delta_i = \xi_i - \xi_i^*$ we obtain:

$$\begin{aligned} &\min_{\vec{w},b,\vec{\delta}} ||\vec{w}||^2 + c\vec{\delta}'S\vec{\delta} \\ \text{s.t.:} & \\ &\vec{w}\cdot\vec{x}_i + b - y_i \leq \epsilon + \delta_i + \xi_i^*, \quad i = 1,\ldots,l \\ &y_i - \vec{w}\cdot\vec{x}_i + b \leq \epsilon - \delta_i + \xi_i, \quad i = 1,\ldots,l \end{aligned} \tag{3}$$

and since when one of the first constraints is active, the related ξ_i^* is 0, and viceversa, when one the second constraints is active, the related ξ_i is 0, we can write:

$$\begin{aligned} &\min_{\vec{w},b,\vec{\delta}} ||\vec{w}||^2 + c\vec{\delta}'S\vec{\delta} \\ \text{s.t.:} & \\ &\vec{w}\cdot\vec{x}_i + b - y_i \leq \epsilon + \delta_i, \quad i = 1,\ldots,l \\ &y_i - \vec{w}\cdot\vec{x}_i + b \leq \epsilon - \delta_i, \quad i = 1,\ldots,l \end{aligned} \tag{4}$$

Finally we obtain:

$$\begin{aligned} &\min_{\vec{w},b,\vec{\delta}} ||\vec{w}||^2 + c\vec{\delta}'S\vec{\delta} \\ \text{s.t.:} & \\ &-\epsilon \leq \vec{w}\cdot\vec{x}_i + b - y_i - \delta_i \leq \epsilon, \quad i = 1,\ldots,l \end{aligned} \tag{5}$$

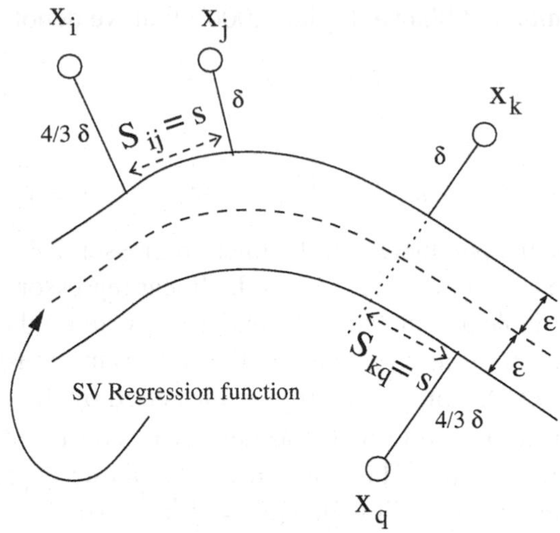

Figure 1. In our generalized quadratic loss, the error configuration generated by patterns $\vec{x}_i$ and $\vec{x}_j$ is more expensive than the error configuration generated by patterns $\vec{x}_k$ and $\vec{x}_q$. Here we assume that $S_{ij} = S_{kq} = s$.

A solution of this problem is a function with the best tradeoff between its smoothness and a uniform error on the training set. In addition, since we are considering signed slack variables ($\vec{\delta}$), we penalize errors on close patterns of the same sign, preferring errors with opposite signs. In Figure 1 we give a graphical exemplification about which type of error co-occurrence we prefer to penalize. Let X be the $l \times d$ matrix of input patterns. Given problem (5) the corresponding Lagrangian objective function is:

$$L = ||\vec{w}||^2 + c\vec{\delta}' S\vec{\delta} + \vec{\alpha}'(X\vec{w} + b\vec{1} - \vec{y} - \vec{\delta} - \epsilon\vec{1}) + \vec{\alpha^*}'(\vec{\delta} - X\vec{w} - b\vec{1} + \vec{y} - \epsilon\vec{1}) \quad (6)$$

where $\alpha_i \geq 0$, $\alpha_i^* \geq 0$ for $i = 1, \ldots, l$.

The Kuhn Tucker conditions for optimality are:

$$\begin{array}{l} \frac{\partial L}{\partial \vec{w}} = 2\vec{w} + X'(\vec{\alpha} - \vec{\alpha^*}) = 0 \Rightarrow \vec{w} = \frac{1}{2}X'(\vec{\alpha^*} - \vec{\alpha}) \\ \frac{\partial L}{\partial b} = (\vec{\alpha} - \vec{\alpha^*})'\vec{1} = 0 \Rightarrow (\vec{\alpha^*} - \vec{\alpha})'\vec{1} = 0 \\ \frac{\partial L}{\partial \vec{\delta}} = 2cS\vec{\delta} - (\vec{\alpha} - \vec{\alpha^*}) = 0 \Rightarrow \vec{\delta} = \frac{S^{-1}(\vec{\alpha} - \vec{\alpha^*})}{2c} \end{array} \quad (7)$$

if S is invertible. Supposing that S^{-1} exists, substituting (7) in (6) gives:

$$\begin{array}{l} \max_{\vec{\alpha},\vec{\alpha^*}} (\vec{\alpha^*} - \vec{\alpha})\vec{y} - \epsilon(\vec{\alpha^*} + \vec{\alpha})'\vec{1} - \frac{1}{2}(\vec{\alpha^*} - \vec{\alpha})'\frac{1}{2}(K + \frac{S^{-1}}{c})(\vec{\alpha^*} - \vec{\alpha}) \\ \text{s.t.: } (\vec{\alpha^*} - \vec{\alpha})'\vec{1} = 0, \;\; \alpha_i \geq 0, \alpha_i^* \geq 0 \;\; i = 1, \ldots, l \end{array} \quad (8)$$

Notice that when S^{-1} exists, problem (8) is equivalent to a hard margin SVR problem with a kernel matrix equal to $\frac{1}{2}(K + \frac{S^{-1}}{c})$, while the regression function is defined over the feature space induced by kernel K. Actually, in this case it is also possible to explicitly build a feature map. Let consider the following mapping $\phi : \mathbb{R}^d \longrightarrow \mathbb{R}^{d+l}$ that, for all $i \in [1,\ldots,l]$, maps $\vec{x}_i \mapsto \phi(\vec{x}_i)$: $\phi(\vec{x}_i) = [\vec{x}_i', (\sqrt{\frac{S^{-1}}{c}}\vec{e}_i)']'$ where $\vec{e}_i$ is the i-th vector of the canonical base of $\mathbb{R}^l$. It is not difficult to see that the kernel matrix obtained with this transformation is equal to $K + \frac{S^{-1}}{c}$. In the following we denote the overall method with QLSVR.

3. Definition of the similarity matrix

The dual solution of problem (5) is based on the inversion of S. Note that when all patterns are distinct points and S is generated by a Gaussian RBF kernel then S is invertible ([Micchelli, 1998]). Under some experimental conditions, however, a similarity matrix defined in this way may be ill-conditioned and inversion can be problematic.

For this reason we also considered an exponential kernel $e^{\nu K}$, defined by $e^{\nu K} = \sum_{i=0}^{+\infty} \frac{\nu^i}{i!} K^i$. A kernel matrix obtained by this formula is always invertible and its inverse is $(e^{\nu K})^{-1} = e^{-\nu K}$. Experimentally we never had problems in computing the inverse of the exponential matrix.

A similarity matrix generated by an RBF kernel can be understood as a way to take into account local similarity between patterns, where the amount of locality is regulated by the width of the RBF function. The exponential kernel, besides to guarantee the invertibility of the S matrix, has been proposed in the context of discrete domains [Kondor and Lafferty, 2002], and it appears to be particularly suited when the instance space is composed of structured objects, such as sequences or trees.

4. Experiments

To measure the performance of the regression methods we used the average absolute error ($AAE = \frac{1}{l}\sum_{i=1}^{m} |y_i - f(\vec{x}_i)|$) and the average squared error ($ASE = \frac{1}{l}\sum_{i=1}^{m}(y_i - f(\vec{x}_i))^2$). Since the reported performances are averaged across different shuffles, we also report their standard deviation computed as $\sigma = \sqrt{\frac{1}{n-1}\sum_{i=1}^{n}(E_i - \mu_E)^2}$, where n is the number of data shuffles, E_i is the AAE (or ASE) error on the i-th shuffle and μ_E is the mean AAE (or ASE) error on the shuffles set.

We tested the two regression methods on two datasets: the Abalone dataset from the UCI repository and a QSPR problem involving alkanes, i.e. chemical compounds represented as trees. For both datasets we report the results obtained by SVR and QLSVR. We employed a modified version of SVMLight 5.0 [Joachims, 1998] enabled to work with a kernel matrix generated by Scilab 2.7 ©INRIA-ENPC.

The Abalone dataset comprises 3000 training patterns and 1177 test patterns and the input patterns are normalized to zero mean and unit variance coordinate-wise. We considered 10 independent shuffles of the Abalone dataset and we calibrated the hyperparameters using a split of each original training set. The calibration procedure is based on the first 2000 patterns for training and on the last 1000 patterns for validation.

For the SVR algorithm we adopted a RBF kernel $K(\vec{x},\vec{y}) = e^{-\gamma||\vec{x}-\vec{y}||^2}$ for the input feature space. We applied on each shuffle of the dataset a calibration process that involved a 5×5 mesh of powers of 10 starting from $10, 0.1$ for c and γ, while the ϵ parameter was increased by steps of size 0.3 starting from 0 up to 1.2. For each shuffle we selected the hyperparameters set that gave the best performance in terms of ASE, we trained the SVR on the original training set, and finally the obtained regressor was evaluated on the original test problem.

For QLSVR we considered the same setting as the SVR and a similarity matrix S generated by an RBF kernel with parameter γ_S. During the calibration phase γ_S was varied from 4 to 24 by steps of size 5. Hyperparameters selection and final evaluation were performed using the same procedure as adopted for SVR.

We also considered a QSPR problem consisting in the prediction of the boiling point for a group of acyclic hydrocarbons (alkanes). The dataset comprises 150 alkanes with up to 10 carbon atoms, each represented as a tree (for more details, see [Bianucci et al., 2000; Bianucci et al., 2003]). The target values are in the range [-164 , 174] in Celsius degrees.

In order to deal with trees as input instances, we have chosen the most popular and used Tree Kernel proposed in [Collins and Duffy, 2002]. It is based on counting matching subtrees between two input trees.

For the calibration of SVR hyperparameters, we shuffled the 150 compounds and we created 30 splits of 5 patterns each. The calibration involved a set of 3 parameters: the SVR training error weight constant c, the Tree Kernel downweighting factor λ and the SVR regression tube width ϵ. On the last 3 splits we applied a 3-fold cross validation that involved a 5×5 mesh of powers of 10 starting from $10, 0.1$ for c and $\sqrt{\lambda}$, while the ϵ parameter is increased by steps of size 0.01 starting from 0 up to 0.04. We selected the parameter vector that gave the median of the best AAE on the three splits and then we used these parameters on 10 different splits of the original dataset to obtain the final test results.

For QLSVR we considered the same setting as the SVR and a similarity matrix generated by an exponential kernel ($S = e^{\nu TK}$), since the exponential kernel has been proposed in the context of discrete domains [Kondor and Lafferty, 2002], such as set of trees. During the calibration phase ν was varied

Table 1. Results for the Abalone dataset. We report also the unbiased standard deviation measured on the 10 different shuffles of the dataset. SVR_{Chu} refers to [Chu et al., 2004].

Method	*AAE tr*	*ASE tr*	*AAE ts*	*ASE ts*
SVR_{Chu}	-	-	0.454±0.009	0.441±0.021
SVR	0.432±0.008	0.397±0.017	0.456±0.010	0.435±0.020
QLSVR	0.006±2.2E-4	3.4E-5±2.9E-6	0.461±0.009	0.424±0.019

from 0.5 to 0.65 by steps of size 0.015. Hyperparameters selection and final evaluation were performed using the same procedure adopted for SVR.

The results for the Abalone dataset, both for the training set (tr) and the test set (ts), are shown in Table 1 where we report also the results obtained for SVR in [Chu et al., 2004]. From the experimental results it can be concluded that the proposed approach and the SVR method give a similar result in terms of the absolute mean error, while the quadratic loss produces an improved mean squared error with a reduced standard deviation.

Table 2 reports the results obtained for the Alkanes dataset, including the values for the hyperparameters, as returned by the calibration process described above. Also in this case we got a similar result in terms of the absolute mean error, while the quadratic loss produces an slightly improved mean squared error, but with an increased standard deviation.

These results, however, should be considered very preliminary for the QLSVR method, since the presence of an additional hyperparameter for the generation of the similarity matrix S, as well as the possibility to use different methods for its generation, require a more intensive set of experiments in order to get a better coverage for S.

Table 2. Results for the alkanes dataset. We report also the unbiased standard deviation measured on the 10 different shuffles of the dataset.

Method	*Parameters*	*AAE tr*	*ASE tr*	*AAE ts*	*ASE ts*
SVR	$c = 1E5$ $\lambda = 0.25$ $\epsilon = 0.02$	1.68±0.03	3.19±0.08	3.82±0.97	30.27±32.08
QLSVR	$c = 1E4$ $\lambda = 0.25$ $\epsilon = 0.02$ $\nu = 0.8$	1.67±0.02	3.16±0.06	3.82±1.09	30.00± 32.63

5. Conclusions

In this paper we proposed a generalized quadratic loss for regression problems that exploits the similarity of the input patterns. In fact, the proposed generalized quadratic loss weights co-occurrence of errors on the basis of the similarity of the corresponding input patterns. Moreover errors of similar patterns of the same sign are discouraged. We derived a SVR formulation for the proposed loss showing that if the similarity matrix is invertible the problem is equivalent to a hard margin SVR problem with a kernel matrix which depends also on the inverse of the similarity loss matrix. Experimental results on two regression tasks seem to show an improvement in the performance.

A problem with this approach is the need to invert the similarity matrix and how to define it in a meaningful way. Thus further study will be devoted to these issues and to the extension of the framework to multiclass and ranking problems. Finally, the robustness of the approach should be studied, both theoretically and empirically.

References

Bianucci, A.M., Micheli, A., Sperduti, A., and Starita, A. (2000). Application of cascade correlation networks for structures to chemistry. *Journal of Applied Intelligence (Kluwer Academic Publishers)*, 12:117–146.

Bianucci, A.M., Micheli, A., Sperduti, A., and Starita, A. (2003). A novel approach to QSPR/QSAR based on neural networks for structures. In Sztandera, L.M. and Cartwright, H.M., editors, *Soft Computing Approaches in Chemistry*. Springer-Verlag.

Chu, W., Keerthi, S. S., and Ong, C. J. (2004). Bayesian support vector regression using a unified loss function. *IEEE Trans. on Neural Networks*, 15(1):29–44.

Collins, M. and Duffy, N. (2002). Convolution kernels for natural language. In *NIPS 14*, Cambridge, MA. MIT Press.

Cristianini, N. and Shawe-Taylor, J. (2000). *An Introduction to Support Vector Machines and other Kernel-based Learning Methods*. Cambridge University Press, Cambridge.

Joachims, T. (1998). Text categorization with support vector machines: learning with many relevant features. In *Proceedings of ECML-98, 10th European Conference on Machine Learning*, pages 137–142.

Kondor, R. and Lafferty, J. (2002). Diffusion kernels on graphs and other discrete input spaces. In *Proceedings of the Int. Conf. on Machine Learning, 2002.*

Micchelli, C.A. (1998). Algebraic aspects of interpolation. In *Proceedings of Symposia in Applied Mathematics*, pages 36:81–102.

Portera, Filippo and Sperduti, Alessandro (2004). A generalized quadratic loss for support vector machines. In *Proceedings of* 16th *European Conference on Artificial Intelligence*, pages 628–632.

Vapnik, V.N. (1998). *Statistical Learning Theory*. Wiley, New York.

Zhang, T. and Oles, F. J. (2001). Text categorization based on regularized linear classification methods. *Information Retrieval*, 4:5–31.

A FLEXIBLE ICA APPROACH TO A NOVEL BSS CONVOLUTIVE NONLINEAR PROBLEM: PRELIMINARY RESULTS

Daniele Vigliano, Raffaele Parisi and Aurelio Uncini
Dipartimento INFOCOM, Università di Roma "La Sapienza" – Italy Via Eudossiana, 18, 00184 Roma – Italy, daniele.vigliano@poste.it; parisi@infocom.uniroma1.it; aurel@ieee.org;

Abstract. This paper introduces a Flexible ICA approach to a novel blind sources separation problem. The proposed on line algorithm performs the separation after the convolutive mixing of post nonlinear convolutive mixtures. The Flexibility of the algorithm is given by the on line estimation of the score function performed by Spline Neurons. Experimental results are described to show the effectiveness of the proposed technique.

Key Words: Blind Source Separation, Flexible ICA, Spline Adaptive function, Mutual Information.

1. Introduction

The first studies about Independent Component Analysis aimed at resolving the famous Cocktail party problem first in static, then in reverberant environments. A critical issue is that linear mixing models are too unrealistic and "poor" in a lot of real situations. The approach to nonlinear convolutive problems are not too widely diffused until now.

Important theoretical results in nonlinear static ICA are in [Hyvarinen et al., 1999]. Several papers considers Post Nonlinear Mixing problem (PNL) in static [Taleb, 2002] and in convolutive [Milani et al., 2002][Zade et al., 2002] environment but only few of them (see [Taleb et al., 1999][Hyvarinen et al., 1999]) explore the existence and uniqueness of the solution. Recent advances in BSS of nonlinear mixing models have been reviewed in [Jutten et al., 2003]. A growing interest is also in the so called Flexible ICA since it improves the quality of separation introducing a better pdf matching and allows a faster learning.

Actually recent studies try to improve the severity of mixing models moving from single block nonlinear structures (convolutive or at least static) to multi block structures. In [Solazzi et al., 2004] sources are recovered from a PNL mixing followed by an instantaneous mixing; in [Vigliano et al., 2004][Vigliano et al., 2004] the mixing environment is composed by a PNL

B. Apolloni et al. (eds.), Biological and Artificial Intelligence Environments, 217–224

mixing block followed by a convolutive one. This paper explores the solution of the BSS problem in a novel, more severe, convolutive nonlinear mixing environment: the convolutive mixing follows a PNL convolutive mixing block.

2. The nonlinear issue

This section introduces BSS problem in nonlinear environment. Considering an N vector of independent sources **s**[*n*] and a vector of signals **x**[*n*] received by a N-sensor array. The general formulation of the hidden mixing model is:

$$\mathbf{x}[n] = \mathsf{F}\left\{\mathbf{s}[n],\ldots,\mathbf{s}[n-L]\right\} \tag{1}$$

in which $\mathsf{F}\{\cdot\}$ is a dynamic nonlinear distorting function. The solution of the BSS problem can be expressed as: $\mathbf{y}[n] = \mathsf{H}\ \{\mathbf{s}(n)\} = \mathsf{G}\ \circ \mathsf{F}\ \{\mathbf{s}(n)\}$. In instantaneous environments ICA recovers the original sources up to some trivial acceptable non-uniqueness: outputs can be scaled and delayed version of flipped inputs. Convolutive mixing environments add a stronger non-uniqueness: the filtering indeterminacies. Convolutive mixtures are separable but applying channel-by-channel filters to the independent recovered signals, outputs are still independent.

This indeterminacy may be unacceptable since it can strongly distort the sources. In any case after separation it is possible to equalize the outputs producing acceptable results. According to these reasons filtering indeterminacy will no more considered in the rest of this paper.

In the more general convolutive nonlinear case (1), the issue of separating mixture with the only constraint of independent output signals and no other a priori assumption is affected by a strong non uniqueness [Jutten et al., 2003]. Several well known examples show that some maps, given independent inputs, produce independent outputs even with non diagonal Jacobian matrix. Independence constraint alone is not strong enough to recover original sources from generic nonlinear mixing environments [Taleb, 2002].

The main issue for generic nonlinear problems is to ensure the presence of conditions (in term of sources, mixing environment, recovering structure) granting at least theoretically the possibility to achieve the desired solution. In [Hyvarinen et al., 1999] authors proposed a constructive way (a Gram-Schmidt like method) to obtain solutions of the separation problem in a static nonlinear mixing environment; in order to grant the uniqueness of the solutions some constraints have been applied to the mixing environment.

The idea introduced is general: adding some "soft" constraint to the problem (like a priori "trivial" assumptions) can produce the uniqueness of the solution. In this paper the a priori knowledge of the mixing model is exploited to design the recovery network: the so called "mirror" demixing model is used.

3. The mixing-demixing structure

This section explores the recovery of separated sources from nonlinear convolutive mixing; the a priori knowledge of the mixing model has been used to design the recovering network. The mixing environment modelled in this paper is represented in figure 1. In which $\mathbf{A}[k]$ and $\mathbf{B}[k]$ are $N \times N$ FIR matrices with respectively L_a and L_b filter taps and $\mathbf{F}\left[\mathbf{p}[n]\right]=\left[f_1\left[p_1[n]\right],\ f_N\left[p_N[n]\right]\right]^T$ is the $N \times 1$ vector of nonlinear distorting functions.

The closed form for mixing model is: $\mathbf{x}[n]=\mathcal{F}\ [\mathbf{s}]=\mathbf{B}[n]*\mathbf{F}\left[\mathbf{A}[n]*\mathbf{s}[n]\right]$; it enlarges the set of mixing environments from which it is possible to recover separated signals. According to the uniqueness requirements expressed in the previous section the recovering structure mirrors the mixing model. The closed form for recovered outputs is:

$$\mathbf{y}[n]=\mathcal{G}\ [\mathbf{x}]=\mathbf{Z}[n]*\mathbf{G}\left[\mathbf{W}[n]*\mathbf{x}[n]\right]=\sum_{h=0}^{K_Z-1}\mathbf{Z}[h]\mathbf{G}\left[\sum_{k=0}^{K_W-1}\mathbf{W}[k]\mathbf{x}[n-k-h]\right] \quad (2)$$

In which $\mathbf{G}[.]$ is the $N \times 1$ vector of nonlinear compensating functions, one for each channel; $\mathbf{W}[k]$ and $\mathbf{Z}[k]$ are $N \times N$ FIR matrices with K_w and K_z filter taps.

Introducing the knowledge about the particular kind of mixing model is the key to avoid the strict non uniqueness of the solution; such assumption limits the weakness of the output independence condition reducing the cardinality of all possible independent output solutions; with this constraint the problem of recovery the original sources is not ill posed any more.

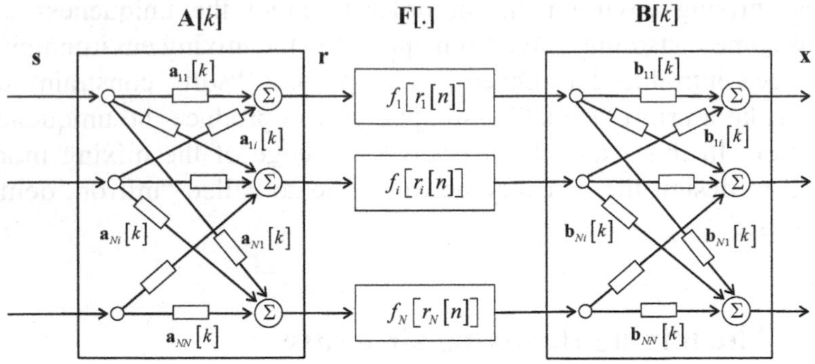

Figure 1. The Block diagram of the convolutive nonlinear mixing model

The use of FIR filter blocks grants the stability of the whole demixing structure.

4. The blind demixing algorithm and the network model

This section explores the blind demixing algorithm, the adaptive network and the network used to compensate the nonlinear distortion. The blind algorithm performs an on-line adaptive learning of the network parameters $\mathbf{\Phi}$ on the base of the output independence estimation. The learning is realized minimizing the Mutual Information $I\{\mathbf{\Phi},\mathbf{y}\}$ between outputs, with a steepest descent algorithm: $\mathbf{\Phi}(k+1)=\mathbf{\Phi}(k)-\eta_{\mathbf{\Phi}}\left[\partial I\{\mathbf{\Phi},\mathbf{y}\}/\partial\mathbf{\Phi}\right]$. The choice of a gradient based minimization procedure lead to terms like:

$$\frac{\partial}{\partial\mathbf{\Phi}}\log\left[p_{y_i}(y_i)\right]=\frac{\partial p_{y_i}(y_i)/\partial y_i}{p_{y_i}(y_i)}\frac{\partial y_i}{\partial\mathbf{\Phi}}=\psi_i(y_i)\frac{\partial y_i}{\partial\mathbf{\Phi}} \tag{3}$$

in which $\psi_i(y_i)$ are the so called Score Functions (SF). In this paper, the Spline Neurons are used to perform the on-line estimation of both Score Functions and nonlinear compensating functions (for a detail about Spline Neurons see [Solazzi et al., 2004][Uncini et al., 2004]). The most attractive property of Spline Neurons, as function estimator, is local learning: for each learning step only the four control points nearest to the training input are considered; no matter how many control points the Spline curve has.

The direct estimation of SF has been performed MSE approach ([Taleb, 2002] for details) but learning rules result still blind:

$$\frac{\partial \varepsilon}{\partial \mathbf{Q}_i^{\psi_j}} = \left[\frac{1}{4} \mathbf{T}_u \mathbf{M} \mathbf{T}_u \mathbf{M} \mathbf{Q}_i^{\psi_j} + \frac{1}{\Delta} \dot{\mathbf{T}}_u \mathbf{M} \right] \tag{4}$$

in which **M** is a matrix of coefficients, **T** is the vector local abscissa and Δ is the distance between the abscissas of adjacent control points.

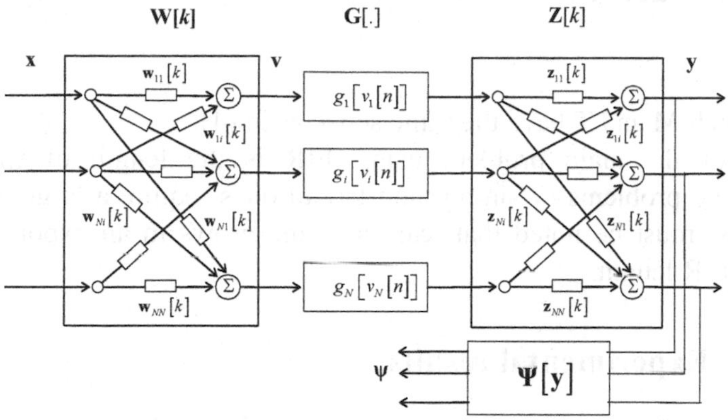

Figure 2. Feed Forward network used for the nonlinear blind deconvolution and separation.

Figure 2 shows the network used to perform the separation, it is a cascade of blocks well described in literature and previously used to resolve more simple problems. Deriving the cost function $I\{\mathbf{\Phi}, \mathbf{y}\}$ with respect the learning parameter $\mathbf{\Phi}$ results:

$$\frac{\partial I\{\mathbf{\Phi}, \mathbf{y}[n]\}}{\partial \mathbf{\Phi}} \simeq \frac{\partial \Im\{\mathbf{\Phi}, \mathbf{y}[n]\}}{\partial \mathbf{\Phi}} = \\ = -\frac{\partial}{\partial \mathbf{\Phi}} \sum_{n=0}^{M} \left[\log\left|\det \mathbf{Z}(0)\right| + \log \prod_{i=1}^{N} g_i\left[v_i[n]\right] + \log\left|\mathbf{W}(0)\right| + \sum_{i=1}^{N} \log p_{y_i}(y_i) \right] \tag{5}$$

In (5) the expected value of the signals has been replaced by the instantaneous value. The learning rules for the elements of the FIR matrices **Z**[*k*] and **W**[*k*], and for the control points $\mathbf{Q}^g$ of the Spline neurons that compensate the nonlinear distorting functions are:

$$\partial\Im / \partial \mathbf{Z}[k] = -\mathbf{Z}[k]^{-T} \delta_k - \mathbf{\Psi}_y{}^T \mathbf{v}[n-k] \tag{6}$$

$$\partial\Im/\partial\mathbf{Q}_i^{g_j} = -\left[\dot{\mathbf{T}}_u\mathbf{M}/\dot{\mathbf{T}}_u\mathbf{M}\mathbf{Q}_i^{g_j} + \mathbf{\Psi}_y\left(\mathbf{Z}[0]\right)_j \mathbf{T}_u\mathbf{M}\right] \tag{7}$$

$$\partial\Im/\partial\mathbf{W}[k] = -\mathbf{Z}[0]^{-T}\delta_k - \left[\ddot{g}_1(r_1)/\dot{g}_1(r_1)\cdots\ \ddot{g}_N(r_N)/\dot{g}_N(r_N)\right]^T \mathbf{x}[n-k] + \\ -\sum_p\left(\mathbf{Z}[p]^T\mathbf{\Psi}\right)\mathbf{v}^T[n-p]\mathbf{x}[n-p-k] \tag{8}$$

in which **M** and **T** have the same sense as in (4).

One of the main problem using FIR is the length of filters: real convolutive problems or simply non trivial ones require a large number of filter taps; must be noted that learning time grows in an exponential way with the FIR length.

5. Experimental results

This section collects the experimental result of the proposed architectures. The algorithm is able to perform the separation of N-channel mixtures but in order to make it possible the proper visualization of results only a pair of sources are considered: a male and a female voice speaking respectively "*Le donne i cavalier l'arme*" and "*Riperdo una seconda volta quegli esigui beni*".

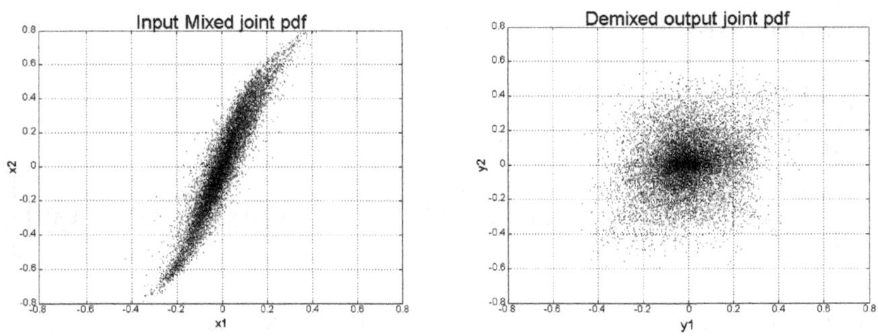

a) b)

Figure 3. a) Joint pdf of input mixture; b) Joint pdf of output demixed signals.

Figure 3 a) shows the pdf of mixed signal (the typical plot of the joint pdf of nonlinearly mixed sources) and figure 3 b) the ones of resulting signals after a 1200 epochs training: the typical plot of the joint pdf of separated signals. The recovering network has 103 Spline control points and a 15 taps FIR matrixes. The nonlinear distortions applied in this test are: $\mathbf{F}\left[f_1(p_1), f_2(p_2)\right] = \left[p_1 + 2p_1^{\,3}, 0.5p_2 + \tanh(7p_2)\right]$.

The mixing environment applied are invertible mixing MIMO channels; with respect to figure 1: $\mathbf{A} = \begin{bmatrix} 0.8 - 0.3z^{-1} + 0.3z^{-2} & 0.5 + 0.2z^{-1} - 0.2z^{-2} \\ -0.5 + 0.6z^{-1} + 0.2z^{-2} & 0.3 + 0.2z^{-1} - 0.1z^{-2} \end{bmatrix}$, $\mathbf{B} = \begin{bmatrix} 0.7 + 0.1z^{-1} + 0.4z^{-2} & 0.4 - 0.3z^{-1} + 0.1z^{-2} \\ 0.6 + 0.5z^{-1} - 0.1z^{-2} & 0.8 + 0.2z^{-1} + 0.3z^{-2} \end{bmatrix}$.

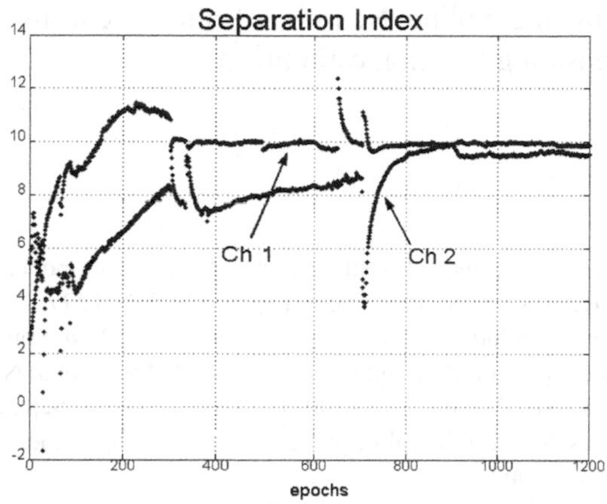

Figure 4. Separation index ratio index during the training.

The Separation index S_j (dB) introduced in [Shobben et al., 1999] measures the separation of the channel *j*-th.

$$S_j = 10\log\left[E\left\{\left(y_{\sigma(j),j}\right)^2\right\} \Big/ E\left\{\sum_{k\neq j}\left(y_{\sigma(j),k}\right)^2\right\}\right] \tag{9}$$

In (9) $y_{i,j}$ is the *i*-th output signal when only the *j*-th input signal is present while $\sigma(j)$ is the output channel corresponding to the *j*-input. The trend of this index (Figure 4) confirms the growing of separation during the training. Figure 4 shows that, after a first period, the algorithm performs the separation of the output signals. The reason of the starting transient has been the number of blocks each of one separately have to converge to the optimum values.

6. Conclusion

This paper explores a novel mixing environment for which the BSS performed by ICA is granted. Preliminary result on separation assures a quite good sources recovery after the convolutive mixing of a PNL convolutive mixtures. Although a good separation level has been reached, we are carrying researches on improving it and on granting better output quality. The FIR recovering network performs the on line estimation of the score function by the Spline Neurons. Spline Neurons perform also the nonlinear compensating function estimation.

References

Hyvarinen, A., Pajunen, P., (1999), "Nonlinear Independent Component Analysis: Existence and Uniqueness Results", Neural Networks 12(2): 429-439, 1999.

Jutten, C., Karhunen, J., (2003), "Advances in Nonlinear Blind Sources Separation", 4th International Symposium on ICA and BSS (ICA2003), April 2003, Nara, Japan.

Milani, F., Solazzi, M., Uncini, A., (2002), "Blind Source Separation of convolutive nonlinear mixtures by flexible spline nonlinear functions", Proc. of IEEE ICASSP'02, Orlando, USA, May, 2002.

Shobben, D., Torkkola, K., Smaragdis, P., (1999), "Evaluation of blind signal separation methods", In Proc. of ICA and BSS, Aussois, France, January 11-15, 1999.

Solazzi, M., Uncini, A., (2004), "Spline Neural Networks for Blind Separation of Post-Nonlinear-Linear Mixtures", In IEEE Trans. on Circuits and Systems I Fundamental Theory and Applications, Vol. 51 , No. 4, pp 817 – 829, April 2004.

Taleb, A., (2002), "A Generic Framework for Blind Sources Separation in Structured Nonlinear Models", In IEEE Trans. on signal processing, vol. 50. no 8 August 2002.

Taleb, A., Jutten, C., (1999), "Sources Separation in post nonlinear mixtures", In IEEE Trans. on signal processing, vol. 47. no 10 August 1999.

Uncini, A., Vecci, L., Piazza, F., (1998), "Learning and approximation capabilities of adaptive Spline activation function neural network", In NN, Vol. 11, no. 2, pag. 259-270 March 1998.

Vigliano, D., Parisi, R., Uncini, A., (2004), "A novel recurrent network for independent component analysis of Post Nonlienar convolutive mixtures", Proc. of IEEE ICASSP'04, Montreal, Canada, May 17-21, 2004.

Vigliano, D., Parisi, R., Uncini, A., (2004), "Nonlinear ICA solution for convolutive mixing of PNL mixture", Proc. of IEEE ISCAS'04, Vancouver, Canada, May 23-26, 2004.

Zade, M. B., Jutten, C., Najeby, K., (2001), "Blind Separating, Convolutive Post nonlinear Mixture", ICA 2001 In Proc. of the 3rd Workshop on Independent Component Analysis and Signal Separation (ICA2001), San Diego (California, USA), 2001, pp. 138–143.

COMPUTING CONFIDENCE INTERVALS FOR THE RISK OF A SVM CLASSIFIER THROUGH ALGORITHMIC INFERENCE

B. Apolloni, S. Bassis, S. Gaito, D. Malchiodi, and A. Minora
Dipartimento di Scienze dell'Informazione, Università degli Studi di Milano
Via Comelico 39/41, 20135 Milano, Italy
{apolloni,bassis,gaito,malchiodi,minora}@dsi.unimi.it

Abstract We reconsider in the Algorithmic Inference framework the accuracy of a Boolean function learnt from examples. This framework is specially suitable when the Boolean function is learnt through a Support Vector Machine, since (i) we know the number of support vectors really employed as an ancillary output of the learning procedure, and (ii) we can appreciate confidence intervals of misclassifying probability exactly in function of the cardinality of these vectors. As a result we obtain confidence intervals that are up to an order narrower than those supplied in the literature, having a slight different meaning due to the different approach they come from, but the same operational function. We numerically check the covering of these intervals.

Keywords: support vector machines, confidence intervals, algorithmic inference, computational learning

1. Introduction

Support Vector Machines (SVM for short) [Cortes and Vapnik, 1995] represent an operational tool widely used by the Machine Learning community. *Per se* a SVM is an n dimensional hyperplane committed to separate positive from negative points of a linearly separable Cartesian space. The success of these machines in comparison with analogous models such as a real-inputs perceptron is due to the algorithm employed to learn them from examples that performs very efficiently and relies on a well defined small subset of examples that it manages in a symbolic way. Thus the algorithm plays the role of a specimen of the computational learning theory [Valiant, 1984] allowing theoretical forecasting of the future misclassifying error. This prevision however may result very bad and consequently deprived of any operational consequence. This is because we are generally obliged to broad approximations coming from more or less sophisticated variants of the law of large numbers. In the paper

B. Apolloni et al. (eds.), Biological and Artificial Intelligence Environments, 225–234

we overcome this drawback working in the Algorithmic Inference framework [Apolloni et al., 2003] with the benefit of computing relatively narrow confidence intervals for the misclassifying probability that numerically prove not exceedingly oversized.

2. Learning SVMs

In their basic version, SVMs are used to compute hypotheses in the class H of hyperplanes in $\mathbb{R}^n$, for fixed $n \in \mathbb{N}$. Given a sample $\{\mathbf{x}_1, \ldots, \mathbf{x}_m\} \in \mathbb{R}^{mn}$ with associated labels $\{y_1, \ldots, y_m\} \in \{-1, 1\}^m$, the related classification problem lies in finding a *separating hyperplane*, i.e. an $h \in \mathsf{H}$ such that all the points with a given label belong to one of the two half-spaces determined by h.

In order to obtain such a h, a SVM computes first the solution $\{\alpha_1^*, \ldots, \alpha_m^*\}$ of the constrained optimization problem

$$\max_{\alpha_1,\ldots,\alpha_m} \quad \sum_{i=1}^{m} \alpha_i - \frac{1}{2} \sum_{i,j=1}^{m} \alpha_i \alpha_j y_i y_j \mathbf{x}_i \cdot \mathbf{x}_j \tag{1}$$

$$\sum_{i=1}^{m} \alpha_i y_i = 0 \tag{2}$$

$$\alpha_i \geq 0 \quad i = 1, \ldots, m\,, \tag{3}$$

where $\cdot$ denotes the standard dot product in $\mathbb{R}^n$, and then returns a hyperplane (called *separating hyperplane*) whose equation is $\mathbf{w} \cdot \mathbf{x} + b = 0$, where

$$\mathbf{w} = \sum_{i=1}^{m} \alpha_i^* y_i \mathbf{x}_i \tag{4}$$

$$b = y_i - \mathbf{w} \cdot \mathbf{x}_i \text{ for } i \text{ such that } \alpha_i^* > 0\,. \tag{5}$$

In the case of a *separable sample* (i.e. a sample for which the existence of at least a separating hyperplane is guaranteed), this algorithm produces a separating hyperplane with *optimal margin*, i.e. a hyperplane maximizing its minimal distance with the sample points. Moreover, typically only a few components of $\{\alpha_1^*, \ldots, \alpha_m^*\}$ are different from zero, so that the hypothesis depends on a small subset of the available examples (whose elements are denoted *support vectors* or SV).

A variant of this algorithm, known as *soft-margin classifier* [Schölkopf et al., 1999], produces hypotheses for which the separability requirement is relaxed, introducing a parameter μ whose value represents an upper bound to the fraction of sample classification errors and a lower bound to the fraction of points that are allowed to have a distance less or equal the margin. The corresponding optimization problem is essentially unchanged, with the sole exception of (3), which now becomes

$$0 \leq \alpha_i \leq \frac{1}{m} \quad i = 1, \ldots, m$$
$$\sum_{i=1}^{m} \alpha_i \geq \mu. \tag{3'}$$

Analogously, the separating hyperplane equation is still computed through (4-5), though the latter equation needs to be computed on indices i such that $0 < \alpha_i^* < \frac{1}{m}$.

3. The associated Algorithmic Inference problem

We assume the following statement of the general problem of learning a Boolean function from examples.

DEFINITION 1 *For a given space $\mathfrak{X}$ and fixed m, a* labeled sample *is a set*

$$\mathbf{z}_m = \{(x_i, b_i),\ i = 1, \ldots, m\}, \tag{6}$$

where $x_i \in \mathfrak{X}$ and b_i are Boolean variables. If we assume that, given a concept class C, for every M and every (labeled) population $\mathbf{z}_M$ a c exists in C such that $\mathbf{z}_{m+M} = \{(X_i, c(X_i)),\ i = 1, \ldots, m+M\}$, then we call learning algorithm *a total function $\mathcal{A} : \{\mathbf{z}_m\} \mapsto \mathsf{H}$ that*

- *for any $\mathbf{z}_m$*
- *for any pair of accuracy parameters $\varepsilon, \delta \in [0, 1]$*

computes another function, that we denote as hypothesis *h, such that the confidence interval $(0, \varepsilon)$ of the measure $U_{c \div h}$ of the symmetric difference $c \div h$ between the two functions has at least confidence $1 - \delta$. In formulas:*

$$\mathrm{P}(U_{c \div h} \leq \varepsilon) \geq 1 - \delta. \tag{7}$$

We can bind the $U_{c \div h}$ distribution law through the following theorem.

THEOREM 2 *[Apolloni and Malchiodi, 2001] For a space $\mathfrak{X}$ and any probability measure P on it, assume we are given*

- *concept classes C and H on $\mathfrak{X}$;*
- *a labeled sample $\mathbf{Z}_m$ drawn from $\mathfrak{X} \times \{0, 1\}$;*
- *a* fairly strongly surjective *function $\mathcal{A} : \{\mathbf{z}_m\} \mapsto \mathsf{H}$*

In the case where for any $\mathbf{z}_m$ and any infinite suffix $\mathbf{z}_M$ of it a $c \in \mathsf{C}$ exists computing the example labels of the whole sequence, consider the family of *random sets* $\{c \in \mathsf{C} : \mathbf{z}_{m+M} = \{(x_i, c(x_i)), i = 1, \ldots, m+M\}$ *for any specification* $\mathbf{z}_M$ *of* $\mathbf{Z}_M\}$. *Denote* $h = \mathcal{A}(\mathbf{z}_m)$ *and* $U_{c\div h}$ *the random variable given by the probability measure of* $c \div h$ *and* $F_{U_{c\div h}}$ *its cumulative distribution function. For a given* $\mathbf{z}_m$, *if* h *has detail* $\mathrm{D}_{(\mathsf{C},\mathsf{H})_h}$ *and misclassifies* t_h *points of* $\mathbf{z}_m$, *then for each* $\varepsilon \in (0,1)$,

$$\sum_{i=t_h+1}^{m} \binom{m}{i} \varepsilon^i (1-\varepsilon)^{m-i} \geq F_{U_{c\div h}}(\varepsilon) \geq \sum_{i=D_{(\mathsf{C},\mathsf{H})_h}+t_h}^{m} \binom{m}{i} \varepsilon^i (1-\varepsilon)^{m-i} \quad (8)$$

Fairly strong surjectivity is a usual regularity condition [Apolloni et al., 2003], while $D_{(\mathsf{C},\mathsf{H})_h}$ is the key parameter of the Algorithmic Inference approach to learning. The general idea is that it counts the number of meaningful examples within a sample, i.e. those examples that prevent $\mathcal{A}$ from computing a hypothesis h' with a wider mistake region $c \div h'$. In greater detail, a *sentry function* [Apolloni and Chiaravalli, 1997] attributes points from $\mathfrak{X}$ to each concept c in order to discriminate it within a class C. Call these points *frontier* of the concept. The frontier size of the most expensive concept attributed by the least efficient sentry function $\mathbf{S}$, i.e. the quantity $\mathrm{D}_\mathsf{C} = \sup_{\mathbf{S},c} \#\mathbf{S}(c)$, is called *detail* of C. Moving to symmetric differences, for another set H of concepts let us consider the class of symmetric differences $c \div \mathsf{H} = \{c \div h \ \forall h \in \mathsf{H}\}$ for any c belonging to C. The detail of a concept class H w.r.t. c is the quantity $\mathrm{D}_{c,\mathsf{H}} = \mathrm{D}_{c\div\mathsf{H}}$ and the overall detail of the class $\mathsf{C} \div \mathsf{H} = \cup_{c\in\mathsf{C}} c \div \mathsf{H}$ is the quantity $\mathrm{D}_{\mathsf{C},\mathsf{H}} = \sup_{c\in\mathsf{C}}\{\mathrm{D}_{c,\mathsf{H}}\}$. Finally, we denote $\mathrm{D}_{(\mathsf{C},\mathsf{H})_h}$ the restriction of $\mathrm{D}_{\mathsf{C},\mathsf{H}}$ to h, i.e. the number of sentry points within the above sup computation to sentinel exactly h.

Analogous results in the PAC learning approach are based on a dual parameter constituted by the Vapnik-Chervonenkis dimension $\mathrm{d_{VC}}(\mathsf{C})$ (for short, VC dimension) of the concept class C [Blumer et al., 1989] counting the number of concepts within C necessary to discriminate all subsets of points within a sample.

A link for comparing the two families of results is represented by the following theorem.

THEOREM 3 *For any concept class* C

$$\mathrm{D}_\mathsf{C} < \mathrm{d_{VC}}(\mathsf{C}) + 1 \,. \quad (9)$$

Finally, we frame the SVM learning problem in the above results thanks to the following lemma.

LEMMA 4 *Let us denote by* C *the concept class of hyperlanes on a given space* $\mathfrak{X}$ *and by* $\sigma = \{x_1, \ldots, x_s\}$ *a minimal set of support vectors of a hyperplane* h *(i.e.* σ *is a support vector set but, whatever* i *is, no* $\sigma \backslash \{x_i\}$ *does the same).*

Then, for whatever goal hyperplane c separating the above set accordingly with h, there exists a sentry function $\mathbf{S}$ *on* $\mathsf{C} \div \mathsf{H}$ *and a subset of σ of cardinality at most $s-1$ sentinelling $c \div h$ according to* $\mathbf{S}$.

Proof: *To identify a hyperplane in an n-dimensional Euclidean space we need to put n* non aligned *points into a linear equations' system, $n+1$ if these points are at a fixed (either negative or positive) distance. This is also the maximum number of support vector required by a SVM. We may substitute one or more points with direct linear constraints on the hyperplane coefficients when the topology of the support vectors allows it. Sentinelling the expansion of the simmetric difference $c \div h$ results in forbidding any rotation of h into a h' pivoted along the intersection of c with h. The membership of this intersection to h' adds from 1 to $n-1$ linear relations on its coefficients, so that at most $\#\sigma - 1$ points from σ are necessary, possibly in conjunction with the direct linear constraints on the coefficients to fix h' to h.*

□

In synthesis, our approach focuses on a probabilistic description of the *uncertainty region* [Shawe-Taylor and Cristianini, 2004], rather than on its geometric approximation [Muselli, 2001].

We must remark that in principle the constraint for h' to contain the intersection of h with c gives rise to $n-1$ linear relations on h' coefficients. These relations may result effective in a shorter number if linear relations occur between them deriving from linear relations, in own turn, between h and c coefficients. Now, as the former are functions of the sampled points, no way exists for computing coefficients that result exactly in linear relation with those of the unknown (future) c if the sample space is continuous (and its probability distribution do the same). We really realize these linear relations if either the sample space is discrete or the algorithm computing the hyperplane is so approximate to work on an actually discretised search space.

Thus we have the following fact.

FACT 5 *The number of sentry points of separating hyperplanes computed through support vector machines ranges from 1 to the minimal number of involved support vectors minus one, depending on the approximation with which either sample coordinates are stored or hyperplanes are computed.*

4. Confidence intervals for the learning error

DEFINITION 6 *Given a random variable with parameter L* [1] *and a real number $0 \leq \delta \leq 1$, (l_i, l_s) is called a $1-\delta$* confidence interval *for L if*

$$\mathrm{P}(l_i < L < l_s) \geq 1 - \delta \tag{10}$$

The quantity δ is called the confidence interval's level.

Equation (8) allows us to compute a confidence interval $I = (u_1, u_2)$ at level δ for $U_{c\div h}$ directly from the inequality

$$F_{\mathrm{U}_{c\div h}}(u_2) - F_{\mathrm{U}_{c\div h}}(u_1) \geq 1 - \delta\,; \tag{11}$$

therefore, getting

$$\Delta F = \sum_{i=\mathrm{D}_{\mathrm{C,H}}+t_h}^{m} \binom{m}{i} u_2^i (1-u_2)^{m-i} - \sum_{i=t_h+1}^{m} \binom{m}{i} u_1^i (1-u_1)^{m-i}$$

as an upper bound to $F_{\mathrm{U}_{c\div h}}(u_2) - F_{\mathrm{U}_{c\div h}}(u_1)$, (11) can be solved by dividing the probability measure outside I in two equal parts in order to obtain a two-sided interval symmetric in the tail probabilities. In this way we obtain a solution to the interval confidence problem from:

$$\sum_{i=\mathrm{D}_{\mathrm{C,H}}+t_h}^{m} \binom{m}{i} u_2^i (1-u_2)^{m-i} = 1 - \frac{\delta}{2} \tag{12}$$

$$\sum_{i=t_h+1}^{m} \binom{m}{i} u_1^i (1-u_1)^{m-i} = \frac{\delta}{2} \tag{13}$$

Let us consider the companion error probability associated to a hypothesis h through the following definition.

DEFINITION 7 *For a given space $\mathfrak{X}$, a distribution probability* P *on it, and fixed m, consider a conept* c *and a random* labeled sample

$$\mathbf{Z}_m = \{(X_i, B_i),\ i = 1, \ldots, m\}$$

where X_i are distributed according to P *and B_i are Bernoullian variables such that $b_i = c(x_i)$ for each pair of specifications of X_i and B_i respectively. For any learning algorithm $\mathcal{A}$ denote by $V(\mathbf{Z}_m)$ the random variable measuring $c \div \mathcal{A}(\mathbf{Z}_m)$ according to* P *and $\nu(\mathbf{Z}_m)$ the corresponding frequency of classification errors computed from the sample according to $\mathcal{A}$ (called* empirical error*).*

We refer to the commonly used confidence intervals stated by Vapnik and Chervonenkis since the late '70 for the risk $V(\mathbf{Z}_m)$. Analogous intervals based on Rademaker complexity prove either not applicable or meaningless in the general cases we are considering [Bartlett and Mendelson, 2002].

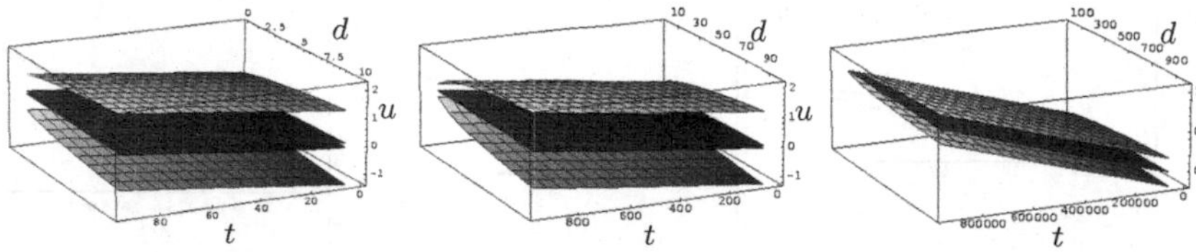

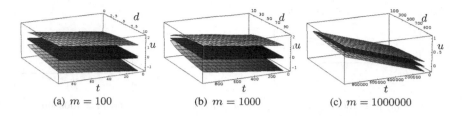

(a) $m = 100$ (b) $m = 1000$ (c) $m = 1000000$

Figure 1. Comparison between two-sided 0.9 confidence intervals for SVM classification error. t: number of misclassified sample points; d: VC dimension; u: confidence interval extremes; m: sample size. Gray surfaces: VC bounds. Black surfaces: proposed bounds.

THEOREM 8 *[Vapnik, 1982] Let* C *be a Boolean concept class of bounded VC dimension* $\mathrm{d_{VC}} = d$. *With the same notations of Definition 7, the event*

$$\nu(\mathbf{Z}_m) - 2\sqrt{\frac{d\left(\log\frac{2m}{d}+1\right)-\log\frac{\delta}{9}}{m}} < V(\mathbf{Z}_m) < \nu(\mathbf{Z}_m) + 2\sqrt{\frac{d\left(\log\frac{2m}{d}+1\right)-\log\frac{\delta}{9}}{m}} \qquad (14)$$

has probability $1-\delta$.

5. Numerical experiments

To appreciate the numerical benefit of our approach, or at least a lower bound to it, in the following example we artificially fill the gap between detail and VC dimension by: 1) referring to both complexity indices and empirical error ν constant with learnt hypotheses and 2) assuming $\mathrm{D}_{\mathsf{C},\mathsf{C}} = \mathrm{d_{VC}}(\mathsf{C}) = d$ ($\leq n+1$). Figure 1 compares two-sided confidence intervals in the two approaches for a set of values of the number of mislabelled points and of support vectors. Following the previous remark, we compute the former quantity in (12) and (13) as $m\nu$. For a sample of 100, 1000 and 1000000 elements respectively, the three graphs show the limits of the 0.9-confidence intervals drawn using both VC (external surfaces) and Detail (internal surfaces) bounds. Moreover, to appreciate the differences even better, in Figure 2 we draw a section with $d = 4$ in function of the number of misclassified points. The figures show that:

- Detail confidence intervals are always more accurate than VC's; this benefit accounts for a narrowing of one order at the smallest sample size, while tends to disappear when the sample size increases.

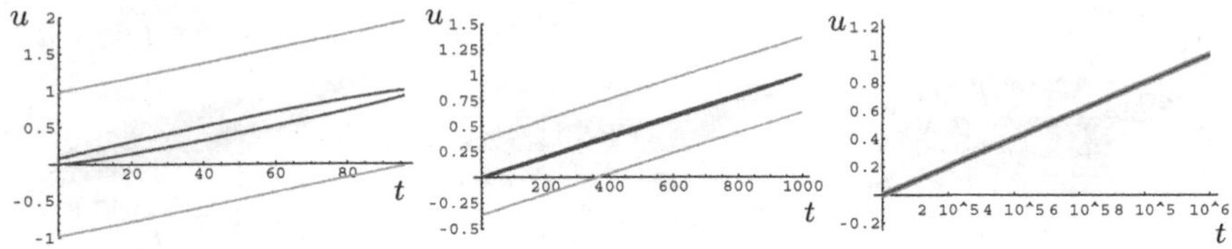

(a) $m = 100$ (b) $m = 1000$ (c) $m = 1000000$

Figure 2. Same comparison as in Figure 1 with $d = 4$.

- Detail confidence intervals are consistent, that is they are always contained in $[0, 1]$;

Finally, in Figure 3 we check the coverage of the above intervals through a huge set of pairs of statistics and error probabilities $\mathrm{P_{err}} = u_{c \div h}$ sampled from learning instances on points uniformly distributed in the unitary hypercube and variously separated by random coefficients hyperplanes. Namely in Figure 3(a) we considered different sample sizes for the number of support vectors fixed to 3, and in Figure 3(b) we conversely maintained the sample size fixed to 100 and considered different numbers ν_h of support vectors as upper bound to $\mathrm{D}_{(\mathsf{C},\mathsf{H})_h}$ plus 1. The slight oversize of the intervals on each abscissa is connected with Fact 5. Indeed from the graph in Figure 4(a) of the percentage of experiments trespassing the confidence intervals for any abscissa with the accuracy μ of the learning algorithm (see (3′)), we see that the design parameter $\delta = 0.1$ is stably reached with the increase of this parameter. Note that for $\mu > 0$ the algorithm works on a superset of the support vectors, thus we rely on the upper bound n (the dimension of the sample space) to their cardinality. Finally, in Figure 4(b) we draw the same confidence region in case the SVM tries to divide two regions non linearly separable. In this case we use a parabolic surface for dividing the hypercube points, hence to label the sample as well. This may induce some mislabeling by the hypothesis even on the sample points. We afford this case just by adding the number of support vectors and the number of mislabelled sample points in the abscissa of the graph and using a parameter $\mu = 0.2$. We have the same confidence intervals in correspondence of the abscissas and $u_{c \div h}$ values well contained in these intervals as well.

Notes

1. See [Apolloni et al., 2003] for a thorough explanation of this definition and of the use of a random variable as parameter.

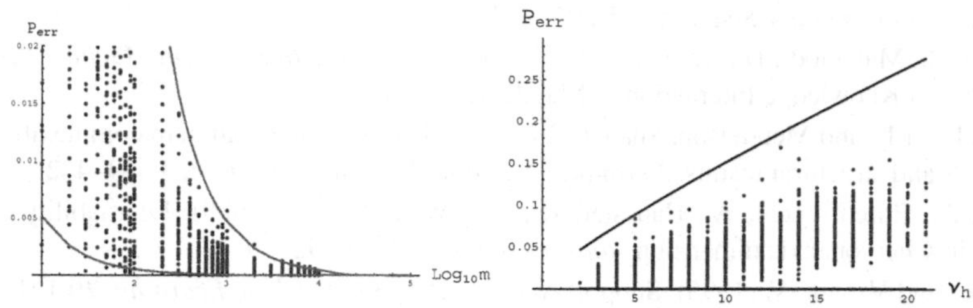

(a) (b)

Figure 3. Course of misclassification probability with the parameters of the learning problem: (a) probability vs. sample size, (b) probability vs. ν_h.

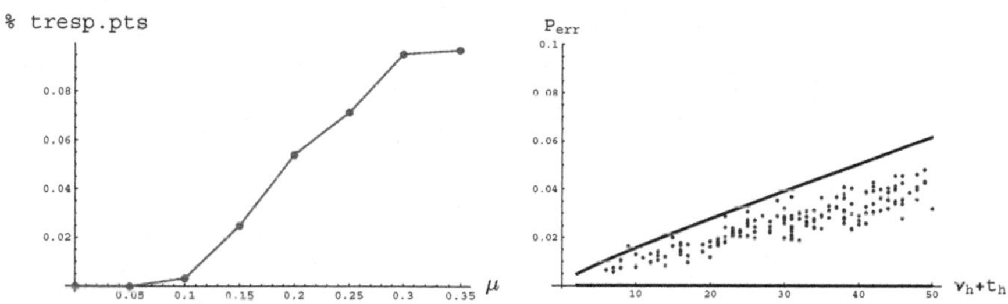

(a) (b)

Figure 4. (a) Course of the experimental confidence level with algorithm approximation. (b) Same picture as in Figure 3(b) for non linearly separable instances. Abscissa: ν_h plus number of wrongly classified sample points t_h.

References

Apolloni, B. and Chiaravalli, S. (1997). PAC learning of concept classes through the boundaries of their items. *Theoretical Computer Science*, 172:91–120.

Apolloni, B. and Malchiodi, D. (2001). Gaining degrees of freedom in subsymbolic learning. *Theoretical Computer Science*, 255:295–321.

Apolloni, B., Malchiodi, D., and Gaito, S. (2003). *Algorithmic Inference in Machine Learning*. Advanced Knowledge International, Magill, Adelaide.

Bartlett, Peter L. and Mendelson, Shahar (2002). Rademacher and Gaussian complexities: Risk bounds and structural results. *Journal of Machine Learning Research*, 3:463–482.

Blumer, A., Ehrenfreucht, A., Haussler, D., and Warmuth, M. (1989). Learnability and the Vapnik-Chervonenkis dimension. *Journal of the ACM*, 36:929–965.

Cortes, C. and Vapnik, V. (1995). Support-Vector networks. *Machine Learning*, 20:121–167.

Muselli, M. (2001). Support Vector Machines for uncertainty region detection. In Marinaro, M. and Tagliaferri, R., editors, *Neural Nets: WIRN VIETRI '01, 12th Italian Workshop on Neural Nets (Vietri sul Mare, Italy, 17–19 May 2001)*, pages 108–113, London. Springer.

Schölkopf, B., Burges, C. J. C., and Smola, A. J., editors (1999). *Advances in kernel methods: Support Vector learning*. MIT Press, Cambridge, Mass.

Shawe-Taylor, J. and Cristianini, N. (2004). *Kernel Methods for Pattern Analysis*. Cambridge University Press.

Valiant, L. G. (1984). A theory of the learnable. *Communications of the ACM*, 11(27):1134–1142.

Vapnik, V. (1982). *Estimation of dependencies based on empirical data*. Springer, New York.

LEARNING CONTINUOUS FUNCTIONS THROUGH A NEW LINEAR REGRESSION METHOD

B. Apolloni, S. Bassis, S. Gaito, D. Iannizzi, and D. Malchiodi
Dipartimento di Scienze dell'Informazione, Università degli Studi di Milano
Via Comelico 39/41, 20135 Milano, Italy
{apolloni,bassis,gaito,iannizzi,malchiodi} @dsi.unimi.it

Abstract We revisit the linear regression problem in terms of a computational learning problem whose task is to identify a confidence region for a continuous function belonging in particular to the straight lines family. Within the Algorithmic Inference framework this function is deputed to explain a relation between pairs of variables that are observed through a limited sample. Hence it is a random item within the above family and we look for a partial order relation allowing us to state a cumulative distribution function over the function specifications, hence a pair of quantiles identifying the confidence region. The regions we compute in this way is theoretically and numerically attested to *entirely* contain the goal function with a given confidence. Its shape is quite different from the analogous region obtained through conventional methods as a collation of confidence intervals found for the expected value of the dependent variable as a function of the independent one.

Keywords: linear regression, confidence intervals, algorithmic inference

1. Introduction

We focus on the classical model of linear regression [Morrison, 1967] which we formalize as follows

DEFINITION 1 *Given the space $\mathfrak{X} \times \mathfrak{Y} \subseteq \mathbb{R}^*$ and a sample of size m whose general form is*

$$\mathbf{z}_m = \{(x_i, y_i) : x_i \in \mathfrak{X},\ y_i \in \mathfrak{Y},\ i = 1, \ldots, m\} \subseteq (\mathfrak{X} \times \mathfrak{Y})^m \quad (1)$$

we assume that a function c exists within a class C such that, for any suffix $\mathbf{z}_M$ of $\mathbf{z}_m$ (i.e. any continuation of the observed data), and for any (x_i, y_i) belonging to the concatenated sequence $\mathbf{z}_{m+M}$

$$y_i = c(x_i) + \varepsilon_i, \quad i = 1, \ldots, m + M \quad (2)$$

B. Apolloni et al. (eds.), Biological and Artificial Intelligence Environments, 235–243

where the ε_i *values are specifications of a set of corresponding random variables* E_i *(modeling an additive noise).*

The easiest and best known instance of regression problem is the following

- $\mathfrak{X}$ and $\mathfrak{Y}$ are subsets of $\mathbb{R}$;
- the concept class is $\mathsf{C} = \{a' + bx : a', b \in \mathbb{R}\}$;
- the random variables E_i are assumed to be independent, identically distributed and with null mean.

To facilitate the future computations, we adopt the special representation of a line whose $\mathfrak{X}$ coordinate is centered around $\overline{x} = \frac{1}{m}\sum_{i=1}^{m} x_i$, hence relying on the model

$$y_i = a + b(x_i - \overline{x}) + \varepsilon_i, \quad i = 1, \ldots, m \tag{3}$$

This is without loss of generality, since it corresponds to shift the origin of the $\mathfrak{X}$ axis by $\overline{x}$ in the framework where c is represented through $a' + bx$ with $a' = a - b\overline{x}$.

2. A twisting argument for regression lines

Since many different z_M sequences (call them populations) may constitute suffixes of the observed z_m (in the hypothesis that a same phenomenon underlies both sequences) we have that a and b in (3) represent specifications of random variables A and B respectively, whose distribution laws we will discover in the frame of the Algorithmic Inference [Apolloni et al., 2003]. A *twisting argument* is the logical tool we will use for relating sample properties with population parameters through a particular mapping called *sampling mechanism.* The mapping is stated from a standard random variable to the one we are studying through a function involving the parameters we are questioning on. In our case exactly (3) will constitute a sampling mechanism mapping from E to Y having the X specifications for given. After some elementary algebra on (3) we discover the following logical implications constituting twisting arguments for A and B

$$(a \leq \widetilde{a}) \Leftrightarrow \left(\sum_{i=1}^{m} y_i \leq \sum_{i=1}^{m} \widetilde{y}_i\right) \tag{4}$$

$$\left(b \leq \widetilde{b}\right) \Leftrightarrow \left(\sum_{i=1}^{m} y_i\,(x_i - \overline{x}) \leq \sum_{i=1}^{m} \widetilde{y}_i\,(x_i - \overline{x})\right) \tag{5}$$

where $\widetilde{y}_i$ corresponds to the value we would observe in place of y_i with the tilded parameters. These relations start from a definite order relation on both statistics and parameter values. Hence, it is possible to reverse them in probability terms. Namely, introducing the variables $S_{\mathsf{E}} = \sum_{i=1}^{m} \mathsf{E}_i = \sum_{i=1}^{m}(Y_i - ma)$, for any $a \in \mathbb{R}$, and $S'_{\mathsf{E}} = \sum_{i=1}^{m} \mathsf{E}_i(x_i - \overline{x}) = \sum_{i=1}^{m} Y_i(x_i - \overline{x}) - b\sum_{i=1}^{m}(x_i - \overline{x})^2$, for any $b \in \mathbb{R}$, we obtain the cumulative distribution function (c.d.f.) of the parameters A and B from the distribution of E:

$$F_A(\widetilde{a}) = 1 - F_{S_{\mathsf{E}}}\left(\sum_{i=1}^{m} y_i - m\widetilde{a}\right) \tag{6}$$

$$F_B(\widetilde{b}) = 1 - F_{S'_{\mathsf{E}}}\left(\sum_{i=1}^{m} y_i(x_i - \overline{x}) - \widetilde{b}\sum_{i=1}^{m}(x_i - \overline{x})^2\right) \tag{7}$$

In order to state an analogous relation involving the entire regression line we need to introduce an order relation also in the lines' family. We do this through a contour lines' family $\{D_k\}$ constituted by the envelope of: i) either a set of straight lines $y = a^* + b^*(x - \overline{x})$ such that $b^* \geq 0$ and $a^* + b^*$ equals a thresholding parameter k, and ii) a set of straight lines such that $b^* < 0$ and $a^* - b^* = k$. Each D_k partitions the family line in a set I_k and its complement such that: a) each line $\ell \in I_k$ lies completely under D_k, and b) for each $k' < k$ contour $D_{k'}$ lies completely under D_k. Fig. 1(a) gives a qualitative picture of I_k. We will consider it as the intersection of two regions bounded either before $\overline{x}$ (call it I_k^l) or after $\overline{x}$ (call it I_k^r).

First of all we notice that the right part after $\overline{x}$ of a line $y = a' + b'(x - \overline{x})$ lies completely under the line $y = a + b(x - \overline{x})$ if and only if both parameters a' and b' are less than or equal to the corresponding parameters a and b. Namely

$$\left(a \leq \widetilde{a} \wedge b \leq \widetilde{b}\right) \Leftrightarrow \left(a + b(x - \overline{x}) \leq \widetilde{a} + \widetilde{b}(x - x), \; \forall x \geq \overline{x}\right) \tag{8}$$

Moreover, we recognize that parameters a and b of a line ℓ have a sum less than or equal to $\widetilde{k}$ if and only if two numbers a' and b' exist with a sum less than or equal to $\widetilde{k}$ as well which are parameters of a line lying over ℓ for each $x \geq \overline{x}$. I.e.

$$\left(\exists a', b' \text{ s.t. } (a' + b' \leq \widetilde{k}) \wedge (a + b\,(x - \overline{x}) \leq a' + b'\,(x - \overline{x}) \;\forall x \geq \overline{x})\right) \Leftrightarrow \left(a + b \leq \widetilde{k}\right) \tag{9}$$

Following (4) and (5) we may also state:

$$\left(a+b\leq\widetilde{k}\right)\Leftrightarrow\Bigg[\exists a',b'\text{ such that }\left(a'+b'\leq\widetilde{k}\right)\\ \wedge\left(\widetilde{y}_i=a'+b'\left(x_i-\overline{x}\right)+\varepsilon_i\;\forall i=1,\ldots,m\right)\wedge\\ \left(\sum_{i=1}^{m}y_i+m\frac{\sum_{i=1}^{m}y_i(x_i-\overline{x})}{\sum_{i=1}^{m}(x_i-\overline{x})^2}\leq\sum_{i=1}^{m}\widetilde{y}_i+m\frac{\sum_{i=1}^{m}\widetilde{y}_i(x_i-\overline{x})}{\sum_{i=1}^{m}(x_i-\overline{x})^2}\right)\Bigg] \tag{10}$$

since the last brackets read $(ma+mb\leq ma'+mb')$.

Joining (9) and (10) we have:

for each a,b such that $a+b\leq\widetilde{k}$ it exists $a',b'\leq\widetilde{k}$ such that

$$\Bigg[\left(\widetilde{y}_i=a'+b'\left(x_i-\overline{x}\right)+\varepsilon_i\;\forall i=1,\ldots,m\right)\\ \wedge\left(\sum_{i=1}^{m}y_i+m\frac{\sum_{i=1}^{m}y_i(x_i-\overline{x})}{\sum_{i=1}^{m}(x_i-\overline{x})^2}\leq\sum_{i=1}^{m}\widetilde{y}_i+m\frac{\sum_{i=1}^{m}\widetilde{y}_i(x_i-\overline{x})}{\sum_{i=1}^{m}(x_i-\overline{x})^2}\right)\Bigg]\\ \Leftrightarrow\left[\left(a+b(x-\overline{x})\leq a'+b'(x-\overline{x}),\;\forall x\geq\overline{x}\right)\right] \tag{11}$$

For $\breve{k}\in\mathbb{R}$ we can therefore consider the *ceiling family*

$$D^r_{\breve{k}}=\{(a^r,b^r)\}_{\breve{k}}=\left\{\arg\sup{}^r\left\{(a',b')\text{ s.t. }a'+b'\leq\breve{k}\right\}\right\} \tag{12}$$

representing the top contour of $I^r_{\breve{k}}$, where $\arg\sup^r$ means any pair (a^r,b^r), with $a^r+b^r=\breve{k}$ of parameters of a line ℓ such that no line $y=a'+b'(x-\overline{x})\in I^r_{\breve{k}}$ lies even partially over the envelope of ℓ when $x\geq\overline{x}$. Thus the membership of line $y=a'+b'(x-\overline{x})$ to $I^r_{\breve{k}}$ is checked for a suitable element of $D^r_{\breve{k}}$ through the implication:

$$\left(a+b(x-\overline{x})\leq a^r+b^r(x-\overline{x})\right)\Leftrightarrow\\ \left(\sum_{i=1}^{m}y_i+m\frac{\sum_{i=1}^{m}y_i(x_i-\overline{x})}{\sum_{i=1}^{m}(x_i-\overline{x})^2}\leq\sum_{i=1}^{m}\widetilde{y}_i+m\frac{\sum_{i=1}^{m}\widetilde{y}_i(x_i-\overline{x})}{\sum_{i=1}^{m}(x_i-\overline{x})^2}\right) \tag{13}$$

with $\widetilde{y}_i = a^r + b^r(x_i - \overline{x}) + \varepsilon_i$. Therefore if we introduce the random variable

$$S''_{\mathsf{E}} = S_{\mathsf{E}} + S'_{\mathsf{E}} \frac{m}{\sum_{i=1}^{m}(x_i - \overline{x})^2} = \sum_{i=1}^{m} \mathsf{E}_i \left(1 + m \frac{x_i - \overline{x}}{\sum_{i=1}^{m}(x_i - \overline{x})^2} \right)$$

we obtain the following distribution function

$$\widetilde{F}_{I^r_K}(I^r_k) = P(I^r_K \subseteq I^r_k) =$$
$$= 1 - F_{S''_E} \left(\sum_{i=1}^{m} y_i - ma^r + m \frac{\sum_{i=1}^{m} y_i(x_i - \overline{x})}{\sum_{i=1}^{m}(x_i - \overline{x})^2} - mb^r \right) \quad (14)$$

Analogous considerations can be done for the c.d.f. of the random variable I^l_K, corresponding to $x < \overline{x}$, whose c.d.f. reads:

$$\widetilde{F}_{I^l_K}(I^l_k) = P(I^l_K \subseteq I^l_k) =$$
$$= 1 - F_{S''_{\mathsf{E}}} \left(\sum_{i=1}^{m} y_i - ma^l - m \frac{\sum_{i=1}^{m} y_i(x_i - \overline{x})}{\sum_{i=1}^{m}(x_i - \overline{x})^2} + mb^l \right) \quad (15)$$

The latter cumulative distribution function in (15) still refers to the variable S''_{E} if E is symmetric around 0, and S_{E} and S'_{E} are linearly independent. We easily verify this property when the covariance $\mathrm{Cov}[S_{\mathsf{E}}, S'_{\mathsf{E}}] = 0$ and assume henceforth this property.

Regarding the distribution of observed points, since $Y = A + B(x - \overline{x}) + \mathsf{E}$, we may set $a' = a + \varepsilon$ and repeat the previous passages, obtaining an equality similar to (14), substituting the statistic S''_{E} with $S'''_{\mathsf{E}} = S''_{\mathsf{E}} + m\mathsf{E}$.

With these c.d.f. we are looking for a region G where to find the regression line L with a given confidence γ [Wilks, 1962]. Namely

$$P(L \subseteq G) = 1 - \gamma \quad (16)$$

Now, read the second member of (14) and (15) respectively as $(1 - F_{S''_{\mathsf{E}}}(-\Delta a - \Delta b))$ and $1 - (1 - F_{S''_{\mathsf{E}}}(-\Delta a + \Delta b))$, then get $-\Delta a - \Delta b = z''_{\gamma/4}$ and $-\Delta a +$

$\Delta b = z''_{\gamma/4}$ as the solutions of the equations

$$\begin{aligned} 1 - F_{S''_{\mathsf{E}}}(-\Delta a - \Delta b) &= 1 - \frac{\gamma}{4} \\ 1 - F_{S''_{\mathsf{E}}}(-\Delta a + \Delta b) &= 1 - \frac{\gamma}{4} \end{aligned} \tag{17}$$

where z''_α is the α quantile of S''_{E}. In the hypothesis that the corresponding random variables ΔA and ΔB are independent and Gaussian (which holds for instance when E_i are both independent and Gaussian), we have that $-\Delta A - \Delta B$ and $-\Delta A + \Delta B$ are also independent variables. In this case the inequalities

$$\begin{aligned} -\Delta A - \Delta B &\geq z''_{\gamma/4} \\ -\Delta A + \Delta B &\geq z''_{\gamma/4} \end{aligned} \tag{18}$$

define a $(1-\gamma/4)^2 \simeq 1-\gamma/2$ (for small γ) upper bounded confidence region I_k like the one in Fig. 1(a) for the line $A + B(x - \overline{x})$, provided we make this region definite by fixing an interval for one of the two addends, for instance for a', in (12). Actually, region in Fig. 1(a) has been drawn as the span of all straight lines satisfying (18) with $0 \leq \Delta A < (s_{\mathsf{E}} - z_{\gamma/2})/m$, where z_α is the α quantile of S_{E}, and all parallels to the previous ones for $\Delta A < 0$ to fill D_k functionality. Putting any negative infinitely low value of ΔA in (18) would allow any infinitely low and any infinitely high value of ΔB, thus filling the plane and losing any operational meaning to the filled region. *Vice versa*, we get the analogous lower bounded region for the line $A + B(x - \overline{x})$ in Fig. 1(b) having $-\Delta a - \Delta b = z''_{1-\gamma/4}$ and $-\Delta a + \Delta b = z''_{1-\gamma/4}$, as solutions of analogous equations analogous to (17-18), with $(s_{\mathsf{E}} - z_{1-\gamma/2})/m < \Delta A < 0$, as constraints on the spanning line.

The intersection between the two regions removes exactly the additional parallel straight lines (see Fig. 1(c)), maintaining all lines satisfying the relations

$$-z''_{1-\gamma/4} + |\Delta A| \leq \Delta B \leq z''_{1-\gamma/4} - |\Delta A| \tag{19}$$

$$(s_{\mathsf{E}} - z_{1-\gamma/2})/m \leq \Delta A \leq (s_{\mathsf{E}} - z_{\gamma/2})/m \tag{20}$$

which jointly insure a $1-\gamma$ two-side confidence interval I for A centered around $\sum_{i=1}^m y_i/m$, and a global $(1-\gamma/2) - 2\gamma/4 = 1-\gamma$ (for small γ) two-side confidence region having the shape of the double cone in Fig. 1(c), for the entire regression line.

3. Numerical examples

We apply the learning method to two distributions of the noise E: i) the usual normal distribution $N(0, \sigma)$, and ii) the symmetric exponential one [Feller,

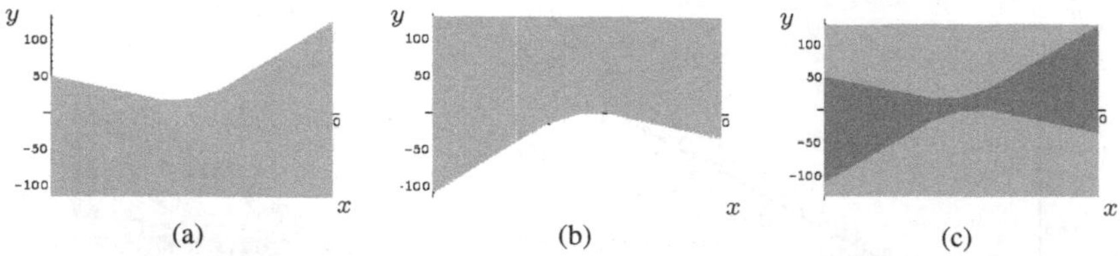

Figure 1. Upper (a) and lower (b) bound of the algorithmic confidence region (c) for the straight line in the linear model (3).

1960] for which conventional methods are not able to supply specific solutions. Fig. 2(a) shows for the former the 90% confidence regions obtained for regression lines and sampled points using the previous formulas, with reference to a 20-sized sample of observations having set as reference value $a = b = 15$ and $\sigma = 20$ for generating them. Due to the E_i distribution law, the variables $\frac{S_{\mathsf{E}}}{m}$, S'_{E}, $\frac{S''_{\mathsf{E}}}{m}$ and $\frac{S'''_{\mathsf{E}}}{m}$ follow a Gaussian distribution of null mean and variance $\frac{\sigma^2}{m}$, $S_{xx}\sigma^2$, $\left(\frac{1}{m} + \frac{1}{S_{xx}}\right)\sigma^2$, and $\left(1 + \frac{1}{m} + \frac{1}{S_{xx}}\right)\sigma^2$, respectively, where $S_{xx} = \sum_{i=1}^{m}(x_i - \overline{x})^2$. This allows us to compute the quantiles $z"_{0.975}$ and $z_{0.95}$ as referred to the straight line. With a slight extension of the above arguments we also draw the confidence region for the distribution of the observed points. In the figure we also compare these regions and the corresponding ones obtained using standard statistical theory [Sen and Srivastava, 1990]. While from a mere computational perspective the two regression methods are both quadratic in the sample size, the comparison is somehow improper since $E[Y]$ stands for a fixed line $a + b(x - \overline{x})$ originating any pair (X, Y) with the addition of noise E_i. In any case we expect to find a straight line that explains our past and future observation pairs. As it concerns the shape of the confidence regions, we note that those coming from our inferential framework include almost completely the other corresponding ones. Is this broadening necessary? To check it we extend the numerical experiments in Fig. 2(a). Namely, for a fixed sample $\{x_1, \ldots, x_m\}$ and a same pair of statistics $s_1 = \sum_{i=1}^{m} y_i$ and $s_2 = \frac{\sum_{i=1}^{m} y_i(x_i - \overline{x})}{\sum_{i=1}^{m}(x_i - \overline{x})^2}$, hence for the same confidence regions, we got 100 samples $\{(x_i, y_i),\ i = 1, \ldots, 20\}$ as follows. We draw 100 samples $\{\varepsilon_i, i = 1, \ldots, 20\}$ from a Gaussian variable of 0 mean and standard deviation 20, as specified for E_i; then, starting from (3), rereading $s_1 = \sum_{i=1}^{m} y_i = a + \sum_{i=1}^{m} \varepsilon_i$ and $s_2 = \sum_{i=1}^{m} y_i(x_i - \overline{x}) = b + \sum_{i=1}^{m} \varepsilon_i(x_i - \overline{x}) / \sum_{i=1}^{m}(x_i - \overline{x})^2$, we compute a and b for each sample, hence the y_i's. Fig. 2(b) shows that the whole

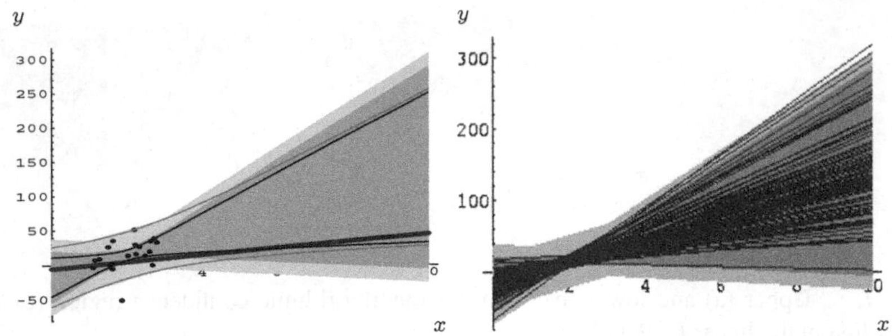

(a) (b)

Figure 2. Algorithmic confidence region for a regression line and points scattering with Gaussian drifts with $\mu = 0$ and $\sigma = 20$ around the reference line $y = 15 + 15(x - \overline{x})$, with X uniform in $[0, 20]$. Bold line: reference line. Dark shadow region: 90% confidence region for the regression line. Light shadow region: 90% confidence region for random points. Dark curves: delimiters of 90% standard confidence region for the regression line. Light curves: delimiters of 90% standard confidence region for points. (b) Coverage of the algorithmic inference regions in (a) by 100 reference lines having the same confidence regions.

90% confidence region computed from these statistics is spanned by the lines. Idem for the generated points; however we avoided plotting them for sake of readability.

In Fig. 3(b) we report analogous confidence regions when the shifts E_i are exponentially spread around the origin as in Fig. 3(a) according to the distribution

$$f_{\mathsf{E}_i}(e; \lambda) = \frac{\lambda}{2} \mathrm{e}^{-\lambda |e|}, \quad i = 1, \ldots, m \tag{21}$$

The distribution of the relevant variables have still a close though complex form. In this case S_{E} has the following distribution density

$$f_{S_{\mathsf{E}}}(\varepsilon; \lambda) = \frac{d_m(\lambda |\varepsilon|)}{(m-1)! 2^{m-1}} \frac{\lambda}{2} \mathrm{e}^{-\lambda |\varepsilon|} \tag{22}$$

where the functional coefficient d_m is defined through the following recurrent relations

$$\begin{aligned} d_i(x) &= (2(i-1)-1) d_{i-1}(x) + x^2 d_{i-2}(x) \qquad \forall i \geq 3 &(23)\\ d_2(x) &= x + 1 &(24)\\ d_1(x) &= 1 &(25) \end{aligned}$$

Then the procedure works in perfect analogy with what has been done in the previous example. In particular, since the moment generating function of standardized normal distribution and standardized symmetric exponential one almost coincide around the zero of their argument, the condition on $\Delta a + \Delta b$ and

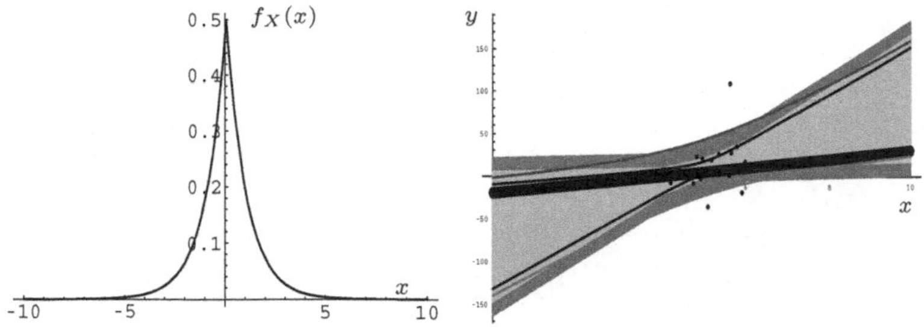

(a) (b)

Figure 3. (a) Graph of the symmetric exponential density for measurement errors, for $\lambda = 0.0513$. (b) Algorithmic confidence region for a regression line and points scattering with the above distribution law around the reference line $y = 5 + 5(x - \overline{x})$, with X uniform in $[0, 20]$. Same notation as in Fig. 2(a).

on $\Delta a - \Delta b$ is satisfied also in this case. In Fig. 3(b) we draw also standard regions obtained for the same data under the usual Gaussian approximation on E_i. We have a similar shape difference as in the previous example and the benefit of working with exact solutions in our approach.

As a conclusion, learning continuous functions may be an affordable task that can be dealt with through exact methods. The key point is to identify meaningful statistics and frame them in a suitable statistical framework, that in the present case is constituted by the Algorithmic Inference. In essence, this framework constitutes a proper logical cadre to manage confidence interval computations underlying the learning problem as much as the classical Kolmogorov framework is well suited to decide hypothesis tests. It is exactly the shift from the latter to the former that renders the learning of continuous function a feasible task.

References

Apolloni, B., Malchiodi, D., and Gaito, S. (2003). *Algorithmic Inference in Machine Learning*. Advanced Knowledge Intenational, Magill, Adelaide.

Feller, W. (1960). *An Introduction to Probability Theory and Its Applications*, volume 1. John Wiley & Sons, second edition.

Morrison, D. F. (1967). *Multivariate Statistical Methods*. McGraw-Hill, New York.

Sen, A. and Srivastava, M. (1990). *Regression Analysis, Theory, Methods and Applications*. Sprenger-Verlag.

Wilks, S. S. (1962). *Mathematical Statistics*. Wiley Publications in Statistics. John Wiley, New York.

A NOVEL KERNEL METHOD FOR CLUSTERING

Francesco Camastra
INFM - DISI, University of Genova, Via Dodecaneso 35, 16146 Genova, Italy
camastra@ieee.org

Alessandro Verri
INFM - DISI, University of Genova, Via Dodecaneso 35, 16146 Genova, Italy
verri@disi.unige.it

Abstract Kernel Methods are algorithms that implicitly perform a nonlinear mapping of the input data to a high dimensional Feature Space. In this paper, we present a novel Kernel Method, *Kernel K-Means* for clustering problems. Unlike other popular clustering algorithms that yield piecewise linear borders among data, Kernel K-Means allows to get nonlinear separation surfaces in the data. Kernel K-Means compares better with popular clustering algorithms, on a synthetic dataset and two UCI real data benchmarks.

Keywords: Kernel Methods, Clustering, K-Means

1. Introduction

Kernel Methods [Cristianini and Shawe-Taylor, 2000] are algorithms that implicitly perform, by replacing the inner product with an appropriate Mercer Kernel, a nonlinear mapping of the input data to a high dimensional Feature Space. Powerful supervised Kernel Methods have been developed to solve classification and regression problems. As far as we know no effective Kernel Methods to solve clustering problems have been developed. In this paper, we present an effective Kernel Method, *Kernel K-Means* for clustering problems. Kernel K-Means maps data from the Input Space to a high dimensional Feature Space using a Mercer Kernel. Then it considers K centers and computes for each center the smallest ball that encloses the data that are closest. Kernel K-Means uses a K-Means-like strategy, i.e. it moves repeatedly the centers, computing for each center the smallest ball, until any center changes. Unlike other popular clustering algorithms that yield piecewise linear borders among data, Kernel K-Means allows to get nonlinear separation surfaces in the data. This is the main quality of the algorithm. The plan of the paper is as follows.

B. Apolloni et al. (eds.), Biological and Artificial Intelligence Environments, 245–250

In Section 2 we review K-Means that inspired Kernel K-Means and the Support Vector Clustering, the basic step of the Kernel K-Means; in Section 3 we present the Kernel K-Means algorithm; in Section 4 some experimental results are reported; finally some conclusions are drawn in Section 5.

2. Preliminaries

Let $D = (x_1, x_2, \ldots, x_m)$ be a data set with vectors $x_i \in \mathbf{R}^N$. We call *codebook* the set $W = (w_1, w_2, \ldots, w_{k-1}, w_k)$ where each element $w_c \in \mathbf{R}^N$ and $k \ll m$. The *Voronoi Set* (V_c) of the codevector w_c is the set of all vectors in D for which w_c is the *nearest vector*. The most popular clustering technique is K-Means [Lloyd, 1982]. K-Means works by repeatedly moving all codevectors to the arithmetic mean of their Voronoi sets. K-Means consists of the following steps:

1 Initialize the codebook W to contain K with vectors chosen *randomly* from the training set D.

2 Compute for each codevector $w_i \in W$ its Voronoi Set V_i.

3 Move each codevector w_i to the mean of its Voronoi Set.

4 Go to step 2 if any codevector, in the step 3, w_i has been changed.

K-Means is an *Expectation-Maximization* (*EM*) algorithm [Dempster et al., 1977].
Since each EM algorithm is convergent, the convergence of the K-Means algorithm is guaranteed.
Support Vector Clustering (*SVC*) [Ben-Hur et al., 2001], called also *one-class SVM*, is a unsupervised Kernel Method based on support vector description of a data set. In Feature Space, SVC computes the smallest sphere that encloses the image of the input data. Let $D = (x_i \in \mathbf{R}^N, \; i = 1, 2, \ldots, m) \subseteq \mathcal{X}$, with $\mathcal{X} \subseteq \mathbf{R}^N$. We project the data x_i in some Feature Space $\mathcal{F}$ using a non-linear transformation $\Phi : \mathcal{X} \rightarrow \mathcal{F}$. Then we look for the smallest sphere of radius R, in the Feature Space, that encloses the data projections $\Phi(x_i)$. This is described by the constraints:

$$\|\Phi(x_j) - a\|^2 \leq R^2 \quad j = 1 \ldots m,$$

where $\|\cdot\|$ is the Euclidean norm and a is the center of the sphere.
The constraints can be relaxed by using *slack* variables ξ_j:

$$\|\Phi(x_j) - a\|^2 \leq R^2 + \xi_j$$

with $\xi_j \geq 0$. We solve the problem of finding the smallest sphere introducing the *Lagrangian*

$$L = R^2 - \sum_j^m (R^2 + \xi_j - \|\Phi(x_j) - a\|^2)\beta_j - \sum_j^m \xi_j \mu_j + C \sum_j^m \xi_j$$

where $\beta_j \geq 0$ and $\mu_j \geq 0$ are Lagrange multipliers, C is a constant and $C \sum_j^m \xi_j$ is a penalty term. After differentiating w.r.t R, a, ξ_j we may eliminate the variables R, a and μ_j, turning the Lagrangian into a function $\mathcal{W}$ of the variables β_j:

$$\mathcal{W} = \sum_j^m \Phi(x_j)^2 \beta_j - \sum_i^m \sum_j^m \beta_i \beta_j \Phi(x_i) \cdot \Phi(x_j).$$

The point $\Phi(x_j)$ can be classified as follows: if $\beta_j = 0$ it lies inside the surface; if $\beta_j = C$ it lies outside the sphere; if $0 < \beta_j < C$ it lies on the surface of the Feature Space sphere. Such a point will be referred to as a *support vector* (*SV*). Now we compute the inner products $\Phi(x_i) \cdot \Phi(x_j)$ by an appropriate Mercer kernel $G(x_i, x_j)$ (*kernel trick*). The usual choice is to use the Gaussian kernel. We have adopted this choice in the experimentations described in the Section 4. After using the kernel trick, the function $\mathcal{W}$, becomes

$$\mathcal{W} = \sum_j^m G(x_j, x_j)\beta_j - \sum_i^m \sum_j^m \beta_i \beta_j G(x_i, x_j).$$

It can be shown that the position of the center a can be unknown. Nevertheless, for each point x the distance $R(x)$ between the center a and its image in Feature Space $\Phi(x)$ can be computed:

$$R^2(x) = \|\Phi(x) - a\|^2 = G(x, x) - 2 \sum_j^m \beta_j G(x_j, x) + \sum_i^m \sum_j^m \beta_i \beta_j G(x_i, x_j).$$

3. Kernel K-Means

Since SVC can detect only one cluster, the goal of our research is to formulate a Kernel Method, based on the support vector description of the data set. We propose an algorithm, *Kernel K-Means* for clustering. Given a data set D, we map our data in some Feature Space $\mathcal{F}$, by means a nonlinear map Φ. Unlike SVC, we consider K, whose value is apriori fixed, centers in Feature Space ($a_i \in \mathcal{F}$ $\quad i = 1, \ldots, K$). We call the set $A = (a_1, \ldots, a_K)$ *Feature Space Codebook* since in our representation the centers in the Feature Space play the same role of the codevectors in the Input Space. In analogy with the codevectors in the Input Space, we define for each center a_c its *Voronoi Set* in Feature Space. The *Voronoi Set in Feature Space* (FV_c) of the center a_c is the set of all vectors x_i in D such that a_c is the *closest vector* for their images $\Phi(x_i)$ in the Feature Space

$$FV_c = \{x_i \in D \mid c = arg\min_j \ \|\Phi(x_i) - a_j\|\}$$

Now we describe the *Kernel K-Means* algorithm. Kernel K-Means uses a K-Means-like strategy, i.e. moves repeatedly all centers a_c in the Feature Space, computing SVC on their FV_c, until any center changes. In order to make more robust Kernel K-Means than K-Means with respect to the outliers SVC is computed on $FV_c(\rho)$ of each center a_c. $FV_c(\rho)$ is defined as

$$FV_c(\rho) = \{x_i \in FV_c \ \ and \ \ \|\Phi(x_i) - a_c\| < \rho\}.$$

$FV_c(\rho)$ is the Voronoi set in the Feature Space of the center a_c without outliers, that is the images of data points whose distance from the center is larger than ρ. The parameter ρ can be set up using model selection techniques [Bishop, 1995]. Kernel K-Means has the following steps:

1 Project the data Set D in a Feature Space $\mathcal{F}$, by means a nonlinear mapping Φ. Initialize the centers $a_c \quad c = 1, \ldots, K \quad a_c \in \mathcal{F}$

2 Compute for each center a_c $FV_c(\rho)$

3 Apply SVC to each $FV_c(\rho)$ and assign to a_c the center yielded, i.e.

$$a_c = SVC(FV_c(\rho))$$

4 Go to step 2 until any a_c changes, otherwise return the Feature Space codebook.

Kernel K-Means is an EM algorithm since its second and third step are respectively the expectation and maximization stage of an EM algorithm. Hence Kernel K-Means convergence is guaranteed, since each EM algorithm is convergent.

4. Experimental Results

Kernel K-Means has been tried on a synthetic data set (*Delta Set*) and on two UCI data sets, that is the *IRIS* Data [Fisher, 1936] and the *Wisconsin's breast cancer* database [Wolberg and Mangasarian, 1990]. Delta Set is a bidimensional set formed by 424 points of two classes nonlinearly separated. Therefore the two classes cannot be separated by clustering algorithms that use only two codevectors in the Input Space, since two codevectors permit only linear separation of the data. To confirm that, we tried K-Means, using two codevectors, on Delta Set. As shown in the figure 1, K-Means cannot separate the

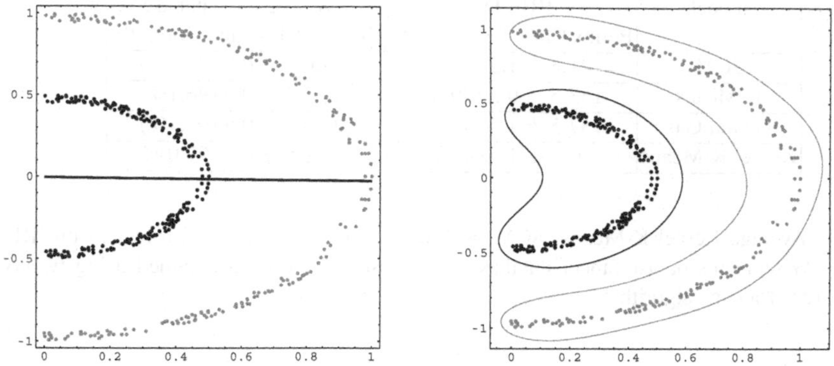

(a) K-Means (b) Kernel K-Means

Figure 1. (a) K-Means on Delta Set. The solid line indicates the separation line determined by K-Means. (b) Kernel K-Means on Delta Set. The region delimited by the black line identifies the input data whose images in the Feature Space have distance from the center a_1 less than 0.75. The region delimited by the gray line identifies the input data whose images in the Feature Space have distance from the center a_2 less than 0.84.

clusters. K-Means shares this limitation with other not-kernel-based clustering algorithms, e.g. SOM [Kohonen, 1982] and Neural Gas [Martinetz and Schulten, 1993]. Then we tried Kernel K-Means on Delta Set using only two centers. As shown in figure 1, Kernel K-Means can separate the two clusters, unlike other clustering algorithms. Iris Data is formed by 150 points, that belong to three different classes. One class is linearly separable from the other two, but the other two are not linearly separable from each other. Wisconsin's breast cancer database collects 699 cases for such diagnostic samples. We have removed 16 database samples with missing values, therefore the database considered in the experiments has 683 patterns. The patterns belong to two different classes, the former has 444 samples, the latter has 239 samples. We tried Kernel K-Means, K-Means, Neural Gas and SOM on IRIS data and Wisconsin database, using respectively two and three centers. The table 1 shows the average performances of the algorithms on 20 runs, obtained changing algorithm inizializations and parameters. As shown in the table, Kernel K-Means performances are better than other clustering algorithms on both datasets.

5. Conclusion

In this paper we have presented a novel clustering algorithm, Kernel K-Means. Under this aspect Kernel K-Means compares favourebly with clustering algorithms such as *Self Organizing Maps* and *Neural Gas*, whose convergence is not guaranteed. Kernel K-Means is a batch clustering algorithm, therefore its performance is not affected by the pattern ordering in the training

model	IRIS Data Points Classified Correctly	Wisconsin Database Points Classified Correctly
SOM	121.5 ± 1.5 (81.0%)	660.5 ± 0.5 (96.7%)
K-Means	133.5 ± 0.5 (89.0%)	656.5 ± 0.5 (96.1%)
Neural Gas	137.5 ± 1.5 (91.7%)	656.5 ± 0.5 (96.1%)
Kernel K-Means	142 ± 1 (94.7%)	662.5 ± 0.5 (97.0)%

Table 1. Average Kernel K-Means, SOM, K-Means and Neural Gas performances on IRIS Data and Wisconsin's breast cancer database. The results have been obtained using twenty different runs for each algorithm.

set, unlike on-line clustering algorithms. The main Kernel K-Means quality consists, unlike most clustering algorithms published in the literature, in producing nonlinear separation surfaces among data. Kernel K-Means compares better with K-Means, Neural Gas and SOM, on a synthetic dataset and two UCI benchmarks. These results encourage the use of Kernel K-Means for the solution of real world problems.

Acknowledgments

This research has been partially funded by the FIRB Project ASTA

References

Ben-Hur, A., Horn, D., Siegelmann, H.T., and Vapnik, V. (2001). Support vector clustering. *Journal of Machine Learning Research*, 2:125–137.

Bishop, C. (1995). *Neural Networks for Pattern Recognition*. Cambridge University Press.

Cristianini, N. and Shawe-Taylor, J. (2000). *An Introduction to Support Vector Machines*. Cambridge University Press.

Dempster, A.P., Laird, N.M., and Rubin, D.B. (1977). Maximum likelihood from incomplete data via the em algorithm. *Journal Royal Statistical Society*, 39(1):1–38.

Fisher, R.A. (1936). The use of multiple measurements in taxonomic problems. *Annals of Eugenics*, 7:179–188.

Kohonen, T. (1982). Self-organized formation of topologically correct feature maps. *Biological Cybernetics*, 43:59–69.

Lloyd, S.P. (1982). An algorithm for vector quantizer design. *IEEE Transaction on Communications*, 28(1):84–95.

Martinetz, T.E. and Schulten, K.J. (1993). Neural-gas network for vector quantization and its application to time-series prediction. *IEEE Transaction on Neural Networks*, 4(4):558–569.

Wolberg, W.H. and Mangasarian, O.L. (1990). Multisurface method of pattern separation for medical diagnosis applied to breast citology. *Proceedings of the National Academy of Sciences, USA*, 87:9193–9196.

GENETIC MONTE CARLO MARKOV CHAINS

STEFANO HAJEK
DSI - Università degli Studi di Milano

Abstract: Bayesian Neural Networks – considering priors and averaging model results accordingly with weights probabilities - can be an important resource in solving classification problems whose learning sets have few samples. Hybrid Monte Carlo Markov Chains (HMCMC) are typically used to numerically solve the integrals involved in learning procedures; in this work a Genetic Algorithm is proposed as alternative to gradient measure to hybridize MCMC so that multimodal distribution can be better fitted and derivative calculation needed for gradient information can be omitted.

Keywords: Bayesian Neural Networks, Genetic Algorithms, Monte Carlo Markov Chains, Metropolis Algorithm.

1. BAYESIAN NEURAL NETWORKS

Multidimensional discriminant analysis is the goal of many machine learning applications; in different areas neural networks represent an important approach to data mining and pattern recognition.

In financial risk management, for example, Basilea committee is now developing methods to estimate capital requirements needed to mitigate bank's operational losses; causal analysis is proposed to classify relationships between critical environmental factors and extreme loss events.

Due to the exceptionality of extreme losses, statistical samples are often not representative of possible scenarios, so that it's important to include in loss models special assumptions that make up for the lack of past experience.

These assumption are:

B. Apolloni et al. (eds.), Biological and Artificial Intelligence Environments, 251–259

prior information available about model;

production of predictive results as weighted composition of various results, each depending from the likelihood of the particular model that originated it.

Bayesian learning provides an interesting framework to conjugate priori information with observed likelihood in which posterior probability of the model given observed data is derived from the probability of the model and from the probability of data given the model; formally:

$$p(x|y) \propto p(y|x)p(x)$$

Bayesian Neural Networks are based on bayesian learning: priors are given by the probability distributions of networks weights, likelihoods are the net errors computed feeding with input data the nets updated with the different sets of prior weights:

$$\hat{\mathbf{y}}_{n+1} = \int_{R^N} f(\mathbf{x}_{n+1}, \mathbf{w})\, P(\mathbf{w} \mid (\mathbf{x}_1, \mathbf{y}_1), \ldots, (\mathbf{x}_n, \mathbf{y}_n))\, d\mathbf{w}$$

"In the bayesian approach to statistical prediction one does not use a single "best" set of network weights, but rather integrates the predictions from all possible weight vectors over the posterior weight distribution which combines information from the data with a prior bias toward more plausible weights ... with integration, a weight vector that fits data only slightly better than others contributes only slightly more to the prediction than completely dominating, as happens with maximum likelihood estimation." [Neal, 1992]

2. MONTE CARLO MARKOV CHAINS

Integrations involved in bayesian neural networks are very complex and difficult to compute analitically; a class of numerical solutions is then proposed for posterior probability approximation, the class of "Montecarlo Methods".

The fundamental idea of Montecarlo Methods is related to the fact that an integral can be expressed as an expectation of a function $f(x)$ over the probability $p(x)$ [Walsh, 2002].

$$\int_a^b h(x)\,dx = \int_a^b f(x)\,p(x)\,dx = E_{p(x)}[\,f(x)\,]$$

Thus, if we draw a large number $x_1,\ldots,x_n$ of random variables from the density $p(x)$ then:

$$\int_a^b h(x)\,dx = E_{p(x)}[\,f(x)] \simeq \frac{1}{n}\sum_{i=1}^{n} f(x_i)$$

Hence, for bayesian integration we have:

$$I(y) = \int f(y\,|\,x)\,p(x)\,dx = \frac{1}{n}\sum_{i=1}^{n} f(y\,|\,x_i)$$

In many complex problems proposal distribution *p(x)* is far from draw values covering target distribution; MCMC is a strategy for generating samples using a Markov chain.

For any starting point, the chain will convergence to the desidered invariant distribution *f(x)*, as long as T is a stochastic transition matrix that obeys the following properties:

Irreducibility.

For any state of the Markov chain, there is a positive probability of visiting all other states; that is, all states communicate with each other, as one can always go from any state to any other state (although it may take more than one step).

Aperiodicity.

A chain is said to be aperiodic when the number of steps required to move between two states (say x and y) is not required to be multiple of some integer. Put another way, the chain is not forced into some cycle of fixed length between certain states.

Metropolis Algorithm is a routine that generates Markov Chains meeting irreducibility and aperiodicity requirements:

1. Start with any initial value μ_0 satisfying $f(\mu_0) > 0$.
2. *Using current μ value, sample a* ***candidate point*** *μ^* from some* ***jumping distribution*** *$q(\mu_1; \mu_2)$, which is the probability of returning a value of μ_2 given a previous value of μ . This distribution is also referred to as the* ***proposal*** *or* ***candidate-generating distribution****. The only restriction on the jump density in the Metropolis algorithm is that it is symmetric, i.e., $q(\mu_1; \mu_2) = q(\mu_2; \mu_1)$.*
3. Given the candidate point $\mu*$, calculate the ratio of the density at the candidate (μ^*) and current (μ_{t-1}) points,

$$\alpha = p(\mu^*)\,/\,p(\mu_{t-1}) = f\;\mu^*\;\;/f\,(\mu_{t-1})$$

Notice that because we are considering the ratio of $p.(\xi)$ under two different values, the normalizing constant ***K*** cancels out.

4. If the jump increases the density ($\alpha > 1$), accept the candidate point (set $\mu_t = \mu^*$) and return to step 2. If the jump decreases the density ($\alpha < 1$), then with probability α accept the candidate point, else reject it and return to step 2.

Metropolis algorithm, although widely used, perform poorly because it explore the space by a slow random walk; to improve its performances, it can include additional information to reduce random walk behaviour in state transition.

The Hybrid MCMC [MacKay] uses gradient information to find candidate directions in which changes have higher probability of being accepted.

Despite its efficency, HMCMC algorithm has relevant teoretical and pratical limitations:

first, it's affected from local minima convergence and lacks in exploring multimodal distributions; second it only works if gradient information is available, i.e. if the distribution to fit is known and derivable. From the implementative point of view, developement of complex applications with gradient calculation could be very expensive and an alternative way to gain information about function's variation could be preferred.

Genetic Algorithms are optimization routines that reach the maximum of a function random generating and selecting candidate values (like Montecarlo Methods) and extracting the "building blocks" of optimal candidates from previous selected candidates; GA can hence substitute gradient descent in rectifying candidates for Metropolis algorithms.

3. GMCMC ALGORITHM

In our experiment we follow the suggestion to start the chain as close to the center of the distribution as possible, for example taking a value close to the distribution's mode. [Storn et al., 1995].

The test distribution is a classical bimodal one [Andrieu et al., 2003] defined from the equation:

$$P \bullet 0.3 \exp(-0.2x^2)+0.7 \exp(0.2(x-10)^2)$$

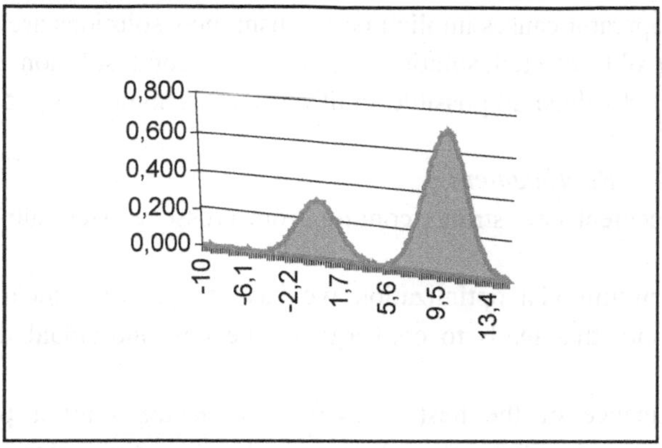

Figure 1. The test distribution

To intercept multiple modes we determine various function maxima with a GA an then we use those maxima as Metropolis starting values where chains are parallelized; multimodal optimization requires multi-niche optimization in GA obtained via opportune replacement technique.

Step 1 – Initial population generation

Accordingly with basic GA procedure [Goldberg, 1989] initial GA population consist of a fixed number of randomly generated binary strings.

Step 2 – Selection

Random selected pairs of strings are decoded in the corresponding decimal values which are passed through the fitness function (the function to optimize); for each pair the string with higher fitness is admitted to the next step. Selection is repeated as many times as the size of the population.

Step 3 – Crossover

Bits from random selected pairs of strings are recombined, a string exchanges its bits in randomly selected positions with bits in corresponding positions of another string.

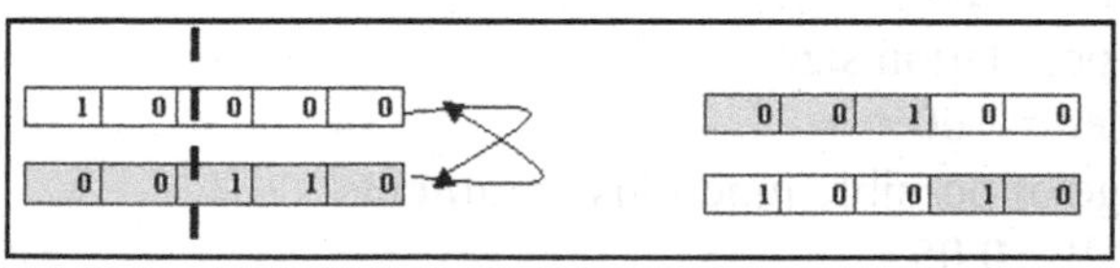

Figure 2. Crossover

Crossover operator causes implicit parallelism: new solutions are composed with elements from old selected solutions so, when a good solution is selected are intrinsecally good valued all possible solutions having some component in common with it.

Step 4 – Replacement

With replacement new strings coming from crossover step substitute previous population.

To obtain multimodal optimization we have to preserve local maxima from evolutive pressure that tends to converge to the best individual discarding each other.

Total dominance of the best is avoided replacing only a portion of past generation and choosing, for each replacement, the old individual most similar to the new generation's individual that overwrites it.

Similarity between strings is given by their euclidean distance. [Cedeno et al., 2001]

Step 5 – Reiterate n times from Step 2

Step 6 – Apply Metropolis algorithm

For each resulting individual Metropolis routine restarts from the decimal value decoded from corresponding string; it cosequently produces as many chains as the population's size.

4. RESULTS

"The quality of an MC algorithm is given by the number of run until the chain approaches stationarity; slower the algorithm longer the flat periods corresponding to all candidates being rejected." [Walsh, 2002]

The aim of our experiment is to generate a MCMC that fits a multimodal distribution rapidly achieving stationarity.

Algorithm parameters are setted to obtain fast convergence on various sub-optimal Hasting starting values:

NIters = 10

Is the number of iterations for GA

NGenes = 10

Is the length of binary strings

NIndividuals = 20

Is theGA population size

Max_Coded = 100

Is the range of possible functions arguments

Mutation_P = 0.05

Is the mutation rate

Replacement_P = 0.3

Is the new individual's replacement rate
XOver_P = 0.5
Is the crossover rate
NSteps = 30
Is the number of MC steps
MC_step = 1
Is the maximum chain's transition step

As you can see in the next graph the Markov processes create a diffusion around the most likely values found by GA:

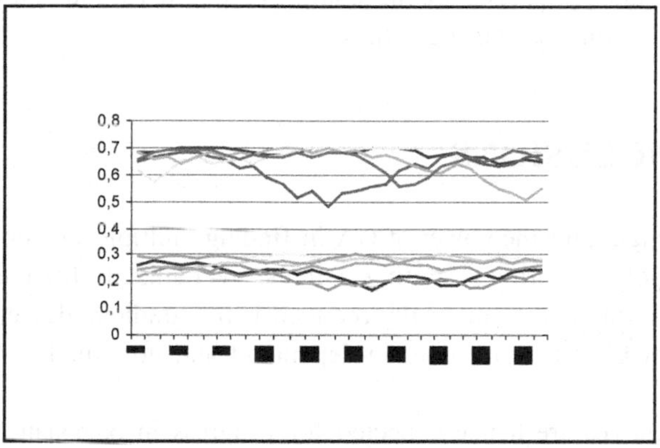

Figure 3. GA polarizes MCMC starting values

Convergence test is needed to assess whether stationarity has indeed been reached; Geweke test compares values early in the sequence with those late in the sequence [Watanabe et al., 2004].

Given $X(i)$ the i th draw of a parameter in the recorded m draws, Geweke proposes the following statistic called convergence diagnostics (CD).

$$\mathrm{CD} = \frac{\bar{X}_A - \bar{X}_B}{\sqrt{\hat{\sigma}_A^2/n_A + \hat{\sigma}_B^2/n_B}},$$

where σ^2_A / n_A and σ^2_B / n_B are standard errors of A and B. If the sequence of $X(i)$ is stationary, it converges in distribution to the standard normal.

In the run we are discussing, convergence diagnostic gives these result:

Table 1. Convergence statistic

Z-Value	0,132512
P - Value	0,55271

It confirms the stationarity of the chain composed by the sub-chains derived from previously optimized starting values.

5. CONCLUSIONS

This work highlights the power of GA in finding multiple sub–optimal values to use as Metropolis algorithm starting values; recognized distribution's modes, MCMC burn-in time is drammatically reduced while gradient–descent optimization tecniques are avoided because domain-dependent and not suitable for multimodal distributions.

Good persectives are hence expected for progress in bayesian neural network learning although genetic optimization in neural networks weights causes redundances dued to network's simmetry: different weight's strings originate equivalent nets [Whitley, 1995].

Alternative net's representations can be investigated to improve bayesian neural networks efficency.

REFERENCES

Andrieu, C., De Freitas, N., Doucet A. and Jordan, M. (2003): An Introduction to MCMC for Machine Learning

Cedeno W., Vemuri V.R. and Slezak T. (2001): Multi-Niche Crowding in Genetic Algorithms and its Application to the Assembly of DNA Restriction-Fragments - Department of Applied Science University of California

Goldberg, D. E. (1989): Genetic Algorithms in Search, Optimization, and Machine Learning, Addison Wesley Professional

Haario, H., Saksman, E. and Tamminen J. (2001): An adaptive Metropolis algorithm. Bernoulli , 7, 223-242.

Laskey, K.B. and Myers, J.W. (2003): Population Markov Chain Monte Carlo. Mach. Learn., 50, 175-196.

MacKay, D.J.C. :Introduction To Monte Carlo Methods

Neal, R. (1992): Bayesian Training of Back Propagation Networks by the Hybrid Monte Carlo Methods

Storn,R. and Price, K. (1995): Differential Evolution - a simple and efficient adaptive scheme for global optimization over continuous spaces TR-95-012. Berkeley: International Computer Science Institute

Walsh, B. (2002): Markov Chain Monte Carlo and Gibbs Sampling, Lecture Notes for EEB 596z, B.

Watanabe and T. Omori, Y (2004): A multi-move sampler for estimating non-Gaussian time series models: Comments on Shephard & Pitt, Faculty of Economics, Tokyo Metropolitan University, Faculty of Economics, University of Tokyo.

Whitley, D (1995): Genetic Algorithms and Neural Networks in Genetic Algorithms in Engineering and Computer Science – John Wiley and Sons

CONSISTENCY OF EMPIRICAL RISK MINIMIZATION FOR UNBOUNDED LOSS FUNCTIONS

Marco Muselli[1] and Francesca Ruffino[2]

[1]*Istituto di Elettronica e di Ingegneria dell'Informazione e delle Telecomunicazioni Consiglio Nazionale delle Ricerche, Genova, Italy*
marco.muselli@ieiit.cnr.it

[2]*Dipartimento di Scienze dell'Informazione, Università di Milano, Milano, Italy*
ruffino@dsi.unimi.it

Abstract The theoretical framework of Statistical Learning Theory (SLT) for pattern recognition problems is extended to comprehend the situations where an infinite value of the loss function is employed to prevent misclassifications in specific regions with high reliability.

Sufficient conditions for ensuring the consistency of the Empirical Risk Minimization (ERM) criterion are then established and an explicit bound, in terms of the VC dimension of the class of decision functions employed to solve the problem, is derived.

Keywords: Loss function, Empirical Risk Minimazation, Consistency.

1. Introduction

Pattern recognition problems deal with the important task of performing a binary classification of data pertaining to a given physical system by examining a finite collection of examples, usually called *training set*.

A variety of different methods have been proposed for solving pattern recognition problems; normally, the theoretical framework employed to establish the consistence of the followed approach is the one proposed by Vapnik & Chervonenkis more than thirty years ago [Vapnik and Chervonenkis, 1971; Vapnik, 1982; Vapnik, 1998] and currently referred to as Statistical Learning Theory (SLT).

In this framework the solution of any pattern recognition problem is shown to be equivalent to a proper functional optimization problem, where the (probability) measures involved are totally unknown and must be (implicitly)

B. Apolloni et al. (eds.), Biological and Artificial Intelligence Environments, 261–270

estimated through the examples contained in the training set. In particular, the functional to be minimized, called *expected risk*, is the expected value of a binary *loss function* that assumes value 1 in correspondence with a given input data, if a misclassification occurs.

The adoption of a binary loss function amounts to treat in the same manner all the examples in the training set; consequently, no a priori information is supposed to be available about the reliability of the data at hand. In fact, if this information would be accessible, a possible way of taking into account the highest confidence associated with a specific subset of the input space could be to increase the value of the loss function in that region.

In the limit case we could assign an infinite value of the loss function in correspondence with the data belonging to the region with high reliability, thus preventing any misclassification inside it. However, the adoption of this choice violates a basic requirement for the application of SLT, since the consistency of the Empirical Risk Minimization (ERM) criterion (usually adopted in pattern recognition techniques) is established only if the expected risk is always finite.

In this paper an extension of the theoretical framework of SLT is proposed to comprehend the case of pattern recognition problems where the loss function can assume an infinite value. In particular, it is shown that the finiteness of the VC dimension for the class of decision functions employed is still a sufficient condition for the consistency of the ERM criterion. An explicit upper bound for the error probability is provided, depending on the size of the available training set.

Due to space limitations, some proofs have been omitted.

2. The theoretical framework for pattern recognition problems

Consider a general pattern recognition problem, where vectors $x \in D \subset \mathbb{R}^d$ have to be assigned to one of two possible classes, associated with the values of a binary output y, coded by the integers -1 and $+1$. Every solution for the pattern recognition problem at hand is given by a binary function $\varphi : D \to \{-1, 1\}$, called *classifier* or *decision function*.

Usually, a sufficiently large set of classifiers $\Gamma = \{\varphi(x, \alpha), \alpha \in \Lambda\}$ is considered and the best decision function $\varphi(x, \alpha^*)$ that minimizes the expected risk

$$R(\alpha) = \int Q(z, \alpha) dF(z) \, , \qquad \alpha \in \Lambda$$

is selected. Here, $F(z)$ is the joint cumulative distribution function (c.d.f.) of $z = (x, y)$, whereas Q is called *loss function* and is given by

$$Q(z, \alpha) = |y - \varphi(x, \alpha)| = \begin{cases} 0 & \text{if } y = \varphi(x, \alpha) \\ 1 & \text{if } y \neq \varphi(x, \alpha) \end{cases} \tag{1}$$

However, when solving real world pattern recognition problems, usually we do not know the distribution function $F(z)$, but have only access to a training set S_l containing l samples (x_j, y_j), $j = 1, \ldots, l$, supposed to be obtained through l i.i.d. applications of F.

In this case we have not sufficient information to retrieve the minimum of the expected risk. A possible way to proceed is to apply the *Empirical Risk Minimization* (ERM) method, which suggests to calculate the function in Γ that minimizes the empirical risk, i.e. the risk computed on the training set.

$$R_{emp}(\alpha) = \frac{1}{l} \sum_{j=1}^{l} Q(z_j, \alpha) \tag{2}$$

It is then important to obtain necessary and sufficient conditions for the consistence of the ERM approach. Vapnik [Vapnik, 1998, page 82] has shown that a stronger definition of consistency allows to rule out trivial situations:

DEFINITION 1 *The ERM method is* strictly consistent *for the set of functions* $\{Q(z, \alpha),\ \alpha \in \Lambda\}$ *and the probability distribution function* $F(z)$ *if for any non-empty subset* $\Lambda(c) = \{\alpha \in \Lambda : R(\alpha) \geq c\}$ *with* $c \in (-\infty, +\infty)$ *the following convergence holds*

$$\inf_{\alpha \in \Lambda(c)} R_{emp}(\alpha) \xrightarrow[l \to \infty]{\mathbf{P}} \inf_{\alpha \in \Lambda(c)} R(\alpha)$$

Necessary and sufficient conditions for strict consistency are provided by the following theorem [Vapnik, 1998, page 88].

THEOREM 2 *If two real constants a and A can be found such that for every $\alpha \in \Lambda$ the inequalities $a \leq R(\alpha) \leq A$ hold, then the following two statements are equivalent:*

1 *The empirical risk minimization method is strictly consistent on the set of functions* $\{Q(z, \alpha),\ \alpha \in \Lambda\}$.

2 *The uniform one-sided convergence of the mean to their matematical expectation takes place over the set of functions* $\{Q(z, \alpha),\ \alpha \in \Lambda\}$, *i.e.*

$$\lim_{l \to \infty} \mathbf{P} \left\{ \sup_{\alpha \in \Lambda} (R(\alpha) - R_{emp}(\alpha)) > \varepsilon \right\} = 0, \quad \textit{for all } \varepsilon > 0$$

Vapnik also gives an upper bound for the rate of convergence [Vapnik, 1998, page 130]:

$$\mathbf{P}\left\{\sup_{\alpha\in\Lambda}\left(R(\alpha)-R_{emp}(\alpha)\right)>\varepsilon\right\}\leq 4\exp\left\{\left(\frac{G^{\Lambda}(2l)}{l}-\left(\varepsilon-\frac{1}{l}\right)^{2}\right)l\right\} \tag{3}$$

where $G^{\Lambda}(m)$ is the so called *Growth function*.

The quantity $\exp(G^{\Lambda}(m))$ represents the highest number of different classifications achievable by the functions in Γ on a sample of m points; note that $G^{\Lambda}(m)$ depends only on Λ and m. Furthermore it can be shown that the growth function assumes only two possible behaviors: linear for all values of m or linear for all $m \leq h$, where h is a positive integer called *VC dimension*, and logarithmic for $m > h$. This result allows to characterize completely the consistence of the ERM approach; in fact for any c.d.f. $F(z)$, a sufficient condition for the consistency of the ERM method is that the set Γ has a finite VC dimension.

3. A natural extension to unbounded loss functions

The theoretical framework described in the last section treats all the examples (x_j, y_j) of the training set in the same way; no information is supposed to be known about the confidence of the output value y_j assigned to the input vector x_j. On the other hand, if this kind of information is actually available, we can properly modify the loss function Q to take into account the different reliability associated with each portion of the input space.

In the limit case, if we have high confidence in output values included in samples belonging to a given subset $C \subset Z$, we can assume that the loss function Q takes an infinite value in these points. Denote with

$$C^{+} = \{x \in D : (x, +1) \in C\}\,, \qquad C^{-} = \{x \in D : (x, -1) \in C\}$$

the subsets of C with positive and negative label respectively, and with

$$D_{\alpha}^{+} = \{x \in D : \varphi(x, \alpha) = +1\}\,, \qquad D_{\alpha}^{-} = \{x \in D : \varphi(x, \alpha) = -1\}$$

the partition of X in two regions made by the function $\varphi(x, \alpha) \in \Gamma$.

With this definition only the classifiers $\varphi(x, \alpha)$ such that both the intersections $D_{\alpha}^{-} \cap C^{+}$ and $D_{\alpha}^{+} \cap C^{-}$ are empty can lead to a finite value of the expected risk. This condition can be viewed as a too strong constraint on the solution we are searching for. In fact, even if the measure of the subset

$$T_{\alpha} = (D_{\alpha}^{-} \cap C^{+}) \cup (D_{\alpha}^{+} \cap C^{-})$$

is negligible, the expected risk goes to infinity.

To relax this constraint we can accept as possible solutions also the decision functions $\varphi(x, \alpha)$ for which the measure of T_α is smaller than a prescribed tolerance $\tau > 0$. The corresponding value of the expected risk $R(\alpha)$ can be kept finite if the following loss function is employed:

$$Q_\tau(z, \alpha) = \begin{cases} Q'(z, \alpha) & \text{if } \mu(T_\alpha) \geq \tau \\ Q(z, \alpha) & \text{if } \mu(T_\alpha) < \tau \end{cases} \tag{4}$$

where

$$Q'(z, \alpha) = \begin{cases} 0 & \text{if } y = \varphi(x, \alpha) \\ 1 & \text{if } y \neq \varphi(x, \alpha) \text{ and } (x, y) \notin C \\ \infty & \text{if } y \neq \varphi(x, \alpha) \text{ and } (x, y) \in C \quad \text{(i.e. if } x \in T_\alpha) \end{cases} \tag{5}$$

Using these definitions, the expected and the empirical risk become respectively

$$R_\tau(\alpha) = \int Q_\tau(z, \alpha) dF(z), \qquad R_{\tau,emp}(\alpha) = \frac{1}{l} \sum_{j=1}^{l} Q_\tau(z_j, \alpha)$$

Now, we want to extend results on consistency of the ERM method to this new setting. To this aim a generalization of Vapnik's theory is required to include situations where the loss function assume values in the range $[0, \infty]$.

Denote with $\Lambda_\tau = \{\alpha \in \Lambda : \mu(T_\alpha) < \tau\}$ the subset of Λ including only parameters α which provide a finite loss function and with Λ_∞ the complement of Λ_τ in Λ. Note that if $\alpha \in \Lambda_\tau$, the expected risk $R_\tau(\alpha)$ assumes a finite value, while $R_\tau(\alpha) = \infty$ for all $\alpha \in \Lambda_\infty$.

It can be easily seen that the definition of strict consistency for ERM method can be directly generalized to the present case. Note that, according to the hypothesis of Theorem 2, we suppose that two real constants a and $A \in \mathbb{R}$ exist such that for every $c \leq a$, $\Lambda(c) = \Lambda(a)$ and for every $c \geq A$, $\Lambda(c) = \Lambda_\infty$. Then, we can consider only the real values $c \in [a, A]$ and the case $c = \infty$.

The following three lemmas provide specific results that are needed to generalize Theorem 2. Denote with $\Lambda_\tau(c) = \{\alpha \in \Lambda_\tau : R_\tau(\alpha) > c\}$ the subset of $\Lambda(c)$ containing the parameters which provide a finite expected risk. Note that, for all $c \in [a, A]$,

$$\Lambda(c) \setminus \Lambda_\tau(c) = \Lambda(\infty) = \Lambda_\infty \tag{6}$$

LEMMA 3 *If*

$$\inf_{\alpha \in \Lambda_\infty} R_{\tau,emp}(\alpha) \xrightarrow[l \to \infty]{\mathbf{P}} \inf_{\alpha \in \Lambda_\infty} R_\tau(\alpha) \tag{7}$$

then

$$\lim_{l\to\infty} \mathbf{P}\left\{\left|\inf_{\alpha\in\Lambda(c)} R_{\mathcal{T},emp}(\alpha) - \inf_{\alpha\in\Lambda_\tau(c)} R_{\mathcal{T},emp}(\alpha)\right| > \varepsilon\right\} = 0 \qquad (8)$$

for every $\varepsilon > 0$ *and every* $c \in [a, A]$.

Proof. If (8) would not be valid, then, by using (6) we obtain for every $\varepsilon > 0$

$$\lim_{l\to\infty} \mathbf{P}\left\{\left|\inf_{\alpha\in\Lambda(c)} R_{\mathcal{T},emp}(\alpha) - \inf_{\alpha\in\Lambda_\infty} R_{\mathcal{T},emp}(\alpha)\right| > \varepsilon\right\} = 0 \qquad (9)$$

and it can be easily shown that (7) leads to

$$\inf_{\alpha\in\Lambda(c)} R_{\mathcal{T},emp}(\alpha) \xrightarrow[l\to\infty]{\mathbf{P}} \inf_{\alpha\in\Lambda_\infty} R_\tau(\alpha) = \infty$$

This is not possible since $R_{\mathcal{T},emp}(\alpha) \in \mathbb{R}$ for all $\alpha \in \Lambda(c)$ with $c \in [a, A]$. □

LEMMA 4 *Under hypothesis (7) the following two statements are equivalent for all* $c \in [a, A]$*:*

$$\lim_{l\to\infty} \mathbf{P}\left\{\left|\inf_{\alpha\in\Lambda(c)} R_\tau(\alpha) - \inf_{\alpha\in\Lambda(c)} R_{\mathcal{T},emp}(\alpha)\right| > \varepsilon\right\} = 0 \textit{ for every } \varepsilon > 0 \qquad (10)$$

$$\lim_{l\to\infty} \mathbf{P}\left\{\left|\inf_{\alpha\in\Lambda_\tau(c)} R_\tau(\alpha) - \inf_{\alpha\in\Lambda_\tau(c)} R_{\mathcal{T},emp}(\alpha)\right| > \varepsilon\right\} = 0 \textit{ for every } \varepsilon > 0 \qquad (11)$$

Proof At first we can note that for all $c \in [a, A]$

$$\inf_{\alpha\in\Lambda(c)} R_\tau(\alpha) = \inf_{\alpha\in\Lambda_\tau(c)} R_\tau(\alpha) \qquad (12)$$

since

$$\inf_{\alpha\in\Lambda_\infty} R_\tau(\alpha) = \infty$$

Now, let us prove that (10) implies (11); we have

$$\begin{aligned}
&\lim_{l\to\infty} \mathbf{P}\left\{\left|\inf_{\alpha\in\Lambda_\tau(c)} R_\tau(\alpha) - \inf_{\alpha\in\Lambda_\tau(c)} R_{\mathcal{T},emp}(\alpha)\right| > \varepsilon\right\} \\
\leq\ &\lim_{l\to\infty} \mathbf{P}\left\{\left|\inf_{\alpha\in\Lambda_\tau(c)} R_\tau(\alpha) - \inf_{\alpha\in\Lambda(c)} R_{\mathcal{T},emp}(\alpha)\right| > \frac{\varepsilon}{2}\right\} \\
+\ &\lim_{l\to\infty} \mathbf{P}\left\{\left|\inf_{\alpha\in\Lambda(c)} R_{\mathcal{T},emp}(\alpha) - \inf_{\alpha\in\Lambda_\tau(c)} R_{\mathcal{T},emp}(\alpha)\right| > \frac{\varepsilon}{2}\right\}
\end{aligned}$$

Due to (12) and (10) the first term at the right hand side vanishes; for the last term it is sufficient to apply Lemma 3.

To verify that (11) implies (10) we employ Lemma 3 to obtain that

$$\inf_{\alpha\in\Lambda(c)} R_{\mathcal{T},emp}(\alpha) \xrightarrow[l\to\infty]{\mathbf{P}} \inf_{\alpha\in\Lambda_{\mathcal{T}}(c)} R_{\mathcal{T}}(\alpha)$$

from which (10) follows after the application of (12). □

LEMMA 5 *The following equality holds for every $\varepsilon > 0$:*

$$\mathbf{P}\left\{\left|\inf_{\alpha\in\Lambda_\infty} R_{\mathcal{T}}(\alpha) - \inf_{\alpha\in\Lambda_\infty} R_{\mathcal{T},emp}(\alpha)\right| > \varepsilon\right\} = \mathbf{P}\left\{\sup_{\alpha\in\Lambda_\infty}(R_{\mathcal{T}}(\alpha) - R_{\mathcal{T},emp}(\alpha)) > \varepsilon\right\}$$

Using previous lemmas we can prove the following two results which generalize Theorem 2 and the upper bound for the rate of convergence (3).

THEOREM 6 *The following two statements are equivalent:*

1 *The ERM method is strictly consistent on the set of functions $\{Q_{\mathcal{T}}(z,\alpha), \alpha\in\Lambda\}$.*

2 *For every $\varepsilon > 0$*

$$\lim_{l\to\infty} \mathbf{P}\left\{\sup_{\alpha\in\Lambda}(R_{\mathcal{T}}(\alpha) - R_{\mathcal{T},emp}(\alpha)) > \varepsilon\right\} = 0 \tag{13}$$

Proof Since

$$\begin{aligned}
&\lim_{l\to\infty} \mathbf{P}\left\{\sup_{\alpha\in\Lambda}(R_{\mathcal{T}}(\alpha) - R_{\mathcal{T},emp}(\alpha)) > \varepsilon\right\} \\
\le\ &\lim_{l\to\infty} \mathbf{P}\left\{\sup_{\alpha\in\Lambda_\infty}(R_{\mathcal{T}}(\alpha) - R_{\mathcal{T},emp}(\alpha)) > \varepsilon\right\} \\
+\ &\lim_{l\to\infty} \mathbf{P}\left\{\sup_{\alpha\in\Lambda_{\mathcal{T}}}(R_{\mathcal{T}}(\alpha) - R_{\mathcal{T},emp}(\alpha)) > \varepsilon\right\}
\end{aligned} \tag{14}$$

to obtain that 1 implies 2 it is sufficient to prove that the two terms at the right hand side of (13) vanish for every $\varepsilon > 0$.

For the first term we can apply Lemma 5 by noting that, when $c = \infty$, the definition of strict consistency gives

$$\lim_{l\to\infty} \mathbf{P}\left\{\left|\inf_{\alpha\in\Lambda_\infty} R_{\mathcal{T}}(\alpha) - \inf_{\alpha\in\Lambda_\infty} R_{\mathcal{T},emp}(\alpha)\right| > \varepsilon\right\} = 0 \text{ for every } \varepsilon > 0 \tag{15}$$

For the second term we can use Lemma 4, thus obtaining for $c \in [a, A]$ that

$$\lim_{l\to\infty} \mathbf{P}\left\{\left|\inf_{\alpha\in\Lambda(c)} R_{\mathcal{T}}(\alpha) - \inf_{\alpha\in\Lambda(c)} R_{\mathcal{T},emp}(\alpha)\right| > \varepsilon\right\} = 0 \text{ for every } \varepsilon > 0$$

is equivalent to

$$\lim_{l\to\infty} \mathbf{P}\left\{\left|\inf_{\alpha\in\Lambda_{\mathcal{T}}(c)} R_{\mathcal{T}}(\alpha) - \inf_{\alpha\in\Lambda_{\mathcal{T}}(c)} R_{\mathcal{T},emp}(\alpha)\right| > \varepsilon\right\} = 0 \text{ for every } \varepsilon > 0$$

Now, when $\alpha \in \Lambda_{\mathcal{T}}(c)$, we have $Q_{\mathcal{T}}(z, \alpha) = Q(z, \alpha)$; then, Theorem 2 can be employed to ensure that

$$\lim_{l\to\infty} \mathbf{P}\left\{\sup_{\alpha\in\Lambda_{\mathcal{T}}} (R_{\mathcal{T}}(\alpha) - R_{\mathcal{T},emp}(\alpha)) > \varepsilon\right\} = 0 \text{ for every } \varepsilon > 0$$

To verify that 2 implies 1, we note that (13) implies

$$\lim_{l\to\infty} \mathbf{P}\left\{\sup_{\alpha\in\Lambda_{\infty}} (R_{\mathcal{T}}(\alpha) - R_{\mathcal{T},emp}(\alpha)) > \varepsilon\right\} = 0$$

and

$$\lim_{l\to\infty} \mathbf{P}\left\{\sup_{\alpha\in\Lambda_{\mathcal{T}}} (R_{\mathcal{T}}(\alpha) - R_{\mathcal{T},emp}(\alpha)) > \varepsilon\right\} = 0$$

Then Lemma 5 ensure that

$$\lim_{l\to\infty} \mathbf{P}\left\{\left|\inf_{\alpha\in\Lambda_{\infty}} R_{\mathcal{T}}(\alpha) - \inf_{\alpha\in\Lambda_{\infty}} R_{\mathcal{T},emp}(\alpha)\right| > \varepsilon\right\} = 0 \text{ for every } \varepsilon > 0 \quad (16)$$

whereas the application of Theorem 2 yields

$$\lim_{l\to\infty} \mathbf{P}\left\{\left|\inf_{\alpha\in\Lambda_{\mathcal{T}}(c)} R_{\mathcal{T}}(\alpha) - \inf_{\alpha\in\Lambda_{\mathcal{T}}(c)} R_{\mathcal{T},emp}(\alpha)\right| > \varepsilon\right\} = 0 \text{ for every } \varepsilon > 0$$

By using Lemma 4 we obtain therefore

$$\lim_{l\to\infty} \mathbf{P}\left\{\left|\inf_{\alpha\in\Lambda(c)} R_{\mathcal{T}}(\alpha) - \inf_{\alpha\in\Lambda(c)} R_{\mathcal{T},emp}(\alpha)\right| > \varepsilon\right\} = 0 \quad (17)$$

for every $\varepsilon > 0$ and every $c \in [a, A]$. □

THEOREM 7 *The following inequality holds*

$$\mathbf{P}\left\{\sup_{\alpha\in\Lambda}\left(\int Q_\tau(z,\alpha)dF(z)-\frac{1}{l}\sum_{j=1}^{l}Q_\tau(z_j,\alpha)\right)>\varepsilon\right\}$$
$$\leq 4\exp\left\{\left(\frac{G^{\Lambda_\tau}(2l)}{l}-\left(\varepsilon-\frac{1}{l}\right)^2\right)l\right\}$$
$$+\quad 4\exp\left\{\left(\frac{G^{\Lambda_\infty}(2l)}{l}-\left(\tau-\frac{2}{l}\right)^2\right)l\right\} \tag{18}$$

4. A more practical choice for the empirical risk

Unfortunately, in real-world applications the measure μ on the input space D is unknown and only the training set is available. In these cases the empirical risk $R_{\tau,emp}(\alpha)$, which depends on $\mu(T_\alpha)$, cannot be calculated. Thus we have to use a different form of the empirical risk that allows a direct evaluation while ensuring the convergence in probability to $\inf_{\alpha\in\Lambda} R_\tau(\alpha)$ when l increases indefinitely. In this way the replacement does not prejudice the consistency of the ERM method.

A possible choice is the following

$$R'_{emp}(\alpha)=\frac{1}{l}\sum_{j=1}^{l}Q'(z_j,\alpha)$$

where $Q'(z,\alpha)$ is defined in (5).

We can prove that, under mild conditions, this form of the empirical risk shares the same convergence properties of $R_{\tau,emp}(\alpha)$.

If $\Lambda_0=\{\alpha\in\Lambda_\tau:\mu(T_\alpha)=0\}$, the corresponding classifiers $\varphi(x,\alpha)$, with $\alpha\in\Lambda_0$ do not misclassify any point of the certainty region C. Then $\Lambda_{0,\tau}=\Lambda_\tau\setminus\Lambda_0$ includes the values of α for which $0<\mu(T_\alpha)<\tau$.

The following corollary establishes the convergence properties of $R'_{emp}(\alpha)$.

COROLLARY 8 *If*

$$\inf_{\alpha\in\Lambda_0} R_\tau(\alpha)\leq\inf_{\alpha\in\Lambda_{0,\tau}} R_\tau(\alpha) \tag{19}$$

then

$$\inf_{\alpha\in\Lambda} R'_{emp}(\alpha)\xrightarrow[l\to\infty]{\mathbf{P}}\inf_{\alpha\in\Lambda} R_\tau(\alpha) \tag{20}$$

Furthermore, it can be easily proved that the rate of convergence of $R'_{emp}(\alpha)$ to $R_\tau(\alpha)$ can be upper bounded by the right hand side of (17).

References

Vapnik, V. N. (1982). *Estimation of Dependences Based on Empirical Data*. New York: Springer-Verlag.

Vapnik, V. N. (1998). *Statistical Learning Theory.* York: John Wiley & Sons.

Vapnik, V. N. and Chervonenkis, A. Ya. (1971). On the uniform convergence of relative frequencies of events to their probabilities. *Theory of Probability and Its Applications*, pages 264–280.

A PROBABILISTIC PCA CLUSTERING APPROACH TO THE SVD ESTIMATE OF SIGNAL SUBSPACES

M. Panella[1], G. Grisanti[1] and A. Rizzi[1]

[1] *INFO-COM Dpt. - University of Rome "La Sapienza"*
Via Eudossiana 18, 00184 Rome (Italy)
{panella, rizzi}@infocom.uniroma1.it
grisantigianluca@virgilio.it

Abstract In this paper, we investigate the full equivalence, under basic conditions, between the Probabilistic PCA clustering approach and the reconstruction of signal subspaces based on the singular value decomposition. Therefore this equivalence allows the adaptive determination of the clusters identified on data, in order to maximize the quality of the reconstructed signal. Furthermore, using known results in SVD framework, we also introduce a new technique to estimate automatically the dimension of the latent variable subspace.

Keywords: probabilistic PCA clustering, SVD signal estimate, SHEM algorithm

1. Introduction

A deep analysis of the two methods reveals a common interpretation which confirms the investigated purposes. In this paper we can suggest a different "point of view" by which examining the same problem: the determination of meaningful components in noisy data. The general idea, which looks on to a potential similarity of the results of the two methods, is the necessity of selecting a reduced space from the original one, provided from an incoming measurement matrix. The matter which leads to this kind of procedure is that the entire space includes some constructive information and others unknown, noisy elements with no advantages in the right acknowledgment of the signal. In the Probabilistic PCA (PPCA) approach, the concept of the principal space concerns the selection of a subspace, chosen in a suitable way, which represents a compromise between the attempt to have less complexity and the need to not eliminate the useful information. In the same way, the SVD decomposition is intended to the estimation of a signal space and a noisy space with the aim of

B. Apolloni et al. (eds.), Biological and Artificial Intelligence Environments, 271–279

recovering the useful information from the full set of observed data. We shall analyze in the following the common features.

1.1 The PPCA technique

The Probabilistic PCA method [Christopher M. Bishop, 1997] provides a technique for clustering and reconstruction of data space. The computation of the latent space makes use of the "factor loadings" matrix W which allows the projection of the reduced space (described by the variable x_n) onto the whole space (estimate variable $\hat{t}_n$) and the inverse projection using the following:

$$\hat{t}_n = W(W^T W)^{-1} x_n + \mu \qquad and \qquad x_n = W^T(t_n - \mu) \tag{1}$$

where μ describes the mean value of the data matrix from pattern t_n. In the PPCA model, developed for a generic number of clusters, it is usual to determine the W matrix through the maximization of log-likelihood function and the result directly connected with sample covariance matrix S [Christopher M. Bishop, 1997]. Every single block of the W expression can be computed under the hypothesis of isotropic noise by calculating the singular value decomposition of the sample covariance S. The condition leads to the expression of the covariance matrix C of the probabilistic model:

$$C = \sigma^2 I + WW^T \tag{2}$$

where σ^2 represents the variance of the noisy process. It can be obtained (once established the dimension q of the latent space) as the mean value of the remaining d-q eigenvalue terms λ_j on the diagonal of the covariance matrix (decomposed by SVD) $\sigma^2 = \frac{1}{d-q} \sum_{j=q+1}^{d} \lambda_j$. Therefore the expression of W, under the previous assumption about noise [Christopher M. Bishop, 1997] is:

$$W = U_q \left(\Lambda_q - \sigma^2 I_q\right)^{1/2} R \tag{3}$$

where q describes the dimension of the latent space, U_q represents the first q columns of the left eigenvectors matrix of S, Λ_q the correspondent eigenvalues matrix and R is an arbitrary rotational matrix.

The purpose is to find out a formulation of C, pointing out every single term of the last formula (3) in connection with the general data matrix D. Describing D with its singular value decomposition $D = U_D \Lambda_D V_D^T$, the first step is to calculate the correspondent sample covariance matrix S :

$$S = Cov(D) = \frac{D^T D}{N} = \frac{V_D}{\sqrt{N}} \Lambda_D^2 \frac{V_D^T}{\sqrt{N}} \tag{4}$$

Evaluating the covariance matrix S in the form of SVD it is necessary to determinate the correct subspace blocks and later the factor loadings W :

$$S = U_S S_S V_S^T = (U_{S1} \ U_{S2}) \begin{pmatrix} S_{S1} & 0 & S_{S1} \\ & 0 & \end{pmatrix} \begin{pmatrix} V_{S1}^T \\ V_{S2}^T \end{pmatrix} \tag{5}$$

where the index 1 and 2 are referred to the latent space and the rejected space. Comparing the two expressions (4 and 5) we can obtain:

$$U_S = \frac{V_D}{\sqrt{N}} = \frac{1}{\sqrt{N}} [V_q \ V_{d-q}] \tag{6}$$

$$S_S = \Lambda_D^2 = \left[\Lambda_q^2 \ \Lambda_{d-q}^2\right] \tag{7}$$

$$V_S^T = \frac{V_D^T}{\sqrt{N}} = \frac{1}{\sqrt{N}} [V_q \ V_{d-q}]^T \tag{8}$$

From the expression of factor loadings in the PPCA approach (3), the correspondent blocks allow to express the formula in term of SVD of S (5):

$$W = [U_{S1}] \left[S_{S1} - \sigma^2 I_q\right]^{1/2} \left[V_{S1}^T\right] \tag{9}$$

with $U_q = U_{S1}$ (left eigenvectors of the q dimensional subspace), $\Lambda_q = S_{S1}$ (eigenvalues correspondent to the q dimensional subspace), $R = V_{S1}^T$ (depends on the arbitrariness of the rotational matrix R which has to respect the only condition of orthogonality)

If we develop the covariance C (2) illustrated in the sense of W value (9):

$$C = \sigma^2 I + [U_{S1}] \left[S_{S1} - \sigma^2 I_q\right]^{1/2} \left[V_{S1}^T\right] [V_{S1}] \left[S_{S1} - \sigma^2 I_q\right]^{1/2} \left[U_{S1}^T\right] \tag{10}$$

and keeping in mind that: the eigenvalues matrix $\left[S_{S1} - \sigma^2 I_q\right]$ is diagonal then equal to its transposed; is verified the formula $\left[V_{S1}^T\right] [V_{S1}] = I$; we obtain:

$$C = \sigma^2 I + [U_{S1}] \left[S_{S1} - \sigma^2 I_q\right] \left[U_{S1}^T\right] \tag{11}$$

Finally considering the previous (6), (7) and (8) the expression of C will be the following:

$$C = \sigma^2 I + \frac{V_q}{\sqrt{N}} (\Lambda_q^2 - \sigma^2 I_q) \frac{V_q^T}{\sqrt{N}} \tag{12}$$

which represent the covariance in the PPCA model in function of the matrix D.

1.2 SVD technique for signal space estimate

The SVD method for noisy matrix analysis take advantage of the singular value decomposition of the complete observation data matrix M expressed as the sum of a signal matrix E and a noise matrix N, under the conditions $rank(M) = rank(N) = d$ and $rank(E) = q < d$ as shown:

$$M = E + N = (U_{m1} \quad U_{m2}) \begin{pmatrix} S_{m1} & 0 & S_{m2} \\ & 0 & \end{pmatrix} \begin{pmatrix} V_{m1}^T \\ V_{m2}^T \end{pmatrix} \tag{13}$$

where S_{m1} and S_{m2} are the singular values of M, both organized in diagonal matrix. The formula describes a generic SVD form of M and we know it is always possible to decompose the matrix M by SVD to have the eigenvalues in a decreasing order. The separation of the blocks in the matrix describes two different sections, standing for signal and noise part [DeMoor, 1993]. To identify the correct splitting point it is possible to measure the maximum differende (a gap) between eigenvalues along the principal diagonal on the eigenvalues matrix of M. So we can write down the correspondent expressions, obtained developing the sum of E and N in SVD decomposition: $S_{m1} = \sqrt{S_{e1}^2 + \sigma^2 I_q}$ (with S_{e1} eigenvalues matrix of E) and $S_{m2} = \sigma I_{d-q}$ (noise eigenvalues matrix). Among the S_{m1} values and the remaining S_{m2} there is a threshold (gap) caused by the fact that the $d - q$ values σ^2 in S_{m2} are all equal because generated from the same Gaussian noisy process. This threshold is not defined at first and it clearly depends on the specific properties of the data matrix and the additional noise. The matter is that the "gap" feature turns out to be easily identifiable in the determination of the subspace.

The aim is to calculate the unknown signal matrix E from the SVD of the generic data matrix M (which is known). The problem is that we have not enough parameters to determine every single eigenvalues and eigenvectors block from M. The needs is to estimate E using an alternative way, such as the *minimum variance estimate*:

$$\min_{X \in R^{qXq}} \|MX - E\|_F^2 \tag{14}$$

with the consequence that E matrix can be expressed as [DeMoor, 1993]:

$$\hat{E} = [U_{m1}] \left[S_{e1}^2 \left(S_{e1}^2 + \sigma^2 I_r \right)^{-1/2} \right] [V_{m1}^T] \tag{15}$$

As we done previously, we want to underline the final expression of the covariance of E and therefore we have to start from the data matrix M. From the expression of minimum variance of E and considering the $S_{m1} = \sqrt{S_{e1}^2 + \sigma^2 I_q}$ derived from a general analysis of the SVD decomposition of M, it is possible to explicitate the E covariance matrix as below:

$$Cov(E) = \frac{E^T E}{N} =$$

$$= \frac{[V_{m1}]}{N} \left[S_{e1}^2 \left(S_{e1}^2 + \sigma^2 I_q \right)^{-1/2} \right]^T \left[U_{m1}^T \right] \left[U_{m1} \right] \left[S_{e1}^2 \left(S_{e1}^2 + \sigma^2 I_q \right)^{-1/2} \right] \left[V_{m1}^T \right]$$

$$= \frac{1}{N} [V_{m1}] \left[(S_{m1})^{-T} \left(S_{m1}^2 - \sigma^2 I_q \right)^T \right] \left[\left(S_{m1}^2 - \sigma^2 I_q \right) (S_{m1})^{-1} \right] \left[V_{m1}^T \right]$$

$$= [V_{m1}] \frac{\left[S_{m1}^{-1} \right] [S_{e1}]}{\sqrt{N}} \left[S_{m1}^2 - \sigma^2 I_q \right] \frac{\left[S_{m1}^{-1} \right] [S_{e1}]}{\sqrt{N}} \left[V_{m1}^T \right] \quad (16)$$

2. Analytic approach to the equivalence

About the data features on which we develop the analysis, the PPCA technique doesn't require any particular attribute; it is not necessary to have zero mean value because the procedure returns a normalized value by considering the μ quantity. On the contrary the analysis of the data matrix with signal space and noise space method, works with mean value equal to zero.The hypothesis introduced in this paper considers a zero mean value data matrix in case of PPCA analysis. This fact doesn't reduce the validity of the procedure and it doesn't limit its generality.

In both situations we can assume the same noise conditions. The most common one is the isotropy of the noisy process, for example a Gaussian process. In the PPCA method this hypothesis results necessary to assert that the covariance matrix C can be directly connected with the sample covariance S. Consequently it is possible to compute the factor loadings W through SVD analysis. In the space decomposition method the same hypothesis can be considered as essential, in fact it is the consequence of the condition for the existence of SVD decomposition of M, that is $N^T N \propto I$ (proportional to the identity matrix). Moreover the noisy process is to be considered uncorrelated with the signal so we can assert that $Cov(M) = Cov(E) + Cov(N)$.

The MoG model [M. Panella, 2003] based on the probabilistic PCA, used as fundamental structure, provides a local weighed Gaussian process. The prior probability $\pi^{(j)}$ (j index stands for cluster) measures the influence of the data set on the generic cluster and it is expressed by the responsibility function R_{ni}. The hypothesis asserted in this paper concerns to work on a specific cluster, weighed by a unitary responsibility function, which means that we shall consider a single cluster data set matrix. The results obtained in this way will be extended later on the generic data matrix.

From the expressions developed in the approaches (12) and (16) we can examine the correspondence:

- $\sqrt{N}^{-1}[V_q] \Longleftrightarrow \sqrt{N}^{-1}[V_{m1}]\left[S_{m1}^{-1}\right][S_{e1}]$ where V_q and V_{m1} are right eigenvectors in the data matrix D, both referred to the same signal subspace. The term $\left[S_{m1}^{-1}\right][S_{e1}]$ depends on the fact that SVD decomposition generated unitary eigenvectors with the normalization term displaced on the eigenvalues. On the contrary the PPCA provides a normalized latent space. So, it acts as a suited scaling factor.

- $\left[S_{m1}^2 - \sigma^2 I_q\right] \Longleftrightarrow \left[\Lambda_q^2 - \sigma^2 I_q\right]$ both S_{m1} and Λ_q describes eigenvalues with dimension corresponding to the reduced space, each one achieved with the correspondent method.

The results of the formal check in the minimum variance estimate support the concept perceived by intuition: both sequences lead to the same conclusion. Finally we can conclude asserting that: the mean value and the variance of the noise process are the same in both methods; the mean value of the signal can be calculate for each data matrix and we proved that the covariance terms are equal in both approaches; then *if E has Gaussian distribution the $\hat{E}$ minimum variance estimate corresponds to the $\hat{t}_n$ reconstructed with PPCA technique.*

3. Automatic determination of the latent subspace dimension

The main matter about the identification of the subspaces is the selection of the correct $rank$ of E: the q dimension. This value is usually established before starting the analysis of data, therefore we have no adaptive choice. Otherwise q can be evaluate through some energetic considerations: for instance the 95% of the residual variance (the method considered as reference to evaluate the suggested technique in the following tests) or, equivalently, it must be fixed in advance for some constraint. We propose to choose this value using the properties of the SVD estimate, evaluating the existing gap among the eigenvalues in the diagonal of the covariance matrix: $gap \Leftrightarrow \max(\sigma_n^2 - \sigma_{n-1}^2)$. The maximum difference in fact represents the separation between the signal space and the noise space because we speculate there should be a remarkable difference in the variance terms. An approach like this allows to evaluate each reconstructed cluster individually and in a adaptive way, to allow a better dimensional identification.

The PPCA clustering and reconstruction process, applied to a generic data set, provides a global rearranging policy. It distributes the new sets weighting up both aspects of local distance among the pattern and global function reconstruction [Christopher M. Bishop, 1997]. Combining the PPCA technique of clustering-rebuilding of the data space with this method enables a better performance as shown afterwards. Moreover a later improvement has been developed for the gap method, the relative gap approach which results more profitable in order to pick the right q: $relative\ gap \Leftrightarrow \max\left(\frac{\sigma_n^2 - \sigma_{n-1}^2}{\sigma_{n-1}^2}\right)$. This last approach will be our submitted method in the following comparing tests where we shall demostrate how efficient it is in determining the right dimension values.

4. Tests

A major improvement introduced by the present analysis concerns the determination of the subspace dimension. The following tests concern different aspects, related to the correct identification of the dimension space and to the real problem applications as well. To manage the new technique of q dimension recognition we used the SHEM algorithm (Splitting Hierarchical Expectation Maximization) [M. Panella, 2001] based on the MoG (Mixture of Gaussian) [M. Panella, 2003] structure.

4.1 Dimension recognition

In order to evaluate the performance of the proposed gap method, we generated a specific data set with the signal dimension lower than the full space dimension and with noise dimension equal to the maximum. All clusters were developed by a Gaussian distribution, in a more or less overlapped position, and the noise superimposed has a variance value smaller than the signal variance (about 15-20%), zero mean value and it is spreaded on each cluster. The table shows the signal dimension for every cluster separated by "/" item (except for the last case where the cluster number is shown in brackets) and the noise dimension equal to the total dimension. The results columns show the identified dimensions in the reference and suggested methods.

total clusters	signal dimension per cluster	noise dimension cluster	total dimension per cluster	identified dimension 95% method	identified dimension gap method
3	5/5/5	20	20	6/7/7	5/5/5
3	6/8/10	20	20	5/7/9	6/8/10
10	15(10)	20	20	13(9)/14(1)	15(10)

It should be noted that in case of different structures, the signal dimension results correctly identified by the gap method. On the contrary the standard technique of the 95% residual variance cannot recognize the real dimension, in particular when the signal dimension is considerably lower than the complete space dimension. In the 10 clusters case, (on the vertex of an hypercube), it is asserted the better performance of the gap method (all clusters recognized).

4.2 Function approximation

The proposed approach was evaluated also in more complex problems. The first one concerned the real function approximation where we managed tests on three well-known benchmarks [I. Rojas and Prieto, 2000], sampled with a spiral distribution on the input space, with 400 points used for training, $\lambda = 0,5$ C_{max}=40 (SHEM)

test functions	result 95% method	result gap method
$y = \frac{C_a}{1+e^{-C_b X_2}} + 0,45(x_2 - 5)$	30,973 db	30,973 db
$y = C_c \sin^2\left(2\pi \frac{(5-x_1)^2+(5-x_2)^2}{10}\right)$	7,9718 db	8,4158 db
$y = C_d \frac{(5-x_2)^2}{3(5-x_1)^2+(5-x_2)^2}$	16,771 db	21,261 db

From the analysis of the results appears an evident better performance of the suggested approach which ensure a consistent improvement of the error ratio (SNR) particularly for the second and third cases (which have major complexity).

4.3 Prediction problem

Another real world application concerns the prediction performed, for example, on environmental time series [M. Panella, 2001]. In particular we considered three sequences: the Acoustic Noise and Ozone level (acquired sampling the observation data every 5 minutes); the Electric Load required in a particular region (sampling every hour) and at last the Mackey Glass (a benchmark series):

	Acoustic Noise	Ozone	Electric Load	Mackey Glass
95% method	25,539 db	21,569 db	25,955 db	35,854 db
gap method	23,39 db	21,604 db	28,801 db	37,201 db

It is evident, examining the table, that the suggested method performs a better results in the most of the cases, expecially in the Electric Load sequence and in the benchmark one.

4.4 Noise filtering

To evaluate the capability of the algorithm to reconstruct original data set it has been tested on imaging applications. In particular the elaboration has concerned the well known image "Lena". Gaussian noise has been added on this image (variable from a SNR of 10 db to 25 db) and the purpose was to rate the gain of the restored image. The algorithm SHEM provided a training on the full size image and it analyze a 4x4 pixel block each time to restore original data set.

	SNR noise 25 db	SNR noise 20 db	SNR noise 15 db	SNR noise 10 db
95% method gain	+1,35 db	+2,120 db	+0,543 db	+0,28 db
gap method gain	-2,1 db	+1,568	+2,768 db	+2,497 db

From the analysis of results it is clear how satisfying is the performance in case of heavy noise overlaid. The improvement respect the old method becomes more evident when the noise level is higher.

References

Bishop, C.M., Tipping, M.E. (1997). Mixture of probabilistic principal component analysers. *Technical Report NCRG.*

DeMoor, B. (1993). The singular value decomposition and long and short spaces of noisy matrices. *IEEE transactions on signal processing*, 41.

Panella, M., Rizzi, A., Frattale Mascioli, F.M., Martinelli, G. (2001). constructive em approach to density estimation for learning. *Proceedings of IJCNN'2001 Washington DCA.*

Panella, M., Rizzi, A., Martinelli, G. (2003). Refining accuracy of environmental data prediction by mog neural network. *Neurocomputing*, 55(3-4):521–549.

Rojas, I., Pomares, H., Ortega, J. and Prieto, A. (2000). Self-organized fuzzy system generation from training examples. *IEEE Transactions on fuzzy systems*, 8(1):23–36.

FAST DOMINANT-SET CLUSTERING

Massimiliano Pavan and Marcello Pelillo
Dipartimento di Informatica
Università Ca' Foscari di Venezia
Via Torino 155, 30172 Venezia Mestre, Italy
{pavan,pelillo}@dsi.unive.it

Abstract

Dominant sets are a new graph-theoretic concept that has proven to be relevant in pairwise data clustering problems. We address the problem of grouping out-of-sample examples after the clustering process has taken place. This may serve either to drastically reduce the computational burden associated to the processing of very large data sets, or to efficiently deal with dynamic situations whereby data sets need to be updated continually. Numerical experiments show the effectiveness of the approach.

Keywords: Unsupervised Learning, Incremental Clustering, Graphs, Game Dynamics

1. Introduction

Proximity-based, or pairwise, data clustering techniques are gaining increasing popularity over traditional central grouping techniques, which are centered around the notion of "feature" (see, e.g., [Hofmann and Buhmann, 1997; Shi and Malik, 2000]). We have recently developed a new framework for pairwise data clustering based on a novel graph-theoretic concept, that of a *dominant set* [Pavan and Pelillo, 2003a; Pavan and Pelillo, 2003b]. An intriguing connection between dominant sets and the solutions of a (continuous) quadratic optimization problem allows us to use continuous optimization techniques such as *replicator dynamics* from evolutionary game theory [Weibull, 1995]. Such systems are attractive as can be coded in a few lines of any high-level programming language, can easily be implemented in a parallel network of locally interacting units, thereby motivating analog VLSI implementations [Torsello and Pelillo, 2000], and offer the advantage of biological plausibility. A nice feature of this framework is that it naturally provides a

B. Apolloni et al. (eds.), Biological and Artificial Intelligence Environments, 281–289

principled measure of a cluster's cohesiveness as well as a measure of a vertex participation to its assigned group. It also allows one to obtain "soft" partitions of the input data, by allowing a point to belong to more than one cluster. The approach has proven to be a powerful one when applied to problems such as intensity, color, and texture segmentation, and is competitive with spectral approaches such as normalized cut [Pavan and Pelillo, 2003a; Pavan and Pelillo, 2003b].

However, a typical problem associated to pairwise grouping algorithms in general, and hence to the dominant set framework in particular, is the scaling behavior with the number of data. Moreover, in applications such as document classification or visual database organization, one is confronted with a dynamic environment which continually supplies the algorithm with newly produced data that have to be grouped. In such situations, the trivial approach of recomputing the complete cluster structure upon the arrival of any new item is clearly unfeasible.

Motivated by the previous arguments, in this paper we address the problem of efficiently assigning out-of-sample, unseen data to one or more previously determined clusters. This may serve either to substantially reduce the computational burden associated to the processing of very large (though static) data sets, by extrapolating the complete grouping solution from a small number of samples, or to deal with dynamic situations whereby data sets need to be updated continually. We shall see that the very notion of a dominant set, thanks to its clear combinatorial properties, offers a simple and efficient solution to this problem. The basic idea consists of computing, for any new example, a quantity which measures the degree of cluster membership, and we provide simple approximations which allow us to do this in linear time and space, with respect to the cluster size. Our classification schema inherits the main features of the dominant set formulation, i.e., the ability of yielding a soft classification of the input data and of providing principled measures for cluster membership and cohesiveness.

2. Finding Dominant Sets by Game Dynamics

We represent the data to be clustered as an undirected edge-weighted (*similarity*) graph with no self-loops $G = (V, E, w)$, where $V = \{1, \ldots, n\}$ is the vertex set, $E \subseteq V \times V$ is the edge set, and $w : E \to \mathbb{R}_+^*$ is the (positive) weight function. Vertices in G correspond to data points, edges represent neighborhood relationships, and edge-weights reflect similarity between pairs of linked vertices. As customary, we represent the graph G with the corresponding weighted adjacency (or similarity) matrix, which is the $n \times n$ nonnegative, symmetric matrix $A = (a_{ij})$ defined as:

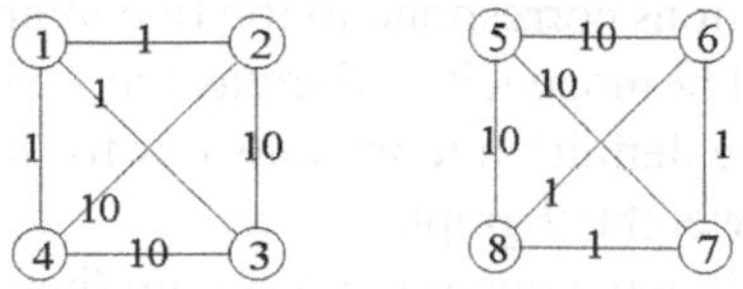

Figure 1. An example edge-weighted graph. Note that $\mathrm{w}_{\{1,2,3,4\}}(1) < 0$ and this reflects the fact that vertex 1 is loosely coupled to vertices 2, 3 and 4. Conversely, $\mathrm{w}_{\{5,6,7,8\}}(5) > 0$ and this reflects the fact that vertex 5 is tightly coupled with vertices 6, 7, and 8.

$$a_{ij} = \begin{cases} w(i,j), & \text{if } (i,j) \in E \\ 0, & \text{otherwise}. \end{cases}$$

Let $S \subseteq V$ be a non-empty subset of vertices and $i \in V$. The *(average) weighted degree* of i w.r.t. S is defined as $\mathrm{awdeg}_S(i) = \frac{1}{|S|}\sum_{j \in S} a_{ij}$, where $|S|$ denotes the cardinality of S.

Moreover, if $j \notin S$ we define $\phi_S(i,j) = a_{ij} - \mathrm{awdeg}_S(i)$, which is a measure of the similarity between nodes j and i, with respect to the average similarity between node i and its neighbors in S.

Let $S \subseteq V$ be a non-empty subset of vertices and $i \in S$. The *weight* of i w.r.t. S is

$$\mathrm{w}_S(i) = \begin{cases} 1, & \text{if } |S| = 1 \\ \displaystyle\sum_{j \in S \setminus \{i\}} \phi_{S \setminus \{i\}}(j,i)\, \mathrm{w}_{S \setminus \{i\}}(j), & \text{otherwise} \end{cases} \tag{1}$$

while the *total weight* of S is defined as $\mathrm{W}(S) = \sum_{i \in S} \mathrm{w}_S(i)$. Intuitively, $\mathrm{w}_S(i)$ gives us a measure of the overall similarity between vertex i and the vertices of $S \setminus \{i\}$ with respect to the overall similarity among the vertices in $S \setminus \{i\}$, with positive values indicating high internal coherency (see Fig. 1).

An alternative, useful way of computing the $\mathrm{w}_S(i)$'s (when $|S| > 1$) is given by the following formula [Pavan and Pelillo, 2003a]:

$$\mathrm{w}_S(i) = \sum_{j \in S \setminus \{i\}} (a_{ij} - a_{hj})\, \mathrm{w}_{S \setminus \{i\}}(j) \tag{2}$$

where h is an arbitrary element of $S \setminus \{i\}$ (it can be shown that the sum in (2) does not depend upon the choice of h).

A non-empty subset of vertices $S \subseteq V$ such that $W(T) > 0$ for any non-empty $T \subseteq S$, is said to be *dominant* if:

1 $\mathrm{w}_S(i) > 0$, for all $i \in S$

2 $\mathrm{w}_{S \cup \{i\}}(i) < 0$, for all $i \notin S$.

The two previous conditions correspond to the two main properties of a cluster: the first regards internal homogeneity, whereas the second regards external inhomogeneity. The above definition represents our formalization of the concept of a cluster in an edge-weighted graph.

Now, consider the following quadratic program (here and in the sequel a dot denotes the standard scalar product between vectors):

$$\begin{array}{ll} \text{maximize} & f(\mathbf{x}) = \mathbf{x} \cdot A\mathbf{x} \\ \text{subject to} & \mathbf{x} \in \Delta_n \end{array} \tag{3}$$

where $\Delta_n = \{\mathbf{x} \in \mathbb{R}^n : x_i \geq 0 \text{ for all } i \in V \text{ and } \mathbf{e} \cdot \mathbf{x} = 1\}$ is the standard simplex of $\mathbb{R}^n$, and $\mathbf{e}$ is a vector of appropriate length consisting of unit entries (hence $\mathbf{e} \cdot \mathbf{x} = \sum_i x_i$). The *support* of a vector $\mathbf{x} \in \Delta_n$ is defined as the set of indices corresponding to its positive components, that is $\sigma(\mathbf{x}) = \{i \in V : x_i > 0\}$. The following theorem, proved in [Pavan and Pelillo, 2003a], establishes an intriguing connection between dominant sets and local solutions of program (3).

THEOREM 1 *If S is a dominant subset of vertices, then its (weighted) characteristics vector $\mathbf{x}^S$, which is the vector of Δ_n defined as*

$$x_i^S = \begin{cases} \frac{\mathrm{w}_S(i)}{\mathrm{W}(S)}, & \text{if } i \in S \\ 0, & \text{otherwise} \end{cases} \tag{4}$$

is a strict local solution of program (3). Conversely, if $\mathbf{x}$ is a strict local solution of program (3) then its support $S = \sigma(\mathbf{x})$ is a dominant set, provided that $\mathrm{w}_{S \cup \{i\}}(i) \neq 0$ for all $i \notin S$.

Note that the components of the weighted characteristic vectors give us a natural measure of the participation of the corresponding vertices in the cluster, whereas the value of the objective function measures the cohesiveness of the class. In order to get a partition of the input data into coherent groups, a simple approach is to iteratively finding a dominant set and then removing it from the graph, until all vertices have been grouped. On the other hand, by finding all dominant sets, i.e., local solutions of (3), of the original graph, one can obtain a "soft" partition of the dataset, whereby clusters are allowed to overlap.

The continuous optimization method we use to solve problem (3) is called *replicator equations*, a class of dynamical systems arising in evolutionary game theory [Weibull, 1995]. In particular, we use the following discrete-time model:

$$x_i(t+1) = x_i(t)\frac{(A\mathbf{x}(t))_i}{\mathbf{x}(t) \cdot A\mathbf{x}(t)} \ . \tag{5}$$

for $i = 1 \ldots n$, which corresponds to a well-known discretization of *first-order* replicator equations (see, e.g., [Weibull, 1995]). It is readily seen that the simplex Δ_n is invariant under these dynamics, which means that every trajectory starting in Δ_n will remain in Δ_n for all future times. Moreover, it can be proved that, since A is symmetric, the objective function $f(\mathbf{x}) = \mathbf{x} \cdot A\mathbf{x}$ of program (3) is strictly increasing along any nonconstant trajectory of replicator equations (5) [Weibull, 1995].

3. Predicting Cluster Membership for Out-of-Sample Data

Suppose we are given a set V of n unlabeled items and let $G = (V, E, w)$ denote the corresponding similarity graph. After determining the dominant sets (i.e., the clusters) for these original data, we are next supplied with a set V' of k new data items, together with all kn pairwise affinities between the old and the new data, and are asked to assign each of them to one or possibly more previously determined clusters. We shall denote by $\hat{G} = (\hat{V}, \hat{E}, \hat{w})$, with $\hat{V} = V \cup V'$, the similarity graph built upon all the $n+k$ data. Note that in our approach we do not need the $\binom{k}{2}$ affinities between the new points, which is a nice feature as in most applications k is typically very large. Technically, $\hat{G}$ is a *supergraph* of G, namely a graph having $V \subseteq \hat{V}$, $E \subseteq \hat{E}$ and $w(i,j) = \hat{w}(i,j)$ for all $(i,j) \in E$.

Let $S \subseteq V$ be a subset of vertices which is dominant in the original graph G and let $i \in \hat{V} \setminus V$ be a new data point. As pointed out in the previous section, the sign of $\mathrm{w}_{S\cup\{i\}}(i)$ provides an indication as to whether i is tightly or loosely coupled with the vertices in S (the condition $\mathrm{w}_{S\cup\{i\}}(i) = 0$ corresponds to a non-generic boundary situation that does not arise in practice and will therefore be ignored).

Accordingly, it is natural to propose the following rule for predicting cluster membership of unseen data:

$$\text{if } \mathrm{w}_{S\cup\{i\}}(i) > 0, \text{ then assign vertex } i \text{ to cluster } S\,. \tag{6}$$

Note that, according to this rule, the same point can be assigned to more than one class, thereby yielding a soft partition of the input data. To get a hard partition one can use the cluster membership approximation measures we shall discuss below. Note that it may also happen for some instance i that no cluster S satisfies rule (6), in which case the point gets unclassified (or assigned to an "outlier" group). This should be interpreted as an indication that either the point is too noisy or that the cluster formation process was inaccurate. In our experience, however, this situation arises rarely.

The next result allows us to compute the sign of $\mathrm{w}_{S\cup\{i\}}(i)$ in linear time and space, with respect to the size of S.

PROPOSITION 1 *Let $G = (V, E, w)$ be an edge-weighted (similarity) graph, $A = (a_{ij})$ its weighted adjacency matrix, and $S \subseteq V$ a dominant set of G*

with characteristic vector $\mathbf{x}^S$. *Let* $\hat{G} = (\hat{V}, \hat{E}, \hat{w})$ *be a supergraph of* G *with weighted adjacency matrix* $\hat{A} = (\hat{a}_{ij})$. *Then, for all* $i \in \hat{V} \setminus V$, *we have:*

$$\mathrm{w}_{S\cup\{i\}}(i) > 0 \quad \Leftrightarrow \quad \sum_{j\in S} \hat{a}_{ij} x_j^S > f(\mathbf{x}^S) \,. \tag{7}$$

Proof: According to equation (2) we have:

$$\mathrm{w}_{S\cup\{i\}}(i) = \sum_{j\in S} (\hat{a}_{ij} - a_{hj})\, \mathrm{w}_S(j) \tag{8}$$

for any $h \in S$ (note that $\hat{a}_{hj} = a_{hj}$ because both h and j are vertices of S). Dividing by $W(S)$, which is non-zero because S is dominant, and recalling the definition of a characteristic vector we get:

$$\frac{\mathrm{w}_{S\cup\{i\}}(i)}{\mathrm{W}(S)} = \sum_{j\in S} (\hat{a}_{ij} - a_{hj}) x_j^S \tag{9}$$

It is immediate to see that the Karush-Kuhn-Tucker (KKT) equality conditions for program (3), i.e., the first-order necessary equality conditions for local optimality [Luenberger, 1984], imply $\sum_{j\in S} a_{hj} x_j^S = \mathbf{x}^S \cdot A\mathbf{x}^S = f(\mathbf{x}^S)$ for any $h \in S$ [Pavan and Pelillo, 2003a]. Hence, the proposition follows from the fact that, being S dominant, $W(S)$ is positive. □

Given an out-of-sample vertex i and a class S such that rule (6) holds, we now provide an approximation of the degree of participation of i in $S \cup \{i\}$ which, as pointed out in the previous section, is given by the ratio between $\mathrm{w}_{S\cup\{i\}}(i)$ and $\mathrm{W}(S \cup \{i\})$. This can be used, for example, to get a hard partition of the input data when an instance happens to be assigned to more than one class. By equation (9), we have:

$$\frac{\mathrm{w}_{S\cup\{i\}}(i)}{\mathrm{W}(S \cup \{i\})} = \sum_{h\in S} (\hat{a}_{hi} - a_{hj}) x_h^S \frac{\mathrm{W}(S)}{\mathrm{W}(S \cup \{i\})}$$

for any $j \in S$. Since computing the exact value of the ratio $\mathrm{W}(S)/\mathrm{W}(S \cup \{i\})$ would be computationally expensive, we now provide simple approximation formulas. Since S is dominant, it is reasonable to assume that all weights within it are close to each other. Hence, we approximate S with a clique having constant weight a, and impose that it has the same cohesiveness value $f(\mathbf{x}^S) = \mathbf{x}^S \cdot A\mathbf{x}^S$ as the original dominant set. After some algebra, we get

$$a = \frac{|S|}{|S| - 1} f(\mathbf{x}^S)$$

which yields $\mathrm{W}(S) \approx |S|a^{|S|-1}$. Approximating $\mathrm{W}(S \cup \{i\})$ with $|S+1|a^{|S|}$ in a similar way, we get:

$$\frac{\mathrm{W}(S)}{\mathrm{W}(S \cup \{i\})} \approx \frac{|S|a^{|S|-1}}{|S+1|a^{|S|}} = \frac{1}{f(\mathbf{x}^S)} \frac{|S|-1}{|S|+1}$$

which finally yields:

$$\frac{\mathrm{w}_{S\cup\{i\}}(i)}{\mathrm{W}(S \cup \{i\})} \approx \frac{|S|-1}{|S|+1} \left(\frac{\sum_{h \in S} \hat{a}_{hi} x_h^S}{f(\mathbf{x}^S)} - 1 \right) .$$

Using the above formula one can easily get, by normalization, an approximation of the characteristic vector $\mathbf{x}^{\hat{S}} \in \Delta_{n+k}$ of $\hat{S} = S \cup \{i \in \hat{V} \setminus V : \mathrm{w}_{S\cup\{i\}}(i) > 0\}$, i.e. the extension of cluster S obtained applying rule (6). With an approximation of $\mathbf{x}^{\hat{S}}$ in hand, it is also easy to compute an approximation of the cohesiveness of the new cluster $\hat{S}$, i.e., $\mathbf{x}^{\hat{S}} \cdot \hat{A}\mathbf{x}^{\hat{S}}$. Indeed, assuming that $\hat{S}$ is dominant in $\hat{G}$, and recalling the KKT equality conditions for program (3) [Pavan and Pelillo, 2003a], we get $(\hat{A}\mathbf{x}^{\hat{S}})_i = \mathbf{x}^{\hat{S}} \cdot \hat{A}\mathbf{x}^{\hat{S}}$ for all $i \in \hat{S}$. It is therefore natural to approximate the cohesiveness of $\hat{S}$ as a weighted average of the $(\hat{A}\mathbf{x}^{\hat{S}})_i$'s.

4. Results and Conclusions

In an attempt to evaluate how the approximations given at the end of the previous section actually compare to the solutions obtained on the dense problem, we conducted the following preliminary experiment. We generated 150 points on the plane so as to form a dominant set (we used a standard Gaussian kernel to obtain similarities), and extracted random samples with increasing sampling rate (i.e., sampling probability), ranging from 1/15 to 1. For each sampling rate 100 trials were made, for each of which we computed the Euclidean distance between the approximated and the actual characteristic vector (i.e., cluster membership), as well as the distance between the approximated and the actual cluster cohesiveness (that is, the value of the objective function f). Fig. 2 shows the average results obtained. As can be seen, our approximations work remarkably well: with a sampling rate less than 10 % the distance between the characteristic vectors is around 0.02 and this distance decreases linearly towards zero. As for the objective function, the results are even more impressive as the distance from the exact value (i.e., 0.989) rapidly goes to zero starting from 0.00025, at less than 10% rate. Also, note how the CPU time increases linearly as the sampling rate approaches 100%.

Next, we tested our algorithm over the Johns Hopkins University ionosphere database[1] which contains 351 labeled instances from two different classes. As

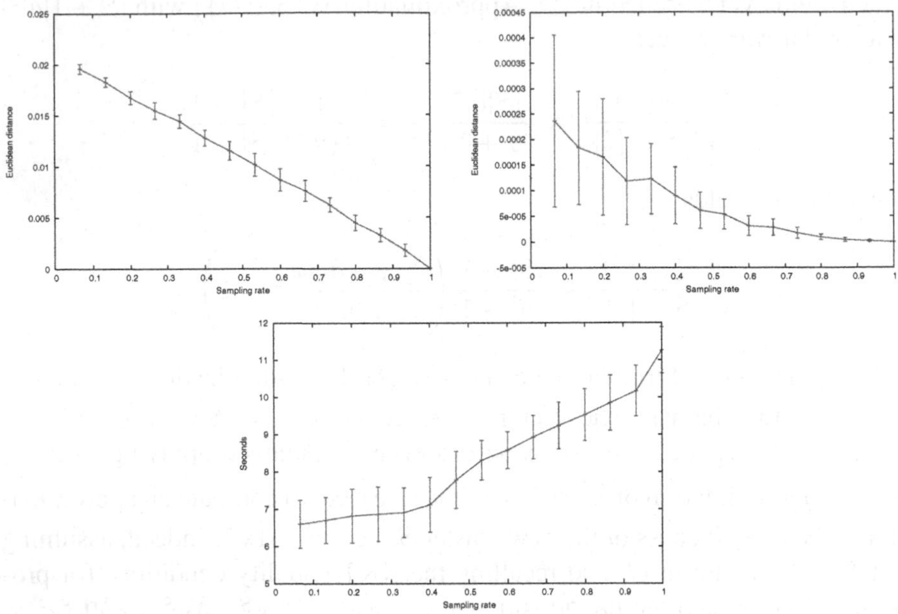

Figure 2. Evaluating the quality of our approximations on a 150-point cluster. Top: average distance between approximated and actual cluster membership (left) and cohesiveness (right) as a function of sampling rate. Bottom: average CPU time as a function of sampling rate.

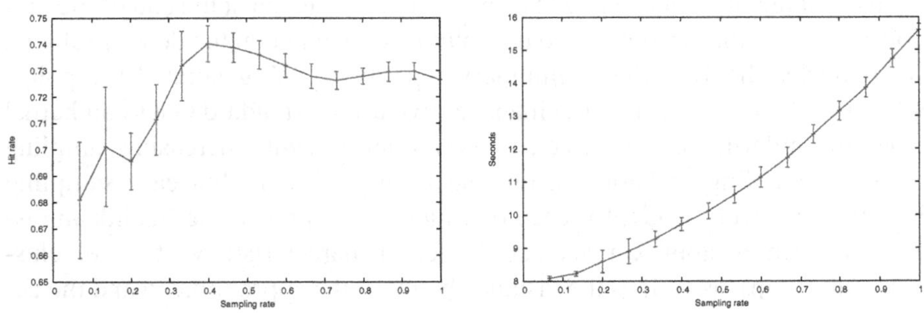

Figure 3. Results on the ionosphere database. Average classification rate (left) and CPU time (right) as a function of sampling rate.

in the previous experiment, similarities were computed using a Gaussian kernel. Our goal was to test how the solutions obtained on the sampled graph compare with those of the original, dense problem and to study how the performance of the algorithm scales w.r.t. the sampling rate. As before, we used sampling rates from 1/15 to 1, and for each such value 100 random samples were extracted. After the grouping process, the out-of-sample instances were assigned to one of the two classes found using rule (6). Then, for each example in the dataset a "success" was recorded whenever the actual class label of the instance coincided with the majority label of its assigned class. Fig. 3 shows the average results obtained. At around 40% rate the algorithm was already able to obtain a classification accuracy of about 73.4%, which is even slightly higher that the one obtained on the dense (100% rate) problem, which is 72.7%. Note that, as in the previous experiment, the algorithm appears to be robust with respect to the choice of the sample data. For the sake of comparison we also ran normalized cut on the *whole* dataset, and it yielded a classification rate of 72.4%.

In this paper, we have provided a simple and efficient extension to the dominant-set clustering framework to deal with the grouping of out-of-sample data. Experiments show that the solutions extrapolated from the sparse data are comparable with those of the dense problem and are obtained in much less time.

Notes

1. `http://www.ics.uci.edu/~mlearn/MLSummary.html`

References

Hofmann, T. and Buhmann, J. (1997). Pairwise data clustering by deterministic annealing. *IEEE Trans. Pattern Anal. Machine Intell.*, 19(1):1–14.

Luenberger, D. G. (1984). *Linear and Nonlinear Programming*. Addison-Wesley, Reading, MA.

Pavan, M. and Pelillo, M. (2003a). A new graph-theoretic approach to clustering and segmentation. In *Proc. IEEE Conf. Computer Vision and Pattern Recognition*, volume 1, pages 145–152.

Pavan, M. and Pelillo, M. (2003b). Unsupervised texture segmentation by dominant sets and game dynamics. In *Proc. IEEE Int. Conf. on Image Analysis and Processing*, pages 302–307.

Shi, J. and Malik, J. (2000). Normalized cuts and image segmentation. *IEEE Trans. Pattern Anal. Machine Intell.*, 22(8):888–905.

Torsello, A. and Pelillo, M. (2000). Continuous-time relaxation labeling processes. *Pattern Recognition*, 33:1897–1908.

Weibull, J. W. (1995). *Evolutionary Game Theory*. MIT Press, Cambridge, MA.

NEURAL NETWORK CLASSIFICATION USING ERROR ENTROPY MINIMIZATION

Jorge M. Santos,[1,3] Luís A. Alexandre,[2] and Joaquim Marques de Sá[1]
[1]*INEB - Instituto de Engenharia Biomédica* [2]*IT - Networks and Multimedia Group, Covilhã*
[3]*Instituto Superior de Engenharia do Porto, Portugal (jms@isep.ipp.pt)*

Abstract

One way of using the entropy criteria in learning systems is to minimize the entropy of the error between two variables: typically, one is the output of the learning system and the other is the target. This framework has been used for regression. In this paper we show how to use the minimization of the entropy of the error for classification.
The minimization of the entropy of the error implies a constant value for the errors. This, in general, does not imply that the value of the errors is zero. In regression, this problem is solved by making a shift of the final result such that it's average equals the average value of the desired target. We prove that, under mild conditions, this algorithm, when used in a classification problem, makes the error converge to zero and can thus be used in classification.

Keywords: Classification, Information Theoretic Learning, Renyi's Quadratic Entropy, Cost Function

1. Introduction

Since the introduction by Shanon of the concept of entropy [Shannon, 1948], and the posterior generalization made by Renyi in [Renyi, 1976], that entropy and information theory concepts have been applied in learning systems.
Shanon's entropy $H_S(x) = -\sum_{i=1}^{N} p_i log p_i$ measures the average amount of information conveyed by the random variable x whose N possible values occur with probability p_i. An extension of the entropy concept to continuous random variables $x \in C$ is: $H(x) = -\int_C f(x) log f(x) dx$ where $f(x)$ is the probability density function (pdf) of the variable x.
The use of entropy and relative concepts have several applications in learning systems. These applications are mostly based on finding the mutual information and the consequent relations between the distributions of the variables involved in a particular problem. Linsker proposed the *Infomax* principle that

B. Apolloni et al. (eds.), Biological and Artificial Intelligence Environments, 291–297

consists on the maximization of Mutual Information between the input and the output of the neural network [Linsker, 1998]. Mutual information gives rise to either unsupervised or supervised learning rules depending on how the problem is formulated. We can have unsupervised learning when we manipulate the mutual information between the outputs of the learning system or between its input and output. Examples of these approaches are independent component analysis and blind source separation [Amari et al., 1996], [Bell and Sejnowski, 1995]. If the goal is to maximize the mutual information between the output of a mapper and an external desired response, then learning becomes supervised.

With the goal of making supervised information-theoretic learning, several approaches have been proposed: 1 - The CIP (Cross Information Potential) tries to establish the relation between the pdfs of two variables. These variables could be the output of the network and the desired targets or the output of each layer and the desired targets [Xu and Príncipe, 1999]. 2- The entropy maximization of the output of the network and simultaneously the minimization of the entropy of the output of the data that belongs to a specific class. This method was proposed in [Haselsteiner and Príncipe, 2000] as a way of performing supervised learning without numerical targets. 3 - The MEE that consists of the minimization of the error entropy between the outputs of the network and the desired targets. This approach was proposed in [Erdogmus and Princípe, 2002] and used to make times series prediction.

We made some experiments with these proposed three methods with the goal of performing supervised classification but we did not achieve good results. This lead us to develop a new approach as described below.

2. Renyi's Quadratic Entropy and Back-propagation Algorithm

Renyi extended the concept of entropy and defined the Renyi's α entropy, in discrete cases, as:

$$H_{R\alpha}(x) = \frac{1}{1-\alpha} \log \left(\sum_{i=1}^{N} p_i^{\alpha} \right) \tag{1}$$

which tends to Shanon entropy when $\alpha \to 1$. If we take the Renyi's Quadratic Entropy ($\alpha = 2$), to continuous random variables, we obtain

$$H_{R2}(x) = -\log \left(\int_C [f(x)]^2 dx \right) \tag{2}$$

Renyi's Quadratic Entropy in conjunction with the Parzen Window probability density function estimation with gaussian kernel allows the determination of the entropy in a non-parametric and computationally efficient way.

Let $a = a_i \in \mathbb{R}^m$, $i = 1, ..., N$, be a set of samples from the output $Y \in \mathbb{R}^m$ of a mapping $\mathbb{R}^n \mapsto \mathbb{R}^m : Y = g(w, x)$, where w is a set of Neural Network weights.
The Parzen window method estimates the pdf $f(y)$ as

$$f(x) = \frac{1}{Nh^m} \sum_{i=1}^{N} K(\frac{x - x_i}{h}) \tag{3}$$

where N is the number of data points, K is a kernel function, and h the bandwidth or smoothing parameter. If we use the simple Gaussian kernel $G(y, I) = \frac{1}{(2\pi)^{\frac{m}{2}}} exp(-\frac{1}{2} y^T y)$, (being I the identity matrix), then, the estimated pdf $f(y)$ using Parzen window and Gaussian kernel will be:

$$f(y) = \frac{1}{Nh^m} \sum_{i=1}^{N} G\left(\frac{y - a_i}{h}, I\right) \tag{4}$$

The Renyi's Quadratic Entropy can be estimated, applying the integration of gaussian kernels [Xu and Príncipe, 1999], by

$$\hat{H}_{R2}(y) = -\log \left[\int_{-\infty}^{+\infty} \left(\frac{1}{Nh^m} \sum_{i=1}^{N} G(\frac{y - a_i}{h}, I) \right)^2 dx \right]$$

$$= -\log \left[\frac{1}{N^2 h^{2m-1}} \sum_{i=1}^{N} \sum_{j=1}^{N} G(\frac{a_i - a_j}{h}, 2I) \right] = -\log V(a) \tag{5}$$

Príncipe calls $V(a)$ the *information potential* [Príncipe et al., 1998] in analogy with the potential field in physics. For the same reason he also calls the derivative of $V(a)$ the *information force* F. Therefore

$$F = \frac{\partial}{\partial a} V(a) = \frac{\partial}{\partial a} \left[\frac{1}{N^2 h^{2m-1}} \sum_{i=1}^{N} \sum_{j=1}^{N} G(\frac{a_i - a_j}{h}, 2I) \right]$$

$$F_i = -\frac{1}{2Nh^{2m+1}} \sum_{j=1}^{N} G(\frac{a_i - a_j}{h}, 2I)(a_i - a_j) \tag{6}$$

This *information force* is back-propagated into the MLP the same way as in the MSE algorithm. The update of the neural network weights is performed using $\Delta w = \pm \eta \frac{\partial V}{\partial w}$. The $\pm$ means that we can maximize (+) or minimize (−) the entropy.

3. Supervised Classification with Error Entropy Minimization

We make use of the information-theoretic concepts, applying an entropy approach to the classification task using the entropy minimization of the error between the output of the network and the desired targets: the Error Entropy Minimization, EEM.

Let $d \in \mathbb{R}^m$ be the desired targets and Y the network output from the classification problem and $e_i = d_i - Y_i$ the error for each data sample i of a given data set. The error entropy minimization approach [Erdogmus and Princípe, 2002] states that Renyi's Quadratic Entropy of the error, with pdf approximated by Parzen window with Gaussian kernel, has minima along the line where the error is constant over the whole data set. Also the global minimum of this entropy is achieved when the pdf of the error is a Dirac delta function.
Taking the quadratic entropy of the error

$$\hat{H}_{R2} = -\log\left[\frac{1}{N^2h^{2m}}\sum_{i=1}^{N}\sum_{j=1}^{N} G\left(\frac{e_i - e_j}{h^2}\right)\right] \tag{7}$$

we clearly see that this entropy will be minimum when the diferences of all the error pairs $(e_i - e_j)$ are zero. This means that the errors are all the same. In classification problems with separable classes, the goal is to get all the errors equal to zero, meaning that we don't get any errors in the classification. In classification problems with non separable classes the goal is to achieve the Bayes error.
In the following we prove that, in classification problems, imposing some conditions to the output range and target values, the EEM algorithm makes the error converge to zero. The objective is to minimize the entropy of the error $e = d - Y$ and, as stated above, to achieve the goal of $e = 0$ for all data samples.

THEOREM 1 *Consider a two class supervised classification problem with a unidimensional output vector.* $Y \in [r, s]$ *is the output of the network and* $d \in \{a, b\}$ *the target vector or the desired output. If* $r = a$, $s = b$ *and* $a = -b$ *then the application of the EEM algorithm makes the errors on each data point be equal and equal to zero.*

Proof: Define the targets as $d \in \{-a, a\}$ and consider the output of the network as $Y \in [-a, a]$. The errors are given by $e = d - Y$.
If the true target for a given input x_i is $\{a\}$ then the error e_i varies in $P = [0, 2a]$.
If the true target for a given input x_j is $\{-a\}$ then the error e_j varies in $Q = [-2a, 0]$.
Since the minimization of the entropy of the error makes the errors all have the

same value, r, we get $e_i = e_j = r$.
r must be in P and Q. $P \cap Q = \{0\}$ thus $r = 0$ and $e_i = e_j = 0$. □

A similar proof can be made for multidimensional data samples.
By minimizing the Renyi's Quadratic Entropy of the error, applying the back-propagation algorithm, we find the weights of the neural network that yield good results in classification problems as we illustrate in the next section.

4. Experiments

We made two experiments, using multilayer perceptrons (MLP), to show the application of the EEM algorithm to data classification. The learning rate η and the smoothing parameter h were experimentally selected. However this is one subject that must be studied with more detail in our subsequent work.

In the first experiment we created a data set consisting of 200 data points, constituting 4 separable classes (figure 1).

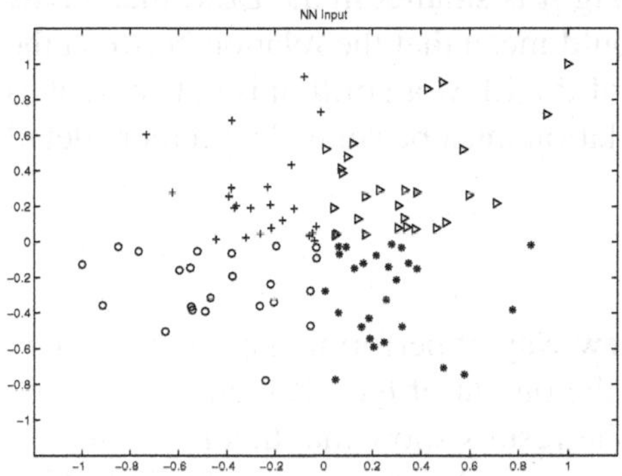

Figure 1 Dataset for the first problem

Several (2;n;2) MLP's were trained and tested 40 times, 150 epochs, using EEM and also for MSE. We made n vary from 3 to 6. Each time, half of the data set was used for training and the other half for testing. The results of the first experiment are shown in table 1.

Table 1. The error results of the first experiment

	n=3	4	5	6	*std*
EEM	2.43 ± 1.33	2.20 ± 1.20	2.01 ± 1.09	2.09 ± 1.02	0.18
MSE	2.93 ± 1.46	2.55 ± 1.24	2.64 ± 1.13	2.91 ± 1.73	0.19

In the second experiment we used the well known Fisher's IRIS data set. It consists of 3 classes, 4 numeric attributes, 150 instances. One class is linearly separable from the other two, but the other two are not linearly separable from each other.

Several (2;n;2) MLP's were trained and tested 40 times, 150 epochs, for EEM and also for MSE. We made n varying from 3 to 8. Each time, half of the data set was used for training and the other half for testing. The results of the second experiment are shown in table 2.

Table 2. The error results for IRIS data set

	n=3	*4*	*5*	*6*	*7*	*8*	*std*
EEM	4.37±1.12	4.43±1.30	4.38±1.34	4.30±1,16	4.42±1,42	4.32±1.27	0.05
MSE	4.72±4.75	4.75±1.27	4.15±1.32	3.97±1,05	5.18±4,74	4.65±1.32	0.44

The results show, in almost every experiments, a small, but better, performance of the EEM algorithm. They also show, especially in the second experiment, that the variation of the error along n is smaller in the EEM than in the MSE (std - tables last column). This could mean that the relation between the complexity of the MLP and the results of the EEM algorithm is not so tight as for the MSE algorithm, although this relation must be studied with more detail in our future work.

5. Conclusions

We have presented, in this paper, a new way of performing classification by using the entropy of the error between the output of the MLP and the desired targets, as the function to minimize. The results show that this is a valid approach for classification and, despite the small diference comparing to MSE, we expect to achieve better results in high dimensional data. The complexity of the algorithm, (N^2), imposes some limitations on the number of samples in order to get results in a reasonable time. Some aspects in the implementation of the algorithm will be studied in detail in our future work: how to choose h and η and make their values adjust during the training phase to improve the classification performance. We have already tested the adjustment of h during the training phase, but we did not achieved good results. We know that the variation of η during the training process improves the performance [Silva and Almeida, 1990]. So, we plan to adjust η as a function of the error entropy instead of adjusting it as a function of the MSE.

References

Amari, S., Cichocki, A., and Yang, H. (1996). A new learning algorithm for blind signal separation. In *Advances in Neural Information Processing System*, volume 8. MIT Press, Cambridge MA.

Bell, A. and Sejnowski, T. (1995). An information-maximization approach to blind separation and blind deconvolution. *Neural Computation*, 7(6):1129–1159.

Erdogmus, D. and Princípe, J. (2002). An error-entropy minimization algorithm for supervised training of nonlinear adaptive systems. *Trans. On Signal Processing*, 50(7):1780–1786.

Haselsteiner, H. and Príncipe, J. (2000). Supervised learning without numerical targets - an information theoretic approach. In *European Signal Processing Conf.*, volume n/a, page n/a.

Linsker, R. (1998). Self-organization in a perceptual network. *IEEE Computer*, 21:105–117.

Príncipe, J., Fisher, J., and Xu, D. (1998). Information-theoretic learning. Computational NeuroEngineering Laboratory, University of Florida.

Renyi, A. (1976). Some fundamental questions of information theory. *Selected Papers of Alfred Renyi*, 2:526–552.

Shannon, C. (1948). A mathematical theory of communication. *Bell System Technical Journal*, 27:379–423, 623–653.

Silva, F. and Almeida, L. (1990). Speeding up backpropagation. In R., Eckmiller, editor, *Advanced Neural Computers*, pages 151–158.

Xu, D. and Príncipe, J. (1999). Training mlps layer-by-layer with the information potential. In *Intl. Joint Conf. on Neural Networks*, pages 1716–1720.

AN ICA APPROACH TO UNSUPERVISED CHANGE DETECTION IN MULTISPECTRAL IMAGES

G. Antoniol[1], M. Ceccarelli[1], P. Petrillo[1], A. Petrosino[2]

[1]*RCOST - University of Sannio*

[2]*ICAR-CNR, Section of Naples*

antoniol@ieee.org,ceccarellli@unisannio.it,alfredo.petrosino@na.icar.cnr.it

Abstract Detecting regions of change in multiple images of the same scene taken at different times is of widespread interest due to a large number of applications in diverse disciplines, including remote sensing, surveillance, medical diagnosis and treatment, civil infrastructure, and underwater sensing.

The paper proposes a data dependent change detection approach based on textural features extracted by the Independent Component Analysis (ICA) model. The properties of ICA allow to create energy features for computing multispectral and multitemporal difference images to be classified. Our experiments on remote sensing images show that the proposed method can efficiently and effectively classify temporal discontinuities corresponding to changed areas over the observed scenes.

1. Introduction

Automatic change detection in images of a given scene acquired at different times is one of the most interesting topics of image processing. Important applications of change detection include video surveillance [Collins et al., 2000; Stauffer and Grimson, 2000; Wren et al., 1997], remote sensing [Bruzzone and Prieto, 2002; Collins and Woodcock, 1996; Huertas and Nevatia, 2000], medical diagnosis and treatment [Bosc et al., 2003; Dumskyj et al., 1996; Lemieux et al., 1998; Rey et al., 2002; Thirion and Calmon, 1999], civil infrastructure [Landis et al., 1999; Nagy et al., 2001], underwater sensing [Edgington et al., 2003; Lebart et al., 2000; Whorff and Griffing, 1992] and driver assistance systems [Fang et al., 2003; Kan et al., 1996]. Despite the diversity of applications, change detection researchers employ many common processing steps and core algorithms.

The core problem is as follows. We are given a set of images of the same scene taken at several different times. The goal is to identify the set of pixels

B. Apolloni et al. (eds.), Biological and Artificial Intelligence Environments, 299–311

that are significantly different between the last image of the sequence and the previous images; these pixels comprise the change mask. The change mask may result from a combination of underlying factors, including appearance or disappearance of objects, motion of objects relative to the background, or shape changes of objects. In addition, stationary objects can undergo changes in brightness or color. A key issue is that the change mask should not contain unimportant or nuisance forms of change, such as those induced by camera motion, sensor noise, illumination variation, non-uniform attenuation, or atmospheric absorption. The notions of significantly different and unimportant vary by application, which sometimes makes it difficult to directly compare algorithms.

Several techniques for detecting changes, specially in remote-sensing images, have been proposed (see for instance the surveys made by Singh [Singh, 1989]). Two principal categories of techniques may be distinguished: *supervised* and *unsupervised*. The former requires the availability of a *ground truth* from which a training set of information about the spectral signature of the changes occurred in the considered area between the two dates could be derived. Instead, the latter require just the considered images.

Therefore, from an practical standpoint, it is clear that using unsupervised techniques is mandatory in many applications, since suitable ground-truth information is not always available. All unsupervised approach are divided in three steps [Bruzzone and Prieto, 2002]:

1 *preprocessing*: at this stage, it is necessary to make perfectly aligned the images to be compared, in both the spatial and the spectral domains. For the spatial domain, the images should be co-registered so that pixels with the same coordinates in the images may be associated with the same area on the ground. Moreover, accurate spatial calibration, as for example that reported in [P.S. Chavez, 1989; Slater, 1987], should be performed in order to correct illumination changes and atmospheric conditions between the two acquisition times.

2 *image comparison*: the co-registered images are compared in a pixel-wise fashion to generate the so-called *difference image* which evidenced temporal discontinuities [Singh, 1989].

3 *analysis of the difference image*: changes can be detected applying a threshold value to the histogram of the difference image. The choice of appropriate threshold value can be done in different ways, although generally made by using non-automatic heuristic strategies [Fung and LeDrew, 1988].

Image analysis problems, such as chenge detection, always require the adoption of image models wich can be used to study the statistical relations between image patches. Frequency models such as Fourier representations and spatial-frequency approaches such as wavelet representations constitute an efficient tool for modeling large number of different images. However, it is well known that the adoption adaptive approaches, where the model parameters adapt to the statical properties of the image data, can give better results [Lee and Lewinksy, 2002]. These adaptive approaches often require a learning phase where image samples are used to compute a new set of basis vectors for representing images. Principal Component Analysis is the simples and most commoly used linear adaptive model. Recently, Independent Component Analysis (ICA) has been proposed as a generic statistical model for images [Harinen et al., 2001]. It is aimed at capturing the statistical structure in images that is beyond second order information, by exploiting higher-order statistical structure in data. ICA finds a linear nonorthogonal coordinate system in multivariate data determined by second- and higher-order statistics. The goal of ICA is to linearly transform the data such that the transformed variables are as statistically independent from each other as possible. ICA generalizes PCA and, like PCA, has proven a useful tool for finding structure in data.

Here we adopt the ICA image model to generate a data dependent filter bank for change detection in multispectral images. The filter bank consists of the ICA basis images, learned from images. These basis images are able to capture the underlying structure of the analyzed scenes, and hence enable us to create features. Our ICA based approach to change detection is aimed at detection of temporal discontinuities in the textural representation of multispectral image patches.

2. ICA Learning and Image Classification

The way we use the ICA model belongs to the so-called filtering method. The basic idea in the filtering methods is that a composite textured image is filtered through a bank of filters, and appropriate features for texture segmentation are generated based on the filter outputs (see for instance [Randen and Husoy, 1999; Ceccarelli and Petrosino, ; Turner, 1986]).

These filters are used to generate energy features for texture description and analysis [Jain and Farrokhnia, 1991]. Here, we use the ICA statistical model for a *data dependent* textural feature description.

The underlying statistical image model in ICA is based on the assumption that an image I can be decomposed into the sum of a set of basis functions multiplied by independent random coefficients:

$$I(x, y) = \sum_i b_i(x, y) s_i. \tag{1}$$

By reshaping the image as a column vector, $\mathbf{x}$, it is easy to realize that equation (1) can be rewritten as

$$\mathbf{x} = A\mathbf{s} \tag{2}$$

which is the well known linear ICA model, where $\mathbf{x}$ is the vector of observed variables, $\mathbf{s}$ is the vector of latent variables, called the independent components or source signals, and A is an unknown constant matrix, called the mixing matrix. The columns $\mathbf{a}_1, ..., \mathbf{a}_N$ of the mixing matrix A are the basis vectors or features of image windows. The matrix A is learnt from observations. The basic idea behind the learning algorithm is to find a linear transformation $\mathbf{y} = W^{+}\mathbf{x}$ yielding a vector whose components are statistically independent. The matrix W^{+} is the pseudo-inverse of A. To estimate such matrix we used the FastICA algorithm [A. and E., 1997], which also includes a PCA preprocessing step for whitening the data.

ICA Extraction from Multispectral Images

Our approach to change detection is based on classifying the difference of the features extracted from multitemporal images. As said before, the features are extracted according to the ICA model. As usual in image and signal processing, if the column vectors of the mixing matrix are considered as basis functions, the coefficients that express the observed data as function of the adopted basis are considered as features. Therefore, given two images I_1 and I_2, we classify the difference between the features extracted from each of them. To do this, we have to exactly state what we consider an observation and how the learning phase is performed in order to make the comparison between features possible.

For the case of change detection, the raw difference between pixel luminance is not enough for efficiently classifying the changes in images, especially for multispectral images. This is due to the difference in conditions and acquisition setup that can be months or years time apart. Therefore, an efficient change detection tool should be able to extract textural information from the images under study. Contextual information carried out by the neighboring values for each analyzed pixel typically contributes in a significant manner to the textural information. Hence, the image is divided into $m \times m$ overlapping patches. We experimentally verified that for our study, using Landsat multispectral images, patch dimensions of 9×9 represent a good compromise between description accuracy and computational efficiency. In order to extract the features from different images in an homogeneous manner, we run the learning algorithm over a set of randomly selected patches for all the images of the same scene at our disposal (see figure 1). Being the image multispectral (in our case 7-band images), each observation consists into a column vector

$\mathbf{x}$ obtained by stacking the $m \times m$ patches for all b bands centered at a given pixel.

In more details, we extract one vector of observation from each of the different bands, and put them together, in the following manner:

$$\mathbf{X} = [\mathbf{x}_1; ...; \mathbf{x}_N] \tag{3}$$

In this way, the extraction of features is performed on information carried out by each band at the same area. The learning algorithm, applied to this vector, produces the mixing matrix A, and the vector of the independent components $\mathbf{s}$. If n is the number of all the possible patches that we can extract from an image, we obtain the same number of vectors of observation, which we can put together, in order to obtain a $(m \times m \times b) \times n$ matrix of observation X, as we can see in figure 2, where each vector $\mathbf{x}_i$ is obtained as described above.

To avoid that the Independent Components depend upon differences in both the matrix W^+ and X, we impose that the matrix W^+ is the same for both images to be compared. To this end, we run the learning algorithm over the set of data obtained by putting together all the observation matrices, obtained for each scene at disposal, in order to create a matrix containing information given by all scenes:

$$\mathbf{X} = [\mathbf{X}_1, ..., \mathbf{X}_N] \tag{4}$$

After applying the learning algorithm on this matrix, we obtain the mixing matrix A and the transformation W^+, which we can use to generate, in this case, a coefficient matrix S:

$$S = W^+ X \tag{5}$$

As S gets the same dimension of X, if we make the inverse of the transformation used to extract the vector $\mathbf{x}$, we can obtain an image having the same dimension of the original scene. We can define this image as *coefficient image*. In particular, each point of it indicates the weight given to the corresponding basis vector. Therefore, the comparison of two coefficient images let us to evaluate the textural differences between them. Given two matrices $\mathbf{X}_1$ and $\mathbf{X}_2$, the equation (5) transforms them by the same basis of representation, then the matrices $\mathbf{S}_1$ and $\mathbf{S}_2$ (and relative coefficient images) present differences due only to the textural features of the original images. Finally, by comparing two coefficient images we are able to estimate the changes occurred on the considered scene in the period between the two acquisitions. In particular, the comparison is based on the difference between the two coefficient images within each image patch:

$$s = \frac{1}{n^2} \sum_{i=1}^{m^2} \mid \mathbf{s}_{1i} - \mathbf{s}_{2i} \mid^2, \tag{6}$$

where:

- s_1 and s_2 are the coefficient vectors relative to a couple of corresponding patches, one for each image;

- s is the value associated to the corresponding point of the difference image.

If we apply the equation(6) to all corresponding patches that it is possible to extract from the images, we obtain the entire difference image.

Difference Image Classification

The final step of our approach is to analise the difference image, obtained by the steps described in the previous subsection. Specifically, the difference image is characterized by grey-level values, each one defining a degree of difference. Thus, it is necessary to define the minimum value of change, value that defines the accuracy of the approach, and that nearly depends on the particular application under study. This value is the *threshold value*, which, once fixed, distinguishes the whole set of pixels in two subsets:

- *changed pixels*: all pixels whose value is greater than the threshold value;

- *unchanged pixels*: all pixels whose value is less than threshold value.

Therefore the classification process results into a binary image. Several techniques have been proposed for choosing a suitable thresholding value [Fung and LeDrew, 1988]. Here we adopt an heuristic technique, by setting as threshold the value:

$$threshold = \frac{min + max}{7} \tag{7}$$

where min and max represent the lower and the higher grey-level values respectively, which demonstrated to give good performance among several test values.

3. Preliminary Results

Here we want to demonstrate the behavior or our methods on the temporal analysis of the images in figure (1) which represents three images of the same scene acquired in August 1999, 2000 and 2001. In particular, we take as reference image that acquired in 2000, and we want to analyze the differences with the others.

Applying the reported method, a qualitative analysis of these images leads to the results shown in figure 3. These images are characterized by two types of areas: *black*, which corresponds to an unchanged area between the two images;

% alteration	# pixels	# detected pixels		# missed pixels		% error	
		CNT	proposed	CNT	Proposed	CNT	proposed
20	2601	2102	2589	499	12	19.18	0.46
40	2601	2088	2586	513	15	19.72	0.58
60	2601	2095	2569	506	32	19.45	1.23
80	2601	2074	2592	527	9	20.26	0.35

Table 1. Obtained results with simulated changes as function of the noise percentage, and comparison with the CNT approach

white, which represents a changed area. Some details are reported in figure 4 which evidence how the white areas effectively present changes on the land cover. These images compare some areas of the original scenes corresponding to marked changed areas.

However, these results are not sufficient for giving a quantitative valuation to our approach. Indeed, a quantitative analysis of the performance should rely on a ground truth which, however, we did not have at our disposal. Such data is typically not available in change detection studies, and its development through ground campaign can be very expensive. For the purpouses of this paper we artificially appled a texture-based random alteration between similar images and measured the percentage of corret pixels classified as changed in the area affected by the alteration. This measure is taken as function of the amount of random noise of alteration of each pixel. In particular, once selected a specific area to altered we apply the following multiplicative noise:

$$I'(i,j) = I(i,j) + I(i,j) * \Delta * \eta(i,j)$$

where $I(i,j)$ is the pixel in the original image, $I'(i.j)$ is the altered value, Δ is noise percentage percentage (in our experiments we set $\Delta = .2, .4, .6, .8$) and $\eta(i,j)$ is just an uniform random value in $[0,1]$. The obtained results are summarized in Table 1 and compared with the classical nonautomatic thresholding (CNT) approach [Bruzzone and Prieto, 2002]. As we can see the algorithm is able to efficienlty classify the whole changed area, whereas the classical threshold based method, which dows not take into account the texture, fails at detecting the changed pixles even in presence of high percentage opf noise.

a)

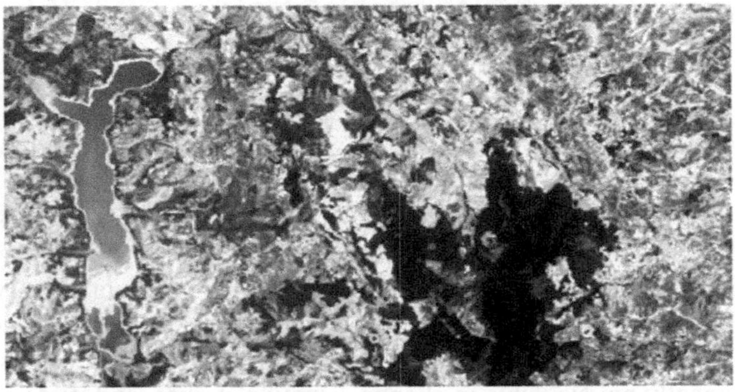

b)

c)

Figure 1. Three multispectral images of the same scene taken at three different times. The images are Landsat scenes of 7 bands (for visualization purposes we display just three of them). The image a) refers to the scene taken in 1999, whereas the figures b) and c) refers respectively to 2000 and 2001.

Figure 2. X matrix corresponding to patches extracted from an image.

4. Conclusions

The main contribution of the paper is to show that the ICA model can be a suitable tool for learning a vector base for feature extraction to design a feature based data dependent approach that can be efficiently adopted for image change detection. The preliminary experimental results over real remote sensing multispectral images show that the proposed method efficiently and accurately detect changed areas in the observed scenes.

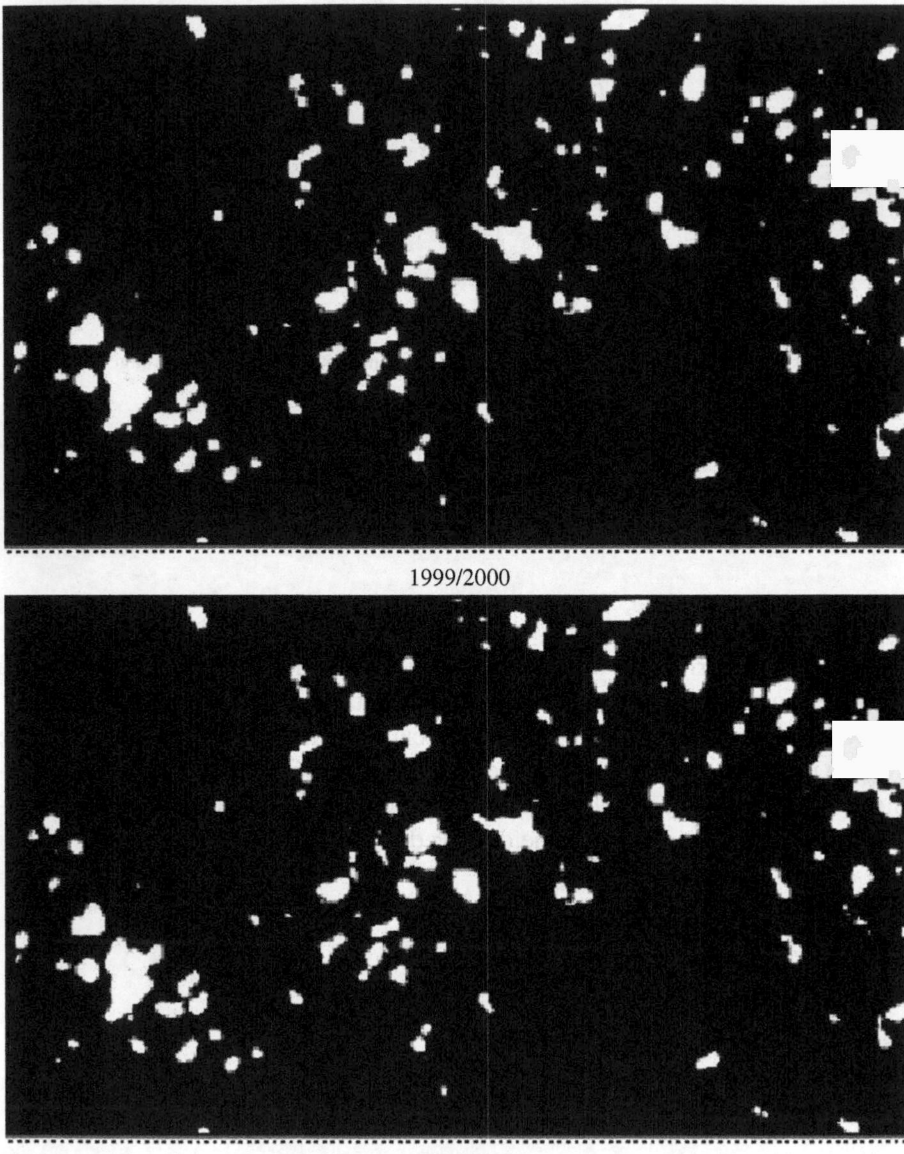

Figure 3. Classified images, obtained applying the threshold value (7).

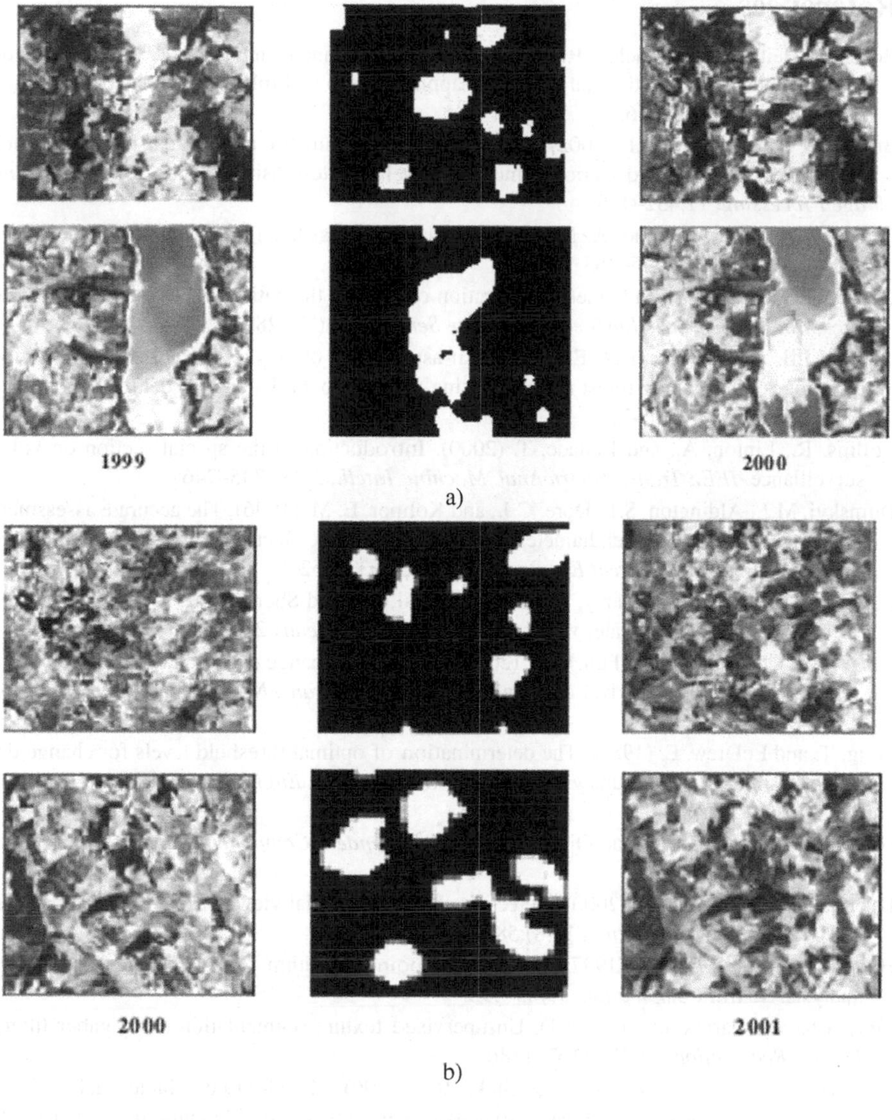

Figure 4. Figure a) shows some changed areas, corresponding to differences between scenes taken at 1999 and 2000; in the same way, figure b) shows the differences between scenes taken at 2000 and 2001.

References

Bosc, M., Heitz, F., Armspach, J. P., Namer, I., Gounot, D., and Rumbach, L. (2003). Automatic change detection in multimodal serial mri: application to multiple sclerosis lesion evolution. *Neuroimage*, 20:643–656.

Bruzzone, L. and Prieto, D.F. (2002). An adaptive semiparametric and context-based approach to unsupervised change detection in multitemporal remote-sensing images. *IEEE Trans. Image Processing*, 11:452–466.

Ceccarelli, N. and Petrosino, A. Multifeature adaptive classifier for sar image segmentation. *Neurocomputing*, 17:345–363.

Chavez, P.S., Jr. (1989). Radiometric calibration of landsat thematic mapper multispectral images. *Photogrammetric Engineering Remote Sensing*, 55(9):1285–1294.

Collins, J.B. and Woodcock, C.E. (1996). An assessment of several linear change detection techniques for mapping forest mortality using multitemporal landsat tm data. *Remote Sensing Environment*, 56:66–77.

Collins, R., Lipton, A., and Kanade, T. (2000). Introduction to the special section on video surveillance. *IEEE Trans. Pattern Anal. Machine Intell.*, 22(8):745–746.

Dumskyj, M.J., Aldington, S.J., Dore, C.J., and Kohner, E. M. (1996). The accurate assessment of changes in retinal vessel diameter using multiple frame electrocardiograph synchronised fundus photography. *Current Eye Research*, 15(6):632–652.

Edgington, D., Dirk, W., Salamy, K., Koch, C., Risi, M., and Sherlock, R. (2003). Automated event detection in underwater video. *Proc. MTS/IEEE Oceans 2003 Conference*.

Fang, C.Y., Chen, S.-W., and Fuh, C.-S. (2003). Automatic change detection of driving environments in a vision-based driver assistance system. *IEEE Trans. Neural Networks*, 14(3):646–657.

Fung, T. and LeDrew, E. (1988). The determination of optimal threshold levels for change detection using various accuracy indices. *Photogrammetric Engineering & Remote Sensing*, 54(10):1449–1454.

Harinen, A., Karhunen, J., and Oja, E. (2001). *Independent Component Analysis*. John Wiley and Sons, Inc.

Huertas, A. and Nevatia, R. (2000). Detecting changes in aerial views of man-made structures. *Image and Vision Computing*, 18(8):583–596.

Hyvarinen, A. and E., Oja (1997). A fast fixed-point algorithm for independent component analysis. *Neural Computation*, 9:483–492.

Jain, A.K. and Farrokhnia, F. (1991). Unsupervised texture segmentation using gabor filters. *Pattern Recognition*, 24(12):1167–1186.

Kan, W.Y., Krogmeier, J.V., and Doerschuk, P.C. (1996). Model-based vehicle tracking from image sequences with an application to road surveillance. *Optical Engineering*, 35(6):1723–1729.

Landis, E., Nagy, E., Keane, D., and Nagy, G. (1999). A technique to measure 3d work-of-fracture of concrete in compression. *J. Engineering Mechanics*, 126(6):599–605.

Lebart, K., Trucco, E., and Lane, D.M. (2000). Real-time automatic sea-floor change detection from video. *MTS/IEEE OCEANS 2000*, pages 337–343.

Lee, T.W. and Lewinksy, M.S. (2002). Unsupervised image classification, segmentation and enhancement using ica mixute models. *IEEE Trans. on Image Processing*, 11(3):270–279.

Lemieux, L., Wieshmann, U., Moran, N., Fish, D., and Shorvon, S. (1998). The detection and significance of subtle changes in mixed-signal brain lesions by serial mri scan matching and spatial normalization. *Medical Image Analysis*, 2(3):227–242.

Nagy, G., Zhang, T., Franklin, W., Landis, E., Nagy, E., and Keane, D. (2001). Volume and surface area distributions of cracks in concrete. *Visual Form 2001 (Springer LNCS 2059)*, pages 759–768.

Randen, T. and Husoy, J.H. (1999). Filtering for texture classification: A comparative study. *IEEE Transactions on Pattern Analysis and Machine Intelligence*, 21(4):291–310.

Rey, D., Subsol, G., Delingette, H., and Ayache, N. (2002). Automatic detection and segmentation of evolving processes in 3d medical images: Application to multiple sclerosis. *Medical Image Analysis*, 6(2):163–179.

Singh, A. (1989). Digital change detection techniques using remotely-sensed data. *Internat. Journal of Remote Sensing*, 10(6):989–1003.

Slater, P.N. (1987). Reflectance and radiance based methods for the in-flight absolute calibration of multispectral sensors. *Remote Sensing of Environment*, 22:11–37.

Stauffer, C. and Grimson, W. E. L. (2000). Learning patterns of activity using real-time tracking. *IEEE Trans. Pattern Anal. Machine Intell.*, 22(8):747–757.

Thirion, J.-P. and Calmon, G. (1999). Deformation analysis to detect and quantify active lesions in three-dimensional medical image sequences. *IEEE Transactions on Medical Image Analysis*, 18(5):429–441.

Turner, M. R. (1986). Texture discrimination by gabor functions. *Biol. Cybern.*, 55:71–82.

Whorff, J. and Griffing, L. (1992). A video recording and analysis system used to sample intertidal communities. *Journal of Experimental Marine Biology and Ecology*, 160:1–12.

Wren, C. R., Azarbayejani, A., Darrell, T., and Pentland, A. (1997). Pfinder: Real-time tracking of the human body. *IEEE Trans. Pattern Anal. Machine Intell.*, 19(7):780–785.

A COMPARISON OF ICA ALGORITHMS IN BIOMEDICAL SIGNAL PROCESSING

B. Azzerboni,[1] M. Ipsale,[1] F. La Foresta,[2,1] N. Mammone,[2] F.C. Morabito[2]

[1]*Dipartimento di Fisica della Materia e Tecnologie Fisiche Avanzate*
Università degli Studi di Messina, Salita Sperone, 31 C.P. 57, 98166 Messina, Italy
(azzerboni,ipsale,laforesta)@ingegneria.unime.it, URL: http://www.eltgroup.polito.it

[2]*Dipartimento di Informatica, Matematica, Elettronica e Trasporti*
Università "Mediterranea" di Reggio Calabria, Loc. Feo di Vito, 89100 Reggio Calabria, Italy
morabito@unirc.it, URL: http://neurolab.ing.unirc.it

Abstract In the last years Independent Component Analysis (ICA) has been applied with success in signal processing and many algorithms have been developed in order to perform ICA. In this paper we review some algorithms, like INFOMAX (Bell and Sejnowski 1995), extended-INFOMAX (Lee, Girolami and Sejniowski 1997), FastICA (OjA, and Hyvärinen 1999), that solve the ICA problem under the assumption of the linear mixture model. We also show an overview of the nonlinear ICA algorithms and we discuss the MISEP (Almeida 2003). In order to test the performances of the reviewed algorithms, we present some applications of ICA in biomedical signal processing. In particular the application of ICA to the electroencephalographic (EEG) and surface electromyographic (sEMG) recordings are shown.

Keywords: Independent Component Analysis, Neural Networks, Artifact Removal, sEMG, EEG, Biomedical Signals.

Introduction

The Independent Component Analysis (ICA) is a computational statistical method able to reveal hidden factors (features) that underlie sets of random variables, measurements, or signals [Hyvarinen et al, 2001]. ICA builds a generative model for the measured multivariate data, in which the data are assumed to be linear or nonlinear mixtures of some unknown hidden variables (sources); the mixing system is also unknown. In order to overcome the underdetermination of the algorithm we assume that the hidden sources have the properties of nongaussianity and statistical independence. These sources are named independent components (ICs).

B. Apolloni et al. (eds.), Biological and Artificial Intelligence Environments, 313–320

The ICA was demonstrated to be a powerful tool in biomedical signal processing [Jung, Humphries et al, 2000], [Jung, Makeig et al, 2000], [Jung et al, 1998], [Azzerboni et al, 2003], [Friston et al, 2000], [Tey and Puthusserypady, 2003]: some kinds of brain imaging data and muscle activity representations seem to be quite well described by the ICA model. In particular, the ICA linear models work well with electroencephalography (EEG) [Jung, Humphries et al, 2000], [Jung, Makeig et al, 2000], [Jung et al, 1998] and electromyography (EMG) [Azzerboni et al, 2003], which are recordings of electric fields of signal emerging from neural currents within the brain and from motor potentials within the muscles motor units. Also the ICA nonlinear models have been applied with success in order to process biomedical signals; in fact , after that Friston [Friston et al, 2000] showed that functional Magnetic Resonance Images (fMRI) are nonlinear mixing of some independent source, Puthusserypady [Tey and Puthusserypady, 2003] investigated successfully an application of post-nonlinear ICA to fMRI.
In this paper we present an overview of the most popular ICA algorithms and we discuss some applications in biomedical signal processing.

1. An Overview of the ICA Algorithms

ICA is a method for solving the blind source separation (BSS) problem whose aim is to recover the independent source signals from some measured mixtures [Hyvärinen et al, 2001]. Using the vector matrix notation, the mixing model is written as

$$\mathrm{x} = \mathrm{F}(\mathrm{s}) \tag{1}$$

where x is the observed data vector, $F(\cdot)$ is the nonlinear mixing function and s is an unknown source vector containing the source signals, which are assumed to be statistically independent. Thus, the ICA resolves the BSS problem under the hypothesis that the source are mutually independent. In the following, we discuss some well known algorithms that solve the ICA problem under the assumptions of linear or nonlinear mixture models.

The general nonlinear mixing model (1), in its post-linear mixing form can be represented as follow:

$$\mathrm{x} = \mathrm{F}(\mathrm{As}) \tag{2}$$

Here the sources are first linear mixed and then the non linear operator F is applied. Post-nonlinear model has been introduced by Taleb and Jutten [Taleb and Jutten, 1999] and various studies proposed some approaches to solve (2). The nonlinear issue was less studied than the post-nonlinear one: a very used algorithm about nonlinear ICA is MISEP [Almeida, 2003], that is based on the minimization of the mutual information of the estimated components as a generalization of the most popular INFOMAX algorithm [Bell and Sejnowski, 1995], [Lee et al, 1999]. A serious problem is that the solution of (1), although it always exists, it is not unique (see ref. [Hyvärinen et al, 2001], pp. 315-319). Another problem is that nonlinear methods are computationally demanding. In the applications we often like better to assume a post-nonlinear model and then to solve (2) because it is an adequate modelling of real world physical systems, since data recording sensors can have a nonlinear characteristics. But, if the mixing process is intrinsically nonlinear, this model is not suitable. Under the assumption of the linear mixture model, the (1) becomes:

$$\mathrm{x} = \mathrm{As} \tag{3}$$

where A is the unknown mixing matrix. In this case, we have to estimate a matrix W such that

$$\mathrm{u} = \mathrm{Wx} \tag{4}$$

where u are the estimated ICs. In the last years many algorithms was implemented in order to solve (4). Bell and Sejnowski implemented an algorithm based on the INFOMAX principle [Bell and Sejnowski, 1995], [Lee et al, 1999] whose aim is to maximize the output entropy, of information flow, of a neural network with nonlinear outputs, as shown in fig. 1.

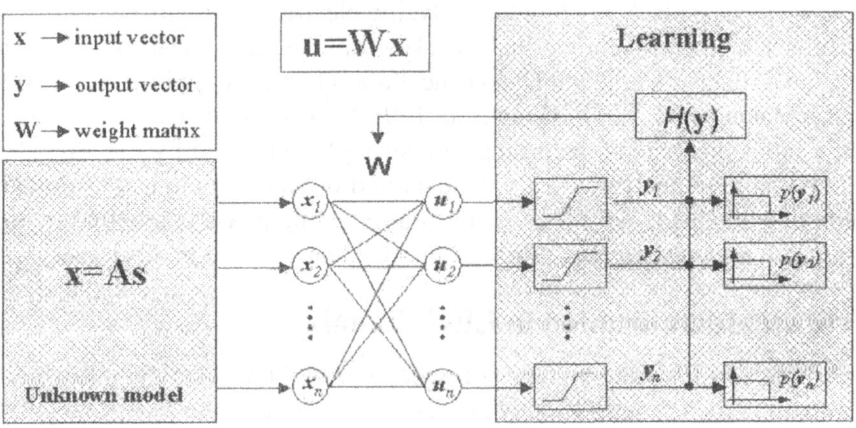

Figure 1. Neural Network architectures for INFOMAX algorithm.

Subsequently, Hyvarinen and Oja proposed a fast fixed point algorithm (Fast ICA) estimating the nongaussianity by the kurtosis (see ref. [Hyvarinen et al, 2001], pp. 178-179) or by the negentropy (see ref. [Bell and Sejnowski, 1995], pp. 188-196). They work on the basis that the ICs can be found by finding directions in which the data is maximally nongaussian. Fortunately, in many practical applications the assumption of linear mixture model is reasonable, and we can apply linear ICA algorithms with good results; for this reason, we put our attention on the solution of the linear mixture model. In particular we base the processing on the extended-INFOMAX[Lee et al, 1999]. The choice of this algorithm is based on its simplicity and its ability to separate sources with sub- an super-gaussian distributions. The kurtosis estimate is the switching criterion in the learning rule,

$$\Delta \mathrm{W} \propto [\mathrm{I} - \mathrm{K}\,tanh(\mathrm{u})\mathrm{u}^T - \mathrm{u}\mathrm{u}^T]\mathrm{W} \tag{5}$$

were K is the diagonal matrix, whose elements are k_i = *sign(kurt(*u_i*))*.
In the next section we discuss some ICA applications for biomedical signals, like EEG and EMG ones.

2. Biomedical Signal Processing by ICA

The biomedical area is a very promising field of application for ICA. So far ICA has been applied to EEG, Magnetoencephalograms (MEG), fMRI , Electrocardiograms (ECG) and surface Electromyographic (sEMG) signal processing [Jung, Humphries et al, 2000], [Jung Makeig et al, 2000], [Jung et al, 1998], [Azzerboni et al, 2003], [Friston et al, 2000], [Tey and Puthusserypady, 2003]. The ICA technique allows to extract important features from the data. Here we focus on ICA as a tool for analyzing electric activity in the brain and in the muscles. In particular we analyze a key topic in biomedical signal processing: the artifacts identification and cancellation [Jung, Humphries et al, 2000], [Jung, Makeig et al, 2000], [Jung et al, 1998], [Azzerboni et al, 2003]. In fact, if the biomedical signal recordings are strongly corrupted by the artifacts, it is impossible to analyze exactly the data and often some clinical information cannot be obtained. For these reasons a processing phase is required in order to remove artifacts. Here we show as the ICA can be used in this issue.

Artifacts Identification in EEG Signals

Artifacts in EEG are signals not generated by brain activity, but by some disturbance such as muscle activity. These signals are quite independent from those related to brain activity, so ICA is a candidate for artifacts rejection. ICA has been successfully applied to EEG for artifacts removal also in an automatic way [Delorme et al, 2001]. Consider 19 channels EEG recordings, 200 Hz sampling rate, as shown in fig. 2a; in this case the assumption of linear mixture model is reasonable, because we can say that every channel record a linear combination of independent sources. The application of ICA algorithm allows to obtain the ICs (see fig. 2b). In order to identify the artifact components, we use markers that are related to the signal's distributions. In particular we compute two markers for every component: the kurtosis, that is highly positive for 'peaked' activity distributions, typical of artifacts, and the entropy (low values of entropy are typical of artifacts) [Barbati et al, 2004]. Here, the distributions of the local entropy and of the local kurtosis were normalized to 0-mean and 1-standard deviation with respect to all ICs for each segment; the thresholds were set at ś1.64 and, if a significant percentage (set at 20%) of segments exceeded rejection threshold, the corresponding IC was marked for rejection. The ICs with the local higher kurtosis were IC_5, IC_{16}, IC_{17}, and IC_{19}, whereas the ICs with the local lower entropy were IC_5, IC_{14}, IC_{17} and IC_{19}. Thus, we can say that IC_5, IC_{17} and IC_{19} are certainly artifacts components.

Artifacts Cancellation in Surface EMG

Let consider two active electrodes that perform a sEMG. The electrodes were put on the pectoral muscles of a healthy co-operating human subject. In particular the first electrodes was put on the left pectoral muscle and the second one on the thorax so that the cardiac activity is recorded (see fig. 3a). It is easy to see that first row of sEMG is corrupted by cardiac activity. The fig. 3b shows the ICs: the cardiac activity is represented by the first IC. Thus, we can remove artifact and we can reconstruct the sEMG, (see fig. 3c). The reconstruction step is based on (3), in fact we compute the mixing matrix A, by the inverse (or pseudo-inverse) of W, and we set to zero the column related to the component that we want remove. Thus we calculate the new data set x that represents the reconstructed signals after artifacts cancellation. Finally, we evaluate the removal artifact goodness by a comparison, in time- and frequency-domain, between the original first channel (ch 1) and the reconstructed one. The fig. 3d confirms the good reconstruction in the time-domain (the liner regression coefficient is equal to 0.987). The Power Spectrum Density (PSD) of the original (dotted line) and the reconstruction signal (continuous line) are shown in fig. 3e. Note that the PSD of reconstructed ch 1 is simply scaled and the frequency range, in which the artifact was localized, is strongly attenuated.

3. Conclusions

In this paper we presented an overview of the ICA algorithms and their applicability to biomedical signal processing. We have discussed the linear and nonlinear mixture models and various algorithms in order to solve them. We have also underlined that nonlinear methods are computationally demanding: for this reason we like better, if it is possible, to approximate the problem under the assumption of the linear mixture model. We have also shown how the application of linear ICA allows the artifacts identification and cancellation in EEG and sEMG data with good results.

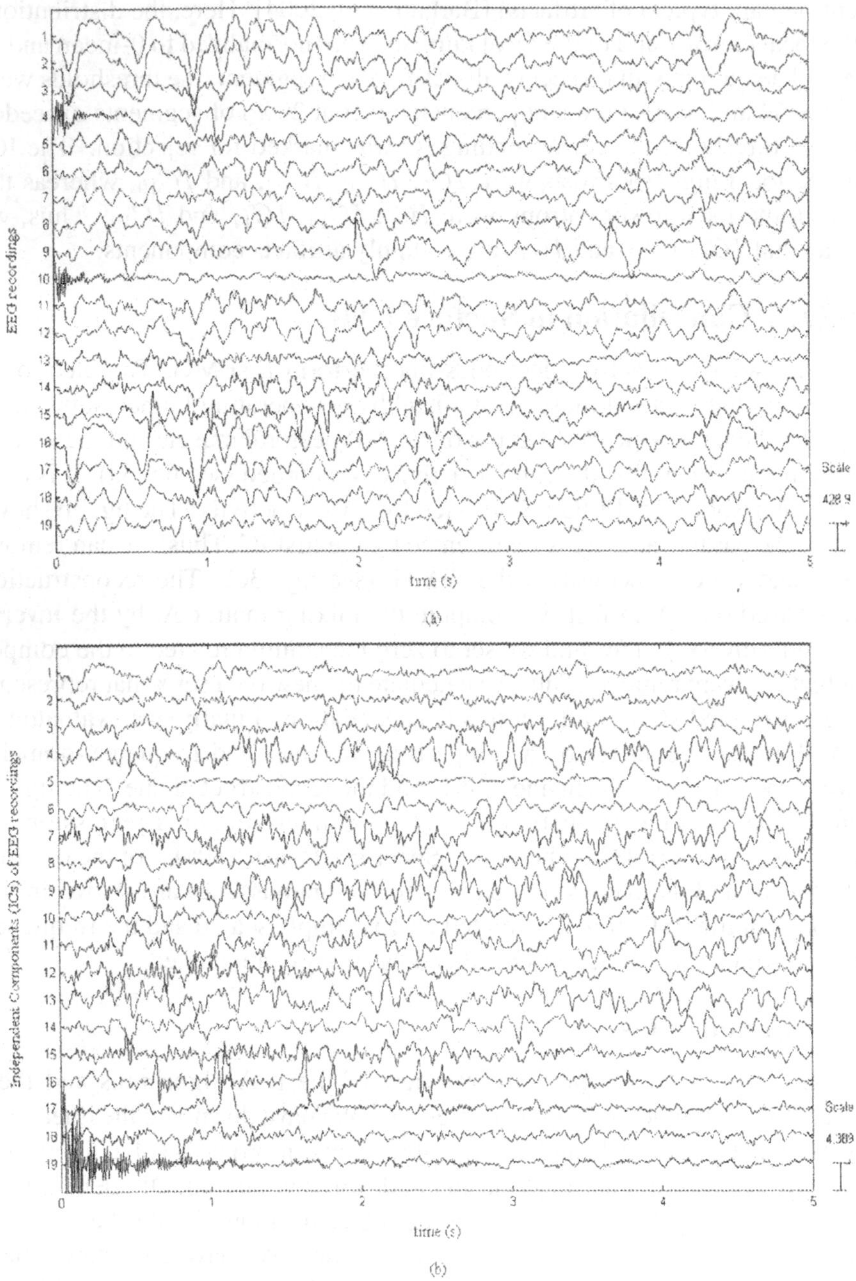

Figure 2. Artifact identification in EEG signals by ICA. (a) The EEG recordings of 19 active electrodes. (b) ICs computed by means of an algorithm based on extended infomax: the kurtosis analysis allows to identify the ICs (1, 5, 16, 19) related to the artifacts.

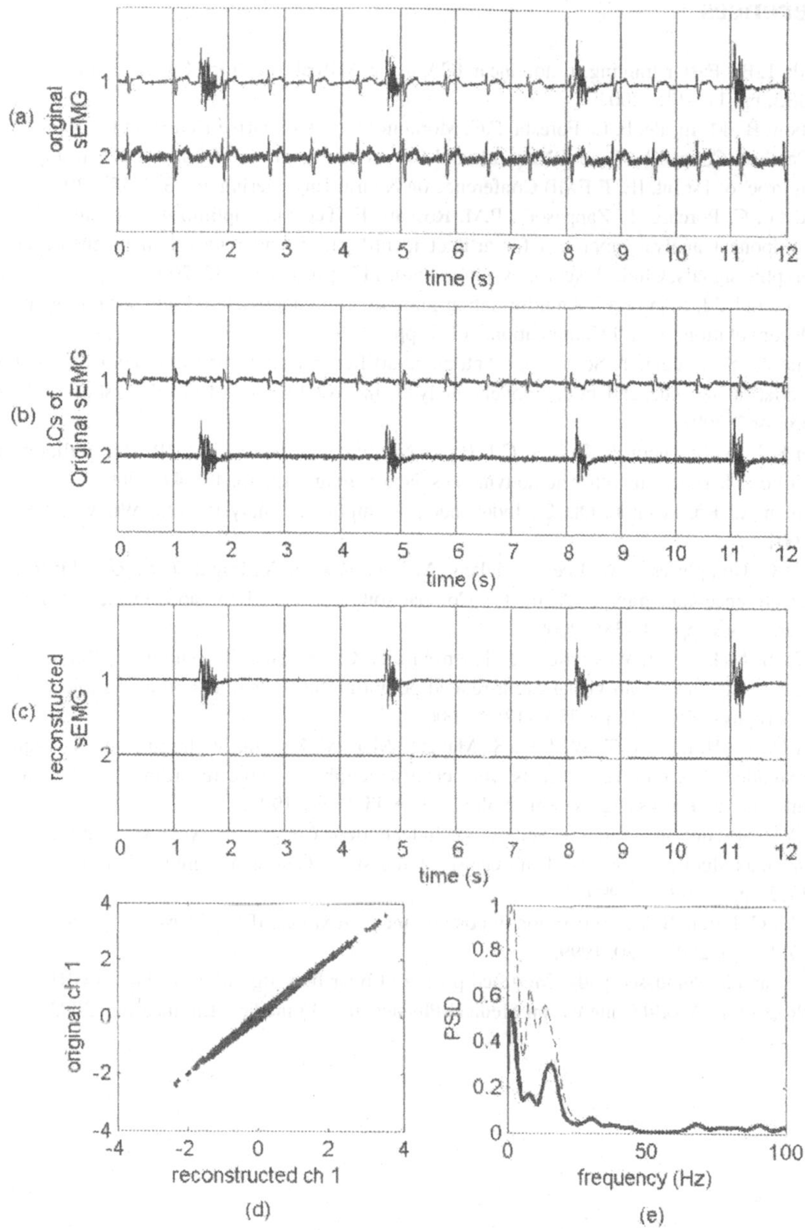

Figure 3. Artifact removal in sEMG by ICA. (a) The recordings of two active electrodes that perform a sEMG. (b) ICs computed by means of an algorithm based on extended infomax: the cardiac activity is represented by the first IC. (c) The Reconstructed sEMG after artifact removal. (d) Comparison on the time-domain between the original ch 1 and reconstructed one: the linear regression coefficient is equal to 0.987. (e) The Power Spectrum Density (PSD) of the original (dotted line) and reconstructed signal (continuous line): the PSD of reconstructed ch 1 is simply scaled and the frequency range, in which was localized the artifact, is strongly attenuated.

References

Almeida L.B.: Faster training in nonlinear ICA using MISEP, in Proc. 4th Int. Sym. on ICA and BSS, pp. 113-118, 2003.

Azzerboni B., M. Ipsale, F. La Foresta, F.C. Morabito: Common Drive Detection for Axial Muscles Cerebral Control by Neural Network and Coherence Analysis of Surface Electromyography, in Proc. of 1st Int. IEEE EMB Conference on Neural Engineering, pp. 352-355, 2003.

Barbati G., C. Porcaro, F. Zappasodi, P.M. Rossini, F. Tecchio: Optimization of an independent component analysis approach for artifact identification and removal in magnetoencephalographic signals, Clinical Neurophysiology, vol. 115, pp. 1220-1232, 2004.

Bell A.J., and T.J. Sejnowski: An information-maximization approach to blind separation and blind deconvolution, Neural Computation, vol. 7, pp. 1129-1159, 1995.

Delorme A., S. Makeig, T. Sejnowski: Automatic artifact rejection for EEG data using high-order statistics and independent component analysis, in Proc. of the 3rd Int. Workshop on ICA, pp. 457-462, 2001.

Friston K.J., A. Mechelli, R. Turner, C.J. Price: Nonlinear responses in fMRI: the Balloon model, Volterra kernels, and other hemodynamics, Neuroimage, 12, pp. 466-477, 2000.

Hyvärinen A., Karhunen J., Oja E.: Independent Component Analysis, John Wiley & Sons, Inc., 2001.

Jung T., C. Humphries, T.W. Lee, S. Makeig, M.J. McKeown, V. Iragui, T. Sejnowski: Removing Electroencephalographic Artifacts: Comparison between ICA and PCA, Computers in Cardiology, pp. 383-386, 2000.

Jung T., S. Makeig, M. Westerfield, J. Townsend, E. Courchesne, T. Senjowski: Removal of eye activity artifacts from visual event-related potentials in normal and clinical subjects, Clinical Neurophysiology 111 pp. 1745-1758, 2000.

Jung T.P., C. Humpries, T.-W. Lee, S. Makeig, M.J. McKeown, V. Iragui, and T. Sejnowski: Extended ICA removes artifacts from electroencephalographic recordings, in Ad. in Neural Information Processing Systems, volume 10, MIT Press, 1998.

Lee T.W., M. Girolami, and T.J. Sejnowski: Independent Component Analysis using an extended infomax algorithm for mixed sub-Gaussian and super-Gaussian sources, Neural Computation, 11(2), pp. 606-633, 1999.

Taleb A., C. Jutten: Source separation in postnonlinear mixtures, IEEE Trans. on Signal Processing, 47(10) pp. 2807-2820, 1999.

Tey E.T. and S. Puthusserypady: Modified post nonlinear ICA algorithm for large fMRI dataset, in Proc. of the World Congress on Medical Physics and Biomedical Engineering, 2003.

TIME-FREQUENCY ANALYSIS FOR CHARACTERIZING EMG SIGNALS DURING FMRI ACQUISITIONS

B. Azzerboni,[1] M. Ipsale,[1] M. Carpentieri,[1] F. La Foresta,[2,1]

[1]*Dipartimento di Fisica della Materia e Tecnologie Fisiche Avanzate Universitàdegli Studi di Messina, Salita Sperone, 31 C.P. 57, 98166 Messina, Italy*
(azzerboni,ipsale,carpentieri)@ingegneria.unime.it, URL: http://www.eltgroup.polito.it

[2]*Dipartimento di Informatica, Matematica, Elettronica e Trasporti Università"Mediterranea" di Reggio Calabria, Loc.Feo di Vito, 89100 Reggio Calabria, Italy*
laforesta@ingegneria.unime.it, URL: http://www.eltgroup.pollto.it

Abstract Research on human sensorimotor functions has hugely increased after electromyogram (EMG) analysis was replaced by functional magnetic resonance imaging (fMRI), that allows to obtain a direct visualization of the brain areas involved in motor control. Very meaningful results could be obtained if the two analysis could be correlated. Our goal is to acquire the EMG data during an fMRI task. The main problems in doing this are related to the electromagnetic compatibility between the resonance coils (very high magnetic fields) and the EMG electrodes. In this study we developed a system that can characterize the entire EMG signal corrupted by the magnetic fields generated by the magnetic resonance gradients. The entire system consists in a hardware equipment (shielded cables and wires) and a software analysis (effective mean analysis and wavelet analysis). The results show that a motor task was correctly delivered by our post processing analysis of the signal.

Keywords: SEMG, FMRI, Time-frequency analysis, Wavelet transform.

Introduction

In the last years functional magnetic resonance imaging (fMRI) has become a very useful method to examine brain activations during motor tasks. To understand the relationship between muscle output and fMRI signals from various cortical fields, EMG information from the muscle is needed. The EMG information can act as a feedback to confirm the fMRI results. Various studies have attempted to measure force during fMRI acquisitions [Dettmers et al, 1996], [Ludman et al, 1996], [Thickbroom et al, 1998], [Ehrsson et al, 1993],

B. Apolloni et al. (eds.), Biological and Artificial Intelligence Environments, 321–328

while other studies were able to record EMG signals in a MRI room during a fMRI task [Liu et al, 2000], [Liu et al, 2002]. These studies reveal that EMG data collected during MRI sequence operation are not readable because of high-voltage noise associated with the sequence. However, they analyze the EMG signals within each gap between two blocks of images, showing that the EMG in a 100-ms window gap reflects the level of muscle activation for the entire contraction. The aim of this paper is to characterize muscle activity through the entire EMG channel, even if it is corrupted by fMRI image scans.

1. System description

The main problems in a joint fMRI-EMG measure are that the EMG signal can interfere with signals from the MRI and that MRI acquisitions can generate unwanted signals that hide the muscle activities in the EMG channels. The measurement system consists of an MRI system with fMRI capability; an EMG measuring system with adeguately shielded cables; a data acquisition board and a control computer. To avoid as much electromagnetic interference as possible, the preamplifiers and the acquisition tools for the EMG signals are placed outside the resonance room. The MRI system requires a highly homogeneous magnetic field that could be corrupted by the EMG amplifiers. A shielded cable bringing all the EMG electrode signals is passed through a narrow cavity between the resonance room door and the floor. Ten healthy volunteers were recruited. All were right-handed and none had contraindications to fMRI or previous history of any neurological or psychiatric disorders. All gave written informed consent. The task under study is a Abductor Brevis Pollicis (ABP) contraction. The simple task that volunteers repeatedly performed during the active phase consisted in finger pinches of the right hand.

MRI system

The MRI system used was a 1.5-T Siemens Vision scanner. In order to test the data acquisition system we collected two types of resonance images: the T1-weighted image that shows the anatomical structure of the skull, and functional images that are able to deliver the Blood Oxygenation Level Dependent (BOLD) signal, related to brain activity. The fMRI analysis measures the contrast differences of brain imaging during active and rest periods. The fMRI signal is related to some changes in the neural activity of the brain. Some increases in local neural activity cause local increases of blood flow with changes in the diamagnetic Oxyhemoglobin (HBO_2) and the weakly paramagnetic deoxyhemoglobin concentrations. Functional brain images were acquired with an ascending multislice gradient Echo Planar Imaging (EPI) pulse sequence. The Field Of View (FOV) for the brain images was 256 x 256 mm, and the matrix size was 64 x 128 mm (interpolated to 128 x 128 mm): thus the pixel size was 2 x 2 mm. The flip angle was 90. Sixteen transverse slices (3 mm slice thickness) were selected for both functional and T1-weighted brain images in the same positions. The distance factor between two adjacent slices was 0.25 mm, making a voxel size of 2 x 2 x 3 mm. The duration of each 16-slice scan that covers the interested brain section was 3 s. In our study, we performed 46 entire brain scans. The initial four scans was discarded (to ensure the stabilization of the magnetic field of the resonance tool) and the other 42 consisted in six 7-scan alternating sessions (rest and active).

EMG measurement system

This system was used to record signals from seven electrodes: four of these recorded EMG activity from the muscles ABP and Flexor Carpi Radialis (FCR), while two electrodes recorded an electrocardiogram (ECG) signal and the last one was used as reference. All the electrode wires were placed in a shielded cable that was passed through a small gap between the floor and the MRI room door. Outside the MRI room the electrode wires were connected to the differential EMG amplifiers whose dynamic amplitude ranged between $-800\mu V$ and $+800\mu V$. After the pre-filters (high-pass at 0.33 Hz and low-pass at 100 Hz) the EMG signals are digitalized (12 bit) at the sampling frequency of 256 Hz. The output was connected to the data acquisition software stored in a laptop computer and the EMG data were stored on the hard disk of the laptop computer.

2. System evaluation

The EMG signals recorded during the fMRI scans are shown in Figure 1. The muscle activity is hidden by the very high fMRI signals and needs a post-processing analysis in order to characterize them. In the next subsection we show the methods used to analyze the EMG signal, whereas in the last subsection we present the results related to the fMRI analysis. All the software processing, both for the EMG and for the fMRI was performed with MATLAB language, by the Mathworks, Inc. The functional analysis was performed by means of the Statistical Parameter Mapping (SPM) toolbox that works on Matlab.

EMG data evaluation

In order to deliver the EMG information buried in this signal we performed a long-time analysis that reflects the functional MRI elaboration. We wanted to find out the differences in signal between the rest scans and the active ones. Other studies carried out in the same way were not able to reveal the EMG within the EPI scans. Here we show that the muscle activity is buried in the acquired signal and there is a method to extract it, based on a effective mean

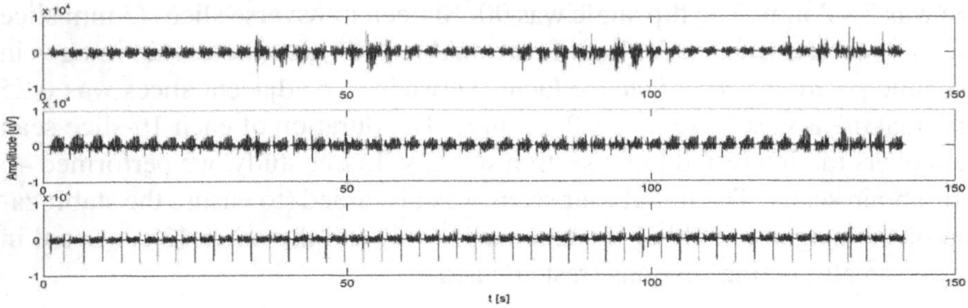

Figure 1. EMG recordings. The first channel records the ABP activity. The second channel records the FCR activity. The third channel records an ECG activity.

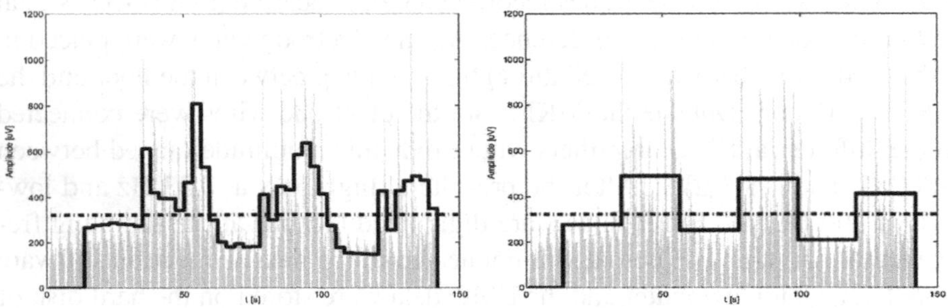

Figure 2. The rectified first channel recording (in background) and the effective mean computed for each fMRI scan (on the left) and for each 7-scan session (in the right). The dash-dotted lines show the mean value of the effective mean computed over the entire time axis. The effective mean trend suggests the discordance between the active time and the rest time range. The muscle is in its activity time when the effective mean overcomes the computed mean value. In the figure the effective mean was amplified by a fixed constant in order to give a better figure visualization.

analysis or on a more sophisticated wavelet analysis. In the next two subsections we present two approaches used in order to reveal the muscle activity.

Effective Mean Analysis. The idea is to create a mean analysis between all the scans belonging to a single session (seven scans), and to assess if there is a meaningful discrepancy between two adjacent sessions (one characterizing the rest time and the other representing the muscle activity). But the recorded signals are practically zero-mean signals and most part of them is distributed around the zero value, making the mean analysis inefficient. For these reasons we introduced signal rectification (absolute value), before performing a mean analysis, calculating an effective mean. In the first step, the effective mean value was calculated for each scan (16 slices), whereas a further computation was carried out applying the effective mean analysis for each session (7 scans of 16 slices each), either when the muscle is at rest, or when it is in its activation time range. The results are shown in figure 2. We can observe that in the EMG channel measuring the ABP activity, there is a very meaningful difference in the effective mean analysis, between the two different kind of sessions (active and rest). In order to authenticate the analysis method, the same study was performed in the others two channels, that recorded the FCR activity and the ECG. As we expected, the same analysis did not reveal a meaningful discordance between the different sessions: in fact, there was no rational motivation that could cause a different signal in a muscle that is not involved in an activity, or in the ECG, that reflect the regular cardiac activity during a motor task. The results are shown in figure 3.

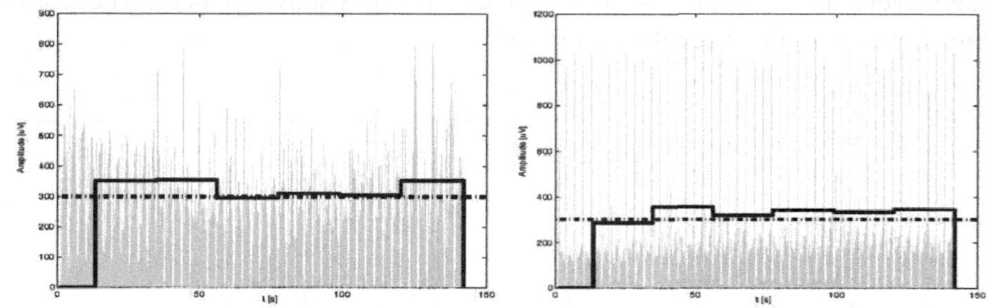

Figure 3. The rectified second channel (left) and third channel (right) recordings (in background) and the effective mean analysis computed for each 7-scan session (solid line). The dash-dotted line shows the mean value of the effective mean computed over the entire time axis. The effective mean trend for each session doesn't reveals any discordance between the active time and the rest time range. In fact, the second channel recorded a muscle activity that was at rest during the entire fMRI task (the FCR), whereas the third channel recorded an ECG activity that obviously was almost constant during the entire fMRI task. In the figure the effective mean was amplified by a fixed constant in order to give a better figure visualization.

Wavelet Analysis. The same analysis was performed by means of the wavelet algorithm. The wavelet analysis is a signal processing tool that is able to extract the time-variant frequency content of a signal. The wavelet analysis can be viewed as a time-variant Fourier Transform, but it has the advantage of a multiresolution approach, that is, it examine the lower spectral components in a larger time lapse, whereas the highest frequencies in the signal are analyzed in narrower temporal time lapses. In [Azzerboni et al, 2003] the authors used a wavelet analysis in order to estimate the applied force in a EMG signal acquired during a dynamic contraction. An analogous analysis can be applied to the EMG signal corrupted by the fMRI magnetic field. Like in the previous analysis, making the signal rectification (absolute value) before performing the wavelet analysis allows to identify the muscle activity buried in the signal. Figure 4 (left) shows the wavelet analysis performed on the first EMG channel that represents the ABP activity. The wavelet analysis was performed using the fourth Daubechies wavelet mother at the ninth level. First we extract an approximate signal by wavelet analysis, then we compute the mean value of this last signal. If we compare the wavelet approximation signal with its mean value, we can notice that the signal overcome the mean value exactly on the time ranges of when the muscle was active. Furthermore, the amplitude of the approximation wavelet signal can be related to the force applied in muscle contraction. The same analysis was performed in the other two channels, that recorded the FCR activity and the ECG. Again, as expected, this algorithm does not reveal a meaningful discordance between the different sessions, and the wavelet approximation kept the same trend almost everywhere. The results are shown in figure 4 (center and right) .

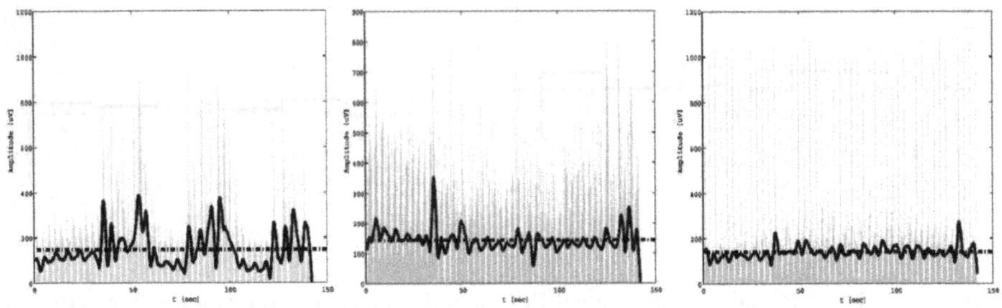

Figure 4. The rectified channel recordings (in background) and the wavelet analysis computed by the fourth Daubechies mother wavelet (solid line). The dash-dotted lines show the mean value of the wavelet signal computed over the entire time axis. (on the left) The wavelet trend, compared with its mean value, suggest the discordance between the active time and the rest time range. The muscle is in its activity time when the wavelet overcomes the computed mean value. Furthermore, the wavelet provides a information that is more accurately related to the applied force in the muscle activity, and thus it more accurately reflects a pure EMG signal. (on the center and the right) The wavelet trend, compared with its mean value, doesn't reveals any discordance between the active time and the rest time range. The FCR and the cardiac activity are not involved in the motor task. In the figure the wavelet was amplified by a fixed constant in order to give a better figure visualization.

fMRI data evaluation

In this subsection we show the results of the fMRI processing when the images are acquired in conjunction with the EMG acquisition. The results show that the presence of the EMG acquisition system does not influence the fMRI analysis. In fact, there is no difference between the obtained results and an analogous fMRI measure collected without the EMG acquisition system. Figure 5 shows on the left the translation and rotation correction at the data, in order to eliminate the motion artifacts from the fMRI data, and on the right the obtained brain activity after the application of a fMRI processing. The results are in agreement with the physiological knowledge about the motor control, showing that the EMG acquisition tool does not influence fMRI measurements. The activation zone is the left cerebrum frontal lobe (Brodmann area 6).

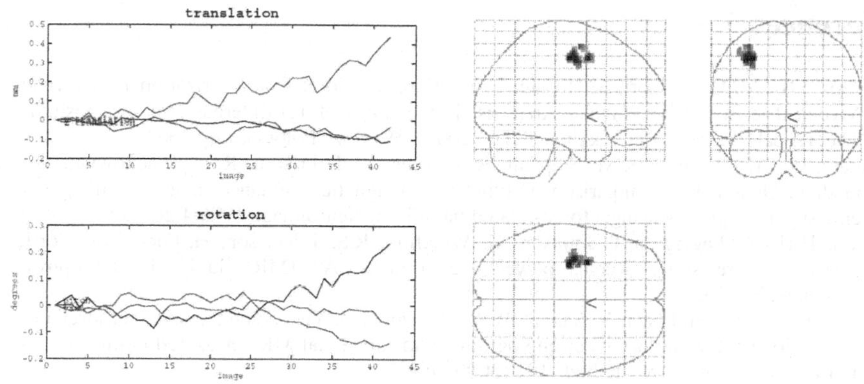

Figure 5. (on the left) The translation and rotation corrections needed to remove the head motion artifacts in fMRI data. (on the right) The brain activity revealed by the fMRI processing. The activation zone is the left cerebrum frontal lobe (Brodmann area 6).

3. Conclusions and discussion

In this paper we presented a tool that reveals the muscle activity in an EMG signal acquired during an fMRI task. The EMG signal was hardly corrupted by the huge magnetic fields generated by the magnetic resonance devices. Using adequate electrodes, wires and shielded cables, we were able to acquire an EMG signal that contained some information about the muscle activity (the amplifiers did not saturate). By means of two post-processing software tools we were able to extract these informations. The software analysis was performed in two step. An effective mean analysis revealed the main differences between the rest time and the activation time. A wavelet analysis allowed to asses the signal hidden in the EMG in depth, providing a force-dependent wavelet approximation signal. In order to reflect muscle activity both software analysis were performed on the rectified signal, since the original signal had a probability density function hardly centered around the zero value. Furthermore, the results from the fMRI processing show that the presence of the suitable EMG acquisition tool does not corrupt the resonance measure. The results are in agreement with the physiological knowledge. This study is the first step in order to create a joint EMG-fMRI study that could better reveal the relationship between a muscle task and the related brain activity.

Acknowledgment

The authors would like to thank Prof. P. Bramanti, Dr. P. Di Bella, Dr. A. Cannata and Dr. N. Muscarà for the data recordings and for their helpful support.

References

Azzerboni, B., M. Carpentieri, M. Ipsale, F. La Foresta: Onset Characterization in a Dynamic Myoelectric Signal by Wavelet Analysis, Proceedings of 12thInternational Symposium on Theoretical Electrical Engineering (ISTET2003), Warsaw, Polonia, July 2003.

Dettmers, C., A. Connelly, K.M. Stephan, R. Turner, K. J. Friston, R. S. Frackowiak, D. G. Gadian: Quantitative comparison of functional magnetic resonance imaging with positron emission tomography using a force-related paradigm, Neuroimage 1996;4:201-9.

Ehrsson, H.H., A. Fagergren, T. Jonnson, G. Westling, R.S. Johansson, H. Forssberg: Cortical activity in precision - versus power - grip tasks: An fMRI Study, J. Neurophysiol. 1993a;69:297-302.

Liu, J.Z., T.H. Dai, T.H. Elster, V. Sahgal, R.W. Brown, G.H. Yue: Simultaneous measurement of human joint force, surface electromyograms, and functional MRI-measured brain activation, Journal of Neuroscience Methods 101 (2000) 49-57.

Liu, J.Z., L. Zhang, B. Yao, G. H. Yue: Accessory hardware for neuromuscular measurements during functional MRI experiments, Magnetic Resonance Materials in Physics, Biology and Medicine 13 (2002) 164-171.

Ludman, C.N., T.G. Cooper, L.L. Ploutz-Synder, E.J. Potchen, R.A. Meyer: Force of voluntary exercise does not affect sensorimotor cortex activation as detected by functional MRI at 1.5 T., NMR Biomed 1996;9:228-32.

Thickbroom, G.W., B.A. Phillips, I. Morris, M.L. Byrnes, F.L. Mastaglia: Isometric forcerelated activity in sensorimotor cortex measured with functional MRI, Exp Brain Res 1998; 121:59-64.

A NEURAL ALGORITHM FOR OBJECT POSITIONING IN 3D SPACE USING OPTOELECTRONIC SYSTEM

Iuri Frosio[1,2], Giancarlo Ferrigno[2] and N. Alberto Borghese[1]

1 Laboratory of Human Motion Analysis and Virtual Reality, MAVR, Department of Computer Science, University of Milano, Via Comelico 39 - 20135 Milano, Italy – http:://mavr.dsi.unimi.it..

2 Department of Biomedical Engineering, Politecnico of Milano, Milano, Italy.

Abstract: Automatic object positioning in 3D space is nowadays required by a great variety of applications. We propose here a new approach to this problem, whose core is constituted by a bank of neural networks; from the measured positions of a set of laser spots generated on the object surface, the nets estimate the position of a set of points rigidly connected to the object. Results on synthetic data are reported, and show that the proposed method is reliable and comparable in accuracy with the most common solutions present in the literature, which are based on Iterative Closest Point (ICP) matching.

Keywords: Object positioning, 3D space, neural bank.

1. Introduction

Automatic positioning of objects to a particular reference position and orientation in 3D space is a task, whose importance is growing more and more inside the industrial, scientific and medical communities. For instance, a precise work-piece positioning is fundamental in many industrial automatic processes, [Hager, 1997]; the pose is a critical parameter for many facial recognition algorithms, [Yang et al., 2002]; in radiotherapy, the efficacy of

B. Apolloni et al. (eds.), Biological and Artificial Intelligence Environments, 329–335

the treatment depends critically on the accuracy in the position and orientation of the patient with respect to the gantry, [Baroni et al., 2003], [Wang et al., 2001].

One of the most used solutions is to resort to a vision system, which monitors the object, and may control its motion towards the reference position. Positioning is then based on the identification of a set of points on the object's surface, called point features. The rototranslation ***[R,T]***, which brings the object from a generic location (*Obj*) to the reference one (Obj_R), can be computed if three or more pairs of features have been localized on both Obj_R and *Obj*. Point features recognition on the image stream is simplified when the features are adequately marked; this approach is followed by many of the existing methods, to guarantee reasonably reliable results. However, use of markers is not allowed in many applications; moreover, incorrect features marking may affect badly object positioning; this was shown to be particularly critical in patient positioning in radiotherapy, [Baroni et al., 2003].

An alternative solution is to provide the 3D coordinates of some points belonging to *Obj* by means of laser beams projected onto *Obj*; however, this data cannot be treated as features, since each laser spot is not rigidly connected with *Obj*. The solution is to define *Obj* and Obj_R as manifolds (for instance 3D meshes), and to cast the problem as non linear optimization: the search for the rototranslation ***[R,T]***, that transforms Obj_R to *Obj*. To the scope, iterative solutions, such as the Iterative Closest Point (ICP) algorithm, [Besl et al., 1992], have been developed. However, their iterative nature badly affects the processing time, which becomes significant when the point clouds representing the two manifolds are composed by a great number of elements.

We present here an alternative solution, based on considering few points, generated as the intersection of *Obj* with a set of laser beams. From the 3D position of these spots, a neural system is used to estimate ***[R,T]*** for a wide range of positions and orientations of *Obj*. Results on simulations and comparison with ICP are reported and discussed. These show that the proposed method is very reliable, and that it is comparable in accuracy with ICP.

2. Methodology

The system is constituted of two components (fig. 1). The acquisition sub-system is composed of a set of *N* laser projectors which project laser spots onto *Obj*. Spots are automatically detected by a set of cameras and their 3D positions, ***{Sj}***, are passed to the second stage. This is constituted of *M* Multi-layer perceptrons (MLP) networks, plus a non linear least squares system solver. Each net receives as input the coordinates of the laser spots, and gives as output the estimated position of a virtual point feature attached to *Obj*. The net output is then processed to estimate the rototranslation ***[R,T]*** from Obj_R to *Obj*.

To train the networks, it is necessary to simulate the rototranslation of the object and to compute the intersection between *Obj* and the laser beams. Therefore both a model Obj_0 and the 3D position and orientation of each laser beam are required. Obj_0 may be obtained by CAD or similar software, when mechanical pieces have to be positioned, or through 3D scanning, as in [Borghese et al., 1998]; in radiotherapy, CT data are often used to extract the patient surface, [Baroni et al., 2003]. For simplicity, and without loss of generality, we consider here Obj_0 equal to Obj_R. The beam parameters are obtained during a preliminary calibration phase, when 3D spots can be generated simply putting a reflecting object along the beam trajectories; from the ensemble of 3D spots, the orientation and position of each beam can be estimated.

Once the setup session has been completed and Obj_R is available, the dataset for net's training is created. First of all, a set of *M* reference virtual point features, $\boldsymbol{VF}^R_1, \ldots, \boldsymbol{VF}^R_M$ is provided by the user; a virtual point feature is defined as a 3D point, which is rigidly connected to the digital object model; the user can freely choose any point of the 3D space to be a virtual point feature. When the object is rototranslated in 3D space by a transformation ***[R,T]***, the displacement of each virtual point feature is described by the same matrix, ***[R,T]***; in this case, the jth virtual point feature will be referred to simply as $\boldsymbol{VF}_j$. The input and desired output vectors of the nets for the training session are obtained by the following procedure: Obj_R is repeatedly moved in the 3D space, by a series of *D* random rototranslation matrixes $[\boldsymbol{R}_1,\boldsymbol{T}_1], \ldots, [\boldsymbol{R}_D,\boldsymbol{T}_D]$; for each rototranslation, the 3D position of the laser spots $\boldsymbol{S}_1, \ldots, \boldsymbol{S}_N$, is computed as the intersection between the laser beams and *Obj*; these points constitute the input vector for training the nets. The desired output vector for the jth net (that is, the jth virtual point feature $\boldsymbol{VF}_j$) is then obtained applying $[\boldsymbol{R}_1,\boldsymbol{T}_1], \ldots, [\boldsymbol{R}_D,\boldsymbol{T}_D]$, to the jth reference virtual feature, $\boldsymbol{VF}^R_j$. Networks are finally trained by means of the Levenberg-Marquardt learning algorithm, [Hagan et al., 1994].

Net training is generally the most time consuming step of the method. However, once the MLPs have been prepared, the position of *Obj* can be estimated in real-time from the *N* laser spots: since the virtual point features are rigidly connected to *Obj*, the rototranslation matrix ***[R,T]***, which brings Obj_R to *Obj*, can be estimated through a non linear least squares system, where the unknowns are the six rototranslation parameters (three for translation and three for rotation). The objective function to be minimized is the following residual error E:

$$E = \sum_{j=1}^{M} \left\| < [\mathbf{R},\mathbf{T}] > \cdot < \mathbf{VF}_{\mathrm{j}} > - \mathbf{VF}^{R}{}_{\mathrm{j}} \right\| \qquad (1),$$

where ***<VF$_j$>*** is the output of the jth net. Once ***<[R,T]>*** has been computed, it can be send to the engine in charge of bringing the object in the reference 3D position.

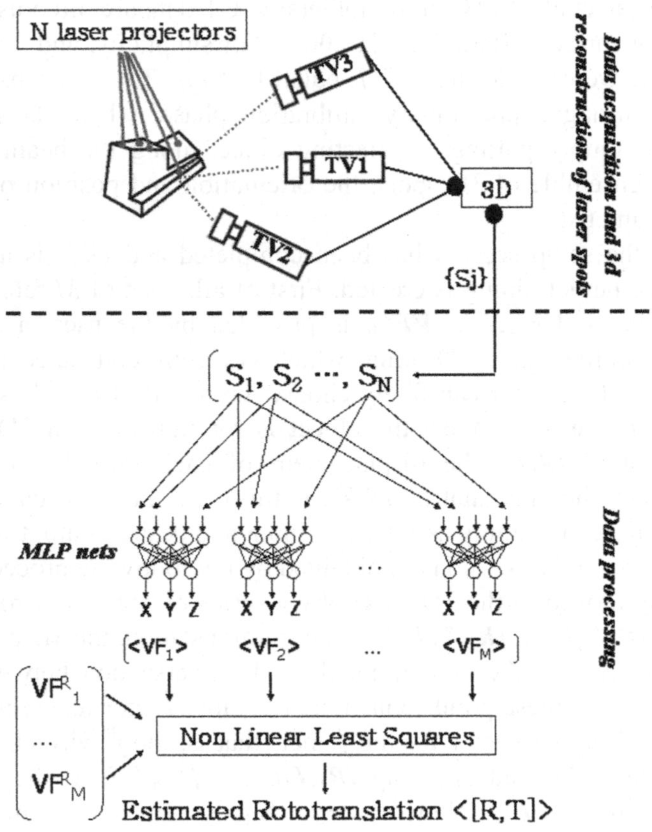

Figure 1. The upper part of the figure describes the acquisition sub-system: *N* laser spots are projected onto the objects' surface; they are detected by a dedicated vision system, which reconstructs their 3D positions. In the lower part, the procedure, which recovers ***<[R,T]>*** from the laser spots, is depicted: first, the 3D positions of the virtual point features, rigidly connected with *Obj*, is computed through a set of MLP networks, each associated to one feature. From the reference positions of the features and the estimated ones, ***<[R,T]>*** can be computed.

3. Results

We tested our algorithm on synthetic data, and compared it with ICP, [Besl et al., 1992], which is one of the most used algorithms for surface matching. The adopted object, Obj_R, is represented in fig. 2. Sixteen laser spots $\boldsymbol{S_1}$, ..., $\boldsymbol{S_{16}}$ are generated by the intersection of sixteen approximately vertical laser beams with the object surface; eleven virtual features are distributed in the 3D space as in fig. 2.

Each MLP is composed by a first layer of nine sigmoidal neurons and an output layer of three linear neurons. The small size of the MLPs avoids the risk of overfitting during the training session. The training dataset was obtained from 1000 rototranslations of Obj_R, where the rototranslation parameters were uniformly spread between ±20 mm for the three translations, ±18° for the three rotations. A testing dataset composed by 100 rototranslation was generated in the same way. To evaluate quantitatively the performance of the neural algorithm, the difference of the reference position and the one obtained by applying the transformation **<[R,T]>** to *Obj*, was computed for all the vertexes of the model. The same was done for ICP. Since we observed that our algorithm works better when initial displacement is small, we decided to iteratively apply it to *Obj*; in this case residual error was further decreased, as demonstrated in table 1, where percentiles for the different methods are reported.

4. Discussion and conclusion

The core of the proposed algorithm is a bank of MLPs, which are used to estimate the position of *M* virtual point features rigidly connected to *Obj*.

Thanks to the adoption of the neural bank, marking of features onto the object is not necessary. This constitutes a great advantage with regards to traditional techniques, since in many applications object features cannot be (reliably) markered. Smart positioning of the virtual point features is helpful to guarantee the residual error to be minimal in a certain zones of *Obj*: for example, features dislocated on a spherical surface (fig. 2) allow repositioning the central point of the sphere at best. Moreover, increasing the number of virtual point features, the algorithm performance does improve.

Although the proposed algorithm reaches the maximum accuracy when *Obj* is close to Obj_R, this is not a strict condition to be satisfied; when *Obj* can be iteratively repositioned, the proposed algorithm can be sequentially applied to *Obj*, to obtain minimal residual errors (table 1); the same cannot be said for ICP, which may converge to bad local minima when *Obj* is too far from Obj_R.

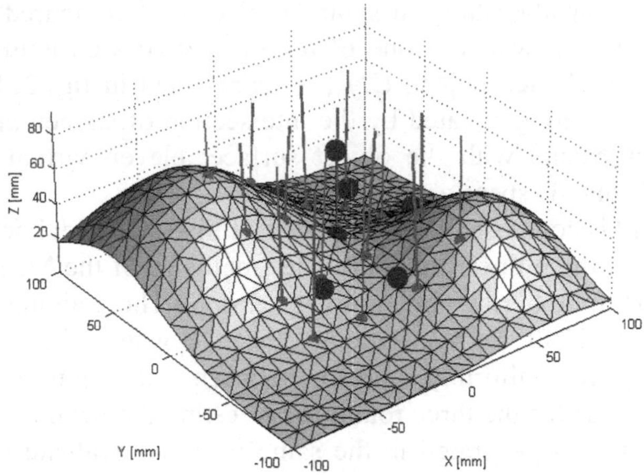

Figure 1. The virtual object used for testing, in reference conditions (Obj_R); it is composed by the sum of two normalized gaussian distributions, with means $\mathbf{\mu}_1$=[-50,50], $\mathbf{\mu}_2$=[65,-35], standard deviations σ_1=45, σ_2=35, multiplied respectively by 7000 and 4000; sampling of Obj_R was performed each 10 mm along the x and y axis. The 11 reference virtual point features are plotted as big spheres (7 of them are totally or partially visible); the 16 laser beams are roughly distributed along the vertical direction.

Table 1. The 25th, 50th and 75th percentile residual errors computed for all the points of the object, for 100 random positioning, are shown: before any correction, after correction with ICP, after correction with the proposed algorithm and after iterative correction with the proposed algorithm.

	25th	50th	75th
Initial displacement	24.24 mm	27.75 mm	30.69 mm
ICP	4.38 mm	5.08 mm	5.94 mm
Proposed algorithm	2.67 mm	3.07 mm	3.51 mm
Proposed algorithm (2nd iteration)	1.04 mm	1.41 mm	2.07 mm

On the test data, our algorithm shows accuracy higher than ICP; this is partially due to the large sampling of Obj_R; in fact increasing the model resolution, the accuracy of ICP increases until it reaches the one of the proposed method. However, also the processing time of ICP increases.

Noise can be added into the training dataset to simulate real conditions. The behavior of the neural system is still robust in this case as far as the number of neurons is increased.

The only critical aspect of the proposed method is the laser beams configuration: it has to be carefully chosen, to guarantee that each the laser spot on *Obj* can be seen by the cameras, and that each ***{Sj}*** effectively contains information about the position and orientation of *Obj*.

In conclusion, we have proposed a new reliable algorithm for rigid object positioning in 3D space. It is faster with respects to traditional methods and it permits to deal with higher initial misplacements. Moreover, feature marking is not necessary for obtaining reliable results. Extension of the method to deformable object is currently under investigation as well as the relationship between the position of the feature points, and the manifold local parameters.

References

Baroni, G., Troia, A., Riboldi, M., Orecchia, R., Ferrigno, G., Pedotti, A. (2003*) Evaluation of methods for opto-electronic body surface sensing applied to patient position control in breast radiation therapy*. Med. Biol. Eng. Comput., 41, pp. 679-688.

Besl, P. J., McKay, N. D. (1992) *A method for registration of 3-d shapes*. IEEE Trans. Pattern Analysis and Machine Intelligence, 14, pp. 239-256.

Borghese N.A., Ferrigno G., Baroni G., Savarè R., Ferrari S. and Pedotti A. (1998) *AUTOSCAN: A flexible and portable scanner of 3D surfaces*. IEEE Computer Graphics & Applications, pp. 38-41.

De Momi E., Frosio I., Baroni G. and Ferrigno G. (2003) *FNNVM, a new fast neurocomputational approach to surfaces alignment in image guided knee replacement*. Procedings of CAOS 2003, Marbella, Spain.

Hagan, M. T., Menhaj, M. (1994) *Training feedforward networks with the Marquardt algorithm*. IEEE Trans. Neural Networks, 5, pp. 989-993.

Hager, G. D. (1997*) A modular system for robust positioning using feedback from stereo vision*. IEEE Trans. On Robotics and Automation, 13, pp. 582-595.

Wang, L. A., Solberg, T. D., Medin P. M. and Boone R. (2001) *Infrared patient positioning for stereotactic radiosurgery of extracranial tumors*. Computer in Biology and Medicine, 31, pp. 101-111.

Yang, M. H., Kriegman, D. J., Ahuja, N. (2002) *Detecting faces in images: a survey*. IEEE Trans. on Pattern Analysis and Machine Intell., 24, pp. 34-58.

HUMAN VISUAL SYSTEM MODELLING FOR REAL-TIME SALT AND PEPPER NOISE REMOVAL

I. Frosio and N. A. Borghese

Laboratory of Human Motion Analysis and Virtual Reality, MAVR, Department of Computer Science, University of Milano, Via Comelico 39 - 20135 Milano, Italy – http:://mavr.dsi.unimi.it.

Abstract: Pixel failures often introduce in digital images a characteristic impulsive noise, known as "salt & pepper". This has to be corrected to get clear digital images. In this paper a new approach to the problem, based on an adequate model of the sensor and on the properties of the Human Visual System, is introduced. The local background luminance is estimated through a 3x3 median filter, and noise standard deviation from the sensor model. Since the filter is based only on local operations, it can work at real-time rates (less than 0.7s for 12 bit, 4.8MPixel images). Its speed may be even improved by using DSP implementation.

Keywords: Salt & pepper noise, switching median filter, human visual system.

1. Introduction

Pixel failures in both sensors and readout hardware often produce degradation in digital images, in the form of bright or dark pixels uniformly spread on the entire image. This kind of noise, known as "salt and pepper", becomes even more evident when the image is treated with filters, which enhance high frequency structures, like contours or lines, [Webb, 1998].

A host of techniques have been developed to eliminate this noise, but few of them are able to reliably operate in real-time on images, which are nowadays of the order of 4÷5 Mpixels. This problem is particularly critical in medical imaging where quantitative measurement and illness diagnoses have to be carried out on them, and large displays are used for optimal visualization.

B. Apolloni et al. (eds.), Biological and Artificial Intelligence Environments, 337–342

The most promising approach is based on a median switching schema: all the pulses are first identified; then the corrupted pixel values are substituted by the median of their neighbours, [Wang et al., 1999], [Zhang et al., 2002]. Pulse detection is the critical element of the filter. Several iterative algorithms, based on switching filters, have been proposed to the scope based mainly on theory of error-correcting code, [Boukerrou et al., 1998], or progressive filtering, [Badulescu et al., 2000]. However, these solutions are not suitable for real-time implementation for large images.

Procedures, which avoid iterative solutions, have also been developed, [Wang et al., 1999], [Rioul, 1996]. However, they fail when high gradients or edges are present in the image. It is shown here how taking explicitly into account the characteristics of the Human Visual System (HVS) and by adopting an adequate model of the sensor, a reliable real-time switching median filter can be realized.

2. Method

The methodology is based on the analysis of the characteristics of the Human Visual System.

2.1 The characteristics of the Human Visual Systems and of the sensor

The ability to detect an object by the HVS is based on three quantities: the object's luminance, the local background's luminance and the local background's noise. These three actors are related by experimentally derived functions.

When background luminance b assumes high values, the *Just Notable Difference* (*JND*) increases linearly with the background luminance, as stated by the Weber's law:

$$JND = C_T \cdot b \tag{1}$$

The *JND* expresses the minimum difference of luminance (Δb) between the background (b) and the object ($b+\Delta b$), which makes it detectable; C_T is the threshold contrast, where contrast is expressed as:

$$C = \frac{|\Delta b|}{b} \tag{2}$$

A pulse is therefore detected if $C>C_T$. In ideal conditions, C_T has been set to 1%, [Ji et al., 1994]. The range of local background luminance to which this law applies, is called “Weber's region”, and it is constituted of the brightest portion of the image dynamics (Fig. 1a).

When background luminance decreases, C_T remains constant. However below a certain value of b, a second factor becomes prominent for detecting objects: the background noise. This situation is summarized in the Rose's criterion, which compares Δb with the local noise standard deviation. Rose's criterion states that an object is visible when:

$$\Delta b > K \cdot \sigma_b \tag{3}$$

where σ_b is the background noise standard deviation. K is known as the Rose number and it has been experimentally set to a quantity between two and five, [Badulescu et al., 2000]. This criterion can be viewed as a signal to noise ratio, where the role of the signal is played by luminance difference, Δb.

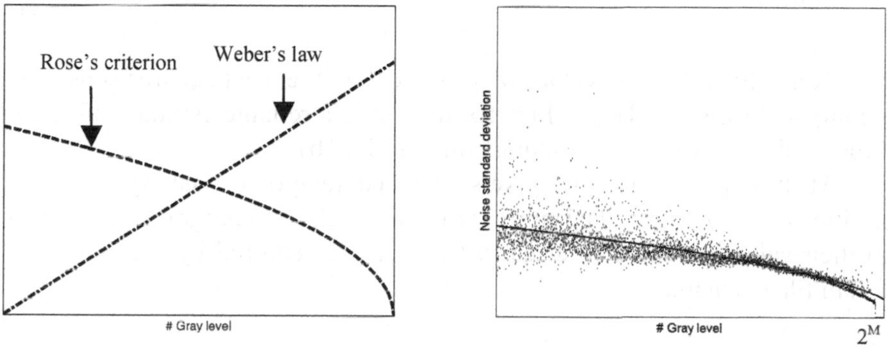

Figure 1. a) Rose's and Weber's laws as they appear for a digital radiography. In the dark region Rose's law provides a more restricting criterion, the opposite in the lighter region. b) Estimated (dots) and modeled (continuous line) noise standard deviation as a function of gray level, for a digital radiography.

The pixel luminance depends on the number of incident photons and on the sensor parameters. This transformation can be modeled as:

$$b(x,y) = G \cdot p_b(x,y) + B \tag{4}$$

where G and B represent the gain and bias of the sensor, and $p_b(x,y)$ is the number of photons reaching the sensor in position (x,y). G and B can be reasonably assumed equal for all the pixels of the same sensors.

2.2 Parameters determination

To identify the pulses, Eq. (2) and (3) are used; the local contrast, $C(x,y)$, and the local Rose number, $K(x,y)$, have to be determined. To the scope, we need to determine the background luminance associated to the pixel, $b(x,y)$, that is to the surrounding pixels; and the local noise standard deviation, $\sigma_b(x,y)$.

$b(x,y)$ can be determined by computing the median value of the surrounding pixels, inside a 3x3 window; $\sigma_b(x,y)$ requires a more careful procedure to obtain a reliable measure. A first estimate of this value can be obtained as follows: all the pixels characterized by the same background luminance, b, are pooled together and the difference between the measured luminance, $l(x,y)$, and $b(x,y)$ is computed: $n(x,y) = l(x,y) - b(x,y)$. The standard deviation of $n(x,y)$ can be assumed as the noise standard deviation associated to b, that is σ_b. By σ_b as a function of the gray levels (cf. Fig. 1b), the need of regularization is evident. To the scope the model of the sensor can be used, in fact the following relationship should hold:

$$b = (1/G)\cdot\sigma_b^2 + B \tag{5}$$

from which the best values of $1/G$ and B in the least squares sense can be computed from the data of Fig. 1b. It follows a reliable estimate of σ_b for all the luminance values (continuous line in Fig. 1b).

At this point, all the pixels that contemporary satisfy the two conditions $C(x,y)>C_T = 0.02$ and $K(x,y)>K_T = 2$, are recognized as pulses and their value corrected from $l(x,y)$ to $b(x,y)$, as required by the switching median filter schema.

3. Results and discussion

The methodology has been widely applied to panoramic and cephalometric radiographies, and it has shown efficient in removing all the corrupted pixels from the images; for 12 bit, 4.8 Mpixels radiographies, the computing time was of 0.67s; the most time consuming step, the median filter, required 0.45s.

A critical condition is verified when only a few pixels assume one luminance value, and among these there is a corrupted pixel. In this situation noise may be over-estimated as shown by the points off the curves in Fig. 1b. However, given the many points used to estimate the sensor parameters, this “outliers” do not produces a meaningful offset of the curve; therefore, more sophisticated and computationally intensive methods based on robust estimate and outliers elimination have not be applied. Highly corrupted images could be problematic in this respect; however, this case should be avoided in modern digital imaging.

It should be remarked that the present algorithm is not badly affected by the presence of local high gradients or edges, as for instance [Wang et al., 1999], [Zhang et al., 2002] or [Boukerrou et al., 1998], as can be seen in Fig. 2. This is due to the global approach in the estimate of σ_b and to the very small window, 3x3, used for median filtering, which guarantees that high gradients or edges do not affect the pulse detector. Few residual pixels may remain visible only in the darkest zones of the radiography, which are usually poor of diagnostic information.

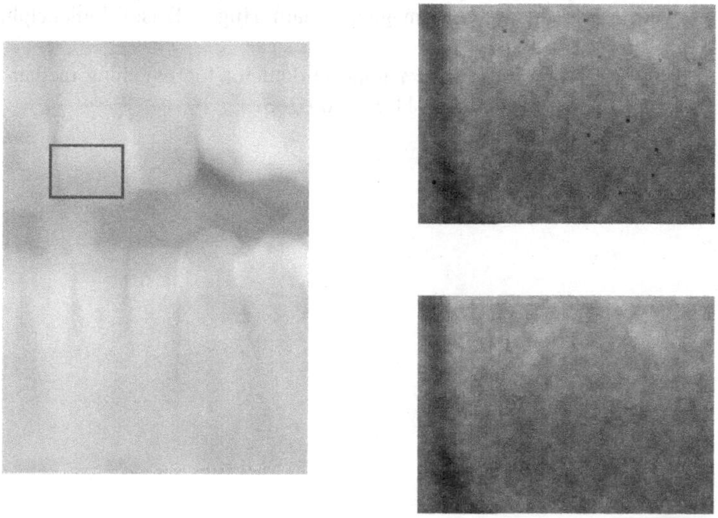

Figure 2. A portion of a typical dental panoramic image, of size 1536x2605, on 12 bits (left panel). A zoom of the same image, treated with unsharp masking filter (mask 13x13, gain 2) is shown in the upper, right panel; the lowest panel demonstrated that our algorithm efficiently removes salt & pepper noise: no pulse is visible after the application of unsharp masking filter. The percentage of pixels corrected on the entire image is 0.7%.

4. Conclusion

The method presented here, conjugates robustness and simplicity. It involves only local operations, with no iterations, making the solution fast. The introduction of the properties of the HVS and of the sensor allows deriving a robust estimate of the parameters used in the pulse detection stage.

References

Badulescu, P. and R. Zacin (2000) A two-state switched-median filter. Proc. CAS 2000, vol. 1, pp. 289-292.

Boukerrou, K., L. Kurz (1998) Suppression of "Salt and Pepper" Noise Based on Youden Designs. Inf. Sci., vol. 110, pp. 217-235.

Ji, T.-L., Sundareshan, and H. Roehrig, H. (1994) Adaptive image contrast enhancement based on human visual properties. IEEE Trans. Med. Imag., vol. 13, no. 4, pp. 573-586.

Rioul, O. (1996) A spectral Algorithm for Removing Salt and Pepper from Images. Proc. 1996 Digital Signal Proc. Workshop, Loen, Norway, pp. 275-278.

Wang, Z. and D. Zhang (1999) Progressive switching median filter for the removal of impulse noise from highly corrupted images. IEEE Trans. Circuits Syst. II, vol. 46, no. 1, pp. 78-80.

Webb, S. The Physics of Medical Imaging. Adam Hilger, Bristol-Philadelphia-New York 1988, pp. 29-32, 571-576.

Zhang, S. and A. Karim (2002) A new impulse detector for switching median filters. IEEE Signal Processing Lett., vol. 9, no. 11, pp. 360-363.

VIRTUAL SENSORS TO SUPPORT THE MONITORING OF CULTURAL HERITAGE DAMAGE

Umberto Maniscalco
I.A.C. Italian National Research Council
Viale del Policlinico 137 00161 Rome, Italy
maniscalco@iac.rm.cnr.it
I.C.A.R. Italian National Research Council
Viale delle Scienze Palermo, Italy
maniscalco@pa.icar.cnr.it

Abstract The present work is part of a wider research activity carried on within the Italian National Project named SIINDA. It shows how physical atmosphere parameters like temperature, humidity, wind direction, can be indirectly estimated in specific points of the monument, if one, or more than one, ambient air monitoring station is present in the neighborhood of the monument itself. We use a connectionist system trained to map the parameters measured by such stations with the parameters measured by the set of installed sensors. The obtained results look like very good and we received the approving by cultural heritage experts who evaluated such a methodology to effective by support monitoring in the field of the conservation state of monuments.

Keywords: Virtual Sensors, Radial Basis Functions, Cultural Heritage.

Introduction

In the field of the conservation of cultural heritage is very important to have non invasive tools able to monitor both physical and chemical conditions of material composing the monuments. In fact, the genesis of the damage is always the result of the interaction among the materials composing the monument and the atmosphere around it.

Therefore, we can consider the monument as a system in which the input is represented by physical and chemical parameters characterizing the atmosphere, the state of the system is represented by physical and chemical parameters characterizing the monument and the output is represented by the observable parameters necessary for the study of the conservation. Of course, it should be essential to know all the system transfer functions to prevent the damage manifestation, but such a task is very complex. However, on the base

B. Apolloni et al. (eds.), Biological and Artificial Intelligence Environments, 343–350

of the human expert knowledge, it is a priori possible to define some values of atmosphere parameters which can become critical for a particular architectonic structure.

As mentioned above, the state of the monument is dynamic and it changes according to the atmosphere parameters. Thus, it is very important for our task, to take in account the period (meaning uninterrupted time) in which the state of the atmosphere remains critical.

Thus, if we want to monitor a monument, we need to know historical series of physical and chemical parameters of the atmosphere around it and historical series of chemical parameters of the composing materials. These series have to be chronologically coherent. This aim can be reached by installing appropriate sensors on the monument and leading several sample campaigns. But, since the monitoring is a long term process, we ought to maintain for long time the sensors on the monument and repeat many times the sample campaigns. Moreover often, such actions are impossible to realize, because they should be very expensive or particularly invasive and reducing the enjoyment of the monument.

As regards the measurement of the atmosphere physical parameters like temperature, humidity and so on, it is possible to indirectly estimate them if one, or better more than one, ambient air monitoring stations (in the following named AAMS) is present in the neighborhood of the monument. In fact, installing on the monument a set of sensors able to measure such parameters, a connectionist system can be trained to map the parameters measured by the AAMS with the parameters measured by the set of installed sensors. In this way, after an opportune training time, the set of sensors on the monument can be uninstalled and parameter values they would have measured can be achieved by using the set of virtual sensors realized by the connectionist system.

The present paper is organized in four parts. At first we sketch out some considerations about the problem, the study case and the kind of data we are considering. Then, the following sections describe both the design of the connectionist system aimed to realize a set of virtual sensors and the implementation with the experimental setup. The last section draws some hypothesis of future work.

1. The study case and data

The present work is part of a wider research activity carried on within the Italian National Project named SIINDA [[Appolonia et al., 2000]].

The research, we are referring to in this paper, is focused on a connectionist system able to realize a set of virtual sensors which are used for non invasive monitoring of several ambient parameters, in order to prevent damage phenomena on the monument.

Table 1. Measured parameters around the pillar and exposition for each sensor.

Sensor Number	Measured Parameters	Exposition
Sensor 1	Air Temperature e Humidity	South
Sensor 2	Air Temperature e Humidity	West
Sensor 3	Air Temperature e Humidity	North
Sensor 4	Air Temperature e Humidity	East
Sensor 5	Contact Temperature	South
Sensor 6	Contact Temperature	West
Sensor 7	Contact Temperature	North
Sensor 8	Contact Temperature	East

We have chosen the roman theater in Aosta city as study case (see Fig. 1) because we have at our disposal suitable sets of chronological series concerning atmosphere parameters measured both by an AAMS located close the theater and by sensors around the faces of a pillar of the theater. The collection of the ambient parameters near the theater is obtained by the surveys carried out from AAMS which is located about at 40 meters from the pillar. This station measures hourly the ambient temperature and the humidity. The collection of the ambient parameters around the pillar is obtained by eight sensors installed on the four faces of it. The collection of the ambient parameters around the pillar is obtained by eight sensors installed on the four faces of it (see Table 1).

Figure 1. The roman theater in Aosta city.

The collection of the ambient parameters around the pillar is obtained by twelve sensors installed on the four faces of it.

Since the pillar's faces are oriented about in according to the cardinal points, we have a very interesting study case. In fact, the shadow in the sunny days, changing its position during the day, has an effect on the sensors causing, for each survey, considerable gaps of values among the surveys on the four faces. Of course, this phenomenon is less meaningful when the sky is overcast. Moreover, since the pillar is a part of an arcade, the wind blowing through the arcade causes a turbulence around it by the Venturi effect. Also this phenomenon influences the sensors, in particular the temperature sensors.

Although, as above described, we have chosen very critical conditions for our experimental setup, very good results have been obtained taking advantage of statistical investigation carried out on the data before the design of the connectionist system.

The analysis of the data shows that:

- the gap between the ambient temperature surveys measured by the AAMS and the temperatures (both ambient and contact) survey obtained by the sensors grows up within the temperature (see left side of Fig. 2);
- the hour of survey has an effect on the gap between the ambient temperature surveys obtained by the AAMS and the temperatures (both ambient and contact) survey measured by the sensors; such effect grows up within the temperature (see right side of Fig. 2);
- the same two considerations, although less tightening, can be made about the humidity.

Thus, our problem can be expressed in terms of following equations (1), where Ta_i, Tc_i, Ha_i, represent, respectively the ambient temperature, the contact temperature and the air humidity in the four points of the pillar. The time is labeled t, the air temperature measured by the AAMS is labeled T and d_i represents the distances between the AAMS and the points on the monument.

$$Ta_i = F(t, T, d_i); Tc_i = F(t, T, d_i); Ha_i = F(t, H, d_i) \text{ where } i \in [1, 4] \tag{1}$$

2. The connectionist system design

On the base of previous items we drawn some hypothesis about the solution of the problem and we concluded that an appropriate tool could be a neural network. In particular, neural networks like multi-layer perceptron [[Rosenblatt et al., 1958]], [[Bryson et al., 1969]], [[Haykin, 1994]], radial basis function [[Lowe, 1995]], [[Light, 1995]] or Hopfield network [[Hopfield et al., 1986]], [[Jordan et al., 1997]] could be able to solve the problem.

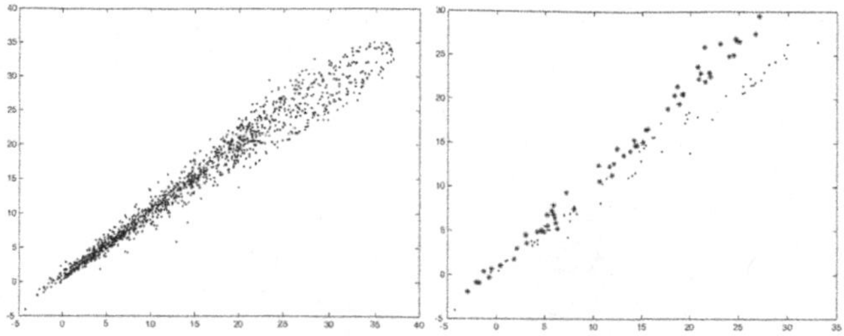

Figure 2. The ambient temperature surveys obtained from thc AAMS versus the ambient temperature surveys obtained from the sensor number 2 (left side). The same parameters at 10 a.m. (*) and at 10 p.m. (.) (right side).

Among these kinds of neural networks, the Hopfield network (or more in general recursive networks) seems to have the more appropriate features with respect the problem. In fact, we were handling physical phenomena which evolve depending on both their actual and previous state. Thus, a recursive neural network as the Hopfield network, that produces its output depending on both its input and all previous states including the present, theoretically could be give more effective results than the other two kinds of neural networks.

The multi layer perceptron has been discarded, because several simple experiments using it have given back not promising results.

Actually, we have at our disposal no timely continuous surveys because the AAMS and the sensors often fault their measures. Thus, we think our training set is not still suitable to train a recursive network because a lot of possible states remain unknown. So, at last we have chosen the radial basis function as show Fig. 3.

It could seems a simplistic model to estimate a very complex phenomenon, but, in this first step of our research, it works only as an associative map between the AAMS surveys and the sensors surveys . Of course, some other phenomena surely influence the measured ambient parameters as the presence of wind. Unfortunately, we have at our disposal only information about the wind coming from AAMS because the powder caused several troubles to installed wind sensors. Thus, we cant take into account this important parameter yet.

In the future, when we will have to our disposal more complete sets of data, we think to design a more complex and recursive system so that we can compare the results.

The statistical evidence pointed out in the previous section, has had an important role also in the design of the connectionist system topology.

We have three input parameters: hour of survey and measures of ambient temperature and air humidity. We would like to estimate, in four different

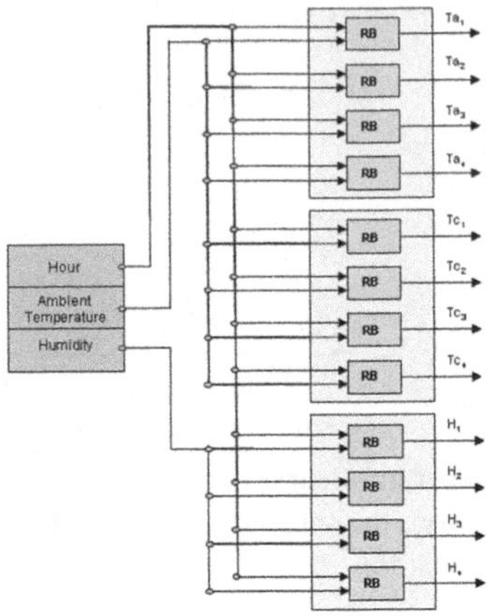

Figure 3. The connectionist system topology. The blocks named RB represent the radial basis function. Ta, Tc and H represent, respectively ambient temperature, contact temperature and air humidity. The subscripts from 1 to 4 represent the four sensors position.

points, the air temperature, the contact temperature and the air humidity. So, at first, we decided the input-output dependences, considering all the outputs always depending on the hour of survey, the output air temperature depending on the input temperature, the output air humidity depending on the input air humidity and the contact temperature depending on input air temperature.

Moreover, deciding to use a single radial basis function for each parameter and each sensor, we designed a connectionist system whose each computational unit can be independently trained and tuned and, if it is necessary to measure the same parameters in other points or new parameters at all, other trained radial basis function can be added to the system making it scalable.

3. Implementation and experimental setup

The implementation and the simulations of the connectionist system have been carried out using the Neural Network MathLab Toolbox. Since at the time of the implementation, we have 1300 usable surveys covering the period between August 2003 and February 2004, we partitioned the surveys in two sets of 650 surveys for each. The first is used for training the radial basis function, the second for testing the system. We chosen to build the two sets using timely alternated surveys, so the two sets cover the same period.

During the experiment we trained and simulated many radial basis function in order to optimize the spread of radial basis neurons of each radial basis functions. Thus, we trained 30 radial basis functions for each parameter using spreads covering the integer interval [10-40]. The results of the simulations, with respect the south sensors, are showed in the Fig. 4. In this figure, along

Table 2. the south sensors mean errors referred to the test set.

	South	West	North	East
Air Temperature (celtius degree)	0.65	0.67	0.64	0.74
Contact Temperature (celtius degree)	0.91	1.10	0.98	1.13
Air Humidity (percentage)	6.54	6.21	6.98	7.21

the X axis the number of surveys and along Y axis the errors are reported. The behaviors of the other three virtual sensors are substantially the same. Using the test set of data we obtained small mean errors as the table 2shows.

Recently, we have had an experimental proof of the effectiveness and robustness of the system testing it by means of a set of input data related to April 2004. Thus, using input data climatically different as regards those used during the training of the system, we substantially obtained the same mean errors for all virtual sensors.

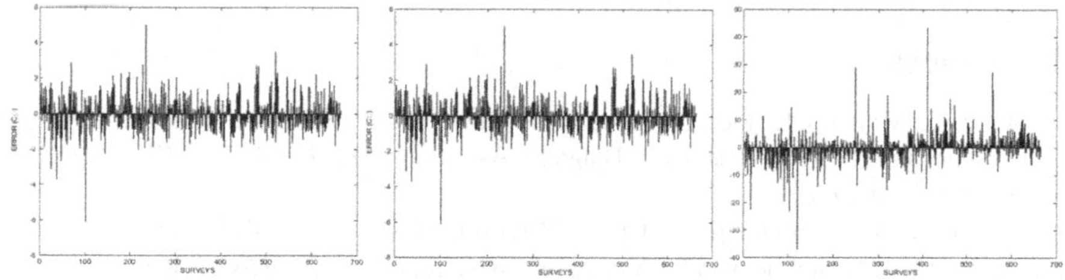

Figure 4. Air temperature, contact temperature and humidity errors for the sensor on south side of the pillar. The graphs are referred to the above described test set (from August 2003 to February 2004).

4. Conclusions

A connectionist system of virtual sensors to support the monitoring of conservation state of monuments has been presented. We showed how is possible to realize a set of virtual sensors in order to replace the physical sensors located on the monument.

We designed a connectionist system having care to guarantee its scalability and portability in terms of different applications. The obtained results look like very good for the application target. In fact, the temperatures (air and contact) means errors, as well as humidity mean error can be considered satisfactory and they guarantee the monitoring process in which is more important the trend of the ambient parameters than the high precision in the measurement.

We also were encouraged to develop our research because we received the approving by the Dr. Lorenzo Appolonia coming from "Soprintendenza ai Beni Culturali della Regione Valle d'Aosta", who evaluates such a methodology effective to support the monitoring of cultural heritage damage.

Our future works will face two new challenges. The first consists in the integration into the system of a new layer of radial basis functions at the aim to refine the results. The second challenge takes into account also the surveys obtained by another AAMS. Moreover, when we will have at our disposal more complete sets of data, we think to design a more complex and recursive system so that we can compare the results with this one.

Acknowledgments

We would like to express our best thanks to full Professor Antonio Chella coming from "DINFO-UNIPA" for his useful suggestions. Moreover our thanks go to to the Dr. Lorenzo Appolonia coming from "Soprintendenza della Regione Valle d'Aosta" for permission to use the data and the validation of our results.

References

Appolonia, L., Moltedo, L., Picco, R., Salonia, P. (2000) Progetto Parnaso, Ricerche e Sviluppi si Sistemi Innovativi di Indagine e Diagnosi Assistita. *Publisher Rivista CNR Rcicerca e Futuro, n.18. 37-43.*

Bryson A.E.,Ho Y.C. (1969) Applied Optimal Control. *Publisher New York, Blaisdell.*

Haykin, S. (1994) Neural networks - A comprehensive foundation. *Publisher Macmillan.*

Hopfield, J.J., and Tank, D.W. (1986) Computing with Neural Circuits: A Model. *Publisher Science(233), August 8, pp. 625-633*

Jordan, M., Ghahramani, Z., and Saul, L. (1997) Hidden Markov decision trees in Advances in Neural Information Processing Systems. *Publisher MIT Press, Cambridge, MA, Vol. 9.*

Light, W.A. (1995) Some Aspects of Radial Basis Function Approximation in Approximation Theory, Spline Functions and Applications. *Publisher S.P. Singh, Kluwer Mathematical and Physical Sciences Series, 356:163-190.*

Lowe, D. (1995) Radial basis function networks. *Publisher MIT Press, Cambridge, MA, pp. 779-782.*

Rosenblatt, F. (1958) The perceptron: A probabilistic model for information storage and organization in the brain. *Publisher Psychological Review, 65:386-408.*

A COMPUTER AIDED ANALYSIS ON DIGITAL IMAGES

Giovanni Luca Masala on behalf of the MAGIC-5 Collaboration
Struttura Dipartimentale di Matematica e Fisica dell'Università di Sassari and Sezione INFN di Cagliari, Italy, via Vienna 2 Sassari, 07100. giovanni.masala@ca.infn.it

Abstract: Purpose of this work is the development of an automatic system which can be useful for radiologists in the investigation of breast and lung cancer. A breast neoplasia is often marked by the presence of microcalcifications and massive lesions in the mammogram. The first are a very small object in a noise background and the second are large object with particular shape. The need for tools able to recognize such lesions at an early stage is therefore apparent. In this article is shown an application of artificial neural network on the imaging analysis in mammography. The results obtained in terms of sensitivity and specificity when it has been tested alone and then used as second reader will be presented. We present also an overview about the methods developed for pulmonary nodule detection in CT images and the preliminary results obtained with a pre-processing filter will be also presented.

Keywords: CAD, neural networks, breast cancer, lung cancer, nodule detections

1. Introduction

Breast and lung cancers are reported as the leading causes of cancer deaths both in United States and in Europe. A reduction of breast cancer

B. Apolloni et al. (eds.), Biological and Artificial Intelligence Environments, 351–357

mortality in asymptomatic women is possible in case of early diagnosis, which is available thanks to screening programs, a periodical mammographic examination performed in general for 49-69 years old women [Feig and Yaffe,1995][Karssmejer,1999][Viborny and Giger,2000]. A breast cancer is often marked by the presence of microcalcification clusters and massive lesions and mammography is widely recognized as the only imaging modality useful for the early detection of such abnormalities. It is usually realized by screen-film modality but digital detectors are becoming widespread. It has been estimated that screening-programs radiologists fail to detect up to approximately 25% breast cancers visible on retrospective reviews and that this percentage increases if also minimal signs are considered. Sensitivity (percentage of pathological images correctly classified) and specificity (percentage of non-pathological images correctly classified) of this examination appreciably increase if two radiologists independently analyze the images. Independent double reading is currently strongly recommended as it allows the reduction of the rate of false negative examinations by 5 to 15%. The recent technological progress has led to the development of several Computer Aided Detection (CAD) systems, which could be successfully used as second readers. The MAGIC5 Collaboration aims at the development of tools that would help in the early diagnosis of breast cancer and in this paper the characteristics of the CALMA CAD software [Bottigli at al.,2002] will be described and its performance will be reported. The case of lung cancer is more complex: the overall 5-years survival rate is only 14% [Gurcan at al.,2002] and in the last two decades there has been no significant improvement, probably due to the lack of a screening protocol tested with reliable results. So an overview about the problems related to lung cancer screening, in terms of opportunity and modalities of lung cancer early detection, will be presented, and an evaluation of the possible impact of CAD also in this field will be discussed.

2. Materials and methods

2.1 Breast

A Computer Aided Detection system (the CALMA CAD), which approach consists in the analysis of each mammogram available per patient, has been developed [Bottigli at all,2002].
The images (18x24 cm^2, digitized by a CCD linear scanner with a 85 μm pitch and 4096 grey levels) are fully characterised: pathological ones have a

consistent description which includes radiological diagnosis and histological data, while non pathological ones correspond to patients with a follow up of at least three years.

The presence of suspicious areas for massive lesions or microcalcification clusters in one or more mammogram results in a possible cancer diagnosis. The relatively large size of a mammogram brings to the need of reducing data input with no loss of information before proceeding to the classification, in order to perform an efficient detection in a reasonable amount of time. Therefore the approach is a multi-level one. The lower levels are demanded to reduce the amount of information without excluding ill regions (demand of sensitivity values close to 100%), whereas the upper levels are requested to perform the classification. In particular, the analysis is organized into three general steps both for massive lesions that for microcalcification clusters search: data reduction (non-interesting regions of the mammogram are eliminated with the consequent reduction of the amount of data passed to the subsequent step); feature extraction (relevant characteristics are extracted out of the selected regions); classification (the selected regions are classified on the basis of a degree of suspiciousness).

Massive lesions are rather large (diameter of the order of cm) objects with very different shapes and show up with a faint contrast slowly increasing with time.

The automated Massive cluster analysis was made using the following approach:

- Select maximum intensity position, by starting from left top corner of the mammogram the absolute maximum of intensity is found
- A set of concentric rings, 5 pixels wide, up to a maximum radius of 247 pixels (~ 2 cm) is built.
- The pixel average intensity in each ring is computed.
- The most external ring, which defines the ROI radius (R), is that ring whose average intensity is less than a given minimum threshold.
- The entire portion inside the ROI radius is then removed and stored for further analysis.
- A new maximum (a new centre) is sought in the remaining matrix.
- Back to the beginning until one of the following condition is verified :
- - 100 maximum are found
- - the n-th maximum intensity is less than a threshold
- For radius, r = R, 2/3 R, 1/3 R , the parameters are used as INPUT in a FFNN with 9 input, 6 hidden, and 1 output neurons to distinguish between pathological and non-pathological ROI.

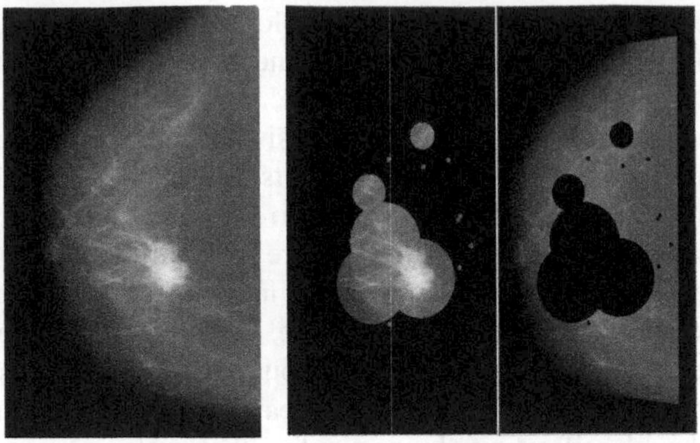

Figure 1. The original mammogram (left), the selected patterns containing the ROIs (middle), and the remaining image (right).

The features extracted to represent ROI are three statistical moments: average, variance, skewness (the last feature being index of distribution asymmetry) of the intensity distribution as functions of *r*. For the case of a massive lesion, the average intensity increases, the variance decreases and the symmetry increases at decreasing *r*.

The adopted Neural Network is a feed-forward back-propagation supervised network trained with gradient descent learning rule with "momentum" to quickly move along the direction of decreasing gradient, thus avoiding oscillations around secondary minima. The software is SNNS v4.1 (Stuttgart University) [Zell et al.,1995]. The weights were determined by training the network with the training set and minimizing the mean squared error (MSE) of the validation set. The minimum MSE value was achieved after 500 training epochs.

2.2 Lung

It has been proven that early detection and resection of lung cancer can improve the prognosis significantly [Itoh et al.,2000]: the overall 5-year survival rate of 14% increases to 49% if the lesion is localized and decreases to 2% if it has metastasized and for Stage I cancer is 67%. The problem is that early curable lung cancers usually produce no symptoms and are often missed in mass screening programs in which chest radiography, which has been used for detecting lung cancer for a long time, is employed [Armato et al.,2002]. Lung cancer most commonly manifests as a non-calcified pulmonary nodule.

We show the application of an effective nodule enhancement filter as a pre-processing step ; the approach reported is made by Q. Li, S. Sone and K. Doi [Li et al.,2003].

The goal consists in a filter able to selectively enhance nodules, blood vessels and airway walls. Assuming dot and line as idealized shapes for nodule and vessels, respectively, the starting point is the construction of enhancement filters for dot and line in 2D image space, which would take into account also the effect of noise and the scale of the object. The method can then be generalized to 3D image space by considering the three idealized basic shapes of dot, line and plane. The filter obtained is based on the eigen value analysis of the Hessian matrix at each location in two-dimensional (2D) of three-dimensional (3D) image space.

3. Results

3.1 Breast

The software developed for the automatic search of massive lesions has been trained on a training set of 515 patterns (102 containing opacities and 413 without) and tested on a test set composed of 515 different images (again 102 containing opacities and 413 without), all extracted from the CALMA database [Bottigli et al.,2002]. The best results obtained by means of this procedure are 90% for sensitivity and 85% for specificity.

The software developed for the automatic search of microcalcification clusters has been tested on a dataset of 676 patterns containing microcalcification clusters and 995 without microcalcification clusters, all extracted from the CALMA database [Bottigli et al.,2002]. In particular, in the training phase 865 patterns (370 with and 495 without microcalcification clusters) were used, whereas the test set consisted in 806 patterns (306 with and 500 without microcalcification clusters). The best results obtained are 92% for both sensitivity and specificity.

The results obtained in the test of the CALMA CAD as second reader in the search of microcalcification clusters [Lauria et al., 2003] are reported in terms of sensitivity and specificity variations in Table 1. The increment in sensitivity of radiologists supported by CALMA ranges from 10.0% (reader B) to 15.6% (reader C) with a slight increase of the number of false positives. The decrease in specificity was more significant for the least experienced of the radiologists. A_z area increased with CALMA, the variation ranges from 0.01 to 0.06, independently of the skill of reader. It is worth noting that no decrement in specificity has been reported for the radiologist A (the more expert one) when CALMA CAD is used as second reader in the search of microcalcification clusters.

Table 1. Sensitivity and Specificity values of radiologists without and with CALMA System

	Sensitivity		Specificity	
	Alone	With CALMA	Alone	With CALMA
A	82.8 %	94.3 %	87.5 %	87.5 %
B	80.0 %	90.0 %	91.7 %	88.4 %
C	71.5 %	87.1 %	74.2 %	70.9 %

The average value of sensitivity for a radiologist alone is 78.1% ±5.9%, the average value of sensitivity with the aid of CALMA CAD is 90.5%±3.6%. These values, are in accord with previous works [Lauria et al, 2003], where an increment in sensitivity is shown when a CAD system is used as second reader.

3.2 Lung

The dot enhancement filter described in [Itoh et al.,2000] has been reproduced and preliminary tested, previously on artificial images and then on real standard spiral CT images. In Figure 2 the results obtained on a non pathological image are reported. We can see that after the processing of the original image (left) with the 2D filter some structures are still present on the processed image (middle). These probably correspond to sections of vessels, and the processing with the 3D filter (right) eliminates them. By contrast, in the case of the pathological image reported in Figure 2, the nodules are effectively enhanced and are well visible in the image processed by the 3D filter.

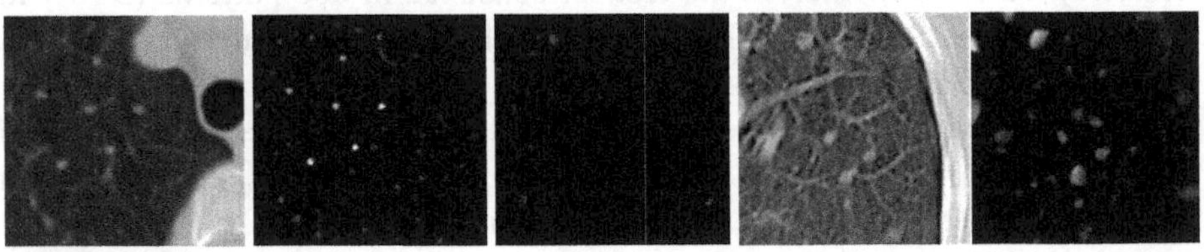

Figure 2. In order it is shown from the left the original image in a non-pathological case, the output of the 2D and 3D filters. Then it is shown the original image in a pathological case and output of the 3D filter.

4. Conclusion

A CAD system for the search of massive lesions and microcalcification clusters has been developed and characterized in terms of sensitivity and specificity on a large database of digitized mammograms obtaining good results. Moreover, it has also been successfully tested as second reader. As it has been happened in mammography, CAD may be a valuable alternative to double reading also for detection of lung cancer on CT images screening. A preprocessing filter able to select and enhance pathological nodules in a background in which are present non pathological structures which appears very similar to pathological nodules in the 2D projections of CT scans has been preliminary tested on clinical images. It can be optimized and become the first step of an automatic system for the search of nodules in lung CT images.

References

Armato S.G., Li F., Giger M.L., MacMahon H, Sone S. Doi K. (2002): 'Lung Cancer: Performance of Automated Lung Nodule Detection Applied to Cancers Missed in a CT Screening Program', *Radiology* 225 pp. 685-692.

Bottigli U., Delogu P., Fantacci M.E., Fauci F., Golosio B., Lauria A., Palmiero R., Raso G., Stumbo S., Tangaro S. (2002): 'Search of microcalcification cluster with the CALMA CAD station', *The International Society for Optical Engineering (SPIE)* 4684 pp. 1301-1310.

Feig S.A., Yaffe M. (1995): 'Digital mammography, computer aided diagnosis and telemammography', *Radiol. Clin. N. Am.* 33, pp. 1205-1230.

Gurcan M.N., Sahiner B., Petrick N., Chan H., Kazerooni E.A., Cascade P.N., Hadjiiski L. (2002): 'Lung nodule detection on thoracic computed tomography images: Preliminary evaluation of a computer-aided diagnosis system', *Med. Phys.* 29(11), pp. 2552-2558.

Itoh S., Ikeda M., Arahata S., Kodaira T., Isomura T., Kato T., Yamakawa K., Maruyama K., Ishigaki T. (2000): 'Lung Cancer Screening: Minimum Tube Current Required for Helical CT', *Radiology* 215 pp. 175-183.

Karssmejer N. (1999): 'Reading screening mammograms with the help of neural networks', *Nederlands Tijdschriff geneeskd*, 143/45, pp. 2232-2236.

Lauria A., Fantacci M.E., Bottigli U., Delogu P., Fauci F., Golosio B., Indovina P.L., Masala G.L., Palmiero R., Raso G., Stumbo S., Tangaro S. (2003): 'Diagnostic performance of radiologists with and without different CAD systems for mammography', *The International Society for Optical Engineering (SPIE)* 5034 pp. 51-56.

Li Q., Sone S., Doi K. (2003): 'Selective enhancement filters for nodules, vessels, and airway walls in two- and three-dimensional CT scans', *Med. Phys.* 30(8) pp. 2040-2051.

Viborny C.J., Giger M.L., Nishikawa R.M. (2000): 'Computer aided detection and diagnosis of breast cancer', *Radiol. Clin. N. Am.* 38(4), pp. 725-740.

Zell A. et al., SNNS Stuttgart Neural Network Simulator – v4.1, University of Stuttgart, report 1995

RECURSIVE NEURAL NETWORKS FOR THE CLASSIFICATION OF VEHICLES IN IMAGE SEQUENCES

Gabriele Monfardini[1]

[1] *Università degli Studi di Siena, Dipartimento di Ingegneria dell'Informazione, Siena, Italy*

Abstract *This paper proposes a new neural network approach to the classification of vehicles in image sequences recorded by a stationary camera. The novelty consists in organizing the tracking data into directed acyclic graphs and in the use of recursive neural networks to discriminate which vehicle is represented in each graph. Some preliminary experimental results from real-world traffic scenes prove the viability of the method.*

Keywords: Vehicles Classification, Recursive Neural Networks, Graphs

1. Introduction

The problem of localizing, tracking and classifying vehicles in image sequences recorded from real-world traffic scenes has been studied extensively in the past ten years [Kastrinaki et al., 2003]. Many approaches to object localization and tracking has been attempted, using a variety of 2D e 3D techniques. Working with a set of tridimensional models [Tan et al., 1998], [Kollnig and Nagel, 1997], [Haag and Nagel, 1999] can lead to good performance but it becomes computationally expensive as the number of models increases. Moreover, this approach can only detect objects that have been modeled in advance, therefore it is less useful if this condition is not completely met, as in generic surveillance tasks [Cavallaro et al., 2002]. Recognition and classification may also be performed directly on the image domain with good results [Gupte et al., 2002], but model-based approach has been proved to be the most accurate and robust against viewpoint changes, although again computationally expensive. In literature there are many papers that use three-dimensional tracking and classification with models of various types of vehicles, expecially cars (e.g. sedan, wagon, etc.), that are projected to image plane and compared with the recorded images [Sullivan, 1992], [Sullivan et al., 1997]. Several researches [Sullivan et al., 1995], [Koller, 1993] have proposed to use detected image fea-

B. Apolloni et al. (eds.), Biological and Artificial Intelligence Environments, 359–366

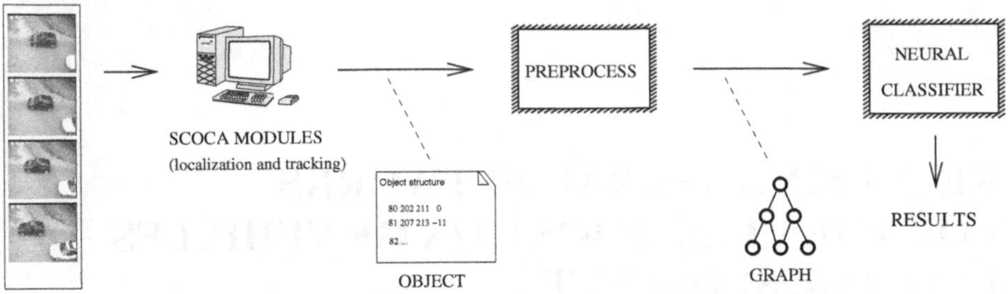

Figure 1. An overview of the system

tures as physical forces that deform vehicle models, as this leads to improved performance.

After the development of the neural paradigm, various attempts have been made to use neural networks in object tracking and recognition and in lane detection for autonomous vehicle guidance.

In this paper we propose to classify vehicles with a particular neural model, called recursive network [Frasconi et al., 2001], that is trained on tracking information. The system used to provide necessary data for localization and tracking of vehicles from image sequences is the SCOCA system (*System for COunting, Classifying and tracking Automatically vehicles in a road intersection*) developed in the TeV (Technology of Vision) group of ITC-irst (Trento, Italy)[1]. It uses background subtraction and region grouping for vehicle detection and tracking, and implements a rather sophisticated two stage classification, with a model-based phase and then a feature-based refinement.

Our goal is to explore the effectiveness of an alternative classifier featuring neural techniques in order to discriminate between five classes of vehicles:

- car
- motorcycle or bicycle
- van
- lorry or bus
- pedestrian

Tracking information from SCOCA system are collected in data structures called Objects. These Objects are preprocessed and coded into graphs which are used to train and test our neural classifier. An overview of the system is shown in Fig. 1.

This paper is organized as follows. Next section outlines data structures resulting from SCOCA tracking module, Sect. 3 describes the proposed approach, while Sect. 4 outlines some preliminary experimental results from real-world traffic sequences. Finally, last section draws some conclusions.

2. Tracking

The tracking phase consists in localizing objects in the scene and detecting their movements from one frame to the next. The SCOCA system's localization module uses *background subtraction* with automatical updating of the background through Kalman filtering [Zanin, 2000]. Thresholding obtained image results in a binary map (the so called *object map* [Gupte et al., 2002], [Koller et al., 1994]), where the detected pixels are grouped together. Before they are assigned to hypothetic objects, regions too small are deleted, as probably caused by noise.

In most cases, this technique provides good global performance, but at the cost of high computational burden. Therefore, real time costraints make applying background subtraction to each frame quite unfeasible with today general purpose hardware. One solution could be to work with frames at lower resolutions but it doesn't lead to satisfactory results. The project developed by TeV reseachers overcomes this problem executing background subtraction not in all frames, but only every five or seven. Between two consecutive subtractions they resort to a less expensive algorithm, which tracks, instead of objects on the whole, only some their local features that are easy detectable, like edges or cornes, i.e. points with high values for intensity gradient.

The information collected during the tracking step is stored in text files. For each hypothetic vehicle a file (called Object file) is created, containing a row for each frame in which it was visible in the camera's field of view. When background subtraction is performed, the row contains a reference to the blob detected by that procedure, with its evaluated position, velocity (in pixels/s) and displacement from previous subtraction. For the other frames, on the contrary, no information about the blob is available, as the tracking algorithm is different (Fig. 2).

During tracking it may happen that two or more vehicles are mixed up in a single object. This is typically due to occlusions among vehicles or to the presence of strong shadows. Often the vehicles, due to their movement, are distinguishable in some frames and merged in the others. In this case the Object file mantains two sets of information until it is possible and then reports only features about the compound resulting from the fusion.

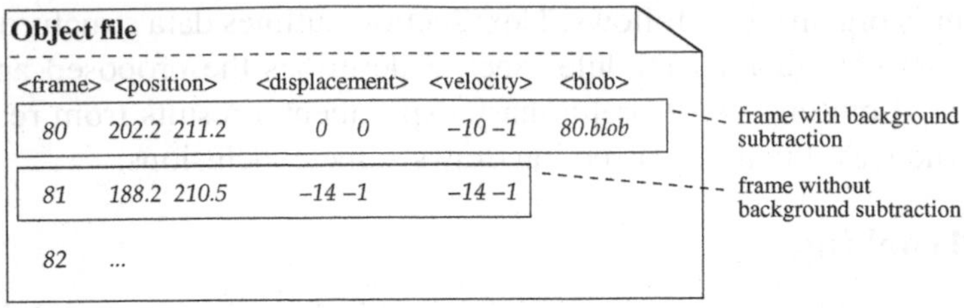

Figure 2. A typical Object file

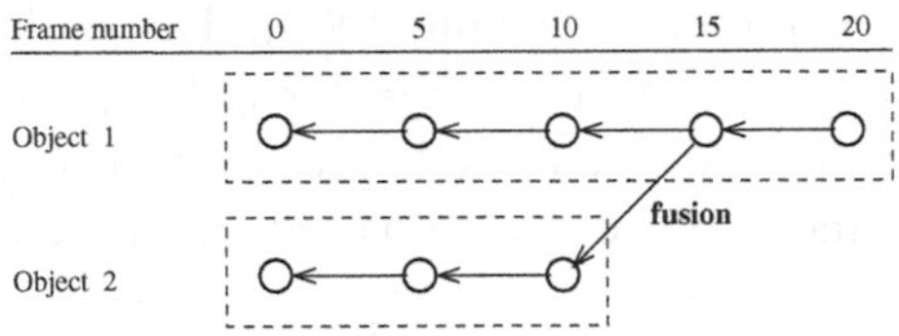

Figure 3. Workflow of the proteomics experiment

Figure 4. Graph structure with fusions

3. Preprocessing phase and neural network classifier

The tracking information collected on each object during all the time in which it was visible are saved in a particular kind of data structure. In order to learn that structure with the recursive neural classifier it must be represented by a DPAG (Directed Positional Acyclic Graph, [Frasconi et al., 2001]).

For each frame in which the object is visible and the background subtraction is performed a node of the graph is built. As a consequence each object will be represented by a sequence of nodes, each one connected to the next with an oriented arc. It is important to remark that we choose to make the connections flow in the opposite direction with respect of time, so that the first node will be associated with the last view of the object in the image sequence. The cases of fusion of one object into another is represented by a ramification in the structure of the graph (Fig. 4).

Given the way in which SCOCA tracking data are built and the rule followed in arcs orientation it is not difficult to understand that the obtained graphs are nothing else than trees, so they surely have a supersource (namely their root)[2].

The label associated with each node contains geometrical features that have been extracted from the blobs detected during the localization phase. In details, the label contains the area of the blob, the principal and secondary axes of blob's convex hull[3] and a concise description of blob's shape.

The principal axis, by definition, is the axis that passes through the center of mass of the convex hull and in respect of which the inertial momentum

Table 1. Results of two tests of recognition of cars. Lines represent true class of the object, while columns report the output of the classifier

	YES	NO	TOTAL	ACCURACY
yes	**53**	9	62	85.48%
no	13	**35**	48	72.92%

TOTAL ACCURACY: 80.00%

	YES	NO	TOTAL	ACCURACY
yes	**72**	3	75	96.00%
no	12	**35**	47	74.47%

TOTAL ACCURACY: 87.70%

is minimum, providing that each pixel is given unitary weight. The secondary axis, on the contrary, is simply the one orthogonal to the principal. The concise description of the shape is given by a fixed length vector, that for our scope was chosen to be a 64-bits vector, or more precisely, a 8×8 matrix that is read line-by-line. Each bit of the matrix represents a square of a grid, suitably scaled and superimposed on the object contour. We set the value of each bit at "1" if the square is crossed by the contour and at "0" elsewhere [Monfardini, 2004].

The proposed classifier consists of five different neural nets, one for each vehicle class, whose aim is to detect the presence in each object of a vehicle of its own class. The reason for this architectural choice is that there is a non negligible percentual of cases in which the tracking structure contains information about more than one vehicle. Therefore, a single net whose output codifies classes in a *one hot* manner is not suitable for the task.

4. Experimental results

The movies used for experiments was acquired in the city of Trento (Italy). The atmospherical conditions were good and there was quite an heavy traffic (but without traffic jams). Tracking phase resulted in more than 500 objects - not all necessarily describing a single vehicle - that have been divided in training, cross-validation and test sets. Due to the reduced number of vehicles of certain classes, we present only the results about recognition of cars and motorcycles (or bicycles).

The architecture of classification nets was chosen with a trial and error procedure; optimal configuration resulted in a three-layer configuration with ten state neurons and ten hidden neurons. Two indipendent tests of recognition of cars yielded the results of Table 1[4].

Table 2. Classification rate in the second car recognition test with different numbers of hidden neurons

# hidden units	Classification Rate
5	77.05%
10	87.70%
20	82.79%

Table 3. Results of two tests of recognition of motorcycles and bicycles

	YES	NO	TOTAL	ACCURACY
yes	4	4	8	50.00%
no	11	91	102	89.22%

TOTAL ACCURACY: 86.36%

	YES	NO	TOTAL	ACCURACY
yes	5	8	13	38.46%
no	18	91	109	83.49%

TOTAL ACCURACY: 78.69%

Varying the number of hidden neurons of the net affects the performance of the classifier. As shown in Table 2 for the second test, ten hidden neurons give the best results.

The classification of motorcycles (and bicycles) has been somewhat harder, as the number of positive examples in training set was considerably minor (Table 3). Since net's behaviour would have been too much conditioned by numeric disparity from positive and negative examples, these results were obtained with an artificially balanced training set.

In order to demonstrate the efficacy of the proposed structural approach some experiments of car recognition with traditional feedforward networks have been made. Obviously this neural model cannot be trained on entire graphs, but it can learn to recognize the presence of a car in a frame from the features evaluated. In details I used a two-layer feedforward networks with sigmoidal activation units and linear output units and the net was trained using resilient backpropagation, a variant of standard backpropagation that offers favourable convergence properties [Riedmiller and Braun, 1993]. First experiment was done without balancing the training set and the results, obtained as mean of five runs and quite insensitive to the number of hidden units, are shown in Table 4. Balancing the training set leads to slightly better performance with ten hidden units, as shown in Table 5.

Table 4. Classification rate in the car recognition test with two-layer feedforward networks with different numbers of hidden neurons and unbalanced training set

# hidden units	Classification Rate
2	67.18%
5	67.65%
10	68.79%
20	68.95%
30	68.44%

Table 5. Classification rate in the car recognition test with two-layer feedforward networks with different numbers of hidden neurons and balanced training set

# hidden units	Classification Rate
2	67.74%
5	66.61%
10	70.97.%
20	67.74%
30	68.39%

As one could expect, results with feedforward networks are significantly worse than using recursive neural model, and this proves that learning the entire image sequence in which each vehicle has been visible helps to improve global classification performance.

5. Conclusions

This paper proposes a new neural network approach to the classification of vehicles from traffic sequences recorded by a stationary camera. The tracking data are organized into DPAGs and used to train recursive neural classifiers. Preliminary experimental results show the effectiveness of this technique w.r.t. the traditional feedforward networks and suggest that it reaches a favourable compromise between computational complexity and quality of generalization on unseen examples.

6. Acknowledgement

This work was partially sopported by ITC-irst (Trento, Italy).
I would like to express my thanks to all TeV people, expecially to S. Messelodi, C. Modena and M. Zanin, for their competence and help. Thanks also to M. Gori of Università degli Studi di Siena for introducing me to neural network models.

Notes

1. For further details see http://tev.itc.it/TeV/Research/SCOCA.html and [Messelodi et al., 2004].

2. The presence of a supersource in each graph is mandatory for the learning scheme adopted.

3. The convex hull of a plane figure is the smallest convex polygon that contains it.

4. In our domain the classification rate can be defined as the number of correct classifications w.r.t. the total amount of objects created in the tracking phase.

References

Cavallaro, A., Steiger, O., and Ebrahimi, T. (2002). Multiple Video Object Tracking in Complex Scenes. In *ACM Multimedia Conference*, pages 523–532, Juan Les Pins, France.

Frasconi, P., Goller, C., Gori, M., Küchler, A., and Sperduti, A. (2001). *A Field Guide to Dynamical Recurrent Networks, J. Kolen and S. Kremer Eds.*, chapter From sequences to Data Structures, pages 351–374. IEEE-Press.

Gupte, S., Masoud, O., Martin, R.F.K., and Papanikolopoulos, N.P. (2002). Detection and classification of vehicles. *IEEE Trans. on Intelligent Transportation Systems*, 3(1):37–47.

Haag, M. and Nagel, H.-H. (1999). Combination of edge element and optical flow estimates for 3d-model-based vehicle tracking in traffic image sequences. *International Journal of Computer Vision*, 35(3):295–319.

Kastrinaki, V., Zervakis, M., and Kalaitzakis, K. (2003). A survey of video processing techniques for traffic applications. *Image and Vision Computing*, 21(4):359–381.

Koller, D. (1993). Moving object recognition and classification based on recursive shape parameter estimation. In *12th Israel Conference on Artificial Intelligence, Computer Vision and Neural Networks*, pages 359–368, Tel-Aviv, Israel.

Koller, D., Weber, J., and Malik, J. (1994). Robust multiple car tracking with occlusion reasoning. In *3rd European Conference on Computer Vision*, volume 1, pages 189–196, Stockholm, Sweden.

Kollnig, H. and Nagel, H.-H. (1997). 3d pose estimation by directly matching polyhedral models to gray value gradients. *International Journal of Computer Vision*, 23(3):283–302.

Messelodi, S., Modena, C. M., and Zanin, M. (2004). A computer vision system for the detection and classification of vehicles at urban road intersection. Technical report, ITC-irst.

Monfardini, G. (2004). Recursive neural networks for the classification of vehicles in image sequences. Technical Report T04-02-06, ITC-irst.

Riedmiller, M. and Braun, H. (1993). A direct adaptive method for faster backpropagation learning: The rprop algorithm. In *Proc. of the IEEE Intl. Conf. on Neural Networks*, pages 586–591, San Francisco, CA.

Sullivan, G. D. (1992). Model-based vision for traffic scenes using the ground-plane constraint. *Phil. Trans. Roy. Soc. (B)*, 337:361–370.

Sullivan, G. D., Baker, K. D., Worrall, A. D., Attwood, C. I., and Remagnino, P. R. (1997). Model-based vehicle detection and classification using orthographic approximations constraint. *Image Vis. Comput.*, 15:649–654.

Sullivan, G. D., Worrall, A. D., and Ferryman, J. M. (1995). Visual object recognition using deformable models of vehicles. *Proc. Workshop on Context-Based Vision*, pages 75–86.

Tan, T. N., Sullivan, G. D., and Baker, K. D. (1998). Model-based localisation and recognition of road vehicles. *International Journal of Computer Vision*, 27(1):5–25.

Zanin, M. (AA 1999-2000). Tecniche di visione artificiale applicate al controllo del traffico: rilevamento di code e conteggio classificato di veicoli. Master's thesis, Università degli Studi di Bologna, Facoltà di Ingegneria.

NEURAL NETWORK IN MODELING GLUCOSE-INSULIN BEHAVIOR

M.Panella[1], F.Barcellona[1], A.M.Bersani[2]

[1] *INFO-COM Dpt., University of Rome "La Sapienza", via Eudossiana 18, 00184 Rome, Italy*

panella@infocom.uniroma1.it

francesco.barcellona@uniroma1.it

[2] *Me.Mo.Mat Dpt., University of Rome "La Sapienza", via Scarpa 16, 00161 Rome, Italy*

bersani@dmmm.uniroma1.it

Abstract In this paper we propose a neural network identification of a mathematical model called MINMOD, which describes the interactions between glucose and insulin in human subjects, in order to realize an adequate model for patients suffering from *Diabetes Mellitus* Type 2. The model has been tested on the basis of clinical data and it can correctly reproduce glucose and insulin reply and temporal evolution, according to experimental data test. Using neural networks, we can predict the glucose temporal evolution without invasive technique for patients, with the aim to determine the clinical effects to be made in case of pathological behaviors.

Keywords: Diabetes Analysis, Glucose-Insulin Interaction, MINMOD Model, MoG Neural Network.

1. Introduction

Insulin is a protein made up of 51 amino acids, which is secreted in small quantities by the pancreas by means of the so-called "β-cells". The insulin secretion can be highly increased in order to answer to several inputs, i.e. sugars (first of them glucose), amino acids, vagus activity. Insulin helps the storage in target cells of glucose and lipids, which are important energy sources. Insulin also affects cells growth and the metabolism of many tissues. Besides, it promotes the protein synthesis, increasing the amino acids transport and stimulating ribosome activity. Finally, it helps glycogen synthesis, restoring it after every muscular activity. Insulin is brought by the bloodstream to specific

B. Apolloni et al. (eds.), Biological and Artificial Intelligence Environments, 367–374

receptors that have been discovered in quite all the tissues membranes. However, biological effects due to the interaction between insulin and receptors have been found in few tissues: liver, muscle and adipose tissue. Glucose is the most important physiological stimulation for insulin secretion. Insulin reply to a protracted glucose stimulation of the β-cells is split into two phases: during all the stimulation period a former high secretion, rapidly decreasing, and a second delayed peak of secretion.

When glucose is no more able to stimulate the β-cells, in the human subject several dysfunctions appear. Among them, one of the most serious is the so-called *Diabetes Mellitus* (DM). It is characterized by hyperglycaemia, due to a complete absence of insulin or to a partial deficit, related to its reduced biological efficiency. DM can be classified into two forms [Faglia, 1997]:

- DM type 1, Insulin-Dependent (IDMM). It is characterized by a quite complete absence of insulin secretion and represents the 10-15 % of all the DM pathologies;
- DM type 2, Non Insulin-Dependent (NIDMM). It is characterized by a low insulin secretion, associated with tissue refractoriness to insulin activity; it represents the 85-90% of all the DM pathologies.

In order to model the mechanism of glucose regulation in the blood, we need to evaluate quantitatively how insulin controls the glucose absorption by the tissues as well as the stimulation action, done by glucose, on insulin production by the pancreas β-cells. This information is clinically considerable, because it permits to diagnose and classify different pathologies, and consequently to distinguish the forms of glucose intolerance due to type 1 or 2 DM. Clinical experience is in general based on experimental tests: Intra Venous Glucose Tolerance Test (IVGTT) and Intra Venous Insulin Tolerance Test (IVITT). Unfortunately, these techniques are invasive and sometimes not efficient. Consequently, many researches on mathematical models suited to reproduce insulin-glucose concentrations and temporal behaviors have recently focused.

Several models have been presented in the literature [G.M.Grodsky, 1972; J.R. Guyton, 1978]. The one called MINMOD, introduced by Bergman and Cobelli in the early Eighties, has found more interesting applications in medical practice. More recently, new interest has been devoted to this topics [G. Baratta, 2002; C. Dalla Man, 2002; A. De Gaetano, 2000], trying to improve the original model or suggesting new ones.

The temporal evolution of insulin and glucose is represented in this model by the compartmental scheme illustrated in Fig. 1 [G. Pacini, 1986].

This model is considered as an optimal one, provided that the following assumptions for the simulation of the kinetics of glucose distribution , following a glucose injection, are met:

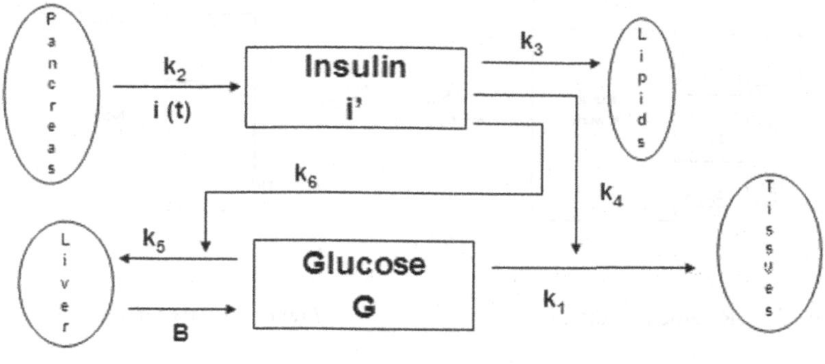

Figure 1. Compartmental scheme for MINMOD.

- it is sufficient to assume that injected glucose distributes into a single compartment;
- glucose disappearance occurs in proportion to thc plasma glucose concentration;
- insulin in a compartment remote from plasma (peripheral) accelerates the disappearance of glucose.

The glucose and insulin compartments are represented by functionals in Fig. 1, which act on the input functions (for example, food ingestion) and whose values are the output functions (i.e., insulin and glucose) of the model. The parameters and variables of the model are the following ones:

- insulin and glucose concentration in plasma: i' and G (in $\mu U/ml$ and mg/dl, respectively);
- concentration of insulin input: $i(t)$ (in $\mu U/ml$);
- glucose concentration in plasma at time $t = 0$ (i.e. the starting time): B_0 (in $mg/dl[minute]^{-1}$);
- concentration of net hepatic glucose: $B = B_0 - \left(k_5 + k_6 i'\right) G$ (in $mg/dl[minute]^{-1}$);
- kinetics of insulin in the remote compartment: k_2, k_3(in $[minute]^{-1}$);
- effect of glucose to enhance its disappearance: k_1, k_5 (in $[minute]^{-1}$);
- effect of remote insulin to enhance glucose disappearance: k_4, k_6 (in $ml/[minute]^{-1}$).

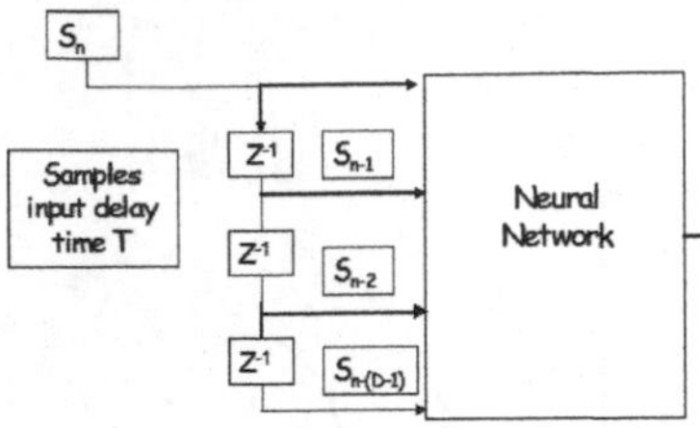

Figure 2. Retarded predictor.

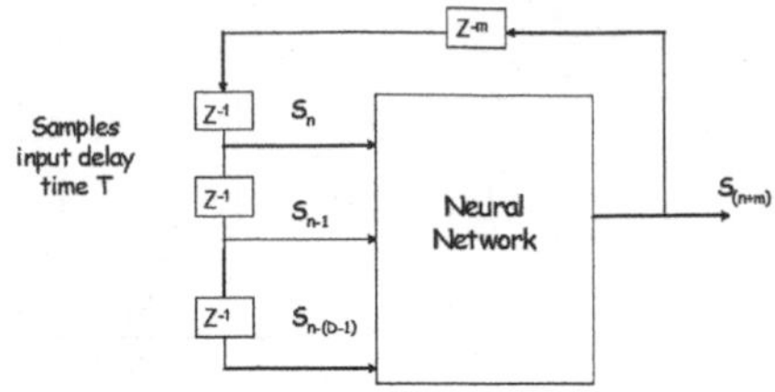

Figure 3. Recursive predictor.

Usually, the analysis for determining the glucose behavior, and the parameters used in the differential equations of MINMOD, is effectuated using IVGTT and least mean squares methods. Unfortunately these techniques are not so effective, because there is a large number of complex variables present in the human organism. Then a robust technique to obtain the correct glucose response is mandatory. In this regard, we propose in this paper a novel approach to forecast the glucose behavior of the MINMOD model, by fitting the response of this model to real data. It is based on a predictive structure, where a neural network is trained to estimate future samples of the glucose time series, based on past samples of the same one.

2. Prediction for Glucose Behavior in MINMOD

For MINMOD glucose behavior prediction we have utilized two different predictors, retarded and recursive, based on neural network. The compartmental scheme of predictors used are shown in Fig. 2 and Fig. 3.

In the first case, with retarded predictor, we have used a samples set input, S_n, delayed of a time T (Time Lag) chosen equal to 1. According to clinical experience in the following we use 3 samples $(D = 3)$ and glucose time series is sampled at a rate of 20 minutes. We remark that the optimal embanding parameters for each time series, T and D, can be chosen using classical methods in time series analysis [Abarbanel, 1986]. However values of T and D larger than the ones previously indicated make the model unsuited for patient's use. Then the net is trained to forecast the sample S_{n+m} at a distance m. In the other case, recursive predictor, we use as inputs the samples $S_n, S_{n-1} \ldots$. Then the prediction of sample S_{n+m} comes from a feedback of the past predictes sample.

We will briefly introduce in this section the architecture of the neural network used in this regard. It is based on a MoG (mixture of gaussian) model, where the distribution of data is the joint space. The joint density of data $p\left(\underline{x}, \underline{y}\right)$ can be estimated with no distinction between input and output variables. The joint density is successively conditioned, so that the resulting $p\left(\underline{y} \mid \underline{x}\right)$

can be used for obtaining the mapping to be approximated [Bishop, 1995]. The density $p\left(\underline{y} \mid \underline{x}\right)$ is based on the determination of a mixture $p\left(\underline{x} \mid \underline{y}\right)$ of C different Gaussian components in in the joint input-output space $D \times N$; i.e.:

$$p\left(\underline{x}, \underline{y}\right) = \sum_{j=1}^{C} \pi^{(j)} G^{(j)}_{\underline{x},\underline{y}}\left(\underline{x}, \underline{y}\right) \tag{1}$$

where $\pi^{(j)}$is the prior probability of the j-th Gaussian component $G^{(j)}_{\underline{x},\underline{y}}$, $j = 1 \ldots C$, which is equal to:

$$G^{(j)}_{\underline{x},\underline{y}}\left(\underline{x}, \underline{y}\right) = \alpha^{(j)} \exp\left[-\frac{1}{2}\left(\underline{z} - \underline{m}^{(j)}\right)^{t} \underline{K}^{(j)^{-1}}\left(\underline{z} - \underline{m}^{(j)}\right)\right] \tag{2}$$

$$\underline{z} = \begin{bmatrix} \underline{x} \\ \underline{y} \end{bmatrix}; \alpha^{(j)} = (2\pi)^{-\frac{D+N}{2}} \left|\underline{K}^{(j)}\right|^{-\frac{1}{2}} \tag{3}$$

with its mean and covariance matrix respectively equal to:

$$\underline{m}^{(j)} = \begin{bmatrix} \underline{m_{\underline{x}}}^{(j)} \\ \underline{m_{\underline{y}}}^{(j)} \end{bmatrix}; \quad \underline{K}^{(j)} = \begin{bmatrix} \underline{K}^{(j)}_{\underline{xx}} & \underline{K}^{(j)}_{\underline{xy}} \\ \underline{K}^{(j)}_{\underline{yx}} & \underline{K}^{(j)}_{\underline{yy}} \end{bmatrix} \tag{4}$$

The density model $p\left(\underline{y} \mid \underline{x}\right)$ is evidently based on a suitable clustering procedure yielding several regions of the input space where the input-output mapping can be locally approximated by the linear functions $\underline{m}^{(j)}_{\underline{y}|\underline{x}}$, j=1...C. In fact, when an input pattern $\underline{x}$ is presented to the network, the corresponding output $\underline{y}$ can be determined in two ways:

Soft Least Square Estimation: $\underline{y}_{soft} = \sum_{j=1}^{C} h_j\left(\underline{x}\right) \underline{m}^{(j)}_{\underline{y}|\underline{x}}$;

Hard Least Square Estimation: $\underline{y}_{hard} = \underline{m}^{(q)}_{\underline{y}|\underline{x}}; q = \arg\max_j \left\{h_j\left(\underline{x}\right)\right\}$

Several preliminary tests encouraged us to use the Soft Least Square Estimation, since its evident smoothness in approximating the mapping can ensure better results. The architecture of the MoG neural network resulting from the determination of the previous density model, i.e. formulas from (1) to (4), is shown in Fig. 4. In order to train an MoG network we can adopt the SHEM (Splitting Hierarchical Expectation Maximization) algorithm proposed in[M. Panella, 2003]. It is based on the maximum likelihood approach for estimating the parameters of the whole Gaussian mixture. The most important benefit of SHEM is the automatic selection of the number C of Gaussian components. It employs a hierarchical approach based on a constructive procedure, where C is increased progressively and only one run of the EM algorithm is necessary for each value of C. In fact, the SHEM algorithm eliminates the random initializations of EM and consequently the necessity to optimize different

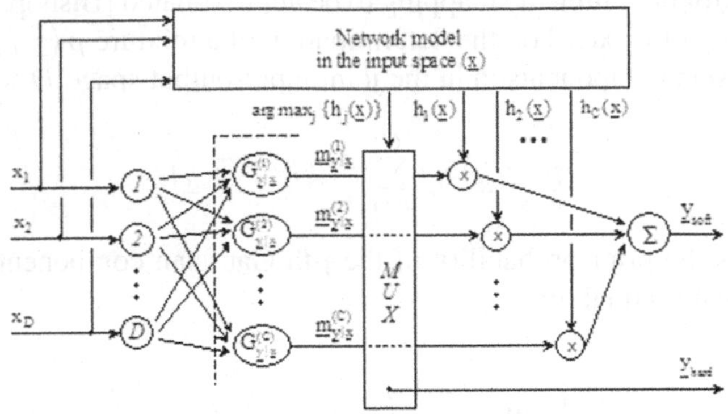

Figure 4. Architecture of the MoG network.

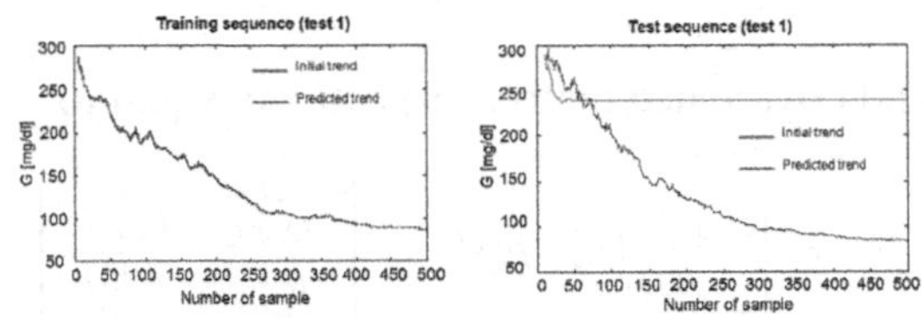

Figure 5. Analysis of retarded and recursive predictor in test 1.

EM solutions for a fixed C. Consequently, the computational cost of SHEM is heavily reduced.

The implementation of a predictor will coincide with the determination of a non-linear data driven function approximation model. For this purpose, in [9] we employed the MoG model illustrated in Sect. 2, trained by the SHEM algorithm; the resulting predictor will be denoted as "MoG Predictor".

Analysis of results

In the following we show in Table 1 the results with a comparison of Signal-to-Noise ratio (SNR) defined by $10\log_{10}\frac{\sum_n S_n^2}{\sum_n (S_n-\hat{S_n})^2}$ where $\hat{S_n}$ represent the predicted value using MoG network that is $\underline{y}_{soft}$. We analyzed different cases using predictors illustrated in Sect.2, and illustrating six different figures that represent the response of the recursive analysis in the different cases. As evidenced in Table 1 the training procedure is performed by progressive increasing the number of sequences (glucose temporal evolution), thus increasing the regularization of the trained MoG network.

Table 1. Comparison between Signal-to-Noise ratio (SNR).

Test	Input set 500 elements set (SNR)	Training predictor test (SNR)	Retarded predictor test (SNR)	Recursive
1	3 sequences for training 2 sequences for predictors	40.504 dB	34.016 dB	2.1381 dB
2	8 sequences for training 7 sequences for predictors	38.524 dB	38.524 dB	9.6571 dB
3	50 sequences for training 30 sequences for predictors	38.024 dB	37.736 dB	28.496 dB

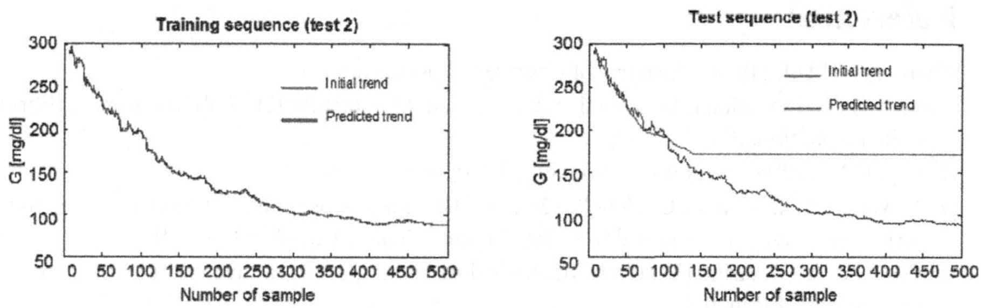

Figure 6. Analysis of retarded and recursive predictor in test 2.

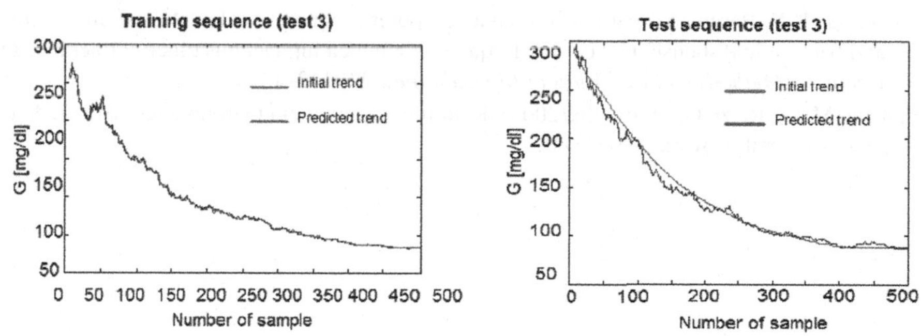

Figure 7. Analysis of retarded and recursive predictor in test 3.

We can observe that with a progressive increasing of input test set, we can follow the complete trend of glucose behavior as shown in previous table.

3. Conclusion

In this paper, we have proved that by means of neural networks, we can predict the glucose temporal evolution for patients. Moreover the analysis of patient's past clinical history has been shown to be effective in order to drastically lower the number of experimental observation needed to fit the correct glucose evolution. Consequently, from a medical and therapeutic point of view, this method may have some interesting implications, in order to single out possible pathological cases, without involving techniques which are invasive for human patients.

References

Abarbanel, H.D.I. (1986). Analysis of observed chaotic data.

Baratta, G., F. Barcellona, G. Lucidi A.M. Bersani M. Coli (2002). Stability and equilibrium points in minmod for glucose.

Bishop, C.M. (1995). Neural networks for pattern recognition.

Dalla Man, C., A. Caumo, C. Cobelli (2002). The oral glucose minimal model: estimation of insulin sensitivity from a meal test. *IEEE Trans. Biom. Eng.*, (49):419–429.

De Gaetano, A., O. Arino (2000). Mathematical modelling of the intravenous glucose tolerance test. Technical Report 40.

Faglia, G. (1997). Malattie del sistema endocrino e del metabolismo.

Grodsky, G.M. (1972). A threshold distribution hypothesis for packet storage of insulin and its mathematical modeling. *J. Cli. Inv.*, (51):2047–2059.

Guyton, J.R., O.F. Foster, J.S. Soeldner M.H. Tan C.B. Kahn L. Koncz R.E. Gleason (1978). A model of glucose-insulin homeostasis in man that incorporates the heterogeneous fast pool theory of pancreatic insulin release. *Diabetes*, (27):1027–1042.

Pacini, G., R.N. Bergman (1986). Minmod: a computer program to calculate insulin sensitivity and pancreatic responsivity from the frequently sampled intravenous glucose tolerance test. *Computer Methods and Programs in Biomedicine*, (23):113–122.

Panella, M., A. Rizzi, G. Martinelli (2003). Refining accuracy of environmental data prediction by mog neural network. *NEUCOM*.

ASSESSING THE RELIABILITY OF COMMUNICATION NETWORKS THROUGH MACHINE LEARNING TECHNIQUES

Claudio M. Rocco S.[1] and Marco Muselli[2]

[1]*Facultad de Ingenieria*
Universidad Central Venezuela, Caracas, Venezuela
crocco@reacciun.ve

[2]*Istituto di Elettronica e di Ingegneria dell'Informazione e delle Telecomunicazioni*
Consiglio Nazionale delle Ricerche, Genova, Italy
marco.muselli@ieiit.cnr.it

Abstract The reliability of communication networks is assessed by employing two machine learning algorithms, Support Vector Machines (SVM) and Hamming Clustering (HC), acting on a subset of possible system configurations, generated by a Monte Carlo simulation and an appropriate Evaluation Function. The experiments performed with two different reliability measures show that both methods yield excellent predictions, though the performances of models generated by HC are significantly better than those of SVM.

Keywords: Reliability, Communication network, Machine learning, Hamming Clustering, Support Vector Machine

1. Introduction

The central role played by communication systems in most real world situations requires an adequate design phase of the networks to be realized or updated. Besides basic constraints concerning the links to be established or the performances to be achieved (connection speed, throughput, etc.), an important issue to be addressed regards the reliability of the communication system.

A convenient way of modeling communication system is to adopt an undirected or a directed connected graph, called *Reliability Block Diagram* (RBD), in which every node is associated with a system component. Edges

B. Apolloni et al. (eds.), Biological and Artificial Intelligence Environments, 375–381

represent links among them and can be associated with a binary variable x_i, assuming value 1 if the corresponding connection behaves correctly or value 0 otherwise. In this way, the whole system can be described by a Boolean vector $\boldsymbol{x} = (x_1, x_2, \ldots, x_d)$, being d the number of edges in the RBD.

Also the state of the whole system can be operating or failed, and is therefore described by a binary variable y. The Boolean mapping that associates every input vector $\boldsymbol{x}$ to its corresponding output y is called Structure Function (SF).

With every component x_i we can associate a real value P_i in the range $[0, 1]$, which represents the probability that the corresponding link behaves correctly. Usually, these probabilities are independent. A measure of the reliability for a communication system is then given by the expected value of its SF. Different definitions for the SF lead to different reliability indexes.

For example, the most widely studied reliability measure ($s - t$ reliability) assumes that two particular nodes, s (the source) and t (the terminal), are fixed: the system is operating if there exists at least a working path from the source node s to the terminal node t. In this case a depth-first procedure [Reingold et al., 1977] can be employed to compute the SF.

However, in communication networks the connectivity is not a sufficient condition for determining an operating state and the success of the network also requires that a sufficient flow is guaranteed, which depends on the capacity of the elements involved. Thus, a communication system performs well if and only if it is possible to transmit successfully the required capacity. In this case, to evaluate if a given state is capable or not of transporting a required flow, the max-flow min-cut algorithm [Reingold et al., 1977] can be adopted.

An important problem with these reliability indexes and their extensions is that in almost all the contexts of interest their evaluation require the solution of an NP-hard problem [Stivaros and Sutner, 1997]. A possible way to reduce the computational burden is to employ Monte Carlo techniques, which attempt to produce an estimate of the network reliability by analyzing a subset of possible system states x.

Generally, Monte Carlo techniques require a large number of SF evaluations to establish the reliability of a system; therefore, it seems to be convenient to employ a machine learning method for approximating the desired reliability expression through a reduced collection of SF values. To this aim several different approaches have been considered in the literature: Neural Networks (NN) [Mitchell et al., 2000], Decision Trees (DT) [Rocco, 2003], Support Vector Machines (SVM) [Rocco and Moreno, 2002] and Hamming

Clustering (HC) [Rocco and Muselli, 2004]. Among them, only DT and HC are able to retrieve an analytical form for the approximated reliability expression of the network. A direct comparison [Rocco and Muselli, 2004] shows that the performance of HC (in terms of accuracy) is significantly superior to that of DT.

Nevertheless, SVM are widely considered as one of the classification devices that achieve the highest values of accuracy in most real-world applications. Although SVM are not able to generate a comprehensible form for the approximated reliability expression, one may wonder if they lead to a minor number of errors in a practical situation. To this aim we compare empirical models, produced by SVM and HC when applied to the samples generated by a Monte Carlo simulation for different SF.

2. Support Vector Machines

Support Vector Machines provide a novel approach to the two-category classification problem [Vapnik, 1998]. Suppose we have to find the unknown decision function $g : \mathbb{R}^d \to -1, +1$ that solves a given classification problem, by employing a set of n examples $(\boldsymbol{x}_1, y_1), (\boldsymbol{x}_2, y_2), \ldots, (\boldsymbol{x}_n, y_n)$, obtained through a random sampling of $g(\boldsymbol{x})$. Like several other classification techniques (e.g. neural networks, radial basis functions networks), SVM searches for a good approximation of $g(\boldsymbol{x})$ by analyzing expressions given by $\text{sign}(f(\boldsymbol{x}))$, where f is a real function $f : \mathbb{R}^d \to \mathbb{R}$ and $\text{sign}(z)$ gives value $+1$ if $z \geq 0$ and value -1 otherwise.

In particular, the following form for the function $f(\boldsymbol{x})$ is considered by SVM:

$$f(\boldsymbol{x}) = b + \sum_{i=1}^{n} \alpha_i y_i K(\boldsymbol{x}_i, \boldsymbol{x}) \tag{1}$$

where the symmetric function $K(\boldsymbol{u}, \boldsymbol{v})$ must be chosen among the kernels of Reproducing Kernel Hilbert Spaces; for example [Vapnik, 1998]:

- the Gaussian radial basis function (GRBF) $K(\boldsymbol{u}, \boldsymbol{v}) = e^{-\|\boldsymbol{u}-\boldsymbol{v}\|^2/2\sigma^2}$
- the polynomial function $K(\boldsymbol{u}, \boldsymbol{v}) = (\boldsymbol{u} \cdot \boldsymbol{v} + 1)^p$.

The scalar quantities α_i in (1) are obtained by solving the following quadratic programming problem:

$$\min_{\boldsymbol{\alpha}} \frac{1}{2} \sum_{i=1}^{n} \sum_{j=1}^{n} \alpha_i \alpha_j y_i y_j K(\boldsymbol{x}_i, \boldsymbol{x}_j) - \sum_{i=1}^{n} \alpha_i$$

subject to the constraints

$$\sum_{i=1}^{n} \alpha_i y_i = 0 \,, \qquad 0 \leq \alpha_i \leq C, \quad \text{for every } i = 1, \ldots, n$$

where C is a real constant that derives from the application of Regularization Theory to the solution of the classification problem at hand.

It can be easily seen that there is a 1-1 correspondence between the scalars α_i and the examples $(\boldsymbol{x}_i, y_i)$ in the training set. In particular, when $\alpha_i = 0$, the corresponding pair $(\boldsymbol{x}_i, y_i)$ does not give any contribution to the sum in (1). Consequently, only the points $\boldsymbol{x}_i$ with $\alpha_i \neq 0$ are considered in the construction of the function $f(\boldsymbol{x})$; these points are called *support vectors*, from which the name Support Vector Machine for the device that implements $f(\boldsymbol{x})$.

The application of SVM to the problem of estimating the reliability expression of a given communication network can be directly performed by employing the above general procedure to obtain a good approximation for the SF. Since SF is a Boolean function we must substitute the output value $y = -1$ in place of $y = 0$ to use the standard training procedure for SVM.

3. Hamming Clustering

As previously observed, the SF of a network can be written as a Boolean function; thus, at least in principle, any method for the synthesis of digital circuits is able to retrieve the desired SF from a sufficiently large training set. Unfortunately, classical methods for Boolean function reconstruction do not care about the output assigned to a case not belonging to the given training set. Better results can be obtained by adopting a new logical synthesis technique, called Hamming Clustering (HC) [Muselli and Liberati, 2002], which is able to achieve performances comparable to those of best classification methods, in terms of both efficiency and efficacy.

It can be easily seen that every system state $\boldsymbol{x}$ can be associated with a binary string with length d. As usual, a simple metric, called Hamming distance, can be introduced in the space of binary strings having the same length d; it is defined as the number $d_H(\boldsymbol{x}, \boldsymbol{z})$ of different bits in the two strings $\boldsymbol{x}$ and $\boldsymbol{z}$:

$$d_H(\boldsymbol{x}, \boldsymbol{z}) = \sum_{i=1}^{d} |x_i - z_i|$$

HC proceeds by grouping together binary strings that belong to the same class and are close to each other according to the Hamming distance. A basic concept in the procedure followed by HC is the notion of cluster, sharing the same definition of implicant in classic theory of logical synthesis.

A cluster is the collection of all the binary strings having the same values in a fixed subset of components; as an example, the four binary strings '01001', '01101', '11001', '11101' form a cluster since all of them only have the values 1, 0, and 1 in the second, the fourth and the fifth component, respectively. This cluster is usually written as '*1*01', by placing a don't care symbol '*' in the positions that are not fixed, and it is said that the cluster '*1*01' covers the four binary strings above.

Every cluster can be associated with a logical product among the components of x, which gives output 1 for all and only the binary strings covered by that cluster. The desired Boolean function can then be constructed by generating a valid collection of clusters for the binary strings belonging to a selected class.

The procedure employed by HC consists of the following four steps:

1 Choose at random an example (x, y) in the training set.

2 Build a cluster of points including x and associate that cluster with the class y.

3 Remove the example (x, y) from the training set. If the construction is not complete, go to Step 1.

4 Simplify the set of clusters generated and build the corresponding Boolean function.

Once the example (x, y) in the training set has been randomly chosen at Step 1, a cluster of points including x is to be generated and associated with the class y. As suggested by the Occam's Razor principle, smaller sum-of-product expressions for the Boolean function to be retrieved perform better; this leads to prefer clusters that cover as many as possible training examples belonging to class y.

However, searching for the optimal cluster in this sense leads to an NP-hard problem; consequently, greedy alternatives must be employed to avoid excessive computation times. One possible choice is to apply the *Maximum covering Cube* (MC) criterion [Muselli and Liberati, 2002], which sequentially introduces a don't care symbol in the position that reduces the Hamming distance from the highest number of training examples belonging to class y, while avoiding to cover training examples associated with the opposite class. Several trials on artificial and real-world classification problems have established the good properties of the MC criterion.

4. The Proposed Approach

To evaluate the performance of the methods presented in the previous sections, the network shown in Fig. 1 has been considered [Yoo and Deo, 1988]. It is assumed that each link has reliability $P_i = 0.90$ and capacity of 100 units.

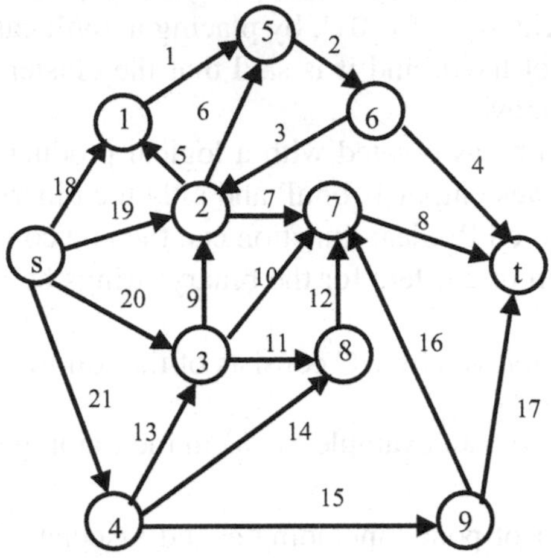

Figure 1. Network considered in experimental analysis [Yoo and Deo, 1988].

The goal of the analysis is twofold: to measure the accuracy of the models produced by the considered techniques and to evaluate the quality of the reliability estimates. The first task is performed through a 10-fold cross-validation on a set of randomly chosen N_T examples $(\boldsymbol{x}, y)$, where $y = SF(\boldsymbol{x})$. Further N_M system states are then required to provide a reliability estimate.

Two different $s - t$ reliability metrics, simple connectivity and guaranteed flow, have been considered in our analysis. In the first case we have selected $N_T = 2000$ and in the latter $N_T = 5000$; the value of N_M has been always set to 10000. Different kernels were tried for the SVM model with different parameter choices; only best results are presented.

Table 1 shows the accuracies obtained for SVM and HC when analyzing simple connectivity. The best SVM corresponds to a fourth order polynomial kernel, based on 675 support vectors. The average system reliability based on a depth-first procedure was 0.9943, while the approximated system reliability obtained with SVM and HC was 0.9941 and 0.9934, respectively.

The accuracies obtained with SVM and HC when analyzing guaranteed flow are shown in Tab. 2. Again the best SVM corresponds to a fourth order polynomial kernel, based on 556 support vectors. The average system reliability based on a max-flow min-cut procedure was 0.8976, while the approximated system reliability using SVM and HC was 0.8989 and 0.8990, respectively.

Table 1. Accuracy results obtained with cross-validation for simple connectivity.

Model	Number of Support Vectors	Training Accuracy (%)	Testing Accuracy (%)
SVM-Polynomial: $d = 4$	675	100	95.15
SVM-Polynomial: $d = 5$	845	100	95.10
SVM-GRBF: $1/2\sigma^2 = 0.016$	481	100	94.60
SVM-GRBF: $1/2\sigma^2 = 0.128$	1529	100	94.10
HC	16.1 (Rules)	100	99.80

Table 2. Accuracy results obtained with cross-validation for guaranteed flow.

Model	Number of Support Vectors	Training Accuracy (%)	Testing Accuracy (%)
SVM-Polynomial: $d = 4$	556	100	98.46
SVM-Polynomial: $d = 5$	693	100	98.36
SVM-GRBF: $1/2\sigma^2 = 0.016$	404	100	98.26
SVM-GRBF: $1/2\sigma^2 = 0.032$	512	100	98.36
HC	25.3 (Rules)	100	99.38

In both cases models derived from SVM and HC correctly classify all the examples in the training set, while showing good generalization capacity. However, the results with HC are better than those obtained with SVM. The reliability measures produced by both methods are always satisfactory.

References

Mitchell, M., Peças Lopes, J. A., Fidalgo, J. N., and McCalley, J. (2000). Using a neural network to predict the dynamic frequency response of a power system to an under-frequency load shedding scenario. In *IEEE Summer Meeting*.

Muselli, Marco and Liberati, Diego (2002). Binary rule generation via Hamming Clustering. *IEEE Transactions on Knowledge and Data Engineering*, 14:1258–1268.

Reingold, E., Nievergelt, J., and Deo, N. (1977). *Combinatorial Algorithms: Theory and Practice*. New Jersey: Prentice Hall.

Rocco, C. M. (2003). A rule induction approach to improve Monte Carlo system reliability assessment. *Reliability Engineering and System Safety*, 82:87–94.

Rocco, C. M. and Moreno, J. M. (2002). Reliability evaluation using Monte Carlo simulation and support vector machine. In *Lecture Notes in Computer Science*, volume 2329, pages 147–155. Berlin: Springer-Verlag.

Rocco, C. M. and Muselli, M. (2004). Empirical models based on machine learning techniques for determining approximate reliability expressions. *Reliability Engineering and System Safety*, 83:301–309.

Stivaros, C. and Sutner, K. (1997). Optimal link assignments for all-terminal network reliabilit. *Discrete Applied Mathematics*, 75:285–295.

Vapnik, Vladimir N. (1998). *Statistical Learning Theory*. New York: John Wiley & Sons.

Yoo, Y. B. and Deo, N. (1988). A comparison of algorithms for terminal-pair reliability. *IEEE Transactions on Reliability*, 37:216–221.

DYNAMICAL RECONSTRUCTION AND CHAOS FOR DISRUPTION PREDICTION IN TOKAMAK REACTORS

Matteo Cacciola, Domenico Costantino, Antonino Greco, Francesco Carlo Morabito, Mario Versaci
Università "Mediterranea" degli Studi di Reggio Calabria
Dipartimento di Informatica Matematica Elettronica e Trasporti (DIMET)
Via Graziella Feo di Vito, I-89100 Reggio Calabria, Italy
morabito@unirc.it, {d.costantino, versaci}@ing.unirc.it

http://neurolab.ing.unirc.it

Abstract Disruption is a sudden loss of magnetic confinement that can cause a damage of the machine walls and support structures. For this reason is of practical interest to be able to early detect the onset of the event. This paper presents a novel technique of early prediction of plasma disruption in Tokamak reactors which uses Neural Networks and Chaos theory. In particular, dynamical reconstruction and chaos theory have been considered for choosing the time window of prediction and to select the inputs set for the prediction system. Multi-Layer-Perceptron nets have been exploited for predicting the incoming of disruption.

Keywords: Disruptions, Tokamaks, Chaos Theory

Introduction to the Problem

Disruption in a Tokamak device is an undesired event of sudden loss of the energy confinement, where the plasma current and the thermal energy content of a Tokamak plasma discharge collapse in an uncontrollable way, thereby generating mechanical forces and heat loads which threaten the structural integrity of the surrounding structures. Therefore, this event is considered a critical issue for the design of future experimental reactors. In this respect, developing reliable tools for the on-line prediction of disruption is a relevant design activity for improving the performance of new devices. Observation of disruptions occurring in operating machines is the main source of information, to be used for understanding the underlying physical mechanisms as well as to study the possible disruption precursors. Recently, the Joint European Torus (JET), some work has been carried out based on the analysis of a block of disruptive shots that have been made available by the JET Team. The main

B. Apolloni et al. (eds.), Biological and Artificial Intelligence Environments, 383–389

objective is to design a signal processor capable to predict the onset of a disruption sufficiently in advance for the intervention of a control action. In the recent literature, some works addressing the same problem have been proposed [Wroblewsky, 1997], [Morabito and al, 2001]. Neural Networks (NN's) and Fuzzy Inference Systems (FISs) appears to be appropriate tools for facing this problem from various perspectives. Firstly, there is a need of fusing various sensory information in order to enhance the detection capability and to exploit different detection mechanisms. Secondly, the network schemes are also more amenable to hardware implementation of the alarm system than traditional approaches. Finally, the FIS can play a relevant role for allowing expert knowledge to be translated in syntactic linguistic rules that are easily embedded in the signal processor. The present study aims to design a processing system that could be able to predict the incoming of disruptions by means of a suitable choice of time windows of prediction. In particular, dynamical reconstruction and chaos theory have been considered for choosing the time window of prediction and to select the inputs set for the prediction system. Multi-Layer-Perceptron nets have been exploited for predicting the incoming of disruption. The goal of the procedure is automatically predict the value of Mode_Lock, strongly linearly correlated with the *ttd*, which is not directly measurable by a physical sensor, in order to in-time alarm the control system. The rest of this paper is organized as follows: In the next section, we describe the features of the available database, that refers to the JET machine. In Section 2, we briefly review the chaos theory. Section 3 describes the way how chaos theory can be applied to the disruption prediction problem. The paper ends with Section 4 which contains the conclusions of the work.

1. The JET Experimental Database

In this database, a set of measurements monitoring the plasma shots are stored. A large number of them were analysed with the purpose to find the technical causes, the precursors and the physical mechanisms of disruptions. The analysed files derives from many years of experimental activity carried out at the Culham Center, Oxfordshire, London (United Kingdom). The database was built starting from the dynamics of a disruption in the zone of flat-top of the plasma current in which the plasma is monitored to obtain a constant plasma current (IPLA) and a stable confinement in terms of shape and position. The choice of the variables to be used as *predictors* among the ones available in the database is always the result of a compromise between the physical availability of measurements and reliability of the related sensors and the peculiarities of the processing model (kind of NNs) carried out in previous works. In the case of missing data, some kind of filtering is used in order to complete the time series. The interval of observation of the variables was limited to the time interval of $[td-440ms; td-40ms]$ according to some physical insight; the left 40ms were omitted as not being relevant, since there is no sufficient time left to control the shot. The time of sampling is 20ms and 20 samples for each channel have been used. In order to test the null hypothesis and verify the percent of false positive occurring, we have considered 1167 shots without disruption, and 701 disruptive shots. A record distinguishes the kind of shot: the outputs of the network are labelled by means of *vtargetTS* for training database, *vtargetVS* for validation database and *vtargetTest* for testing database. The outputs were identified by considering that, in correspondence of a shot without disruption, we have a series of 20 zeros (non disruptive shot). If the shot is a disruptive one, the series of 20 values is a set of numbers in the range (0, 1) and thus a sigmoidal function is used to represent the risk of disruption. In the present approach, the series of 20 numbers is reconstructed on-line after the prediction of the *Mode_Lock* variable.

2. Chaos Theory: a Bird's Eye Overview

A dynamical system is any system that evolves in time. Dynamical systems whose behavior changes continuously in time are mathematically described by a coupled set of first-order autonomous ordinary differential equations $\frac{d\bar{X}}{dt} = \bar{F}(\bar{X}, \lambda)$ where the components of the vector $\bar{X}$ are the dynamical variables of the system, λ is a set of parameters that we denote as *control parameters*, and the components of the vector field $\bar{F}$ are the dynamical rules governing the behaviour of the dynamical variables. There is no loss of generality in the restriction to *autonomous systems*, where $\bar{F}$ is not an explicit function of t is not an explicit function of $\mathbb{R}^n$ can be transformed into an autonomous system in $\mathbb{R}^{n+1}$. Under modest smoothness assumptions about the dynamical rules, the solutions of the dynamical systems are unique and the dynamical system is *deterministic*; that is, the state of the dynamical system for all time is uniquely determined by the state at any one time. The *existence* of unique solution does not necessarily mean that explicit algebraic representations exist. However, if explicit algebraic solutions do exist and they can be used to predict the future behavior of the system for all initial conditions, then the system is said to be integrable. All linear dynamical systems are integrable. Explicit solutions can be constructed for linear systems by first transforming to a new set of dynamical variables in which the governing equations become decoupled. One of the surprising and far-reaching mathematical discoveries of the past few decades has been that the solutions of deterministic nonlinear dynamical systems may be as random as the sequence of heads and tails in the toss of a fair coin. This behavior is called deterministic chaos. Essentially, chaos is a nonlinear behavior that exists between the realms of periodic and random. At first glance, some chaotic systems may appear to regular and periodic, whereas others will appear strictly random; in both cases closer examination topples these assumptions. Chaotic systems are deterministic and, the exact system state can be written as $\bar{X}(t) = [\bar{x}(t), \bar{x}(t - T_0), \ldots, \bar{x}(t - (k-1)T_0)] \in \mathbb{R}^k$ where t is a scalar index for the data series and T_0 is the interval of observations. A key component of chaotic data analysis is Takens' embedding theorem [Kennel et al., 1992].Given a dynamical system, a scalar data measurement, $s(t) = h(\bar{x}(t)) : \mathbb{R}^k \longrightarrow \mathbb{R}$, dependent on the system's complete dynamics can be reconstructed into a $d-$ dimensional vector series $\bar{y}(t) = [s(t), s(t+\tau), \ldots, s(t + (d-1)\tau)]$ where integer τ is called the time lag. Takens' theorem says that, if d is large enough, the vector series $y(t)$ reproduces many of the important dynamical characteristics of the original series, $X(t)$. Thus, one does not need the original vector series in order to analyse many of the system properties of the data series. A scalar function $s(t)$ describing the system is all that is necessary. To apply this theorem effectively, good choices for the lag τ and embedding dimension d are needed. Choice of τ should provide low correlation between adjacent elements in the embedded vector (so that the original data series is not mimicked) without being too long. One can use the first minimum of the average mutual information function $I_{(t)} = -\sum_{ij} p_{ij}(\tau) \ln \frac{p_{ij}(\tau)}{p_i p_j}$ for some partition on the real numbers p_i is the probability to find a time series value in the $i-$th interval, and p_{ij} is the joint probability that an observation falls into the $i-$th interval and the observation time τ later falls into the $j-$th. $I_{(t)}$ measures the average amount of information (bits) shared by two meaurements. According to the embedding theorem, the choice of d requires a priori knowledge of dimension (d_F) of the original attractor, which is unrealistic for experimental data. When d is chosen arbitrarily and happens to be too small as compared to d_F of the original attractor, this may sometimes result is so-called *false nearest neighbours* (FNN) in the reconstructed phase space [Broomhead and King, 1986]. Chaos arises from the exponential growth of infinitesimal perturbations, together with global folding mechanisms to guarantee boundedness of the solutions. This exponential instability is characterized by the spectrum of Lyapunov's Exponents (LEs). LEscan be considered as an estimation of the speed of convergence or divergence of the trajectors in a dynamic system near its attractor set. LEs are useful to classify the asintotical behaviour of the orbits of an dynamical system and gives us a qualitative and quantitative characterization of the beahviour of the system. Each dynamic system, which attractor has at least one positive LE, is defined as "chaotic", and its numerical value gives us the time t after which the mechanisms of the system turn unforseeable. The spectrum of LEs can be defined for continuous and discrete systems and their cardinality is equal to the embedding dimension. A LE is the radius of medium exponential divergence of two adjacent orbits and can be computed as $\lambda_{max} = \lim_{t\to\infty, |\Delta x| \to 0} \frac{1}{t} \ln \frac{|\Delta x(X_0, t)|}{\Delta x_0}$

where $\Delta x(X_0, t)$ represents the separation of two orbits. LE describes the behavior of two nearest points along a direction in the embedding dimension in the time domain; if the points go away then LE will be positive, else negative (null if the distance is constant) [Parker and Chua, 1986]. When a LE is positive, it exists an Horizon of Predictability (HOP); for $t >$ HOP the prediction breaks down. HOP can be calculate by $t_{horizon} \sim O(\frac{\log(a)}{LLE})$ where LLE is the largest LE and $\log(a)$ represents the requested time of variation (average) by two orbits to distance (% dependent by available data) In this work, since data change very quickly, we have choice a divergence of 3.5%.

3. Chaos & MLP for anticipation disruption

In this work we have analyze two disrupted shots (#55548 and #61439) and non-disrupted one (#62488). In order to apply chaos theory, we have verified that the Power Spectral Density (PSD) results distributed on several frequencies. To calculate τ and d we have applied: *(i)* the mutual information method considering first minimum (Figure 1); *(ii)* the FNN method considering the dimension which correspond the null value of the function (Figure 2).

Table 1 reports the achieved results for the embedding parameters.

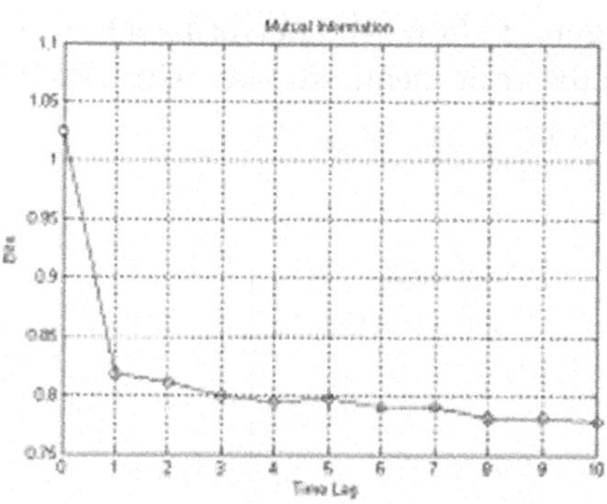

Figure 1. Mutual information for shot #55548. τ=4.

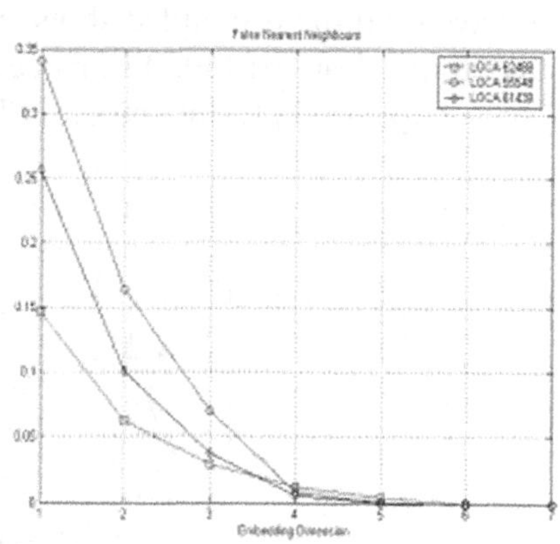

Figure 2. Application of FNN method for the shots under study.

To reduce the computational complexity, we have chosen the dimension that corre-sponds to a percentage of FFN < 1%. In our case, for the examined shots, m is reduced to 5. Table 2 shows LEs for dimension 5.

Shot	Time lag (τ)	Embedding dimension (m)
#55548	4	8
#61439	20	8
#62488	1	9

Table 1. Embedding parameters for shots under study.

Shot	λ_{max}
#55548	0.0553
#61439	0.01176
#62488	0.2389

Table 2. LEs for dimension 5.

Because λ_{max} is positive, the time series are chaotic. Once d and τ are computed, starting from $\bar{X}(t) = [\bar{x}(t), \bar{x}(t-T_0), \ldots, \bar{x}(t-(k-1)T_0)] \in \mathbb{R}^k$ we make the other five $\bar{y}(t) = [s(t), s(t+\tau), \ldots, s(t+(d-1)\tau)]$. In addition, we can compute HOP for each recomputed shot. By means of HOP we have resampled the original shots. In this way, each sample falls in the optimal time window prediction.

For the training step, we have train the MLP (5 inputs, 1 output and 2 hidden layers - logsig - logsig - purelin; Levenberg & Marquardt's learning algorithm) by using the original shots: five consecutive samples for inputs (five is the embedding dimension!) and the following sample for output. In particular, we have made a net for the worst shot (#55548). In the testing step, we have used the resampled shots. Figure 3 shows the performance of the net concerning shot #61439. In this case the root means square error (RMSE) is $7.6888\exp-005$ [Tesla/Ampere] (7.5%).

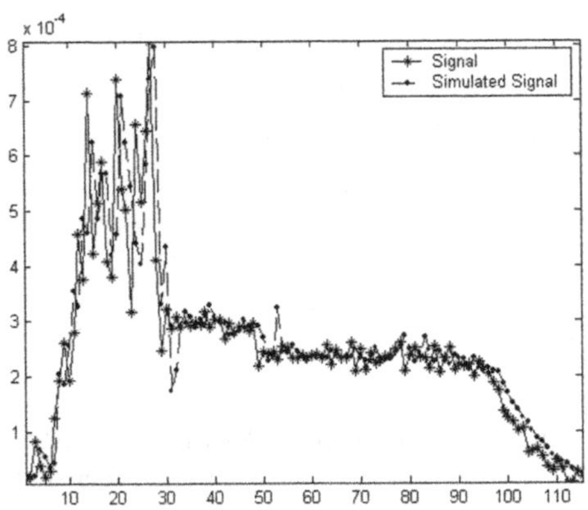

Figure 3. Performance of MLP for shot #61439

4. Conclusions

In this paper a novel technique of early prediction of plasma disruption in tokamak reactors which uses Neural Networks and Chaos theory. In particular, dynamical reconstruction and chaos theory have been considered for choosing the time window of prediction and to select the inputs set for the prediction system. MLP nets have been exploited for predicting the incoming of disruption. The time series under study are chaotic and the time windows prediction have supplied a good prediction of the Mode-Lock in terms of RMSE. The prediction of Mode_Lock, strongly linearly correlated with the *ttd*, which is not directly measurable by a physical sensor, in order to in-time alarm the control system.

References

Broomhead, D. and King, G.P. (1986). Extracting qualitative dynamics from experimental data, physica d. 20:217.

Kennel, M. B., Brown, R., and Abarbanel, H. D. I. (1992). Determining embedding dimension for phase-space reconstruction using a geometrical construction. *Phys. Rev. A 45*, page 3403.

Morabito, F. C. and al (2001). Fuzzy-neural approach to the prediction of disruptions in asdex upgrade, nuclear fusion. 41:1715–172.

Parker, T. S. and Chua, L. O. (1986). Practical numerical algorithms for chaotic systems, springer verlag.

Wroblewsky, D. (1997). Neural network evaluation of tokamak current profiles for real time control. rev. sci. instr. 68:1281.

List of Contributors

N. Nailah Binti Abdullah
Lirmm-University Montpellier II, 161 Rue Ada, Montpellier Cedex 5, France

Giovanni Aiello
DINFO, Dipartimento di Ingegneria Informatica
University of Palermo, Italy.
aiello.giovi@virgilio.it

Luís A. Alexandre
IT - Networks and Multimedia Group, Covilhã

Giovanni Aloisio
CACT, University of Lecce, Italy & SPACI Consortium, Italy
giovanni.aloisio@unile.it

Roberto Amato
Department of Physical Sciences, University of Napoli Federico II, via Cinthia 6, Napoli, Italy

G. Antoniol
RCOST - University of Sannio

Davide Anguita
Dept. of Biophysical and Electronic Engineering,
University of Genova, Genova, Italy.
anguita@dibe.unige.it

B. Apolloni
Dipartimento di Scienze dell'Informazione, Università degli Studi di Milano
Via Comelico 39/41, 20135 Milano, Italy
apolloni@dsi.unimi.it

B. Azzerboni
Dipartimento di Fisica della Materia e Tecnologie Fisiche Avanzate
Università degli Studi di Messina, Salita Sperone, 31 C.P. 57, 98166 Messina, Italy
azzerboni@ingegneria.unime.it, URL: http://www.eltgroup.polito.it

Alan Barbieri
Università di Parma
Dipartimento di Ingegneria dell'Informazione
Parco Area delle Scienze 181/A
43100 Parma - ITALY
barbieri@tlc.unipr.it

F. Barcellona
INFO-COM Dpt., University of Rome "La Sapienza", via Eudossiana 18,
00184 Rome, Italy
francesco.barcellona@uniroma1.it

Flavio Baronti
Dipartimento di Informatica, Università di Pisa
Via Buonarroti, 2 — 56100 Pisa (Italy)
baronti@di.unipi.it

S. Bassis
Dipartimento di Scienze dell'Informazione, Università degli Studi di Milano
Via Comelico 39/41, 20135 Milano, Italy
bassis@dsi.unimi.it

Francesco Baudi
University Magna Græcia of Catanzaro, Catanzaro, Italy

Diego Di Bernardo
Telethon Institute for Genetics and Medicine, Via Pietro Castellino 111 I-80131 Napoli, Italy

INFN - Italian Institure of Nuclear Physics Unit of Naples, via Cinthia 6, Italy

A.M. Bersani
Me.Mo.Mat Dpt., University of Rome "La Sapienza", via Scarpa 16,
00161 Rome, Italy
bersani@dmmm.uniroma1.it

Alberto Bertoni
DSI, Dipartimento di Scienze dell' Informazione,
Università degli Studi di Milano,
Via Comelico 39, 20135 Milano, Italia.
bertoni@dsi.unimi.it

Andrea Boni
DIT, University of Trento
Via Sommarive, 14, 38050 Trento Italy
andrea.boni@unitn.it

N. Alberto Borghese
Laboratory of Human Motion Analysis and Virtual Reality, MAVR, Department of Computer Science, University of Milano, Via Comelico 39 - 20135 Milano, Italy – http:://mavr.dsi.unimi.it

Matteo Cacciola
Università "Mediterranea" degli Studi di Reggio Calabria
Dipartimento di Informatica Matematica Elettronica e Trasporti (DIMET)
Via Graziella Feo di Vito, I-89100 Reggio Calabria, Italy
morabito@unirc.it, {d.costantino, versaci}@ing.unirc.it
http://neurolab.ing.unirc.it

Massimo Cafaro
CACT, University of Lecce, Italy & SPACI Consortium, Italy
massimo.cafaro@unile.it

Stefano Cagnoni
Università di Parma
Dipartimento di Ingegneria dell'Informazione
Parco Area delle Scienze 181/A
43100 Parma - ITALY
cagnoni@ce.unipr.it

Francesco Camastra
INFM - DISI, University of Genova, Via Dodecaneso 35, 16146 Genova, Italy
camastra@ieee.org

Paola Campadelli
Università degli Studi di Milano,
Dipartimento di Scienze dell'Informazione,
via Comelico 39/41,
20135, Milano
Campadelli@dsi.unimi.it
http://homes.dsi.unimi.it/~campadel/LAIV/index.htm

Mario Cannataro
University Magna Græcia of Catanzaro, Catanzaro, Italy

M. Carpentieri
Dipartimento di Fisica della Materia e Tecnologie Fisiche Avanzate
Università degli Studi di Messina, Salita Sperone, 31 C.P. 57, 98166 Messina, Italy
carpentieri@ingegneria.unime.it, URL: http://www.eltgroup.polito.it

Rita Casadonte
University Magna Græcia of Catanzaro, Catanzaro, Italy

Elena Casiraghi
Università degli Studi di Milano,
Dipartimento di Scienze dell'Informazione,
via Comelico 39/41,
20135, Milano
Casiraghi@dsi.unimi.it
http://homes.dsi.unimi.it/~campadel/LAIV/index.htm

D. Cauz, M. Giordani, G. Pauletta, M. Rossi, and L.Santi
Dipartimento di Fisica, Universita di Udine e I.N.F.N. di Udine
Via delle Scienze 208,
33100 Udine, Italia

M. Ceccarelli
RCOST - University of Sannio

Alessio Ceroni
Dipartimento di Sistemi e Informatica, Università di Firenze, Italy
aceroni@dsi.unifi.it

S.A. Cerri
Lirmm-University Montpellier II, 161 Rue Ada, Montpellier Cedex 5, France

Antonio Chella
DINFO, Viale delle Scienze 90128, Palermo, Italy

C.N.R. – ICAR, Viale delle Scienze 90128, Palermo, Italy

Angelo Ciaramella
Department of Mathematichs and Informatics, University of Salerno, Via Ponte don Melillo, I-84084, Fisciano (SA), Italy

Giovanni Cino
Department of Information Technologies, University of Milan, via Bramante 65 –26013 Crema (CR) Italy , e-mail pizzi@dti.unimi.it

M. Claudio S. Rocco
Facultad de Ingenieria
Universidad Central Venezuela, Caracas, Venezuela
crocco@reacciun.ve

Giulio Colavolpe
Università di Parma
Dipartimento di Ingegneria dell'Informazione
Parco Area delle Scienze 181/A
43100 Parma - ITALY
giulio@unipr.it

Domenico Costantino
Università "Mediterranea" degli Studi di Reggio Calabria
Dipartimento di Informatica Matematica Elettronica e Trasporti (DIMET)
Via Graziella Feo di Vito, I-89100 Reggio Calabria, Italy
d.costantino@ing.unirc.it
http://neurolab.ing.unirc.it

Francesco Costanzo
University Magna Græcia of Catanzaro, Catanzaro, Italy

Giovanni Cuda
University Magna Græcia of Catanzaro, Catanzaro, Italy

L. Delfino
IST - Istituto Nazionale per la Ricerca sul Cancro
Largo R. Benzi 10, 16132 Genova, Italy

Ciro Donalek
Department of Physical Sciences, University of Napoli Federico II, via Cinthia 6, Napoli, Italy

Maria Concetta Faniello
University Magna Græcia of Catanzaro, Catanzaro, Italy

Andrea Fantasia
Department of Information Technologies, University of Milan, via Bramante 65 –26013 Crema (CR) Italy , e-mail pizzi@dti.unimi.it

G.B. Ferrara
INFM - Istituto Nazionale per la Fisica della Materia
Via Dodecaneso 33, 16146 Genova, Italy
IST - Istituto Nazionale per la Ricerca sul Cancro
Largo R. Benzi 10, 16132 Genova, Italy

Giancarlo Ferrigno
Department of Biomedical Engineering, Politecnico of Milano, Milano, Italy.

M. Filippone
INFM - Istituto Nazionale per la Fisica della Materia
Via Dodecaneso 33, 16146 Genova, Italy

Sandro Fiore
CACT, University of Lecce, Italy & SPACI Consortium, Italy
sandro.fiore@unile.it

Raffaella Folgieri
DSI, Dipartimento di Scienze dell' Informazione,
Università degli Studi di Milano,
Via Comelico 39, 20135 Milano, Italia.
folgieri@dico.unimi.it

F. La Foresta
Dipartimento di Fisica della Materia e Tecnologie Fisiche Avanzate
Università degli Studi di Messina, Salita Sperone, 31 C.P. 57, 98166 Messina, Italy
(azzerboni,ipsale,carpentieri)@ingegneria.unime.it, URL: http://www.eltgroup.polito.it

Dipartimento di Informatica, Matematica, Elettronica e Trasporti
Università "Mediterranea" di Reggio Calabria, Loc.Feo di Vito, 89100 Reggio Calabria, Italy
laforesta@ingegneria.unime.it, URL: http://www.eltgroup.polito.it

Paolo Frasconi
Dipartimento di Sistemi e Informatica, Università di Firenze, Italy
p-f@dsi.unifi.it

Iuri Frosio
Laboratory of Human Motion Analysis and Virtual Reality, MAVR, Department of Computer Science, University of Milano, Via Comelico 39 - 20135 Milano, Italy – http::/mavr.dsi.unimi.it.

Department of Biomedical Engineering, Politecnico of Milano, Milano, Italy

Salvatore Gaglio
DINFO, Dipartimento di Ingegneria Informatica
University of Palermo, Italy.
gaglio@unipa.it

ICAR-CNR, Istituto di Calcolo e Reti ad Alte Prestazioni,
Consiglio Nazionale delle Ricerche, Palermo, Italy.
{storniolo,urso}@pa.icar.cnr.it

S. Gaito
Dipartimento di Scienze dell'Informazione, Università degli Studi di Milano
Via Comelico 39/41, 20135 Milano, Italy
gaito@dsi.unimi.it

Marco Gaspari
University Magna Græcia of Catanzaro, Catanzaro, Italy

Fabrizio Gelain
Stem Cells Research Institute DIBIT San
Raffaele , via Olgettina 58 – 20132 Milano Italy

Antonio Gentile
ICAR-CNR, Istituto di Calcolo e Reti ad Alte Prestazioni
Consiglio Nazionale delle Ricerche, Palermo, Italy.
{vitabile,pilato}@pa.icar.cnr.it

DINFO, Dipartimento di Ingegneria Informatica
Università di Palermo, Italy.
gentile@unipa.it

Antonino Greco
Università "Mediterranea" degli Studi di Reggio Calabria
Dipartimento di Informatica Matematica Elettronica e Trasporti (DIMET)
Via Graziella Feo di Vito, I-89100 Reggio Calabria, Italy
morabito@unirc.it, {d.costantino, versaci}@ing.unirc.it
http://neurolab.ing.unirc.it

G. Grisanti
INFO-COM Dpt. - University of Rome "La Sapienza"
Via Eudossiana 18, 00184 Rome (Italy)
grisantigianluca@virgilio.it

Pietro Hiram Guzzi
University Magna Græcia of Catanzaro, Catanzaro, Italy

Stefano Hajek
DSI - Università degli Studi di Milano

Jonathan D. Hirst
School of Chemistry, University of Nottingham, University Park, Nottingham, UK

D. Iannizzi
Dipartimento di Scienze dell'Informazione, Università degli Studi di Milano
Via Comelico 39/41, 20135 Milano, Italy
apolloni@dsi.unimi.it

M. Ipsale
Dipartimento di Fisica della Materia e Tecnologie Fisiche Avanzate
Università degli Studi di Messina, Salita Sperone, 31 C.P. 57, 98166 Messina, Italy
ipsale@ingegneria.unime.it, URL: http://www.eltgroup.polito.it

Ignazio Lazzizzera
Dept. of Physics,University of Trento, Via Sommarive 14,
38050, Trento, Italy
ignazio.lazzizzera@unitn.it

M. Liquire
Lirmm-University Montpellier II, 161 Rue Ada, Montpellier Cedex 5, France

Giuseppe Longo
Department of Physical Sciences, University of Napoli Federico II, via Cinthia 6, Napoli, Italy

INFN - Italian Institure of Nuclear Physics Unit of Naples, via Cinthia 6, Italy

Tommaso Loreto
INFOCOM Dept., Facolta' di Ingegneria, Universita' di Roma "La Sapienza"
t.loreto@fastwebnet.it

Valentina Maggini
Dipartimento di Scienze dell 'Uomo & dell'Ambiente - DSUA
Università di Pisa

D. Malchiodi
Dipartimento di Scienze dell'Informazione, Università degli Studi di Milano
Via Comelico 39/41, 20135 Milano, Italy
malchiodi@dsi.unimi.it

Gianpiero Mangano
Department of Physical Sciences, University of Napoli Federico II, via Cinthia 6, Napoli, Italy

INFN - Italian Institure of Nuclear Physics Unit of Naples, via Cinthia 6, Italy

Umberto Maniscalco
I.A.C. Italian National Research Council
Viale del Policlinico 137 00161 Rome, Italy
maniscalco@iac.rm.cnr.it
I.C.A.R. Italian National Research Council
Viale delle Scienze Palermo, Italy
maniscalco@pa.icar.cnr.it

Joaquim Marques de Sá
INEB - Instituto de Engenharia Biomédica

Giuseppe Martinelli
INFOCOM Dept., Facolta' di Ingegneria, Universita' di Roma "La Sapienza"
martin@infocom.uniroma1.it

Giovanni Luca Masala
Struttura Dipartimentale di Matematica e Fisica dell'Università di Sassari and Sezione INFN di Cagliari, Italy, via Vienna 2 Sassari, 07100. giovanni.masala@ca.infn.it

F. Masulli
INFM - Istituto Nazionale per la Fisica della Materia
Via Dodecaneso 33, 16146 Genova, Italy

Dipartimento di Informatica, Universita' di Pisa
Via F. Buonarroti 2, 56125 Pisa, Italy
masulli@di.unipi.it

Giancarlo Mauri
DISCo, Univ. Milano-Bicocca
giancarlo.mauri@unimib.it

Tommaso Mazza
University Magna Græcia of Catanzaro, Catanzaro, Italy

Tassilo Mendl
Polytechnic of Turin,Neuronica Laboratory, INFN sez. di Torino, Corso Duca degli Abruzzi 24,10129 Torino,Italy

Alessio Micheli
Dipartimento di Informatica, Università di Pisa
Via Buonarroti, 2 — 56100 Pisa (Italy)
{baronti,passaro}@di.unipi.it

Gennaro Miele
Department of Physical Sciences, University of Napoli Federico II, via Cinthia 6, Napoli, Italy

INFN - Italian Institure of Nuclear Physics Unit of Naples, via Cinthia 6, Italy

A. Minora
Dipartimento di Scienze dell'Informazione, Università degli Studi di Milano
Via Comelico 39/41, 20135 Milano, Italy
minora@dsi.unimi.it

Maria Mirto
CACT, University of Lecce, Italy & SPACI Consortium, Italy
{giovanni.aloisio, massimo.cafaro, sandro.fiore, maria.mirto}@unile.it

Carmine Del Mondo
Department of Physical Sciences, University of Napoli Federico II, via Cinthia 6, Napoli, Italy

Gabriele Monfardini
Università degli Studi di Siena, Dipartimento di Ingegneria dell'Informazione, Siena, Italy

Walter Moniaci
Polytechnic of Turin,Neuronica Laboratory, INFN sez. di Torino, Corso Duca degli Abruzzi 24,10129 Torino,Italy

Francesco Carlo Morabito
Università "Mediterranea" degli Studi di Reggio Calabria
Dipartimento di Informatica Matematica Elettronica e Trasporti (DIMET)
Via Graziella Feo di Vito, I-89100 Reggio Calabria, Italy
morabito@unirc.it
http://neurolab.ing.unirc.it

Marco Muselli
Istituto di Elettronica e di Ingegneria dell'Informazione e delle Telecomunicazioni
Consiglio Nazionale delle Ricerche, Genova, Italy

M. Panella
INFO-COM Dpt., University of Rome "La Sapienza", via Eudossiana 18,
00184 Rome, Italy
panella@infocom.uniroma1.it

Raffaele Parisi
Dipartimento INFOCOM, Università di Roma "La Sapienza" – Italy Via Eudossiana, 18,
00184 Roma – Italy,
parisi@infocom.uniroma1.it;

Eros Pasero
Polytechnic of Turin,Neuronica Laboratory, INFN sez. di Torino, Corso Duca degli Abruzzi 24,10129 Torino,Italy

Alessandro Passaro
Dipartimento di Informatica, Università di Pisa
Via Buonarroti, 2 — 56100 Pisa (Italy)
passaro@di.unipi.it

Massimiliano Pavan
Dipartimento di Informatica
Università Ca' Foscari di Venezia
Via Torino 155, 30172 Venezia Mestre, Italy
pavan@dsi.unive.it

Marcello Pelillo
Dipartimento di Informatica
Università Ca' Foscari di Venezia
Via Torino 155, 30172 Venezia Mestre, Italy
pelillo@dsi.unive.it

P. Petrillo
RCOST - University of Sannio

A. Petrosino
ICAR-CNR, Section of Naples
alfredo.petrosino@na.icar.cnr.it

Giovanni Pilato
ICAR-CNR, Istituto di Calcolo e Reti ad Alte Prestazioni
Consiglio Nazionale delle Ricerche, Palermo, Italy.
pilato@pa.icar.cnr.it

Rita Pizzi
Department of Information Technologies, University of Milan, via Bramante 65 –26013 Crema (CR) Italy , e-mail pizzi@dti.unimi.it

Filippo Portera
Dipartimento di Matematica Pura ed Applicata
Università di Padova, Padova, Italy
portera@math.unipd.it

Sergio Pozzi
DISCo, Univ. Milano-Bicocca
sergio.pozzi@disco.unimib.it

Barbara Quaresima
University Magna Græcia of Catanzaro, Catanzaro, Italy

Giancarlo Raiconi
Department of Mathematichs and Informatics, University of Salerno, Via Ponte don Melillo, I-84084, Fisciano (SA), Italy

Giuseppe Lo Re
DINFO, Dipartimento di Ingegneria Informatica
University of Palermo, Italy.
lore@unipa.it

ICAR-CNR, Istituto di Calcolo e Reti ad Alte Prestazioni,
Consiglio Nazionale delle Ricerche, Palermo, Italy.
{storniolo,urso}@pa.icar.cnr.it

Sandro Ridella
Dept. of Biophysical and Electronic Engineering,
University of Genova, Genova, Italy.
ridella@dibe.unige.it

Fabio Rivieccio
Dept. of Biophysical and Electronic Engineering,
University of Genova, Genova, Italy.
rivieccio@dibe.unige.it

A. Rizzi
INFO-COM Dpt. - University of Rome "La Sapienza"
Via Eudossiana 18, 00184 Rome (Italy)
rizzi@infocom.uniroma1.it

Riccardo Rizzo
C.N.R. – ICAR, Viale delle Scienze 90128, Palermo, Italy

Danilo Rossetti
Department of Information Technologies, University of Milan, via Bramante 65 –26013
Crema (CR) Italy , e-mail pizzi@dti.unimi.it

Anna Maria Rossi
Dipartimento di Scienze dell'Uomo & dell'Ambiente - DSUA
Università di Pisa

S. Rovetta
INFM - Istituto Nazionale per la Fisica della Materia
Via Dodecaneso 33, 16146 Genova, Italy

Dipartimento di Informatica e Scienze dell'Informazione
Universita' di Genova, Via Dodecaneso 35, 16146 Genova, Italy

Francesca Ruffino
Dipartimento di Scienze dell'Informazione, Università di Milano, Milano, Italy
ruffino@dsi.unimi.it

Jorge M. Santos
INEB - Instituto de Engenharia Biomédica 2IT - Networks and Multimedia Group, Covilhã

Instituto Superior de Engenharia do Porto, Portugal (jms@isep.ipp.pt)

R. Sensi
INFM - Istituto Nazionale per la Fisica della Materia
Via Dodecaneso 33, 16146 Genova, Italy

S.M. Siniscalchi
DINFO, Dipartimento di Ingegneria Informatica
Università di Palermo, Italy.
siniscalchi@csai.unipa.it

Filippo Sorbello
ICAR-CNR, Istituto di Calcolo e Reti ad Alte Prestazioni
Consiglio Nazionale delle Ricerche, Palermo, Italy.
{vitabile,pilato}@pa.icar.cnr.it

DINFO, Dipartimento di Ingegneria Informatica
Università di Palermo, Italy.
sorbello@unipa.it

Alessandro Sperduti
Dipartimento di Matematica Pura ed Applicata
Università di Padova, Padova, Italy
sperduti@math.unipd.it

Antonino Staiano
Department of Mathematichs and Informatics, University of Salerno, Via Ponte don Melillo, I-84084, Fisciano (SA), Italy

Antonina Starita
Dipartimento di Informatica, Università di Pisa
Via Buonarroti, 2 — 56100 Pisa (Italy)
{baronti,passaro}@di.unipi.it

Pietro Storniolo
2ICAR-CNR, Istituto di Calcolo e Reti ad Alte Prestazioni,
Consiglio Nazionale delle Ricerche, Palermo, Italy.
storniolo@pa.icar.cnr.it

Pierosandro Tagliaferri
University Magna Græcia of Catanzaro, Catanzaro, Italy

Roberto Tagliaferri
Department of Mathematichs and Informatics, University of Salerno, Via Ponte don Melillo, I-84084, Fisciano (SA), Italy

INFN - Italian Institure of Nuclear Physics Unit of Naples, via Cinthia 6, Italy

Giuseppe Tradigo
University Magna Græcia of Catanzaro, Catanzaro, Italy

Aurelio Uncini
Dipartimento INFOCOM, Università di Roma "La Sapienza" – Italy Via Eudossiana, 18, 00184 Roma – Italy, daniele.vigliano@poste.it; parisi@infocom.uniroma1.it; aurel@ieee.org

Alfonso Urso
ICAR-CNR, Istituto di Calcolo e Reti ad Alte Prestazioni, Consiglio Nazionale delle Ricerche, Palermo, Italy.
urso@pa.icar.cnr.it

Giorgio Valentini
DSI, Dipartimento di Scienze dell' Informazione, Università degli Studi di Milano, Via Comelico 39, 20135 Milano, Italia.
valentini@dsi.unimi.it

Giorgio Vassallo
DINFO, Dipartimento di Ingegneria Informatica Università di Palermo, Italy.
gvassallo@unipa.it

Pierangelo Veltri
University Magna Græcia of Catanzaro, Catanzaro, Italy

Salvatore Venuta
University Magna Græcia of Catanzaro, Catanzaro, Italy

Mario Versaci
Università "Mediterranea" degli Studi di Reggio Calabria Dipartimento di Informatica Matematica Elettronica e Trasporti (DIMET) Via Graziella Feo di Vito, I-89100 Reggio Calabria, Italy
versaci@ing.unirc.it
http://neurolab.ing.unirc.it

Alessandro Verri
INFM - DISI, University of Genova, Via Dodecaneso 35, 16146 Genova, Italy
verri@disi.unige.it

Angelo Vescovi
Stem Cells Research Institute DIBIT San Raffaele , via Olgettina 58 – 20132 Milano Italy

Daniele Vigliano
Dipartimento INFOCOM, Università di Roma "La Sapienza" – Italy Via Eudossiana, 18, 00184 Roma – Italy, daniele.vigliano@poste.it; parisi@infocom.uniroma1.it; aurel@ieee.org

Lara De Vinco
Department of Mathematichs and Informatics, University of Salerno, Via Ponte don Melillo, I-84084, Fisciano (SA), Italy

Salvatore Vitabile
ICAR-CNR, Istituto di Calcolo e Reti ad Alte Prestazioni
Consiglio Nazionale delle Ricerche, Palermo, Italy.
vitabile@pa.icar.cnr.it

Alessandro Vullo
Dipartimento di Sistemi e Informatica, Università di Firenze, Italy
vullo@dsi.unifi.it

Matthew J. Wood
School of Chemistry, University of Nottingham, University Park, Nottingham, UK

Italo Zoppis
DISCo, Univ. Milano-Bicocca
zoppis@disco.unimib.it

Alessandro Zorat
DIT, University of Trento
Via Sommarive, 14, 38050 Trento Italy
alessandro.zorat@unitn.it